DAYS AND NIGHTS FOR MAKING LOVE

Sexual Timing With Astrology

PAUL ROSNER
JOYCE NUNN

VULCAN BOOKS

L.C. #79-91003

ISBN: 0-914350-39-0

Cover illustration by *BRIDGES*

Astrological glyphs—courtesy of
    Jim Maynard/Quick Silver Productions, Inc.
Typography and graphics by Pacesetters, Inc., Seattle, WA
Book design by Ann Downs
Printed in the United States of America.

To Estelle Winwood
who has lived her whole life
for love

TABLE OF CONTENTS

INTRODUCTION
How To Use This Book

You meet someone who thoroughly enchants you. Everything proceeds beautifully on the first date—the conversation, the rapport, the physical contact. It's one of those evenings when God's in His heaven and all's right with the world and you can't wait to get together again.

But where the first time was all roses and morning glories, the second is dandelions and crabgrass. The glow fades, the conversation is strained, the rapport is abrasive, the sex, if you manage to get to that stage, is mechanical.

You wonder how it could have been so marvelous just a few nights before, and so empty a few nights later. You talk about chemistry and lack of chemistry. You shrug your shoulders and say: "That's the way it goes." You discuss it with your shrink. He says you were deluding yourself, that you were playing with images that weren't real, that you are still clinging to fantasy.

If he told you that it was merely the way certain planets were affecting both your charts, he'd be out of business.

Yet that may be exactly what is happening. Or, conversely, it could happen that the first night is not magical, but you find your interest growing until you find yourself in the midst of a lovely affair.

DAYS AND NIGHTS FOR MAKING LOVE is the first book to give you a valid guide to sexual timing through astrology. It is not based on conjecture or generalization, but on the way the planets in the heavens will be influencing the specific degrees of four planets at your birth. *You need have no knowledge of the complicated mathematics which go into setting up a horoscope. All you have to do is look up your birthdate in Part Two, jot down the degrees and signs of the four planets given, and then check out these degrees and signs in Part Three.*

For example, let us say you were born September 29, 1950. You would find the year 1950 and look down the column for September until you arrived at the 29th. You would then learn that your Sun is in 6 degrees of Libra, your Venus is in 24 degrees of Virgo, your Mars is in 3 degrees of Sagittarius and your Neptune is in 17 degrees of Libra.

Now go to Part Three. Look up the sign of Libra and find 6 degrees. You will discover that if one of your planets is in 6 degrees of that sign, the best days and nights for making love in 1980 and 1981 are:

6 ♎

1980   Jan. 26; Feb. 14; Mar. 26; June 27; July 20, 21; Aug. 13; Sept. 28; Nov. 3, 29; Dec. 27.

1981   Jan. 7, 15, 25; Feb. 8; Mar. 24, 26, 28; May 16, 26; June 9, 13, 27; July 26, 27; Aug. 23; Sept. 28; Nov. 10: Dec. 18, 19, 20, 27, 28, 29, 30.

Jot down these dates on the calendar provided in the back of the book. Then continue with the other three planets and their signs and degrees; 24 degrees of Virgo, 3 degrees of Sagittarius and 17 degrees of Libra. When a date appears more than once, circle it, because that means there is more than one influence at work that day. It is, therefore, a particularly favorable time for making love. In certain instances, dates will appear in bold face type. This means: "Don't you dare stay home and read a book, even this one, unless you're sure someone terrific is coming over!"

This is not to say that these are the **only** days and nights when you will make love. But it's as close as can be predicted without actually consulting an astrologer and paying anything from $50 to $500. Even then, no astrologer is going to take the time to tell you exactly when in the next two years you should get laid.

A few important suggestions:

In Part One, we have presented descriptions of Sun-Venus combinations. If your Sun or your Venus should fall on the cusp of a sign, that is, 29 or 0 degrees, read both portraits. For example: You are a Scorpio with your Venus in 29 degrees of Libra, check out both the Sun in Scorpio and Venus in Libra, and the Sun in Scorpio and Venus in Scorpio, to see which one is more applicable. The same is true if your Sun is in 0 degrees of Gemini and, say your Venus is in 15 degress of Cancer. You would read the Sun in Taurus, and Venus in Cancer, and the Sun in Gemini, and Venus in Cancer.

In Part Two, if you know your time of birth, and it is closer to midnight of the following day than it is to noon, the planetary positions for the day ahead will be more applicable.

In Part Three, you will find that, if you should be residing east of the United States, for instance in Europe or Africa, or if you should vacation there and take this book along, use the date one day **before** the date listed. If you should be residing or vacationing to the west of the United States, for instance in Hawaii, the South Seas, Australia or Asia, use the date one day after the date listed.

You will probably think that Part Three of this book, which lists your actual days and nights for making love, was done by computer. It was not. For those of you who still appreciate craftsmanship, it might interest you to know that it took many grueling hours of working with nothing but our brains, our hands, and the ROSICRUCIAN EPHEMERIS.

Paul Rosner
Joyce Nunn

PART ONE

The Signs
And How They Do It

♈ ARIES

March 21 — April 20

ARIES

Of all the signs in the zodiac, you, Aries, are the least likely to make use of this book. Oh, you'll look up your birthdate all right, and you'll say, yes, my Sun is in such-and-such degree and my Venus is in another, and you may even check out the best days and nights for making love, mostly to see how many there are. But the chances of your following them from month to month are remote. For most of you are going to be guided not by the fortuitous placement of a bunch of planets, but rather by your own natural instincts. However untrustworthy they may be, they are yours. To you, what is yours is a helluva lot more valid than some astrologer's silly calculations.

As far as you're concerned, you don't need to know the best days and nights for making love. It's the challenge of it all—whether it be love or sex, or *lovex*. This is a word we just coined for those of you who have such a difficult time distinguishing between the two. This includes about 315 million Aries throughout the world. The typical Aries, whether male or female, prefers to be the chooser rather than the chosen. You have little fear of rejection as a Taurus a Scorpio has. Like your animal counterpart and symbol, the ram, you rush in where eagles and cows fear to tread. Also like the ram, you can batter your head against the same wall time and time again for, of all the signs, Aries most has the tendency to return again and again to the people and things which have caused him the most pain. The ram can be gentle and inoffensive, but when aroused or in love, he becomes so excitable he often runs against his fellow rams and sometimes will attack the shepherd himself. You may have noticed that when a true Aries gets angry his head lowers as if to charge. Rams have a powerfully developed sense of smell, as do most Aries. Being a sheep, the ram longs for a leader whose steps he will implicitly and blindly follow. So, too, certain Aries will become authority-obsessed, unable to form an opinion which has not been sanctioned by "experts."

There are shy, taciturn Aries in this world, but we haven't met one in years.

Since you're stimulated by challenges, you will often choose a lover who is hard to get over one who melts at the first blink of your eyelash, even though the latter might be considerably more attractive. Hard to get, we said, but never competitive. Which brings up an interesting point. Being just about the epitome of competitiveness, you cherish the idea of wooing and winning someone everybody else wants. Wallflowers and nurds are not for you. But once you get this sought-after individual at least partially involved, you expect them to be—no, you demand them to be—fascinated by every aspect of your daily existence. Whether it be what you had for breakfast, what the garage mechanic said was wrong with your car or how you happened to prick your finger on a rose bush, you require your *inamorata* to hang on every syllable of your monologue.

In the meantime, he or she may have just won the Irish sweepstakes, been awarded the Nobel Prize for physics or received a death threat from the Ayatollah Khomeini, but just let them try and tell you the whole story. *Good God, the chili's boiling over—the cockateel has to be fed—doesn't that aspidistra look like it's dying?* Great listeners you are not.

Great lovers you often are. If someone is looking for generosity, spontaneity, passion and excitement, they've come to the right person. For when you are in love, you are totally and completely so. Each new romance becomes the only one; the others were just a workout for the main event. No matter how many times you are disillusioned or hurt, you enter the latest affair with all the awe and enthusiasm of a child discovering his first soap bubble. To you, life without love is like a hurricane lamp without oil. It may look good, but it doesn't light up.

One of your problems in finding the perfect lover is encountering someone whose sex drive is as strong as yours. That may be why so many Aries wind up with other Aries. Oh, along the way, there could be a Scorpio here, a Taurus there and a couple of Saggitarians and Capricorns thrown in for good measure. But it's really amazing how many of you do wind up with your own sign. If that sounds a bit like narcissism, draw your own conclusions. In bed, unlike in conversation, you will do everything to please your partner. You will, if necessary, experiment in any conceivable way (and some that are inconceivable) to turn them on and keep them turned on. The curious thing is, as much of a blabbermouth as you are vertically, horizontally you suddenly become as mute as Helen Keller. Perhaps it's because the act itself is so totally absorbing and exciting. It's got to be all Roman candles and Catherine wheels! And when it is, then it *must* be love.

Let's say you meet someone you want very badly. You finally get that person in bed, and it's not Roman candles and fireworks — it's more like soggy sparklers. Only to them, it's the earth moving under their feet. The positions are now reversed. You find yourself the pursued rather than the pursuer. You were putty before; now you're granite. You can become insensitive, obstinate, rude, abrupt and sometimes, downright cruel. If the other person happens to be of a slightly masochistic bent, perhaps a Pisces or a Taurus, you suddenly appear the most irresistible creature since that serpent slithered into Eden. After all, there are some people who prefer Mr. Hyde to Dr. Jekyll — and when you're aware of this you can be meaner than Attila the Hun, Uriah Heep and Mommie Dearest combined.

Although you demand admiration and reverence, you disdain subservience and submission. You crave excitement, and, if necessary, you will create it. When things are going smoothly, you will often goad your lover a little in the manner of those Seminole Indians in Florida who poke the alligator with a stick to get him to wrestle. The wonderful thing about a lover's quarrel is that sex is so thrilling once you make up. Sex with a bit of hostility can be a real turn-on and many of you are not adverse to a certain roughness and sense of combat in the act itself. Carried to an extreme, this can lead to a very prevalent contemporary phenomenon: sado-masochism. No, the Marquis de Sade was not an Aries; he was a Gemini. More about him on Page 35.

This brings us to *machismo*. *Machismo* doesn't exactly mean sadism or masochism, but it can lean in that direction. There have been an awful lot of *macho* Aries personalities — from Otto von Bismarck to Kareem Abdul-Jabbar, from Boss Tweed to Howard Cosell, from "The Great White Hope," Jack Johnson to Marlon Brando. Steve McQueen, Warren Beatty and Paul Michael Glazer are Aries. Lest we be accused of sexism, there have been an equal number of female Aries *macho* personalities. Think about Bette Davis, Joan Crawford, Claire Booth Luce, Gloria Swanson, Gloria Steinem, Pearl Bailey, Lucrezia Borgia, Anita Bryant. Aries, every one.

A word about money. Money as such is not an all-consuming goal with most Aries, as it is with certain other signs. The word *security* does not connote happiness; it connotes boredom. But money is essential when it comes to love affairs. The typical Aries derives great satisfaction from lavishing gifts on his lover, taking the adored one on trips, preferably in a limousine or a Learjet, and eating in the kind of restaurant where the waiter doesn't have to ask who ordered what. As long as the money holds out, so does the romance — usually. But in a financial bind, an Aries panics, loses his confidence and sometimes his lover, too. Many of you saw a marriage or an important affair break up during that difficult seven year period from 1969-1976 when Uranus was in Libra forming an opposition to each Aries Sun. You will be glad to know you won't have another period like it for many years to come.

You Aries love to fill your lives with perpetual activity and then claim you don't have a moment to yourself. One Aries lady we know never answers the telephone without huffing and puffing. No matter when you call, you have always caught her in the midst of something pressing. It's not intercourse, either, because the lady is in her late 70's. Upon second thought, with an Aries you can't be too sure.

You are the kind of people who can work from nine to five, attend night school, socialize, screw around, and in your spare time, replace the linoleum in the kitchen. This overabundance of energy is admirable, but to one who gets involved with you, it's like falling in love with a whirling dervish. They can get exhausted just watching you. The one thing you always have time for, though, is sex.

We mentioned replacing the linoleum in the kitchen, and that brings up a point worth observing. Probably more than any other sign, you get bored with your surroundings as you do with everything else (unless you have a predominantly Taurean chart). Sagittarians are the same way, but when this happens, what the Sagittarian does is move. Not you. You often stay in the same place, but you are forever redecorating, rearranging furniture, repapering the hallway, repainting the bedrooms and digging up the garden. You will not only do it for the place you live in, you will want to redecorate the plaes others live in, as well. Maybe that accounts for the fact that there are so many interior designers born under the sign of the ram...some do it professionally and some are just buttinskys.

This overabundance of energy also leads to your being the most impatient people who ever tapped their fingers on any given surface. You are equally impatient in love affairs. Although you are attracted to those who are hard to get, you will not worship from afar like a Pisces or bide your time like a Virgo. Your approach can often be direct to the point of bluntness. One Aries fellow we knew invited a really terrific-looking gal over to his apartment for the first time. She was hardly inside the door when he asked, "Do you want to eat now and fuck later, or fuck now and eat later?" The lady being a Scorpio, you can imagine how late they had dinner.

Involvement is a necessity with you, and so you are equally impatient with a lack of commitment. Although you will pursue with every ounce of your awesome energy, you must eventually get the other person to tell you how much they adore you and how they can't live without you. Aries must be needed, and if you are not, you're going to look around for someone who does need you. In most cases, you will still want the other person as a friend, for you collect people with the same tenacity as you do things.

The conclusions you draw about others are made as quickly as everything else you do. You like or dislike on sight and remain adamant about your perceptions. So it is with *lovex.* Frequently you discover you have chosen while the lights were out the most incompatible mate when the lights go on. But, in typical Aries fashion, you will hold on to that first impression until mayhem ensues.

If you happen to be an Aries with your Venus in Aquarius, chances are you will be more emotionally detached in your relationships. However, emotional detachment to an Aries is equivalent to complete obsession by most other signs.

Mental communication is almost as important as those fireworks, and you are more prone to search for a lover who is also a friend. Since there is the Aquarian reformer instinct combined with the Aries enthusiasm, you will confidently set out to remold your sweetheart to your specifications. Even if it weren't a ridiculous thing to attempt, you would never have the patience to complete the task in the first place. Very soon you will find yourself losing sight of the goal and shouting, "Shape up or ship out!" That's around the time they've decided to ship out anyway.

As sexual as your sign is, most Aries prefer a one-to-one encounter, but with Venus in the socially-oriented sign of Aquarius, you could get your kicks from group activities like coeducational baths, nudist camps and *ménages à trois, quatre, seis, sept,* etc. One of the reasons for this is that you value your freedom and independence. Another is that you like to be in the *avantgarde* and are willing to try just about anything that's new. Still another is that you hate things done in secret, and Lord knows, there is nothing secretive about any of the abovementioned diversions. Especially after you've described them in detail to all of your friends. As a matter of fact, the only person in your wide social circle who may be kept in the dark could be your mate.

Some famous people born with the Sun in Aries and Venus in Aquarius are A. E. Houseman, Robert Frost, Lon Chaney, Akira Kurosowa, Aretha Franklin, Erica Jong, Michael York, Leon Russell and Elton John.

The Aries with Venus in Pisces will be more sensitive and vulnerable. The Aries traits of competitiveness and aggression can manifest themselves in the outside world, and you can be very successful professionally. Where the heart is involved, though, you may feel used and dominated, which would be your own fault, since the Aries self-absorption combined with the Piscean subterfuge can sometimes lead to a peculiar lack of conscience. Gentler and more romantic than the typical Aries, you respond more to Debussy during the sex act than to Ravel's "Bolero." You also respond more to intrigue. While most natives of your sign will blurt out just about anything, Venus in Pisces will make you more secretive, less compelled to be brutally frank—especially if you're playing around on the side. Johannes Bach, Casanova, Hans Christian

Andersen, Emile Zola, Henry James, Nikita Kruschev, Clyde Barrow, Marvin Gaye, Diana Ross, David Cassidy, Kareem Abdul-Jabbar, Francis Ford Coppola and Harry Reasoner are examples of noted people with this combination.

The remarks we have made about Aries in general apply almost in toto to those whose Venus is also in Aries. If ever there was proof that sexual magnetism is a matter of energy rather than dimensions, you are it. This is not to say that there aren't gorgeous people born with this combination, but it's not that important. It's only important for the one you *choose* to be gorgeous. There's an electric aura that seems to emanate from most of you and surely comes through in creative work. Raphael, Van Dyck, Goya, Baudelaire, Tennessee Williams and Stephen Sondheim were all born with this combination.

You are likely to be even more impetuous and impulsive in love, so that commitments are made while the affair is too hot not to cool down. Later, when you realize that it's not one long honeymoon, you may feel cheated out of a romantic ideal which exists only in your mind and in the Collected Works of Barbara Cartland.

It's then that the compromises set in. You hate compromises, but even more you hate to admit you're wrong. Your temper is quick and unpredictable, and your affairs are likely to be stormy...but anything less than a typhoon strikes you as casual. In sex, you love to devour and be devoured.

Venus in Taurus for an Aries is as sensual a position as you're likely to find outside of Pussycat Theatre. This makes you more faithful and always on the lookout for a permanent relationship—if only because all that passion needs some consistent outlet. Your desire for challenge and change can be fulfilled in your professional life, which makes the Sun in Aries-Venus in Taurus often a moneymaking combination. There is an old-fashioned, somewhat traditional side when it comes to love, which gives a stronger leaning towards domesticity and children. By the same token, there is more jealousy and possessiveness.

You are usually attracted to those who are more predictable and conservative than you are and, if you have your choice, less brilliant. This infuses you with the sense of power and control that you need in a lasting attachment. Money plays a significant role in keeping a relationship together, because often there are joint accounts and community property, which you are seldom in a mood to part with.

Some famous personages born with this combination have been: Washington Irving, Henrik Ibsen, Leopold Stokowski, Fatty Arbuckle, Arnold Toynbee, Charlie Chaplin, Arthur Murray, Bessie Smith and Merle Haggard.

Aries is a sign which requires a great deal of variety. So is Gemini. Therefore with the Sun in the former and Venus in the latter, the slightest routine can bug the hell out of you. You are more prone to playing the field than to settling down—unless you happen to find Mr. or Ms. Right during one of your sexual skirmishes. Of course, Mr. or Ms. Right is going to have to be gorgeous, brilliant, witty, talented and a man or woman for all seasons. Then again, you don't want them too gorgeous, brilliant, witty and talented, because that would be more competition than you can handle.

Sometimes those with Venus in Gemini find it more to their liking to have two lovers simultaneously, since one can rarely fulfill all they demand. God knows, you have enough passion to go around. More than other Aries, you can get turned on mentally and play a myriad games before you pop the question "Your place or mine?", a question other Aries will ask before the other person has taken the swizzle stick out of the first drink.

Because you don't wallow in your emotions, you are better able to handle relationships than some of the lovers you choose. There is often a paternal/maternal aura about you, and if you don't become father or mother confessor to those around you, it's simply because you hate to stay in the same place for any length of time. Anatole France, Lowell Thomas, Percy Faith, Al Bloomingdale, Gregory Peck and Bette Davis are among those born with this blend.

♉

TAURUS

April 21 — May 21

TAURUS

Walk up behind a Virgo and start rubbing his back. No matter how good it feels, he will instantly tense up. Whirl around and see who's doing it. If it's someone who does not please his critical eye, that's the end of the physical contact. But do the same with a Taurus, and it doesn't make any difference whose hands are doing the rubbing. If it feels good, that's all that counts.

You Taureans love anything that feels good. Possibly the most tactile sign of the zodiac, you get goosebumps when you touch that which gives you pleasure—from velvet to mink, from leather to brocade, from thick, silken hair to smooth, soft skin.

You also love everything that *looks* good. It's the rare Taurus who can walk or drive down a street without being aware of every gorgeous face and body that passes by. Male Taureans have been permitted by society to be more obvious in their ogling. They can whistle, cheer, hoot or make a pass. What they usually do, though, is keep their admiration to themselves and fantasize. Female Taureans have been forced to be more subtle, but they are not less interested. Years ago they would gape and hide behind their fans. Today they gape and hide behind their sunglasses.

Then there's taste. How you adore everything juicy, succulent, delectable and invariably fattening. Taurus rules the throat; and it is what is ingested that is often most satisfying. The vocal chords being in the throat turn many of you into marathon, compulsive talkers...but, we hasten to add, only in congenial company.

Taurus also rules the ears, and melodious sounds are essential to you. You will seldom encounter a Taurus who is not to some degree or other musical; and you will never meet one who does not get carried away by, as Longfellow called it, "The universal language of mankind." Thus, Taureans need background accompaniment almost constantly when making love. There is one notable exception, however: Taurus musicians. Those who work at it professionally find it a distraction. The only sounds they want to hear in bed are moans, sighs, squeals and the other person crying, "It's never been so good!" But then those sounds appeal to all Taureans.

Your sign also rules the nose, and your sense of smell is just as keen as the other four. So keen is it that it can often pick up scents only Siberian wolfhounds can detect. Taureans make particularly good forest rangers and could save the government a good deal of electronic equipment.

Amyl nitrate or "poppers" exert a special fascination, and, of all signs, yours is most prone to getting hooked on it. Most of you are partial to dousing yourselves in heavy perfume, for the right kind of odor is as much of a turn-on as the face or feel of the other person. Conversely, the wrong kind is an instant turn-off. A lack of proper hygiene will do almost as much to break up a potential romance as financial extravagance.

This brings us to your sixth sense: *money*. This instinct, this proclivity, this obsession becomes tangled up in the skein of your life and consequently, your romantic involvements. We are not going to say that all Taureans are tight with a buck—there are exceptions to every astrological generalization—but, oh, the stories we could tell! We could, for instance, relate the tale of the French Taurus we know. The French are not noted for their prodigal natures, and to be a Taurus only compounds the felony. He has never purchased a can of shaving cream. Why waste all that money when soap is available? And this is not one of those light-skinned fellows with peach-fuzz on his face. This is a typically hairy, heavy-bearded Taurean. He is the kind of guest who will arrive with a pint of ice-cream for four ravenous hyperglycemics. On the other hand, this same fellow drives a Porsche, types on an IBM Selectric and invests every extra penny (if a penny could ever be considered extra to a Taurus) in real estate and Krugerrands. But that makes sense. Real estate and Krugerrands accrue in worth, and Porsches and Selectrics have trade-in value. Shaving cream and ice cream do neither.

Another Taurus we *used* to know once gave a dinner party for six at which he served TV dinners (they weren't even the Hungry Man variety).

Then there's that other Taurus—charming, good-looking, a delightful companion—who will never date a girl who lives more than ten blocks away. He'll tell you he hates to drive (many Taureans will tell you the same), and we have to believe him. However, as the gasoline has gone up, the number of blocks has gone down. It used to be fifteen.

Extreme cases, you say? Perhaps. But even in the most extravagant Taureans, there are strange, unaccountable areas of thrift that would elicit admiration from Ebenezer Scrooge. You know the kind of thing we mean. The Taurus who will spend twenty dollars apiece for the concert seats and go a mile out of his way to avoid the parking fee. This does not make for the greatest happiness in one's love life, especially if such a Taurus happens to become involved with a Leo or a Sagittarian. The truth of the matter is that many Taureans will have to find someone either absolutely mad for them or independently wealthy.

On the other hand...and this is what makes your sign so deucedly frustrating...you can be the most generous people in the world when it comes to a friend in need. Whether your pal requires help painting his new apartment or is hard up financially, you simply cannot refuse him. In these instances, even the aforementioned French Taurus becomes Diamond Jim Brady.

This desire to please also applies to making love. You are intent not only on your own gratification, but on that of your partner. And very often, as in other areas of your life, you will take your cue from someone else. No matter how bull-like a Taurus can appear, he is usually not the aggressor, so that you do not function at your best in singles bars or swinging apartment complexes.

The same is true in bed. Your early sexual experiences are most often conventional, because no matter what your libido may be telling you, you try to refrain from shocking anyone. However, once you make contact with a raunchy Aries or an experienced Aquarian, let's say, it's like Alice going through the looking glass. What a kaleidoscope of pleasure lies beyond! And because those five senses are so highly developed, all the accoutrements and toys available double your pleasure and double your fun. There is also a touch of narcissism involved, which is not unusual in an ever increasingly narcissistic society, and Taureans often get extra satisfaction from not only performing the sex act, but watching themselves at the same time. Thus, Alice's looking glass is not just for going through.

There is also an admirable endurance in your love-making. Seldom do you find a Taurus who is intent on accomplishing the greatest number of orgasms during a single night. You can bide your time, revel in variety and help your partner achieve as much satisfaction as he or she wants. Unlike certain other signs...some Librans and Cancers come immediately to mind...you have no recriminations or resentment if the other person achieves a climax and you do not. To give pleasure to another individual is one of your most gratifying experiences. If they want you to be gentle, you will be gentle. If they want you to be rough, you will be rough. If they want you to be kinky, oh, will you be kinky! The important thing is that they *want* you.

Since you abhor rejection, you are often reluctant at the start of a relationship. The other person usually has to woo you until you are absolutely certain they are sincere and want something more than a disco affair. Security is one of the most potent words in your vocabulary, and you look for it whether you are buying a digital clock or taking the marriage vows. If it were up to the Taureans of the world, there would be no such thing as built-in obsolescence.

You are not, generally speaking, given to passionate outbursts. But the rare times you do, it's like Vesuvius erupting. This is because you find hostility unpleasant, and in the manner of Librans and Scorpios, you let things build up until you can do nothing but bellow out a series of primal screams or put your fist through a door.

There is a tremendous power dormant in Taureans...a power you are often afraid to unleash. When harnessed and disciplined, it can carry you to the heights of genius. The greatest dramatist who ever lived, William Shakespeare, was a Taurus; the greatest novelist, Honore de Balzac; the father of psychiatry, Sigmund Freud, and the father of communism, Karl Marx; the most famous nurse, Florence Nightingale; the incomparable Machiavelli and the incomparable Harry Truman.

In our time alone, we have such formidable talents as Fred Astaire, Larry Hart, Irving Berlin, Bing Crosby, Barbra Streisand, Pierre Balmain, Zubin Mehta, Ella Fitzgerald, Stevie Wonder, Glenda Jackson, Judy Collins, Joseph Heller, Al Pacino and the Hepburn ladies, Katharine and Audrey...to mention just a few.

In other words, whatever you choose to do, you want to be the *best*. There is a sense of perfection in almost every Taurus, just as there is in your opposite sign, Scorpio, which leads to self-criticism. Whatever you've done, you tell yourself you could have done better.

When carried to an extreme, it means that some of you do nothing. It's a shame, too, because most Taureans are naturally talented, especially at making something beautiful out of what others would consider junk or debris. Let an Aries walk along the beach with his lover, and he will immediately want to go swimming. Let a Sagittarian do the same, and he will want it right there on the sand. But put a Taurus on that same beach, and he will be collecting every piece of driftwood and any seashell he can find. When he gets around to it he will create the most extraordinary practical and lovely things. *If* he gets around to it.

We mentioned Katharine Hepburn before as a Taurus, and we're sure that many of you will instantly have protested, "But she's a Scorpio!" Well, she isn't. We discovered her true birth date in a 1934 Astrological Journal. In typical Taurean fashion, she was intent on protecting her privacy, and her privacy included her birth information. Taureans will lie about anything if they feel it's nobody else's business. One Taurus friend of ours is so intent on keeping her life secret, she won't even apply for a credit card. This kind of discretion operates in all areas of your life, so that in sexual terms, like Scorpios and Cancers, you would be the last to kiss and tell.

You are very willing to let sleeping dogs lie. Your motto is "What I don't know won't hurt me." This is because you hate to confront unpleasant situations. If, for example, you have a partner and you both decide to have extracurricular sex...or the other person decides it first, and you have no choice but to go along with it...you can relate the details of your peccadillos (and we do mean *details*), but you don't want to know even the name of the lover your lover is loving.

Now we come to chauvinism . . . both male and female. Taurean men frequently have a rather old fashioned view of the sexes and would be perfectly content with a geisha girl. The fact that you seldom find a geisha girl is because you are invariably attracted to those stronger than you . . . and even more attracted when those stronger lovers pretend to be weaker.

In true 19th Century fashion, you think it's perfectly all right to have your casual flings from time to time while the little lady stays at home crocheting doilies and cooking sauerbraten. As much as you love money, the typical Taurus male does not want his wife to work. Not because she'll neglect the household chores and be too exhausted to satisfy his lust, but because he's afraid of the men she may meet in the outside world who'll take her away from him.

There are certain female Taureans who feel exactly the same way, only in reverse. So convinced are they that they can handle a casual affair, they will go ahead and have one or two — maybe more — and yet be devastated if their mate does the same. Clearly, it's unwise for these kinds of Taureans to be married to other Taureans.

The softest and most gentle Taurus qualities come to the fore when your Venus is in Pisces. Most Taureans find it difficult to say no but Taureans with Venus in this position find it impossible. There is often a lack of confidence evident especially with the opposite sex, and you need constant reassurance that you are wanted and loved. Thus, you will give and give, sometimes to your detriment, but seldom with regret. Occasionally you confuse sympathy with love and then wonder why you attract so many social outcasts and those who take advantage of your generous nature. At the same time, this blend enhances the imagination, creativity, clairvoyance and musical talent. Henry Fielding, Ulysses S. Grant, Lenin, Lionel Barrymore, Ngaio Marsh, Vladimir Nabokov, Kate Smith, Barbra Streisand and Bernadette Devlin are among those born with this combination.

When your Sun is in Taurus and your Venus is in Aries, you will do the opposite for the person we have just described. Rather than be drawn to a lover weaker than yourself, you will search out the strongest and most dominant personality you can find. Frequently, you take on a strength and vitality from this individual so that your ego becomes so intertwined with theirs, you are convinced they would have difficulty surviving without you.

Taureans are naturally paternal and maternal. And you will frequently play tolerant, understanding parent with your lover or mate. If the affair should break up, however, it can be like someone has removed one of those shimmering, revolving objects, composed of a hundred tiny mirrors, that the great hypnotist, Mesmer, employed. You will feel lost, as though your own self-identification had been taken away, and you will immediately search for a replacement...usually the wrong one...to bolster your weakened confidence. Some noted people born with this blend are Machiavelli, James Monroe, John Stuart Mill, Charlotte Bronte, Tchaikovsky, Pierre Curie, Sigmund Freud, Fred Astaire, Duke Ellington, Orson Welles, Willie Mays, Stevie Wonder, Julius Rosenberg and Olga Korbut.

Venus in Taurus accentuates all of the Taurean qualities. You loathe change and cling to permanency. Bargain-hunting becomes more prevalent, and so does saving and conservation. Taking a chance on anything, not only love, is as foreign to your nature as tolerance to a Virgo.

Lusty and expert lovers in the proper surroundings, you can become practically impotent or frigid when faced with discomfort. You are not one for the spontaneous seduction in the back seat of a taxi cab or behind the rhododendrons in Hampton Court (it is wisest not to get hung up on a Sagittarian). Even in our permissive culture, this double Taurean combination is one of the most faithful in all of astrology. Leonardo Da Vinci had it, and so did Oliver Cromwell, Kierkegaard, Karl Marx, L. Frank Baum, Bertrand Russell, Irving Berlin, Adolph Hitler, Glen Campbell, Joe Cocker and Johnny Unitas.

The Sun in Taurus and Venus in Gemini gives a peculiar dichotomy, because the Taurus part of you never fully approves of what the Gemini part is doing. Yet the Gemini part continues to do what it is going to do. It will be unfaithful, for one. Be more spontaneous, for another. More experimental, more flexible, more communicative...and eternally searching for the Fairy Prince or Princess. A fellow we know who has this combination was out buying stockings with his girlfriend. On top of the cellophane package was a photograph of a luscious young lady, and as soon as he saw her, he cried, *"My God, that's my dream girl!"* He insisted on his lover buying the stockings just so he could have the picture. He then took the photo from the package, brought it home and hung it on his bathroom wall. It is still there, fifteen years later. This is a good example of the way people with this combination not only adore youth and beauty, they expect youth and beauty to be suspended in time. This Taurus still looks forward to meeting the lady even though she may have posed for the ad as long as twenty years ago.

There is a very great desire to have someone to talk to...and often that's how affairs begin. There are several dates with just conversation, then one night the conversation leads to the accidental touching of thighs...and you know where that leads, especially if you are a Taurus. We wonder what kind of experiences of this nature others with this combination have had...Socrates, Shakespeare, Kant, Brahms, Anthony Trollope, William Randolph Hearst, Ho Chi Minh, Rudolph Valentino, Benjamin Spock, Joe Louis, Elaine May, Reggie Jackson, and

Malcolm X.

While Venus in Gemini searches for his fairy tale ideal, the Taurus Venus in Cancer actually believes he is going to find it. And after he marries, he insists that he has. Because all Taureans are to some degree or other stubborn, he may continue to insist he has found it long after comfort replaces passion and he has transferred his affections to his children. The Venus in Cancer type is as faithful as the Venus in Gemini type is not; and you will seldom find these people bachelors or spinsters. The endemic fear of rejection is multiplied tenfold so that one often meets one's sweetheart in high school—or third grade—and remains steadfastly loyal from there to eternity. Even when the initial emotional excitement has begun to wane, these individuals often stick to their orignial conviction because they don't want to disappoint their families. *"Mother loves her so much"; "Daddy thinks he's the perfect mate for me"; "I couldn't let Kenneth go. He's so good with the children."* Whatever the excuse, the Taurus with Venus in Cancer would rather do just about anything than alter the status quo. Some famous examples of this blend are Robert Browning, James M. Barrie, Balzac, Harry Truman, Archilbald MacLeish, Margaret Rutherford, James Stewart, Peter Hurkos and Margot Fonteyn.

♊

GEMINI

May 22 — June 20

GEMINI

We told you on page 17 we would tell you about the Marquis de Sade here, and we might as well start with him when talking of Gemini and love and sex. It's not the beginning of the story, but with you Geminis, who cares?

De Sade has gone down in history as possibly the most dissolute, lascivious, unconscionable pornographer who ever tortured an innocent young maiden. The reason for this reputation is because most people have never read De Sade or, if they have, it has been only the most erotic excerpts. De Sade was, in truth, a brilliant writer, a biting satirist and a keen moralist. The whole point of his novels is that in a corrupt society virtue never triumphs. *Vice* triumphs; virtue goes through hell.

This is by way of saying that to most of you Geminis sex is not the be-all and end-all of your lives. Often satire and moralizing, philosophy and communication—anything to do with *ideas*—take precedence. Oh, you can write about it like Gemini de Sade did, or you can personify it like Gemini Marilyn Monroe, or revolutionize it like Gemini Christine Jorgensen, or capitalize on it like Gemini Xavier Hollander. But when it comes to doing it, what leads up to the act is frequently more important that the act itself. It's the game that fascinates you most...the approach, the flirtation, the cerebral discussion with the carnal undertone, the moving forward then moving away, the who-will-get-more-involved and the you-didn't-take-me-seriously syndrome...anything, in fact, that makes life more interesting.

This is not to say that there is no such thing as a horny Gemini. Because Sun Sign astrology is, by its very nature, generalization, we can't possibly take into consideration the Gemini with the basically Taurus chart, with the Scorpio Moon or a Venus-mars conjunction. We are talking here of the *typical* Gemini. Typical Geminis can be a trip-and-a-half, especially if a Scorpio or a Capricorn gets hung up on you. You have methods of enticement both Circe and Merlin would envy. if there's the fellow or the gal with the undulating walk, the come-hither eyes, the skin-tight clothes and the smile that promises a thousand and one

Arabian delights, chances are he or she is born under the Sign of the Twins. Beau Brummel was, and so was Tom Jones.

To add insult to enticement, whether male or female, you are usually the agressor. Since you are seldom shy about talking to strangers, strangers often get the wrong impression. They may think you are on the make, and, in a way you are. Or at least one of the twins is. But the other twin wants to discuss the current international crisis, the current domestic crisis, the current political crisis . . . the current anything as long as it isn't your emotions. Because it's what you *think* that's important, not what you feel. If you are a typical Gemini, you're not really certain what you do feel. But oh, what you *think* You're certain of that because you have at least two dozen facts at your fingertips no matter what subject is being discussed. You Geminis absorb facts like parched soil absorbs rain; and no one could ever accuse you of a one-track mind.

With your stunning assortment of interest, you can make delightful companions. Seldom at a loss for words, there're almost never those embarrassing silences you may get with certain Scorpios, or Capricorns. By the same token, there are almost never those radiant silences when two people are in love and strolling along a country lane hand-in-hand. Let a Gemini stroll along a country lane with the one he or she adores and you may hear something that goes like this: *"Oh look at that cloud formation! Isn't it beautiful! Is it cumulus or cirrus . . . I always forget. Do you know who classified clouds? An Englishman named Luke Howard. Did I tell you I ran into Kevin the other morning? His wife was injured in a car accident. . with her lover . . . a woman named Mickey something. Did you ever read about the survey they did with 100 of the most successful men in the country? They had them fill out these lengthy questionnaires and they discovered that the one thing they all had in common was that none of them owned cats."*

And talking about talking, let's not forget the Gemini wit and humor. It's a wonderful quality on a stage or a screen or across the breakfast table, and you only have to consider such eminent Gemini comedians and comediennes as Rosalind Russell, Bob Hope, Fred Allen, Beatrice Lillie, Stan Laurel, Richard Benjamin, Paul Lynde, Peggy Cass, Andy Griffith, Gene Wilder and Maria Montez.

What is particularly wonderful is how often you can laugh at yourselves. In love, it's another matter. There is a memorable line from an old Irving Berlin song called *You're laughing At Me* which sums it up perfectly: "You have a sense of humor, and humor is death to romance." Irving Berlin is a Taurus, and he should know.

Since variety is so essential to your well-being, once you get down to the sex act itself—and you *do* get down to it from time to time— you are like a smorgasbord of carnal delights. Other signs will read books like *The Joy of Sex* or *The Kama-Sutra,* get their rocks off and then put it away on the shelf. You will read The Joy of Sex and The Kama-Sutra and experiment with every suggestion, usually adding a few innovations of your own. You will try almost anything, not because you are that intent on pleasing your partner, but because you are that intent on never boring yourself. If your partner wants only one entree after the appetizer, he has come to the wrong person. You detest people who have a limited repertoire in bed—unless they happen to be incredibly gorgeous. You will then make concessions, because you adore beauty and youth and love to show off a conquest others will envy.

Your concentration while making love is as tenuous as it is in everything else you do. It is not exceptional for you to interrupt moments of wild passion with a suggestion like "Let's have a cigarette," "You know what I'm dying for right now? some Baskin-Robbins mandarin chocolate", or even "How about a quick game of rummy tiles?" If the person next to you, under you or on top of you happens to be an Aries or a Scorpio, you are in danger of being clubbed to death.

Of all the signs, you Geminis are the most notorious for recording every aspect of your existence. You are the kind who go on vacation and take along three different cameras to capture each single moment of the trip. You are also the kind who insist on showing the results to all your freinds when you get back. Your commentary is invariably so witty they can forgive you—at least the first few times.

You love diaries, scrapbooks, journals, tape recorders, movie cameras and video machines. A young, swinging Gemini bachelor we know has a Betamax and a video camera which records every sexual experience he has. This library is now almost as large as the vaults at M.G.M. Upon request, he will play the latest tape for the particular lady involved—or anyone else who happens to be interested. To him, there is nothing unusual or sacred about this. Sex is a significant part of his life, and if you ask him, he will tell you it's like other people recording baby's first step, baby's first smile and baby's christening.

Just as you appreciate variety in sex, you also appreciate variety in partners. And it all goes back to that symbol of your sign, the Twins. In some of the ancient zodiacs, they were pictured as a man and a woman; in others, as Castor and Pollux holding in their hands a club, an unstrung bow and a harp. Today they're always represented as either holding hands or with their arms about each other. This is not, we venture to say, a completely accurate portrait...with most Geminis, the Twins should be facing in opposite directions, doing two completely different things or wrestling with each other. It is easier to satisfy the traditional Twins than those we have just described, yet ours are the more typical and require greater stimulation to make them content.

The Gemini who settles down for life with a single partner is the rare Gemini and usually the one who has found the ideal mate—a mate who is remarkably tolerant and looks the other way. Most Geminis become bored with fidelity. One Gemini we know, a successful actor-writer, becomes so bored with fidelity he is now on his fifth marriage. His life has certainly been more varied — and so have his alimony payments and his child support. It's astonishing what you will sacrifice to keep boredom at bay.

Like Sagittarians, you prefer sex that isn't planned. You appreciate the spontaneous act in the unusual circumstance — not quite as unusual as Sagittarians, but unusual enough. The one place you will draw the line is in the morning. Sex upon awakening or when half awake is like a dental apppointment at dawn. That marvelous Gemini composer-lyricist, Cole Porter, once wrote a song about this antipathy. It's called *But In The Morning, No*, and you should have a recording of it handy to put on the stereo at 7:00 or 8:00 in case you have a Scorpio or an Aries lover.

The animal counterpart for your sign is the monkey. There are Geminis who resemble this animal with a slightly simian cast to their features, short legs and uncommonly long arms. Like the monkey, Geminis are seldom still; they are curious, clever, superb mimics and strongly attracted to socially organized clans. Monkeys are arboreal, and often in Gemini children you find an inherent joy in climbing trees and swinging from branches. Geminis are notorious for beginning things and not finishing them. Monkeys don't finish things either — except maybe bananas.

The monkey has another significance for your sign. In Chinese astrology, Gemini is represented by the three little monkeys with their hands over their eyes, ears and mouth wherein they "see no evil, hear no evil, and speak no evil." It is uncommon to find a Gemini who gossips. When you reveal information about another person, it is to impart news not scandal. Pisces don't like talemongering either, but with them, they shy away from it out of fear that it will be turned against themselves, whereas you find scuttlebutt unappetizing. There are always exceptions, and Hedda Hopper was one, but no sign's perfect.

One of the most difficult things for a Gemini to understand is the law of cause and effect. You can understand it when it applies to world events, nature or someone else, but not when it applies to you. This generally starts the first time you play with matches and burn your hand. Then the excuses begin, and there are often more excuses in a Gemini's life than at the Nuremburg trials. In love, it's the same way. The typical Gemini has a mighty hard time recognizing the connection between his actions and the results of his actions.

Gemini, as we said, loves variety and Aries adores novelty, so if your Sun is in Gemini and your Venus in Aries you should be one of those most envied in contemporary society: a bona fide swinger. You thrive on singles bars, midnight cruising and those giant stucco apartment complexes where anything goes.

There is the element of love at first sight with this position and it can range from finding it once and for always like Queen Victoria, or six times and for always like Artie Shaw. You can fall in love with an eyebrow or a dimple, usually belonging to someone younger.

Keeping youthful and fit becomes a fetish, e.g. Robert Cummings, and you will try anything from lamb embryo injections to witchcraft in order to remain desirable. If you happen to have a full length portrait of yourself, remember to keep it in the attic. Other famous people born with this combination are Arthur Conan Doyle, Isadora Duncan, Dashiell Hammett, Fred Allen, Marilyn Monroe, Beverly Sills, and we think, Peter Pan.

A greater desire for emotional security exists when your Venus is in Taurus. Your penchant for variety can be fulfilled in your professional life or by a myriad of hobbies and outside interests, rather than in playing the romantic field. Sex as sex becomes more important and the game less so. Money means more to you than to most Geminis and you will hold on to a marriage or a live-in arrangement longer, especially when there are financial involvements. If a divorce or separation occurs, it is most likely because your partner complains of too may extracurricular, not extramarital, activities.

Although often intelligent and well-read, there is sometimes a lack of common sense, and as the years progress you can grow increasingly more eccentric.

Since Taurus rules the sense of touch and Gemini manual dexterity, the things you can do with your hands would prompt admiration from the most experienced Rolfer. Wagner, Mesmer, Walt Whitman, Thomas Hardy, William Butler Yeats, Thomas Mann, Douglas Fairbanks, Jean Paul Sartre, Laurence Olivier, Clint Eastwood, Gene Wilder and Paul McCartney were all born with this blend.

Geminis with Venus in the same sign fall in love more easily with ideas than with individuals. One of the reasons for this is that people make claims upon you, ideas don't. Not Gemini ideas, at any rate. Mental attraction takes precedence over the physical and although you do many things impulsively, marrying is not one of them. A marriage of convenience is not uncommon with this position, because even if it isn't for convenience, eventually you're going to play around anyway. It's not that your passions must be satisfied—your passions aren't like other people's to start with—it's that monogamy is so boring. Even after a few days.

There is more than the usual Gemini charm and wit with this blend. You can also be great teases, and we don't mean that just in the sexual connotation. Talkative and outgoing, you are as much in demand at dinner parties as you are on somebody's chaise, although, if the truth be known, you often prefer the dinner party. Those born under this combination are Paul Gauguin, Richard Strauss, Frank Lloyd Wright, Cole Porter, Lilli Palmer, Rosalind Russell, John F. Kennedy, Bob Dylan and Che Guevara.

A Gemini with Venus in Cancer wouldn't choose the chaise either, unless it goes with the house, the license, the credit cards and the maid. Not that you aren't romantic. You're actually more romantic than most of your fellow Geminis, but the romance is tinged with the need for security and the need for security is tinged with the longing for a surrogate parent. Whereas those other Geminis may be hunting for someone younger, your preference is toward someone older, wiser, stronger and more protective. You want the rock of Gibralter, not a handful of pebbles. If your incurably romantic nature leads you to stray from time to time, there is hopefully that rock to return to. Therefore, unlike many born under your sign, when you stray, you stray discreetly with no compulsion to advertise it in Macy's window. We only hope the rock remains a rock when it comes to in-laws, for what with mommy, daddy and all the aunts, uncles and cousins, your home will seldom be a little love nest for two.

Those also born with the conflict between the Gemini desire to go out dancing and the Cancer need to stay at home are Pascal, Pushkin, G. K. Chesterton, Igor Stravinsky, Hedda Hopper, Stan Laurel, Ian Fleming, Norman Vincent Peale, Joe Namath, Tom Jones and F. Lee Bailey.

Geminis are rarely demanding or possessive, but with Venus in Leo, you can be both. Whereas other Geminis not only practice but understand infidelity, you do not tolerate it at all. Your multi-faceted interests can be demonstrated in non-sexual ways and you can't fathom why others don't do the same. To discover the object of your affections *in flagrante delicto* is enough to lead to complete alienation, if not manslaughter. Not that you don't flirt. You do indeed, since you love attention, but you know when to stop.

Obviously, you would not be well matched with your own sign. There is a love of show here and a desire to choose someone you can proudly present to the rest of the world as a reflection of your impeccable taste. Immanuel Velikovsky, probably the greatest genius of our time, was born with this combination. So were Dorothy McGuire, Malcolm McDowell, Xaviera Hollander, Billy Cunningham and William Calley, Jr.

♋

CANCER

June 21 – July 22

CANCER

Do you remember those Nibbish cartoons that were so popular back in the 50s? There was one of a forlorn, naked young lady with woeful eyes and stringy hair, and the caption underneath was: "Mother loved me, but she died." The young lady must have been Cancer.

The point is that how Mother loved you, to what extent, and whether she loved you at all—not to mention how she loved Father—determines how you will love others. Cancer is the maternal side of the zodiac, just as Capricorn is the paternal, so it's Mother's influence which pervades your sex life like Hamlet's ghost. If her attitude toward sex was uptight or perverse, you can spend years in primal therapy or chanting *Nam yo ho renge kyo* trying to exorcise her power: or, as certain Cancers we know, you can rationalize an unhealthy but externally adoring supremacy by convincing yourself that she was the greatest. You wonder if you will ever find a replacement. Conversely, if Mother's attitudes were wholesome and wise you can go through life with the least sexual neuroses in all of astrology.

Whatever Mama's influence was, we'll keep it strictly between us. We will have to because no matter what they say about Scorpios, you Cancers are the most secretive people in the world. So secretive are you, you're even secretive about being secretive. We wouldn't be surprised if some of you tear out this section before showing the book to friends. Obviously you would have more respect for the publisher if this part were printed in invisible ink.

Among the things you're secretive about is your complexity. You would prefer the world to think what they see is what they get, but nothing could be further from the truth. Your emotions fluctuate like the phases of the moon (often *with* the phases of the moon) and complicate your complexity. Let's take aggressiveness as an example. You can be as timid as a doe when you find yourself in unfamiliar surroundings. Even the most attractive Cancer can become awkward, taciturn or aloof. But on your own home ground, in a place where you really feel comfortable, you can easily approach the one who strikes your fancy.

Most of you have an enormous amount of pride and are terrified of rejection, so that even if you make the first move, you expect the second move to come from the other person. Your favorite attitude is "You propose, I dispose." Because you realize how deeply involved you can get, you generally proceed with caution, unlike the Aries, the Scorpio or the Sagittarian, who will blurt out during the first wild sexual encounter, "For God's sake, let's have an affair!" As much as you long for an affair, you're afraid of getting hurt or of someone making a fool of you. The typical Cancer can laugh at a lot of things in this world, but never himself.

It's not easy for you to laugh at money, either. Just like your opposite sign, Capricorn, money and success have great meaning to you; and in order to impress others, you can bury yourself in *things.* Then you must spend a fortune on burglar alarm systems to protect them. Since you must have the security of a place of your own, what you put into that place often takes on an importance out of proportion to value. Cancers are notorious in home decorating for either complete starkness or filling every available space with objects. One male Cancer we know has an apartment that resembles a hospital room; another Cancer, a German lady, has one that looks like a surrealistic nightmare in which Woolworth's marries a Rexall Drug Store.

You are the same with automobiles. An automobile to the typical Cancer is far more than just a means of getting from point A to point B. It becomes an extension of yourself, and it is the rare Cancer who will choose a car for functional reasons above aesthetic ones. If somebody, a Virgo for instance, tells you not to buy a Jaguar because you can't get Jaguar parts, what difference does that make to you? If you like the looks, you buy it. You buy it, and, oh, the care you take of it! You clean it, you polish it, you pamper it and protect it from finger-prints on the chrome and from cigarette ashes on the carpets. With all that care, you'd think you'd keep it forever, right? Wrong. You will trade it in for the first spiffy model that blinks its headlight at you. And you will continue your romance with the new vehicle with the same passion and adoration as you had with the old.

The analogy here is that you normally choose a lover the same way you do a car. Aesthetics take precedence over practicality. This may be due to your highly developed visual sense. There are a greater number of famous artists throughout history born under the sign of Cancer than any other. Rubens, Whistler, Rembrandt, Pissaro, Andrea del Sarto, Modigliani, Joshua Reynolds, Corot, Delacroix, Degas, Georgio de Chirico, Chagall, John Copley, Rockwell Kent, Buffet, Edward Hopper and both Andrew and James Wyeth. This visual sense also applies to motion pictures, and we have such notable film directors as Billy Wilder, George Cukor, William Wyler, Ingmar Bergman, Vittorio de Sica, Claude Chabrol, Sidney Lumet, Ken Russell and Jean Corteau.

Just like your automobile, you can lavish on your lover the most constant and careful attention...sometimes *too* constant and careful...or there is a romantic streak coursing through Cancerian veins which has some of the qualities of a Mary Pickford movie. For all we know, the Cinderella legend may have originated with a Cancer. Each of you, to some degree or other, believes in it. Even when you grow old, you still believe it. Cancerian Oscar Hammerstein believed in it so much he even set lyrics to it, and his Cancerian collaborator, Richard Rodgers, composed the music. Their work epitomized Cancerian dreams...from the promise that someday you will meet a stranger across a crowded room to the autumn years when you can tell young lovers not to cry because you're alone. The United States is a Cancer country, and never did we have such an apotheosis of the American ideals as in the works of these two men.

It is interesting to note here that Rodgers and Hammerstein were the producers of the original production of *I Remember Mama*, and that 35 years later, Richard Rodgers chose to set it to music. Who else but a Cancer would keep remembering her...and remembering her?

Like Rogers and Hammerstein, you believe love should last forever and most of you struggle to make that dream come true. You've got to have a dream, if you don't have a dream, how you gonna have a dream come true? If you don't succeed...although you'll seldom admit it, for invariably it's the other person's fault...you have amazing recuperative powers. As with automobiles, you go on to the next one with your ideals securely intact. You know that somewhere there's a someone just for you. If it should happen that you reach a grand old age without having found that someone, you are sentimental enough to look back on your life as though you had. It may have been a person who smiled at you on a deserted beach, someone you glimpsed from a passing train or a brief vacation romance...ships that pass in the night...but you will still fantasize over what might have been. Almost every Cancer has a dream lover stashed away in the recesses of his imagination, for it is part of your indomitable spirit that reality seldom daunts you.

Most of you know that both the symbol and the animal counterpart of your sign is the crab. A lot of you even move like crabs with a sidelong gait. You also know that crabs latch on to something and refuse to let go, that the hard shell is a protection for the soft interior, that the crab carries his home with him, that he loves water and swims with great dexterity and that he casts off his skin several times in the process of maturing. Those are things you have read in dozens of astrological books. What most of you don't know is there's another animal counterpart for your sign: the cat. This is a different type of Cancer...or sometimes another side to the crab personality. Some Cancers move with the feline grace of a cat, and like the cat, are nocturnal, dislike water, become more attached to places than to people, love to go carousing, especially in back alleys, are extremely agile and positively adore being stroked. Unlike dogs, cats are determinedly independent and demand affection when they want it, rather than when someone else chooses to give it.

Cancer is the sign that rules the stomach and the breasts, and it's significant to note how both play a vital role in your lives. The stomach, of course is the natural habitat of those butterflies which flutter about whether you are applying for a job or seeing that stranger across a crowded room. The stomach is quite apt to rebel when you eat or drink too much...two not uncommon Cancerian tendencies. As for the breasts, the larger they are, the better. Cancer men are almost never leg-men or ass-men, they are eternally breast-men. Cancer women feel very insecure unless they're built like their sister Cancers, Jane Russell, Gina Lollobrigida or Janet Leigh. The breasts are also a primary erogenous zone for both sexes, whether you are the feeler or the feelee.

Most Cancers are conservative by nature. One Cancer girl we know, in the usually liberal entertainment field, would have died before marijuana touched her lips. For years when the joint was handed around, she would dilate her nostrils, shake her head and pass it on. It wasn't until the early 70s, when her associates were either going back to alcohol or ahead to cocaine that she finally discovered grass. Now they call her "Reefer Rita."

This conservative attitude applies as much to sex as it does to other pleasures. During your first serious affair (that means the person you plan to introduce to your family) you could be shocked to tears if the one you adore, the one you have placed on a pedestal, suddenly decides to try something a bit unconventional. It's like not only your Mother, but all the Mothers in the world, are watching, saying, "That's not nice, dear."

Later on when you discover that not just one or two isolated debauchers are enjoying the unfamiliar, you could have a change of heart. One Cancer lady acquaintance had to be taught by her Aquarian friend the techniques of oral sex at the age of 47. Her husband is still thanking the Aquarian every time he sees her. For once you do get into something, you get into it with every fiber of your being and become as expert as the Aries or the Sagittarian who first introduced you to it. Then you become the teacher and introduce others to these delights as if you'd been doing them for years.

With the tenacity of Cancer and the endurance of Taurus, when your Sun is in the former and your Venus is in the latter, you want to settle down for life. Anything short of that is a one-night stand. Even when a relationship is not right, you hold on as though your fingers were made of Krazy Glue, for you loathe change and fear the unknown. As far as you're concerned, whatever is wrong with what you have is still better than what you might get.

Even more than the normal Cancer, family and security and children mean everything to you. With this position, your partner could never complain about lack of sexual interest. If there's any complaint, it's probably a surfeit of sexual interest, so try to avoid Virgos and Geminis.

Fear of rejection is more prevalent so that invariably you wait for the other person to make the first move. If he doesn't, you go home, lie in bed and curse your timidity. Some celebrities born with this combination are Jean Cocteau, Richard Rodgers, Carly Simon, Tom Stoppard and Shirley Knight.

The Sun in Cancer and Venus in Gemini requires more mental stimulation, whether for good or bad. Sometimes those with this combination find themselves attracted to people who abuse them psychologically. It's not the most pleasant kind of relationship, but as far as you're concerned, it's better to be abused than bored to death. (If this be true, look for a Virgo.) You are not as faithful in love as most Cancerians. A casual fling is perfectly acceptable and very often stimulates an affair or marriage. For extra stimulation, if you find a partner who'll go for it, you are not adverse to bringing in a third party...maybe even a fourth or fifth.

Some of you spend your lives searching for your high school ideal and frequently will worship from afar. Listening to the problems of others can become a pastime, which may sometimes be turned into a profession. Abigail Van Buren and her twin sister, Ann Landers, were born with this position. Others were Henry VIII, Rembrandt, Jean Jacques Rousseau, Henry David Thoreau, Franz Kafka, Rube Goldberg, Ringo Starr, Linda Ronstadt, John Glenn and Cat Stevens.

Those with both the Sun and Venus in Cancer would make wonderful members of the Mafia...and sometimes are. Family takes precedence over everything else, and if the object of your affection does not meet with the approval of mummy, daddy and conceivably the Godfather, he'd just better bug off and find himself a Sagittarian. By the same token, you accept your partner's family with the intense love and devotion you shower upon your own. If the one you choose happens to be estranged from his family you will move heaven and earth to reunite them. Family then becomes like potato chips...once you start, you can't get enough. Should a separation occur between you and your mate (and it's never your fault, of course), you are the kind who will remain bosom friends with your in-laws.

You are extremely giving people, but as in the case of so many born under your sign, the giving has strings attached. There is also a touch of martyrdom in your love. Eventually, even though your mate may be older than you, you will wind up playing the role of parent. It is a role you start training for about the time you feed the first spoonful of pablum to your baby sister or brother. Famous people who probably fed pablum to their siblings are John Calvin, Calvin Coolidge, Helen Keller, Modigliani, Pearl S. Buck, Ernest Hemingway, Wilma Rudolph, Kris Kristofferson, Pete Maravich and O.J. Simpson.

With Venus in Leo, there is just as much giving as with Venus in Cancer only less martyrdom. The result is you do not attempt to hide the psychological tally sheet you maintain in all relationships. This position strengthens the love of beauty. You would rather save your money and buy the real thing than rush out and get the imitation. Your desire is to have your inamorata admired by one and all. It also intensifies your ego and makes you more overtly possessive and jealous. The Moon rules Cancer and the sun rules Leo, therefore, you must be the Sun and the Moon to the person you love. In fact, you must be the Sun and the Moon to most people . . . with a few stars thrown in for good measure. Because the insecurity of Cancer is at war with the confidence of Leo, you demand constant approbation, and if a romance breaks up, it's often due to the other person getting tired of telling you how marvelous you are and virtually never because you are lousy in bed. Rubens, George Sand, Mary Baker Eddy, Stephen Foster, Whistler, Gustav Mahler, Jack Dempsey, P. T. Barnum, Georges Pompidou and Neil Simon were all born with this combination.

There is less chance of settling down for life when your Sun is in Cancer and your Venus is in Virgo. It isn't that you aren't as family oriented as others in your sign. You may be even more so. The reason is you simply have never met anyone who is good enough for you. Oh, at the beginning of an affair, you'll make certain concessions and think this may be the one. But you are merely being led by that romantic Cancerian side. After you are certain the other person is thoroughly involved, the Virgo nit-picking begins. You start to see, even *look* for all the imperfections as if you were Louis Pasteur examining bacilli under a microscope. If you were only half as tolerant with your partners as you expect them to be with you, your love affairs would be infinitely more successful. But it's not easy finding someone who has just descended from Mount Olympus.

Most Cancers with this position have such a cleanliness fetish that one we used to know . . . a male, not a female . . . once dreamt he was the Old Dutch Cleanser lady and awoke the next morning utterly exhausted. Because Cancer has an innate sense of what the public wants and Virgo is so clever, those with the combination usually find more success in their profession than in their personal lives. Some examples: John Quincy Adams, Degas, John D. Rockefeller, Marcel Proust, Marc Chagall, Rose Kennedy, Buckminster Fuller, Stephen Vincent Benet, Irving Stone, Ginger Rogers, Marshall McLuhan, Terry Thomas and Ilie Nastase.

♌

LEO

July 23 — August 22

LEO

There have been all kinds of astrological surveys over the years. We know, for instance, that there are more Aquarians in *Who's Who of American Biography* than any other sign. We know also that Taurus is most common among popular singers, Pisces and Aries among dancers, Capricorn and Aquarius among matadors, Gemini and Leo among lawyers, Libra and Scorpio among chemists and Virgo among surgeons. But, to our knowledge, no one has ever made a study of astrology and hustlers. If they did, we wouldn't be at all surprised to learn that the predominant sign was Leo.

Hustlers, we said, not hookers. For there is a wealth of difference between what the male and the female Leo will do to earn a living. It all goes back to your symbol and your animal counterpart: the Lion. The lion is a noble beast . . . fierce, courageous, indomitable, loyal. He is gorgeous to look at, awe-inspiring in his roar, king of the jungle. His sole function in life is to protect the pride. Otherwise, he sits on his duff and suns himself. It's the lioness who does all the work.

This is not to say that the only thing the male Leo wants to do is sit on his duff in the sunlight and let his woman toil from morn till nightfall. We have throughout history such industrious Leos as Simon Bolivar, Napoleon Bonaparte, Frederick of Prussia, Emperor Franz Joseph, Henry V, Benito Mussolini and Fidel Castro.

Leo men generally consider themselves so special, so attractive and so extraordinary that they see no reason in the world why they shouldn't let the one who is in love with them take care of all those mundane matters like food, shelter and clothing. It's not that they're unwilling to work. They would love to work. But how many armies are there to lead and how many countries to rule on this tiny planet? Start at the bottom, you say? Work your way up? Don't be ridiculous.

Take the case of a young Italian Leo we know. An Italian Leo is equivalent to a Cuban Scorpio or a Jewish Cancer . . . it's like carrying coals to Newcastle. In fact, both the country of Italy and the city of Rome are ruled by Leo. This young lion is a very sexy fellow who rather resembles Sylvester Stallone. He sleeps till 12, spends the afternoons working out at the gym and the nights carousing with his buddies while his sister and his mother operate a small pizzeria. He has dreams of being like his Leo idol, Mick Jagger, except in his dreams, he just wakes up one day and there he is starring at the Universal Amphitheatre. One of these mornings, when his sister and his mother can no longer support him in the style he is gradually becoming accustomed to, he will probably leave for Hollywood and find some wealthy woman . . . or women, or maybe even men . . . to set him up in elegance and style.

Female Leos are no less self-absorbed, but, like the lioness, they are willing to work their asses off in order to gain the money and the prestige essential to every Leo. It is, in truth, this passion for independence which can screw up their love lives. They are so intent on taking command of every situation, it is difficult for them to find a man they feel can do a better job. This is true in sex as well.

Most Leo women like to be on top, and they will tell you that the reason is that the man can admire their bodies, when the real reason remains that they cannot bear being in a vulnerable or subservient position. Long before Leo Bella Abzug and Aquarian Germaine Greer, the greatest Leo of them all, Mae West, was making marvelous comedies in which the male-female roles were reversed. She was the aggressor; she was the tomcat; she was really Clark Gable in drag. So much so that when approached by Taurian Anita Loos in the thirties to co-star with Gable, she politely refused. After all, they were both playing the same role.

So if the Leo woman spends most of her life complaining she cannot find a man strong enough, why then, one would ask, doesn't she get herself a Leo man? She could work all day, direct those activities that her male counterpart couldn't care less about, and come home to find a lusty, muscular stud waiting to satisfy her own passionate needs. Not only that, but he wouldn't put up with any of those domineering qualities which make other men quake in their boots, and she could bide her time until he becomes President of General Motors or Emperor of a banana republic. Sounds ideal, doesn't it? Of course, it doesn't. It would be sheer disaster . . . and usually is. That's why you so seldom find Leo's married to other Leos. They will go on complaining and choose a Libra or a Pisces who will do what they command . . . or wind up by themselves.

We have, for effect, given you the extremes. The lazy hustler with the dreams of glory on the one hand, and Clark Gable in drag on the other, so now let's talk about Leos in general. You love the preliminaries of the sex act as much as the act itself. You adore the candlelit dinners at the very posh restaurant where the maitre d' considers you one of the family. You adore the rented limousine...or preferably the limousine that isn't rented...the imported wine, the violinist who comes to your table to play "your" song, which is often *You Oughta Be In Pictures* or *You Are Too Beautiful For One Man Alone*. You revel in the compliments, the gifts, like the simple diamond necklace or the ruby cufflinks, and you're thrilled by hearing your name paged in the middle of dinner and seeing it in print the next day in the society column. You adore, in fact, everything that used to be associated with Hollywood's Golden Era. That's probably the reason Hollywood's Golden Era boasted so many Leo celebrities: William Powell, Myrna Loy, Norma Shearer, Robert Taylor, Emil Jannings, Clara Bow, Dolores del Rio, Rudy Vallee, Joe E. Brown, Ann Harding, Sylvia Sidney, Ethel Barrymore, Billie Burke, Lucille Ball, Van Johnson, Esther Williams, Maureen O'Hara, Jack Warner, Cecil B. De Mille, John Huston, Alfred Hitchcock, Samuel Goldwyn, and, of course, the venerable Ms. West. It's no wonder that the Metro symbol was a lion and that the head of the studio and the greatest mogul of them all, Louis B. Mayer, was also a Leo.

If that name-dropping sounds familiar, that's because it's one of your favorite pastimes. One Leo lady we know uses reverse psychology. She drops all the names to show you whom she is *not* impressed with. The typical Leo will line every available wall space with photographs of himself with celebrities, or celebrities alone...all bearing personal inscriptions. That's why so many Leo dens resemble the bar at Sardi's. Yet when it comes to affairs or marriage, you almost never choose someone on the same professional or social level. If you are ambitious, you will select one who is subservient...rather like the courtier paying homage to the monarch. If you are not ambitious for yourself, you will seek out the person to whom you can be the power behind the throne.

Monarch, throne, king, queen, emperor, royalty, regality...these are always the words most frequently used in astrological descriptions of your sign. That's why it's not easy for you to find the right partner in life. After all, the selection of worthy mates for the rulers of old was extremely limited. Hence, you will sometimes go out into the world in disguise as happened in those old operettas in which the prince masquerades as his own servant and falls in love with Jeanette MacDonald...or Jeanette masquerades as her lady-in-waiting and falls in love with Nelson Eddy. In either case, if you should bring them back to the palace, it is tacitly understood they are not to the nobility born.

When you do go out into the world, whether in disguise or not, you are the chooser. If someone approaches you in an aggressive manner, you will draw up to your full height, even if you're only as tall as Napoleon, and regard them as a beggar at the Gates of Paradise. Familiarity breeds contempt, unless it's your own familiarity, which is never really that familiar. Your approach is cautious and subtle, for there is much leonine pride involved, and you do not relish being turned down. If you are turned down, you don't wither like a Libra or a Cancer, but quickly regain your composure and go on to someone else. Dignity and determination are two of your foremost qualities.

In the sex act itself, you hate to be rushed or interrupted. You lose yourself in the ecstasy of it and also lose your sense of time, which may account for why so many Leos are attracted to Scorpios and vice-versa. As we said before, you like to be on top in command of the situation and are not known for your extreme versatility. Your enjoyment arises from lust and involvement, rather than from sexual acrobatics. Unlike Taureans, you do not please for the sake of pleasing. You please because you want the admiration of the other person and, at the same time, expect them to please you. You are not a creature that does somersaults when your partner reaches a climax and you don't.

There is a vulnerable area in your egocentricity, which few suspect unless they really get to know you. When you have accepted someone as a friend or lover, you are just about the most tolerant of all twelve signs. You will overlook all shortcomings, except when they embarrass you or attack your ego, as long as they remember to tell you they love you. The interesting thing, though, is that many do not reveal what they really are when they're with you, but rather what you want them to be. Such is the power of your personality. But that also has to do with the fact that, unless you are a highly evolved Leo, you, too, are playing a role. It's a role in which you are eternally presenting your best face for the world to see. You are reluctant to show any inner turmoil, any emotional crisis, any personal setback to any but those who are closest to you.

Because you appear as a stone pillar through fire, flood and earthquake, you find yourself being mother or father confessor to most of those around you. It's a role you enjoy and play to the hilt. Solving the problems of others is infinitely easier than solving your own . . . as any Virgo can tell you. But, unlike Virgo, you always feel that your problems are different. From time to time, you view yourself as so isolated from humanity at large, you don't even expect to get the same diseases as other people. Your diseases, like everything else in your lives, are rare and unique.

Truly rare and unique also are your courage, loyalty and ability to handle almost every obstacle fate throws in your path. We know of no other sign who can so casually cope with disaster without falling apart or running to an analyst. If you had been on that space ship in *Alien,* more than just Sigourney Weaver would have come back alive. In addition, there is not one ounce of self-pity in your make-up and you detest pity from others. Unlike Cancer, Pisces and Libra, you will never hold somebody to you out of sympathy or guilt. The evolved Leo, the one who is able to free himself from the mundane restrictions of materialism and show, can be as marvelous a companion as one could wish for.

You Leos are often homebodies and much prefer entertaining at your own place rather than going to someone else's. However, if you were born with your Venus in Gemini, you'll take every opportunity to bolt out the front door. All somebody has to do is ask you, and there you are with your overnight case. All somebody has to do is make the suggestion and there you are, attending a lecture or trying that new restaurant where the atmosphere isn't much but the food is supposed to be terrrific. This is opposed to other Leos, who'll take atmosphere over food any day of the week. You have less of the Leo feeling of isolation and far less of the snobbery. What you search for in a lover is not necessarily someone you want to show off, but one who stimulates you mentally as well as physically. This combination frequently bestows a multiplicity of talents with the ability to write being particularly strong. You are less absorbed in yourself and more interested in what's going on around you. Therefore, success can sometimes be achieved as a columnist or journalist.

It decreases the sex drive and increases the sense of humor, which is always beneficial when the sex drive is diminished. Famous Leos with their Venus in Gemini are Petrarch, Max Heindel, Amelia Earhart, Eric Hoffer, Dag Hammarskjold, Alfred Tennyson, Gracie Allen, Myrna Loy and Peter Duchin.

All Leos are possessive, but when you're a Leo with your Venus in Cancer everything that is yours is terrific, everything that is someone else's can't be much. This is especially true of lovers. You can search a long time and once you have found it, you will do anything to keep it. Leos usually have a high standard of moral conduct, and you do, too, except when it means holding on to the object of your passion. You may *have* to hold on, especially if that object goes in for sexual pleasures detailed in magazines like *Hustler* or *Penthouse,* since your tendency is to be a bit on the conservative side. For some of you, anything other than the missionary position is considered kinky. The depth of your devotion, however, is admirable, whether it's your lover, your family or your friends; and you will display more outward affection, especially in public, than most Leos. Napoleon Bonaparte, Herman Melville, Annie Oakley, Carl Jung, Mata Hari (some of you *do* know more than the missionary position), Cecil B. De Mille, Benito Mussolini, Aldous Huxley, Dustin Hoffman, Buck Owens, Princess Anne of England, Valerie Harper and Francis Gary Powers are some of those born with this combination.

When both your Sun and your Venus are in Leo, respect becomes mandatory. If you do not respect the one you love, the relationship is doomed no matter how exciting it can be when the lights are out. All the Leo requirements of display, grandeur, regality and dominance are underscored, but so are the capacities to love and to give.

As much as you admire success and wealth, no amount of it will provide happiness unless there's someone with whom to share it. It's not easy finding that person, because the attention you crave is overwhelming to ordinary mortals. You can be as jealous as Othello, but your ego is too great to allow yourself to compete for anyone's favor. If you discover the one you love loves another, it can be absolute trauma although you would be the last to let anyone know. You would then cut off the relationship with a butcher knife and perhaps some of you would cut *up* the relationship with a butcher knife. You'd steadfastly refuse to speak to the person again.

Well-known people with this combination are Sir Walter Scott, George Bernard Shaw, Claude Debussy, John Galsworthy, Raymond Chandler, Yves St. Laurent, Don Drysdale, Stanley Kubrick, Isaac Hayes and Jacqueline Susann.

When your Venus is in Virgo, you could become so discriminating you might function better in a monastery or a convent. Practically no one can measure up to your standards for any length of time. You are the type of person who, if the Venus de Milo passes by, you will say she has an arm missing. However, if you do decide to remain in this imperfect world, you do eventually choose mates . . . and, as so often happens when you are that particular, you can make the worst possible selection. But then just think of what the other person has to put up with . . . a cross between the Leo egotism and the Virgo censure. If perchance you do discover that rare individual for whom you've been searching, your whole life becomes enriched and their flaws infinitesimally minimized. Sometimes Leos with Venus in Virgo find a mate with health problems in order to play nurse or doctor. Famous personages born with this blend are Alexandre Dumas, both pere and fils , Guy de Maupassant, Henry Ford, Herbert Hoover, Lawrence of Arabia, John Huston, Vida Blue, Evonne Goolagong, Neil Armstrong, Andy Warhol, Fidel Castro, Robert De Niro and Wilt Chamberlain.

When your Venus is in Libra and you are not born into the Jet Set or the House of Rothschild, it's really a drag. That's where you were meant to be . . . and you would be the first to agree.
You cherish class, breeding, luxury, beauty and everything that pertains to life beneath the Mediterranean sun or a crystal chandelier. Finding fascinating friends and playmates is as important as finding the perfect lover, so it is wiser not to settle down with one who is jealous. They will never approve of or understand your need to table-hop through life. Not that you aren't generous and devoted. You are. Only you apply these qualities to many, not just one and the more congenial companions you have, the happier your life will be. Once you have established a relationship, it is more difficult for you to break it off than for other Leos. You will do anything to avoid confrontation, and thus try to manipulate the affair so the other person is the one to leave. We wonder if Davy

Crockett, Helena Blavatsky, Orville Wright, Ethel Barrymore, Samuel
Goldwyn, Frank Gifford, Robert Culp and Princess Margaret ever found
themselves in that position.

♍

VIRGO

August 23 – September 22

VIRGO

Pick up almost any astrological book and read the description of Virgo. You may fall asleep along about the third paragraph. After all, who wants to go thorugh life being known as a fussy analytical, nit-picking, methodical, conscientious picture-straightener? And consider the other associations with the sign. It rules the sixth house, which is the house of health, employment, small animals, servants, service and insects. Isn't that exciting! And how about the symbol of the sign? A virgin with a shaft of wheat in her hand. She's not exactly the kind of girl you would love to take to a hot-tub party. And we won't even comment on the part of the body Virgo rules, except to tell you, in case you didn't know, it's the bowels. When you put it all together, it's quite a parlay, wouldn't you say? No wonder so many Virgos born on either cusp will pretend they're either Leo or Libra.

Well, we're here to tell you that the books have got to be rewritten. As a matter of fact, they have *been* rewritten in ancient times by someone spurned by a Virgo lover. Thousands of years ago, the symbol of Virgo was not the virgin standing before you with that simpering smile on her face. She was lying down prostrate, a postion many of you automatically assume at the least provocation.

Few of you know there's an animal counterpart to your sign: the Fox. The fox is surely one of the most fascinating creatures in the animal kingdom, and we'll tell you about him in just a bit.

Another interesting side light is that many astrologers do not believe Mercury is the ruler of your sign. There is a growing feeling you are governed by a still to be discovered planet some have already named Vulcan. If you remember your mythology, Vulcan was the god of metal-working and fire, a brilliant craftsman who also happened to be crippled. But fact and theories aside, Virgos can be stimulating, exciting and dazzling people . . . especially if you like truth. If you're a Pisces, Libra or Cancer, you'd better keep your distance.

Now let's take those items individually. First, let's consider the virgin lying prostrate on the ground. She also, like her more recent counterpart, has a shaft of wheat in her hand. We don't know exactly what she's doing with that shaft, but we can conjecture. We are not saying that Virgo is the sign that masturbates the most, but there's always the possibility. Two reasons come immediately to mind. One is that you are so discriminating, you would rather love yourself in the evening than hate yourself in the morning. Secondly, although you can be the most intricate game-players in the entire zodiac, you are not the sort who pounce on someone to whom you are really attracted. You will make extremely subtle and tentative moves, and if they don't respond, you always have you to fall back on. No, Philip Roth is not a Virgo, he is a Pisces. We never did get Portnoy's birthdate.

As we said, the prostrate position is a favorite one, even though the books will have you believe the only position a Virgo is capable of getting into is sitting at a desk perhaps. You are not the great workers everyone says you are. That's a myth which probably began with some unemployed Virgo. As a matter of fact, you hate to do anything you don't want to do, and, in that reclining state, you can spend so much time *thinking* about working, you are much too exhausted to do anything but watch television or fall asleep.

Then there's the fox. If you consider the many complexities of this creature, you will get a perceptive insight into your sign. Some Virgos even resemble foxes. The late Lyndon Johnson did. Johnson had wheels within wheels within wheels. He could do almost nothing straight-forwardly. He once called a press conference to announce a new appointment. He spoke about everything else. Finally, one impatient newsman (probably an Aries) raised his hand and said, "But, Mr. President, who have you selected for the job?" At last Johnson revealed the name. Afterwards, someone came up to him and said, "Mr. President, what would have happened had that reporter not asked you the question?" To which Johnson replied, "Oh, I had somebody planted in the audience for that purpose."

There was no reason for this kind of subterfuge and it doesn't make sense . . . unless you happen to be another Virgo. We daresay that had it been Johnson, rather than Nixon, involved in Watergate, no one would ever have traced it back to the White House. Tape-recordings in the Oval office? A Virgo would have whispered conservations in an igloo in Iceland instead! It goes back to the foxiness. Remember that foxes are skillful at deceiving pursuers and avoiding traps. They are extremely fast with very keen senses and can never be fully tamed. In wilderness areas, they say a fox can behave like a shy but friendly dog. Yet he remains a fox.

Thus it is with Virgos at the beginning of a relationship. When you really want someone badly enough, you will play anything that other person expects you to play. Ah, what perfect lovers you make when everything is fresh and new! But when the affair begins to wane, then the true Virgo personality emerges from the shadows of perfection like some monster hidden in the dark at the top of the stairs. The other person can only gape in shock or flee for his life. So convincing are you in whatever role you assume, that even the most sagacious Scorpio or Aquarian could never perceive the masquerade.

Foxy has another connotation in our time. It's used to describe very special sexy people, and it's no wonder that Virgo, the sign of all those nit-picking little picture-straighteners, has some of the foxiest: Sophia Loren, Raquel Welch, Sean Connery, Vittorio Gassman, Tuesday Weld, Englebert Humperdinck, Jacqueline Bisset, Valerie Perrine, Arnold Palmer, Jimmy Connors, Twiggy and Leonard Bernstein.

We said before that Vulcan was a superb artisan who happened to be crippled. In symbolic sense, this is applicable to your sign. There are the Virgos with the glittering minds and talents who have, as in Greek tragedy, some fatal flaw which prevents them from making full use of their potential. One Virgo we know...and one of the most brilliant...recently said, "I get so sick of everybody trying to find himself. I found myself years ago. What I'm trying to do is *lose* myself." Often the fatal flaw is purely and simply ego. Ego can always impede progress, and the Virgo ego insists on being right. You hate making mistakes so much that you often make more mistakes than had you not been afraid of making them in the first place. In terms of a brief affair, this flaw is negligible. In a long standing romance, you can drive your partner to drink.

Another thing that can drive them to drink...or grass or coke or Hershey bars...is, as you know, your criticism. Although you have no hesitation in criticizing everything and everyone around you, you cannot bear criticism against yourself. It has to be done by someone you absolutely adore, and then in a voice more mellifluous than Cal Worthington. Your criticism is also aimed at yourself, and practically nothing anyone can tell you will be worse than what you have told the reflection in the looking glass.

In our chapter on Gemini, we mentioned the fact that they do not understand the laws of cause and effect and, therefore, live their lives with more excuses than were found at Nurembery. You, on the other hand, understand only too well the laws of cause and effect, but you'll be damned if you'll let anyone else know. Your best defense is always an offense. In response to any attack you will usually do a 20-minute number which consists of more doubletalk than a tobacco auctioneer and a land promoter combined. We don't know who invented police language, but we wouldn't be surprised if he were a Virgo. Invariably, you take one of two tacks: you either turn it all against your poor unsuspecting opponent or you accuse him of picking on you. If love is never having to say you're sorry, you would be the most desirable mates in the zodiac.

At your best, no one can be a wiser counselor than you. That is if one is looking for honest advice. If he's looking for gooey sympathy, he'd better find a Cancer or Pisces. Often you will seek out a partner actively involved in some field in which your wisdom and expertise becomes indispensable. For you can analyze a situation and be able to predict what the outcome should be in each of several courses of action as well as how every character will react under different sets of circumstances. This is a phenomenal talent, which works like a charm in any situation except the one in which you are personally involved. It's then that your perceptions go straight out the window and the games begin. So skilled are you, as we said, at these defensive ploys that the other person will feel he's not only got a lover, but he's also got the entire collection from the Parker Brothers. That's why a relationship between two Virgos is well nigh impossible. It would be akin to China going to war with Russia; the result would be no winners...just total destruction.

We have talked about a great many things aside from sex, because, with certain exceptions, sex is not the motivating force in your life. Mental stimulation can reach a peak of such exhilaration, it's equivalent to a wild orgasm for certain other signs. It is just such exhilaration that you search for in art, life, conversation and love affairs. Unlike Erica Jong, who is an Aries, you have no fear of flying. Flying is what you want to do every hour of every day, and the trouble is so much of living means being earthbound. That's why when you find someone you can fly with, you want to keep them forever. Combine that with what we said before about hating to make mistakes. It is interesting to note that Virgos have the fewest multiple marriages among film personalities, traditionally famous for multiple marriages. The list of both living and dead is impressive: Maurice Chevalier, Charles Boyer, Fredric March and Florence Eldridge (a rare case of two Virgos who made a go of it), Sophia Loren, Fred MacMurray, Lauren Bacall, Yvonne de Carlo, Alan Ladd, Paul Muni, Gene Kelly, Kitty Carlisle, Anne Bancroft, Vittorio Gassman, Rossano Brazzi. Then there's Mickey Rooney. But he was born exactly on the cusp of Libra, and you know how Libra likes to be married.

Finding the right person is so important you are willing to make all sorts of sexual concessions or adjustments if the individual turns you on mentally. Seldom considered unselfish, in bed you can become the server. Often those who serve the least outside of bed serve the most when the lights are out. Oral sex is often a particular specialty and so is anal sex. It all depends on the other person, for you have the distinction of being the one sign in astrology who will always choose to be the lover rather than the loved. You learn at an early age that when you are the lover you win in the long run, and if there's one thing essential to you it's winning.

Virgo is not naturally a family oriented sign, but if your Venus is in Cancer, this changes. There is more desire for domesticity and the home. As a rule, Virgos are not big on children...somehow their egos do not need to reproduce, possibly because they can be bolstered in so many other ways. However, here there would be a greater desire for the patter of little feet. In most cases, it's not just little feet, but little paws as well. Virgos can heap as much love on an animal as on a person . . . if not more so. A curious thing is that though yours is not a sign that must reproduce, you love reproduction in everything else, whether it's puppies, guppies or African violets. In your case, it's all of the above.

You will be more overtly emotional than other Virgos and more vulnerable. This means if someone should hurt you, you'll only cut off their little finger instead of their whole hand. Notable people who have this same combination are Oliver Wendell Holmes, Lyndon Johnson, Fred MacMurray, William Saroyan, Walt Kelly, Patsy Cline and Raquel Welch.

Taste is important to every Virgo, but extra important to those of you who have your Venus in Leo. More than other Virgos, you go for outward display, and unlike other Virgos, you don't mind paying for what you get. Louis XIV had this combination, so it is not surprising that many of you picture yourselves with the lover of your dreams living in a little abode not unlike the palace of Versailles. Not only do you appreciate things that look good, you like lovers that look good, also. Maybe that's why you are so often attracted to those in athletics or the entertainment world. You are, as a rule, less critical, especially of yourself . . . and this makes you freer to express yourself creatively. Leo Tolstoy, Grandma Moses, Claudette Colbert, James Wong Howe, O. Henry, Leonard Bernstein, Sherwood Anderson, Darryl F. Zanuck, Greta Garbo and Jose Feliciano are a few of the many artists born with this polarity. Virgos are terrified of failure, and Venus in Leo increases this fear. (Garbo, the consummate actress, quit rather than face the possibility of a waning career). This applies to your love lives, too.

When both your Sun and your Venus are in Virgo, you can go through dozens of people . . . sometimes hundreds . . . before you find the one who is right for you. Somehow, with your incredible intuition, you know him immediately and if necessary will pursue him to the ends of the earth, because you've waited so long. In a strange way, you are more fortunate than many other Virgos, since invariably he *is* that one person and he could remain a long, long time. If he should go out of your life, you will not sever the relationship; you will try to maintain contact, for its inconceivable to you that two people can live together for years and not remain friends. *They* may not always feel as kindly, since you are not the softest, most pliable folks to fall in love with. Goethe, Aubrey Beardsley, Charles Boyer, Harry Reems, Jean-Claude Killy, Eldridge Cleaver, Lilly Tomlin, Jimmy Connors, Kate Millet and Brian Epstein were all born with this combination.

There is even more need to find the right person in life when your Venus is in Libra, but you usually can't wait as long as those with Venus in

Virgo. Just to have someone, you may settle for second best unless you happen to have been Elizabeth I of England, who used her Libran Venus to solidify her empire rather than to occupy her bed.

You are usually gentler and more politic in expressing yourself, so that the stinging Virgo criticism is tempered with a bit of Libran frosting. You don't like to argue or fight as much as others of your sign, and since you offend less people, your social circles are larger. In a love relationship, you will at least make an effort to see your partner's point of view, a very un-Virgo characteristic. Rather than demand, you will persuade . . . but still try to get your own way. Some Virgos with Venus in Libra will go to great lengths for love . . . Ingrid Bergman, for instance. Some will go to great lengths for things besides love . . . like Jesse James. Other Sun in Virgo-Venus in Libra combinations belong to Samuel Johnson, Lafayette, Hegel, James Fenimore Cooper, Bret Harte, Theodore Dreiser, Sean Connery, Buddy Holly, Jacqueline Bisset and Mary Shelley.

There is always an element of detachment, even in the most passionate Virgo's love, unless you were born with your Venus in Scorpio. This is the one position that can become obsessed with a lover especially when you are young. There is more jealousy here and in the long run, less tolerance. Unlike other Virgos, when an affair is over, it's *over.* You do not take rejection easily and you can hold a grudge as long as a full-blooded Scorpio. Well, maybe not quite *that* long. Privacy is carried to the point of secrecy, and now and again there may be a certain shyness when you make contact with the outside world. Agatha Christie was born with this combination, and it's not uprising that she chose the form of fiction she did. Virgos can make a mystery out of anything . . . from what they had for breakfast to where they live. And Scorpios are natural born detectives. With this position, unlike most Virgos, you can usually find what you've mislaid. Aside from Miss Christie, we have H. G. Wells, Arnold Schonberg, Rosemary Harris, Joni James, B. B. King, Charlie Byrd, Sid Caesar and Jackie Cooper.

LIBRA

September 23 — October 22

LIBRA

A dear Libran friend of ours is one of the most remarkable people we have ever known. Sweet, considerate, genuinely concerned for the welfare of others, she endures every sling and arrow of outrageous fortune with utter equanimity. Never does she complain; never does she elicit sympathy. She accepts each human being exactly as he is and bestows love and responsibility on her husband, her children, and her friends without expecting anything in return. It was only a few months ago that we learned her secret. In answer to our question, "How on earth do you do it?" she replied, "It's easy. I've been taking Valium every day for the past twenty years."

Now we are not saying that all Librans need Valium or quaaludes or alcohol to survive in this world, but it helps.

The problem is that you Librans are so sensitive, so in need of peace and harmony...whether you are choosing between two brands of apple juice or having the love affair of your life...reality is often too discordant to cope with. And it all has to do with your symbol: those scales of justice. In trying to continually balance them, one keeps getting lower than the other, so you go running over to the second one, trying to pull it down, but then the first one goes too far up and you have to pull that down, and by the time you're finished, they're out of balance anyway, and you're utterly exhausted.

And so it goes with your romantic involvements. Ah, if only life could be a series of brief affairs! For what hosts and houseguests you make! You can disappear into the wallpaper when the other person wants to be alone, and when he doesn't want to be alone, he has only to clap his hands and out you come...the most congenial, witty and sparkling companion anyone could wish for. Since you are naturally extravagant, you will insist on buying gifts and paying for as much as you can. You are also as tidy as a Swiss maid...even tidier at someone else's place than at your own. If there were a Michelin Guide for hosts and visistors, each and every one of you would get four stars.

But the reason life cannot be a series of brief affairs is not because of the nature of life, but because of the nature of you. You long for attachment and need a soul mate like a Virgo needs something to worry about. (If your soul mate happens to be a Virgo, which is unlikely, he will have plenty to worry about.) You will meet someone terribly attractive (Librans like terribly attractive people), and so warm, so giving and so agreeable will you be that, unless the other person is incredibly perverse and wants combat rather than love, he or she will invariably ask to see you again. If you find them equally as appealing...and sometimes it's difficult to tell with a Libran because you so desperately want to ingratiate yourself with everybody...that's when the real problems start. Or, we should say, the real problems don't start until the first sign of conflict arises. Up till then, it's all champagne bubbles.

There is bound to be conflict where there are human beings...an axiom of life you would prefer to ignore. Because of this, during the first conflict, you will continue to smile sweetly and tell yourself and the other person that everything's all right. Then comes the second one. Your smile will be a little less sweet, but again you will try to overlook whatever might have been offensive to you. Around the fifth time, you begin retreating into a corner to brood over whatever has happened and relive the other four times...with a dozen comebacks you should have said but didn't. It's a while later that out of the clear blue sky, over what is usually an absurdly insignificant point, you suddenly pick up that fragile old heirloom that's been in your lover's family for at least three generations and smash it to smithereens. Using expletives the other person never even thought you knew, you will then proceed to blame your beloved for everything from having entrapped you into this goddamned affair to start with to having caused the massacre in Guyana. You will storm out, go to your closest friend (you usually have a lot of close friends) and tell them everything that transpired. You will then get the assurance you were looking for that it certainly wasn't your fault. How *could* it be your fault after the version of the story you've just told? Soon you will cool off and return to your adored one...and unless he or she should happen to be a Scorpio, in which case their door will be doublebolted and never opened again, this is the beginning of an almost perfect Libran sado-masochistic affair.

There are and there have been, of course, certain Librans who do not play sweetness and light before the heirloom hits the wall. Barbara Walters, Groucho Marx, George C. Scott, Trevor Howard, Gore Vidal, Rex Reed, Melina Mercouri and Walter Matthau come immediately to mind, but generally speaking, every Libra longs for the kind of romance where seldom is heard a discouraging word and the skies are not cloudy all day.

It's this sort of idyllic relationship you look for from the moment you approach the Marina del Rey, if you're in Southern California, or its swinging equivalent anywhere in the world. You Librans are at your best in any social situaiton, except orgies, and you can be at your best there, too, provided it's to please someone else. Therefore, you take every opportunity to go out in the hopes that this will be the night you will meet the lover of your dreams. The stay-at-home Libra has either just found the lover of their dreams or is three and half months pregnant. Although you may be quiet and reticent before you get there, once you enter the arena, it's as though you are the main attraction. An irresistible magnetism suddenly emanates from you as though you were encased in a million fireflies.

Because your egos are basically fragile, you protect them by having others come to you so that it puts you in the position you like best: *love me, want me and perhaps I'll love and want you.* But even in this preliminary stage, if the slightest off-key note is sounded, or you detect an imperfection which may bug you later, you will graciously reject any further advances. For you are not like most of the people you are with unless it happens to be a Libran convention. You are not seeing one night of wild pleasure. No, you are envisioning the morning after, the lips that can hardly tear themselves apart, the endless telephone calls, the flowers, the dinners, the trips. The minister and the looks on your parents' faces. It's *involvement* you want, not temporary excitement; only your involvement is more in the nature of a Baldwin novel. Faith, we mean, not James...James is a Leo, and Leos know better.

Once you are at home with the person, it is gradual seduction...never rape. After the wine and the music and the charming conversation comes the physical contact, which seems at first to be inadvertent. Librans love to touch and be touched, and this can go on for hours, since you are not one for tearing off another's clothes and doing it beneath the glass-top coffee-table. You don't dig roughness, not because it doesn't turn you on as much as it is because you cannot bear to have your apparel or your hair mussed. If you are a true Libran, you will always look tumble-dried.

When you finally get to the bedroom...which you will insist on doing unless the other person is a Scorpio or a Sagittarian, when you might as well forget it and remain under the coffee-table...you will want the lights on if you are proud of your body and the lights off if you are not. There is a vanity in almost every Libran which borders on narcissism; and whatever is not real about you (whether it be the hair, the eyelashes or any part of the anatomy), you will strive to maintain the illusion. From there on in, you will try like hell to please. Librans are not by nature kinky, but they can become so if turned on to an unusual fetish by one they love. More than any other sign, you depend on other people. Even in masturbation. A Libran will seldom masturbate alone, but that's because you hate to do anything alone. On the other hand, you will not hesitate to masturbate with someone else if that's what that someone else prefers.

But even if you do get kinky, if you use cockrings or whipped cream or hang from the chandelier, the astounding fact is it's well nigh impossible for you to be vulgar. Vulgarity is as foreign to you as irregularity to Pavlov's dog. When you think of Libran actresses, you think of great ladies such as Deborah Kerr, Greer Garson, Helen Hayes, Julie Andrews, Ina Claire, Lillian Gish and Joan Fontaine. Even the sex symbols like Rita Hayworth, Catherine Deneuve, Brigitte Bardot, Linda Darnell, Lizbeth Scott and Nita Ekberg never showed the slightest trace of vulgarity. This applies to Libran men, too. Whether they command the fleet of an empire like Lord Nelson or become president of a nation like Jimmy Carter and Dwight D. Eisenhower or write of passion and violence like Eugene O'Neill they remain gentlemen.

If this were a more rigid age, having your Sun in Libra and your Venus in Leo would not be the happiest of combinations. For you insist on choosing your own lover, rather than having your choice made for you; and you have very definite ideas on ideals. The ego is stronger and more overt than the average Libran, and it requires a good deal of regular stimulation. Often those with this position will settle down with someone who satisfies their physical and social requirements and be turned on by others who don't. These others are the ones who are set up in a *pied a terre* or kept secretly in the background. Children give satisfaction; and although Librans are not famed for being the most perfect parents, Venus in Leo will help you be more consistent in the way you raise them.

Impressed by wealth and fame, you would prefer every party to be filled with a guest list right out of Earl Blackwell's *Celebrity Register*. But even if they aren't, this won't deter you from grabbing every possible chance to socialize. Persons of renown born with their Sun in Libra and Venus in Leo are Sarah Bernhardt, Walter Lippmann, Thomas Wolfe, Carole Lombard, Marcello Mastroianni, Ray Charles, Glenn Gould, Maury Wills and Rex Reed.

Venus in Virgo sharpens the Libran intellect and gives more objectivity with less of an inclination to be led by your emotions. This is probably why it's such an excellent combination for success. There are more Libran celebrities born with their Venuses here than in any of the other four positions . . . for example Samuel Taylor Coleridge, Friedrich Neitzche, James Whitcomb Riley, Emily Post, P. G. Wodehouse, Eleanor Roosevelt, Bonnie Parker, Johnny Mathis, Don McLean, Mario Puzo, Catherine Deneuve, Groucho Marx and Julie Andrews.

In love, your search is more for character value than for external beauty. The person you choose will be one with whom you will want to spend as much time as possible . . . often to the exclusion of the rest of the world, thereby reducing the Libran passion for socializing. At the same time, all aspects of domesticity do not equally enchant you. Take children, for instance. You do not make the most disciplined of parents; and, although you may truly love the little buggers, you would prefer their upbringing to be supervised by someone else. Librans, in general do not like messy things, and with Venus in Virgo, the sight of sticky faces, soiled diapers and globs of oatmeal congealing on the high chair is as appealing to you as sauerkraut for breakfast or a honeymoon in Bangladesh.

It's a human failing to judge a person not by what he is, but by whether he likes you. With the Sun and Venus both in Libra, this can be carried to such an extreme, it might obliterate any true evaluation of human beings. In love, you are often swept away by one who pretends adoration, and it is only later you wake up one morning and discover the person next to you isn't Tristan or Isolde, but Count Dracula. (Yes, Bela Lugosi was a Libra, although his Venus was in Sagittarius.) This isn't always as bad as it may appear, since both males and females with a Libran Venus are often looking for someone to dominate and direct them. If perchance, Count Dracula turns out to be a pussycat and refuses to sink his teeth into your neck, you might be so disappointed, you could do it to him instead.

Outside of a love affair in which anything goes, courtesy and politeness are even more imperative than they are to others of your sign. Self discipline can be a struggle, and although Librans are artistic and talented, there is the problem of getting them down to the actual creative work. But then there's the problem of getting them down to any kind of work for any length of time. You need to have cooperation to such an extent that the slightest sign of conflict on a job can cause you to run for the unemployment office. The career, even to men with this combination, is always secondary to love. That's why so many of you settle down at an early age with the one you adore. When you no longer adore the one you adored or they no longer adore you, you don't ever say, like a Capricorn, for instance, "never again" and throw yourself with a vengeance into the professional world. No, you simply find another one to adore and after that, perhaps a third, a fourth, a fifth, ad infinitum. Those with this heavy Libran influence are the kind who eventually become the talk to the old folks' home or the senior citizens complex by playing around with the occupant down the hall. Cervantes, Noah Webster, Arthur Rimbaud, Aleister Crowley, David Ben-Gurion, F. Scott Fitzgerald, Lester Maddox and Barbara Walters are examples of this combination.

If Venus in Libra wants the heart, Venus in Scorpio must have the mind, the soul and every inch of the other person's anatomy as well. Sex and love are so engulfing that the Scorpio passion invariably upsets the Libran balance, and before you know it those scales are swinging around in mid-air like two wayward yo-yos. It's then you vow, unlike those other Librans, "never, *never* again" and decide to make your mark in a loveless profession. Unless you become a Mormon missionary or a Buddhist monk, this declaration is usually short lived, and as soon as sex again rears its tantalizing head, you are ready, even eager to go through the whole process again. This time, however, most of you will begin to differentiate between love and sex and realize you can have one without the other. By the time this occurs, you are often on your way to becoming president of IBM or the first female four-star general.

Most Librans do not have great confidence in their abilities, no matter how talented they are, but when your Venus is in Scorpio, you can promote yourself with such bravado, you soon begin to believe your own publicity. The same applies to your sex appeal. You don't have to look like Aphrodite or Apollo to convince others you are irresistible. You have only to turn up the rheostat you are all born with. If there's any word of caution, as in the case of Oscar Wilde, it's when having an affair, don't send postcards. Those who didn't were Franz Liszt, Giuseppe Verdi, John Dewey, Mahatma Ghandi, Buster Keaton, George Gershwin, Timothy Leary, Chubby Checker, Linda Lavin, Lee Harvey Oswald and Mickey Mantle.

A far greater conflict exists if you're Libran with your Venus in Sagittarius. Libra wants marriage and Sagittarius wants freedom so you may feel a little like that old Jimmy Durante song about did you ever get the feeling that you wanted to go and yet you have the feeling that you wanted to stay. This makes you more daring and adventurous than most of those born under your sign (*e.g.* Evel Knievel and Lenny Bruce).

You would not be totally satisfied with a physical or emotional attachment; you would demand a mental one, also. This means that finding the perfect person is that much harder for you. If your tendency is to be unfaithful, it's because you need more stimulation than most Librans . . . whether it be through conversation, travel, sports or a vibrator.

You also need more "romance." Romance does not have the same goosepimply, airborne connotation in our time as it used to. It has fallen into similar ill repute as "joy" . . . words which no longer apply to people's lives but to shampoo commercials or gothic paperbacks. They have been preempted by uppers, downers and poppers. Yet a Libran with Venus in Sagittarius, no matter how young, knows exactly what we're talking about. Mention romance and he sees shadows on the sand and smells night jasmine and hears Japanese windbells. Famous people include Eddie Rickenbacher, Dwight D. Eisenhower, Arthur Schlesinger, John Dean, Dizzy Gillespie and Dory Previn.

♏ SCORPIO

October 23 — November 22

SCORPIO

We'll call her Linda. She was a singer, and an excellent one. In passing it's interesting to note how many fine female singers are born under the sign of Scorpio...Galli-Curci, Ethel Waters, Jane Froman, Mahalia Jackson, Dorothy Collins, Helen Reddy, Grace Slick, Melba Moore, Joni Mitchell, Bonnie Raitt, Lynn Anderson and Cleo Laine. She was very young and very beautiful. Her boyfriend fell ill and died. His death was not unexpected, but, as in all cases where the illness is terminal, the reality still came as a shock. But Linda did not cry or sit alone in her apartment and grieve. She called another young man she happened to know. He invited her over, and she spent the afternoon and the night having as much sex as she possibly could.

At first glance, Linda might seem cold and callous, but she was not. She felt the death as deeply as anyone could. It was just that the only release she could think of, the only release that was complete and totally self-absorbing, was physical intercourse. To her, it was a reaffirmation of life. It happens that way with Scorpios, for it's the sign that rules sex, death and revitalization.

When people who are born under other signs are emotionally distraught or have just suffered some serious setback, they could not possibly think of making love. But for a Scorpio...it's a release, a catharsis. A Pisces may take to the bottle, a Libra to tranquilizers and a Cancer to his mother, but a Scorpio will take to his bed...usually with someone else.

Aside from the fact that sex is the most immediate escape, there is still another reason for this. His emotions are usually so pent-up and he has such difficulty expressing them to other people that the safest release is lust. Rather than permit his mind and his feelings to explode, it is easier for the true Scorpio to let his body do so. That way at least the other person gets some enjoyment, too. Oh, there may be a few scars or monkey-bites, but they don't hurt half as much as a Scorpio tongue run amuck.

After that opening, you're going to think us schizoid when we tell you that too much has been made of Scorpios and sex. There was a time when Scorpio was the most maligned sign of the zodiac. You had only to go to a party and when asked (for, God knows, you would never confess it unless asked) you would shyly admit that you were born under the sign of the Scorpion. Many people would nod politely and take the first excuse to move away. Others would be tolerant enough to say things like "Some of my best friends are Scorpios" or "I don't care what anyone says. I *like* Scorpios," but they would never in a million years have let their sisters marry one.

All that changed somewhere in the 60s when the hair came down along with the restrictions. No longer were you to be pitied or feared . . . you were to be envied. And it was all because of the section of the body your sign rules. In nineteenth century astrology it was called "the private parts." In contemporary America it can well be called "the public parts." So those with the most superficial knowledge of the zodiac hear the word Scorpio and they conjure up some delicious fantasy image. The male counterpart becomes a sullen Marlboro man who has joined the Hell's Angels; the female symbol seems to be a voluptuous leather-clad lady sitting in a window on the Reeperbahn, that notorious section of Hamburg, brandishing a whip. Nothing could be further from the truth. If there is any sign that does not *play* at sex, it's yours. The men may project strength and vitality like General Patton or Richard Burton, and the women beauty and mystery like Vivien Leigh and Gene Tierney, but all those look-at-me-aren't-I-sexy games are as far from the Scorpio image as you can get. Because there is such a wealth of passion swirling below, you will use everything to cover it up . . . from coldness to humor, from aloofness to preoccupation. As a matter of fact, when cruising, you Scorpios sometimes appear to others as so formidable, nobody, except maybe Jack the Ripper or Betty Friedan, would dare approach.

It's all defense-mechanism, at least in most cases. Because you fully realize the extent of your capacity for invovlement, you're afraid of it, just as you're afraid of your temper. You often retreat into a shell of self-containment which others find difficult to break through. If, however, someone makes the effort, they could discover an intensely loyal, devoted human being, who is eager to communicate everything he thinks and feels. It's a little like opening Pandora's Box. The other person is seldom prepared for all that's inside and frequently runs for his life.

You are, of course, *the* sign of extremes. Like a Russian play, you can go from the heights of elation to the depths of depression in a matter of moments. You can be completely disciplined or thoroughly uncontrolled. You can be charming and gregarious or silent and anti-social. You can be joyous, you can be hostile, optimistic or negative. Just take the antonym of any synonym and you will have an insight into the complexity of the typical Scorpio.

Remember, yours is a sign ruled by not one, but two different planets, Mars and Pluto...Mars representing aggression, combat, impulse and energy, and Pluto representing degeneration, regeneration, death and the life force. Then, too, you have a double animal counterpart. There is the scorpion, that poisonous insect which has no herd or pack instinct and prefers to live by itself. The scorpion does not actively seek food, but waits for his prey to come to his lair. Inhabitants of warm areas, they tend to become sluggish during cold periods. They usually avoid other scorpions, but when confronted, they will fight to the death, the victor devouring the vanquished. The scorpion once had the distinction of being the only creature, besides man, who could commit suicide. The legend was that when surrounded by a ring of fire or entrapped so there was no escape, it would turn its sting upon itself. Although in recent years this theory has been scientifically discredited, it remains an accurate one in describing a certain part of the Scorpio personality.

The other animal counterpart is the eagle, for centuries the symbol of empire, of courage and of military powers. Though more formidable than any other bird, the eagle allows them to build near his royal nest without fear of molestation. These nests are usually made by the sea or great rivers, and the eagle will continue to build his nest on the same tree until that tree literally falls. When translated into human terms, no other sign has quite the indefatigability of yours...and no other sign can soar higher. Certain Scorpios even resemble eagles (*e.g.* Ruth Gordon).

The extremes and the complexity are as applicable to every aspect of the mating game, from the moment you make the intital contact till the time the affair ends. This can be fifty years later or the following morning. When you go in search of a lover, you have the distinction of knowing exactly what you want when you see it. There is no indecision, no wondering whether or not the chemistry is there, no having to spend precious moments of passion in small talk, no having to become friends first. You know instantly who you are attracted to, much like Miss Piggy seeing Kermit the Frog for the first time in *The Muppet Movie*. We cannot tell you whether or not Miss Piggy is a Scorpio since she refuses to reveal her birth information. The person of your choice may not feel the same about you, and if this should happen, you can become either bitingly sarcastic or graciously dignified...or leave.

Let's say the other person *is* attracted to you. That still does not mean your instinct was right. Your instinct, in fact, is often not right, and Scorpios will generally find that their long-standing affairs are with those who have sought them out, rather than vice-versa.

You Scorpios are as definite about what turns you on in bed as you are about what turns you on out of bed. You're a little too definite, perhaps. Many other signs will experiment, alternate or try to go along with what the other person wants. You expect the person to go along with what you want. And since it's so difficult for you to compromise, it's equally as diﬁfcult for you to find that rare individual with whom you want to set up house. Interestingly enough, a few years ago in Germany a survey was conducted on astrology and marriage. They discovered that the least divorced group was Scorpio men and the most divorced was Scorpio women. Obviously, it would indicate there is a wide schism between the males and females of your sign. Is there really that wide a schism? Is it not more because of society's restrictions, rather than astrology's? Doesn't it show rather that all Scorpios want to rule (there have been more Scorpion Presidents of the United States than any other sign), and until recently, ruling has been the male prerogative?

Scorpio is not a sign that likes to take a back-seat in marriage or in anything else. You are not as overt about it as a Leo or an Aries, but you find it uncomfortable to follow the dictates of another person unless you are dead sure he knows more than you do or, in more materialistic types, has a more successful track-record. You will then make all kinds of concessions, but it means absolute trust. And how many times in a Scorpio's life does he trust absolutely?

Let's say, now, that you have met someone you are really attracted to and they are attracted to you and you go home with each other and find that sex is terrrific... *really* terrific. You will put aside social, economic, intellectual, professional and astrological differences and you will insist on beginning an affair. It's silly, you know, and there may be no hope of any real relationship, but it's like trying to tell a moth to stay away from the flame. It does not good whatever. And when you get hooked, oh, how you get hooked! You will make compromises unthinkable in other areas of your life. You will give your heart, your time, your money, your freedom. At least, to *you*, it seems that you are giving all these things. To the other person, you may be giving far less than you think...or you may be giving everything but what they really want.

In certain instances, you may be giving too much. Sometimes people are attracted to you because you represent a challenge, and they are disappointed when that challenge is too easily removed. Scorpios give off a natural aura of strength and power, and those who are fascinated by challenges often confuse toughness with strength. The fact is that a strong person is almost never tough and a tough person is almost never strong. You, too, are attracted to challenge...but challenge having to do with yourself, not with other people. You love to be able to remold yourself into new images and towards new goals.

Because you can be so easily led by those "private parts" and therefore find yourself making silk purses out of sow's ears, many of your relationships are doomed from the moment you say, "Do you live around here? And the damned thing is that you *know* they're doomed and you will go ahead and make the same error. This, by the way, is a proclivity which does not apply to other areas of your life. But then, you know as well as anyone else, gonads do not a successful career make.

When the affair is over, you react in true Scorpio fashion. You dream of tortures more violent than any used by the Spanish Inquisition. Some of you may even try to put them into practice. One Scorpio we know made the statement, "We Scorpios don't get angry, we get even." The idea of revenge is never far from your consciousness, but this applies to all Scorpios, not just lovers. If you are an eagle-type, you will toy with a hundred and one odd ways of destruction, but never act upon them. If you are a scorpion-type, you will not only act upon them, you can wait twenty-five years to do so.

One of your favorite methods of torture is to stop speaking. This can drive a Leo, a Virgo, an Aquarian…just about any sign…up the bloody wall. You will, if necessary, stop speaking for any length of time you choose from an afternoon to a lifetime. This is not something you have trained yourself to do just to irritate or vex. As we said before, you are afraid of the violence of your temper and, in a way, you feel you are doing the other person a favor by being totally silent, rather than slicing them to shreds with your tongue or a machete. One Leo lady we knew married a Scorpio man who proved to be a good provider, an exciting lay, a fine father and a gentlemen. But she divorced him after 24 years because she simply could no longer bear those interminable periods of calculated muteness.

There's another rather curious Scorpio method of revenge, but it invariably applies only to Scorpio women. For some strange reason, when they are angered by their lovers, they have a penchant for ripping up his clothes. Just why this is we can't say, unless it's because clothes are very important to Scorpios in general and all Scorpios tend to believe that other people react to things exactly as they do. One of the greatest shocks in a Scorpios' life comes on the day he discovers that other people think and feel differently from him.

Scorpios are perfectionists. So are Virgos. If your Sun is in the former and your Venus in the latter, you are particularly difficult to please. Much of your sex life will be lived out in fantasies, and since your imagination is so vivid, it isn't easy to duplicate them in reality. One of the problems is that you want to play it safe, and the kind of strobe-light, wildly orgasmic sex you dream of seldom comes with living like Ozzie and Harriet. While you're conjuring up raw and savage encounters with Marilyn Chambers or John Holmes, you remain sitting in front of the fireplace, sipping brandy and playing Scrabble. Scorpios are basically home-bodies and dislike crowds. With the Virgo mixture, the major reason you can see for leaving the house is to earn a living or to meet Marilyn or John…provided it's prearranged. In your job, your sense of perfection is an asset to everyone, except perhaps to those who work under you. Yet you still command their respect and admiration for upholding craftsmanship and integrity in an increasingly lax world. Famous people born with this combination are Johann Strauss, Stephen Crane, Ezra Pound, Chiang Kai-Shek, Evelyn Waugh, Mahalia Jackson, H.R. Haldeman and Cleo Lane.

As we mentioned before, the Scorpion is the one creature in nature with no pack or heard instinct. But the Scorpio with Venus in Libra has a powerful need for attachment. There is a great love of harmony and beauty, and you will look for both in a partner. Because Scorpio fears his own violent tendencies and Libra loathes hostility, you will go to extremes to avoid conflict. At the same time, this increases the artistic ability and bestows considerable charm on a sign not noted for its beguiling ways.

The desire to please applies also in bed where you will be even more concerned with your partner's satisfaction than with your own. The Scorpio sexual magnetism is enhanced by the Libran diplomacy, so that those with this position usually have no difficulty attracting either friends or lovers.

Although you can work alone, you do not get as much pleasure from solitude as others of your sign. You want someone to share any pleasure that comes your way, whether it be great strides in your career or a cheese danish.

Many Scorpios cherish a feeling of enclosure and therefore, prefer dark rooms, especially when making love. In your case, however, you want the sun to shine through and don't at all mind the lights being on during the sex act. As a matter of fact, you will probably turn the lights on because it give you the opportunity of watching the other person…and sometimes yourself. Those who probably did it with the lights on are St. Augustine, Daniel Boone, Friedrich Schiller, James A. Garfield, Warren G. Harding, Leon Trotsky, Pablo Picasso, Nehru, Prince Charles of England and Lynn Anderson.

The classic Scorpio…you know, the jealous, possessive, intense, obsessed sex maniac…if found at all, would conceivably have both the Sun and Venus in the same sign. No other combination can go to such extremes. On the other hand, you have those to whom sex becomes as necessary as breathing. We mentioned to one Scorpio with this combination that the difficulty is that sex becomes one of the most important things in life, to which he replied, "One of the most important? It's the only thing!" Enormous sacrifices will be made when sex is terrific…or so it will appear to disapproving friends and family. To you it will seem the most natural thing in the world to give up anything from your citizenship to your futures in soy beans and pork bellies for the lover who turns you on and keep turning you on. Although you may appear to others as possessive and domineering, in a wild love relationship you can lose all perspective and willpower, so that the object of your desire plays master to your slave. For all we know, both Medea and Oedipus could have had this combination.

There is another side to the Sun and Venus in Scorpio. The passions being so overwhelming can force you to the other extreme of inhibition or sublimation. When the latter is accomplished, all that energy directed into a different channel can result in your founding a new sect (like Martin Luther), discovering a new element (like Marie Curie) or ruling the world. Others born with this blend are Voltaire, Marie Antoinette, John Philip Sousa, Ed Wynn, Fred W. Friendly, Charles Manson and Goldie Hawn.

Romance is not a word commonly associated with Scorpio. But if your Venus is in Sagittarius, your love relationships revolve around it. So much so, you are the kind of person who looks for it even in a one-night stand. As far as you're concerned, it's easier to find it in a one-night stand than in the dreary routine of a steady relationship. Although sex is as cathartic to you as it is to other Scorpios, it is not physical compatability that determines the long-standing affair as much as the mental stimulation. Since your ideas are usually further out than those of most Scorpios, you want someone who'll share and substantiate them. In truth, what you are looking for is more of a co-conspirator than a sweetheart. If such a person is found, you are willing to make sexual concessions because you know you can always go elsewhere for lust.

From your point of view, love is sacred, but your body is not. Thus, it's vital to find someone who understands this aspect of your nature and does not demand complete fidelity. Sagittarius cherishes freedom, and you must feel that you have this sort of sexual liberation even though you may not take advantage of it.

The Scorpio-Sagittarius blend also gives a greater desire to travel, to experiment, to study and to involve oneself in metaphysics. All Scorpios improve their souls once they leave the material for the spiritual. With this combination, you are more likely to achieve this than the average Scorpio. George Eliot, Rodin, Claude Monet, Robert Louis Stevenson, Theodore Roosevelt, Jean Girardoux, Charles de Gaulle, Charles Atlas, Louise Brooks and Johnny Carson were are born with this blend.

Venus in Capricorn is another position of extremes of a Scorpio, especially when it come to love. You are alternately attracted to someone older, wealthier and more successful or to someone younger, poorer and invariably unemployed. What's behind this dichotomy is your basic need for security. When you don't have it, you look for it in someone else. When you do have it, you will generously give it to one you feel will benefit from it. Of course, the one who benefits from it may also benefit you, horizontally speaking. In either case, you are strongly motivated by those private parts we mentioned earlier, since Scorpio-Capricorn happens to be one of the most dynamic sexual fusions you willl find in all of astrology. Most Scorpios are more impressed with value and merit than with atmosphere and glamour. However, with your Capricorn Venus, you may pass up the crummy dive with the splendid food for the splendid place with the crummy food.

You crave fame, position and money...and probably have a lot of Leo friends. Notable persons born with this polarity are Ivan Turgenev, George Patton, Burgess Meredith, Indira Gandhi, Jame Froman and Dick Cavett.

SAGITTARIUS

November 23 — December 22

SAGITTARIUS

Some years ago there was a brilliant Italian comedy called *Casanova 70,* in which Marcello Mastroianni portrayed a man who could not have sex unless there was an element of danger involved. If none existed, he would create it. The fellow was obviously a Sagittarian.

We have mentioned from time to time in discussing the sex habits of the other signs how you adore the spontaneous seduction in the unusual setting. From puberty on, the typical Sagittarian will want to do what is most forbidden in a prohibited place with someone who is tabu. It's not that you are natural born rebels or reactionaries; it's just that you crave excitment. The Sagittarian who can settle down into a mundane routine and do the same thing day in and day out without going bonkers is either a Maryknoll nun or dead.

It all begins in the playpen (that's what bed is to you anyway . . . a playpen). Give a Taurus or a Scorpio baby a little stuffed animal and he will cuddle it, nurse it and keep it until the stuffing is literally coming out of the seams. But give a Sagittarian baby that same animal and he will hug it madly for a little while and soon discard it in favor of a different toy, which will soon be discarded in favor of a third. If Charles Foster Kane had been a Sagittarian, he would never have died with "Rosebud," on his lips.

While other babies are still struggling with "Dada" and "Ma-ma," you Sagittarians will probably be spouting whole sentences. One of the first of these is likely to be, "Let me out of this goddamn playpen!", which incorporates two of your most common traits: bluntness and claustrophobia. Your parents will have to get used to them, as they will get used to your endless questions: "Why is the sky blue, daddy?" . . . "Where does ice come from?" . . . "Why can't I fly?" . . . "What does the newspaper say?" . . . "Why can't I drive the car?" At first your precocity will seem so stunning, your parents, especially if they're Leos, Aries or Cancers, will want to show you off to other parents. But, as time passes, your quiz kid genius will become a little less adorable when they discover you in the act of trying to drive the car or they invite the boss to dinner and you sit at the table and say something like, "Why does Mr. Jones eat so much?" No wonder so many Sagittarians are adopted out.

But let's assume your parents are extremely tolerant and do not send you to a foster home, but simply fend off or ignore you. You then go out in the world and find playmates. And how many playmates there are, just waiting for most Sagittarians! These playmates will fall into one of two categories: the ones from whom you learn and the ones whom you teach. Very often while you are learning from one, you will be teaching another exactly what the first is teaching you. This passion for learning and teaching continues all the way through elementary school, high school, college and graduate school. Even if you don't actually go through all of this formal education, you will think you have and act as though you have and, in this world, that's the important thing.

You will impress your teachers, but the moment you are on the verge of mastering something, you are already on to something else. You are the kind of people who can return to your old school twenty years later and find your English teacher saying, "A garage mechanic? I always thought you'd be a writer...you had so much talent". Or, conversely, "Prime Minster of England? Why, I don't remember your ever opening a book." Whatever the reaction, it is bound to be one of surprise, for you love to surprise everyone, including yourself.

What is established in those early days usually remains: the need for excitement, the compulsion for variety, the endless curiosity, the dozens of playmates, the love of learning and teaching, the bluntness, the claustrophobia, the multitude of talents and the desire to shock. When translated into sex, you can become either the most fascinating or frustratring lover...often times both...any poor unsuspecting Pisces, Cancer or Taurus ever got involved with. Come to think of it, even those other fascinating and frustrating signs, Virgo and Scorpio, will find you quite a load to handle.

First off, you seldom have any compunction about approaching whoever it is you want to make. You will look directly into their eyes, and if they should avoid your stare, you will, if necessary, walk to the other side of them and continue to do the same. If they prove singularly aloof, you can circle them several times like a buzzard stalking his prey. When you're ready to go in for the kill, however, you will often stop short, especially if the other person becomes too responsive. It's the challenge and the games that most appeals. No wonder they call you the Don and Donna Juans of the zodiac.

That is not to say you don't like sex. You adore sex. When you're finally alone with the other person in the bedroom...wait, we take that back! When you're finally alone with the other person in the backseat of a

Porsche, in the jacuzzi or the gazebo, behind the Griffith Observatory, under the boardwalk in Atlantic City, on the floor of the Grand Canyon, on a ski lift long up the Jungfrau, or on top of a billiard table, you are seldom disappointing.

Since making love is a relatively short experience, you can give it the total concentration you give any relatively short experience and when you concentrate, you are a powerhouse. This brings up an interesting sidelight concerning the time factor. If you have a whole night, you can prolong the act for hours, or because of your admirable resiliency, you can do it over and over, especially if your partner happens to be another Sagittarian. But if you are pressed for time…if, let's say, you have only ten minutes between planes or a fifteen minute coffee-break, you can then give the condensed version, which is no less sensational, only shorter.

Sensational…that's a good word to describe you and sex. According to *The Random House Dictionary* it means "intended to produce a startling effect, strong reaction or intense interest, especially by exaggerated, superficial or lurid elements" and "is extraordinarily good, conspicuous or phenomenal". But if sex is to be performed with the same person in the same way in the same place at the same time, your partner may have a little difficulty finding you. You will probably be in Tangiers or in somebody else's bathtub.

That's why long love affairs and marriage are so difficult for you. If there's any sign that longs for the perpetual honeymoon, it's yours. As soon as it comes down to "What time are you going to be home?" "What's for dinner?" and "Did you remember to put the cat out?" not only your involvement, but your sexual drive diminishes.

We have known Sagittarians who were happily living in unwedded bliss until they made it legal. Just the idea of being restricted by a license was equivalent to a stranglehold placed against their adam's apple. As soon as you feel the slightest pressure on the throat, the brain or the genital organs, you want to run for your life. To most of you, running for your life isn't as bad as it sounds. Because you love to travel anyway, the end of a romance is always a good reason to recuperate in Biarritz or Winnipeg or Plato's Retreat.

When the affair is still going strong, no one can be as demonstrative in public as you. This may be part of that sense of danger and doing what is forbidden, for you will not hesitate to fondle, paw, or grope your lover wherever you happen to be, whether you are at someone else's dinner party, strolling the Champs Elysees, on the Pirates of the Caribbean ride, in the cocktail lounge of a 747 or on the unemployment line. You will not only use your hands, your thighs and your knees, you will use your not inconsiderable vocabulary, promising such sensual delights that you can have the other person foaming at the mouth. You can then go home and suddenly develop a sick headache, a sudden impulse to bake a *sacher torte,* a compelling desire to watch the Late show or pick a fight. How you adore being unpredictable!

This unpredictability applies to other areas as well. You are the kind of people who love to drop in unannounced and when least expected, and you love to leave as precipitously as you arrived. Sagittarians are notorious for never hemming and hawing at the moment of departure like Libra or a Pisces, for example, who will politely announce ahead of time that gee, it's late and I should be going and I will, right after I finish one more cigarette. No, you just get up, say, "I'm going" and go. This proclivity combined with your often blurting out things without thinking can give the impression that you are a graduate of the Auschwitz School of Charm.

You are more predictable when it comes to jealousy and possessiveness. At the beginning of a romance, you're as consuming as any Aries you will ever meet. You will go to extremes to get the other person involved to the point of obliterating any competition. You long for them to be just as jealous and possessive as you. When they become so, you start complaining, telling them to leave you alone, and you soon lose interest. It is the Sagittarian nature to insist on being the first one out the door, and if you are not, you get very upset.

Your sign is ruled by the planet Jupiter, and in astrology, Jupiter is the planet of luck. Almost all Sagittarians are lucky. You can put in an inch of effort and get a yard of reward in return. Maybe that's why it's difficult for you to put very much effort into anything. Sagittarians we have known can get theselves into the stickiest messes and come out smelling like roses.

Your sign is also the one which rules the ninth house, which is the house of travel, higher education, philosphy, religion and publishing.All of these are significant elements in the lives of most of you. A Sagittarian without a philosophy or a religious belief of some kind is like a rudderless boat. Often you will go through many philosphies and several religions before you find the one that suits you best. It's rather akin to your search for a lover. You expect perfection and for all your doubts to be resolved.

As for publishing, all Sagittarians love to read and most enjoy writing, even if it's just a hobby. There is an astounding number of famous writers born under your sign...more, in fact, than are born under any other single constellation. Whether novelists, playwrights, poets, lyricists, cartoonists or journalists, the number is mindboggling. Horace, Lope de Vega, Lawrence Sterne, Jonathan Swift, William Blake, Jane Austen, Emily Dickinson, Joseph Conrad, Thomas Carlyle, Gustave Flaubert, Christina Rosetti, William Cowper, Alfred de Musset, Mark Twain, John Greenleaf Whittier, Louisa May Alcott, Andre Gide, Joyce Kilmer, Willa Cather, Georges Feydeau, Stefan Zweig, Henrich Heine, Saki, Res Stout, Maxwell Anderson, Noel Coward, Erskine Caldwell, Joseph Wood Krutch, George Santayana, Albert Moravia, Christopher Fry, Garson

Kanin, Brooks Atkinson, Nikos Kansantzakis, Jean Genet, Max Lerner, Rebecca West, Ira Gershwin, Adolph Green, James Thurber, Eric Severeid, Dalton Trumbo, Marc Connelly, Drew Pearson, Betty Smith, Margaret Mead, Shirley Jackson, Murray Schisgal, Arthur C. Clarke, John Osborne, James Agee, Alexander Solzhenitsyn, Charles Schulz, Woody Allen.

You write beautifully, make love beautifully, play sports beautifully, sing, dance, act and tell jokes beautifully, but when it comes to leading, forget it. With the exception of the remarkable Winston Churchill and the remarkable Disraeli, there has not been a first-rate Sagittarian leader in all of history. Sagittarian leaders are more of the caliber of Nero and Mary Queen of Scots…rulers more concerned with personal pleasure than with the needs of the people. It's no wonder, because most of you don't want to lead. You just want to be let alone.

The symbol of your sign is the half-archer, half-horse; and it's unquestionably the only zodiacal symbol that has the slightest sexual overtones. So much for what the ancients thought about you. Like the archer, you always want to get to the point and hit the mark. Also like the archer, you love physical activity. Like the horse, you are extremely sensitive, highly intellilgent and lovers of freedom. Horses form habits difficult to eradicate. They have a sixth sense when it comes to unknown and unseen dangers, and they can discriminate at long range between enemies and friends. It is not surprising how many Sagittarians or those with Sagittarius rising resemble horses and love to ride. As a matter of fact, you Sagittarians love all animals…especially those belonging to other people. Born gamblers, there are probably more Sagittarians at any racetrack in the world than Cancers at all weight-reduction centers put together.

Images are what you're looking for if you're a Sagittarian with your Venus in Libra. You are after a physical ideal, and as long as the exterior is pleasing to the eye, you will invest the interior with your dreams. This, of course, never works, but that doesn't stop you. It's part and parcel of your particular brand of excitement to always be searching for the real thing. The Libran influence will make you more affable, less inclined to put your foot in your Sagittarian mouth. The typical archer doesn't often mind coming home to an empty house, since he's not going to stay there for very long anyway. But when you Venus is in Libra, you would like a gorgeous face and body to greet you. You have a stronger need for marriage and sharing. You are usually not as competitive as most Sagittarians, especially in love. Dueling pistols and scratching somone's eyes out are not your style. Friedrich Engels, Boris Karloff, Woody Allen and Lou Rawls were born with this combination.

The true Sagittarian hunter or huntress usually has Venus in Scorpio. You are the kind who consider yourselves sexually devastating, and so convincing are you in the role that others invariably consider you so, too. Sex becomes as essential to you as it does to the archetypal Scorpio, but whereas Scorpio can confine it to one lusty individual, you prefer the pick of the graduating class at Radcliffe or the entire Olympic swimming team. That's because the chase is more rewarding than the catch.

Sometimes with this position you can be a bit sadistic in leading people on and then reneging at the last minute. As a result, you may find others playing the same game with you, so it becomes a little like Godzilla against the Thing.

You so hate that which is dull and boring, you will often create conflict just to get some kind of excitement going. Now and again those with this combination go to the other extreme because they are fearful of the extent of their passion. They will sublimate the energy into their careers and marry someone to whom they are not overwelmingly attracted so the other person can't manipulate their sexual vulnerability. But this comes only when the Sagittarian under discussion has been truly hurt in the past. Usually you with your Venuses in Scorpio are the ones to do the hurting. Some notable people born with this mixture are Jane Austen, Disraeli, Joseph Conrad, George Santayana, Paul Klee, J. Paul Getty and Mary Martin.

The person who is able to snare the Sagittarian with his Venus in the sign would have to be a genius or Frank Buck. Of all the combinations of the Sun and Venus in each of the signs, it is here we find those least able to come to grips with a long term love affair or marriage. The need for freedom is so overwhelming that the slightest encroachment will have you running for the bushes like a terrified doe. When we say slightest, we *mean* slightest. It can be a simple question like "But I thought you were going to call last night," or "I've made reservations for Hawaii for your vacation" or "I've arranged for you to meet my family." Those with this blend are frequently born with an abundance of physical attributes, and this only increases the aversion to settling down. Yet, at the same time, you often feel you are missing something meaningful in life whenever you come upon a *gemutlicht* family scene. But not for long. Your loathing of commitment is too powerful, and it doesn't apply only to your love lives.

You are the sort who can arrive at a party an hour early, two hours late or not at all, according to the whim of the moment and whom you may have met along the way. Many a Cancer, Taurus or Scorpio may still be waiting by the phone. Mark Twain, Samuel Butler, Martin van Buren, William S. Hart, Billy the Kid, Charles Schulz and Jimi Hendrix are Sagittarians borns with this blend.

While the Sagittarian with Venus in Scorpio will spend most of his time talking about sex and impersonating sex, you who have your Venuses in Capricorn will do it...and do it magnificently, especially if the other person is wealthier or more successful than you. This is a singularly horny combination, but also a clever one, and you are willing to sacrifice your freedom if there is the prospect of social prestige, money and security. Well, you'll sacrifice it for a while. The irresponsible Sagittarian side is forever interfering with the practical Capricornian side, so that eventually you will be torn between playing house or doing the Latin Hustle out the door. You will *surely* do the Latin Hustle out the door if the money runs out.

All Sagittarians love to neck, but you may well be the best kissers in the entire zodiac. We wonder what kind of kissers Spinoza, William Blake, Beethoven, Zachary Taylor, Louisa May Alcott, Lillian Russell, Toulouse-Lautrec, Hector Berlioz and Harpo Marx were.

Sagittarius is not a sign noted for its platonic relationships, for platonic relationships take too long. Sagittarians love things to start fast, get to the point fast and end fast. However, when your Venus is in Aquarius you are not only capable of platonic relationships, but they often become the most rewarding and exciting ones. Talent means a tremendous amount to you, and you will likely value creative potential above physical proportions.

Since you Sagittarians are impulsive, you with your Venus in Aquarius may marry at an age before your own personality is fully developed and before you are certain of what it is you want in a relationship. In almost every case, the marriage turns out to be disaster. Later in life, you can develop a highly successful liaison, but it has to be a really special person who will be as much of a friend as a lover.

Those with this position are often interested in social movements and humanitarian causes. You can be fascinated by the sexual proclivities of others and more faithful than the average Sagittarian. Both Walt Disney And Margaret Mead were born the this mixture. Ms. Mead brilliantly investigated the rites and practices of remote tribes and Mickey Mouse was forever faithful to Minnie. Besides Mead and Disney, we have Flaubert, Maxwell Anderson, Edward G. Robinson, Douglas Fairbanks, Jr. and Sammy Davis, Jr.

CAPRICORN

December 23 — January 19

CAPRICORN

$\mathbf{B}$ack in the 20s Eddie Cantor used to sing a song about a girl who wasn't much in a crowd, but when you got her alone, you'd be surprised! Fifty years later, Charlie Rich recorded a number about a girl who was very proper in public, but when you got behind closed doors and she lets her hair come down, you'd be just as surprised, Clearly, they are the same girl...both Capricorns.

Not just females, mind you, but males born under the sign of Capricorn don't seem sexy on the surface. There are exceptions, of course. One immediately thinks of Muhammed Ali, Marlene Dietrich, Cary Grant, Elvis Presley and Ava Gardner. For the most part though, the typical Capricorn appears, as does the typical Scorpio, aloof, self-contained, businesslike and occasionally formidable. There's that no nonsense approach which makes others think that sex is the furthest thing from your minds. And there is nothing in the astrological canons to indicate you would be any more carnal on a water bed than at a conference table.

After all, yours is the sign most associated with ambition, social standing, power, practicality and the establishment. It's ruled by the dreariest planet of all, Saturn, which governs responsibility, self-discipline, hard work, old age, delays and limitations... those glorious things which make life worth living. The part of the body which Capricorn rules is the knees. Just how sexy can a knee be? Remember that the symbol and animal counterpart is the goat, who will deprive himself of almost anything to reach his objective. He is one of the least costly animals to keep and can survive on the most barren mountainside. He is easily tamed, capable of a considerable degree of friendship and fond of high and solitary places. This is hardly a personification of lust in the animal kingdom, and goats do, of course, have sex. Otherwise we would never have any little goatlings. But when was the last time you heard anyone say, "He's hung like a goat" or "He comes on like a goat" or "He screws like a goat?" No wonder no one ever associates mad passion with Capricorn.

There are other reasons aside from the astrological ones. When you are wearing blinders and trying to work your way step by step to the top of the mountain, love is a deterrent. It's perfectly all right to marry the one who fits your preconceived notions and have 2.5 children, but when it comes to that wild, wonderful affair you sometimes dream about, you won't let yourself be sidetracked.

A great many Capricorns will capitalize on the sex drives of others. They will become symbols of it like Dietrich or Presley or Gardner, or use it to become successful in other areas like Gypsy Rose Lee, or cater to vanity like Helena Rubenstein or make films to titillate like Howard Hughes, or write "turn-on" novels like Henry Miller.

All of these observations tend to obscure the fact that you are really one of the horniest signs of the zodiac. Your stamina can be awe-inspiring. We met one young Capricorn advertising executive who insisted he must have sex at least four times a day . . . if not with a person, then with his hand. And the story goes that Howard Hughes had to have a different woman every night of the week. Lest you be led astray by the male references, let us hasten to add that the same applies to the female of the species. Earlier in life, sex can be a release from the pressures of business. Later in life, when you Capricorns appear to get younger as everyone around you ages, it can become an obsession. In either case, there are few signs that so enjoy sex for the sake of sex itself.

Capricorn has always been such a sign. The trouble was that in previous eras when sex without the legal tie was a no-no, there were an awful lot of sneaky or frustrated Capricorns running around this globe. For yours is a sign tht lives by the rules . . . at least to outside appearances; and no Capricorn could conceivably jeopardize his career or his social position as Libra Oscar Wilde or Virgo Ingrid Bergman or Gemini Isadora Duncan did. Nor would you defy your family. Your blood ties are as powerful as those of your opposite sign, Cancer, for while Cancer represents Mother, Capricorn represents Father. There are many similarities between these two signs and , as with Cancer, much depends on the way your were raised as to what your sex lives will be like. As a matter of fact, a Capricorn without a strong sex drive, and this is rare indeed, will try to simulate one because it's what everybody else is doing.

So now that we have *Cosmopolitan* telling you how to turn your mate on with a vibrator rather than an apple pan dowdy, you Capricorns can behave the way you've wanted to behave for centuries. This doesn't mean that you'll be any the less ambitious, or that you'll start confusing love with lust. It just means that, unless you happen to be a Quaker or a Jehovah's Witness . . . in which case you wouldn't be reading this book to start with . . . you won't have to slink about in back alleys or panic when you register at a motel with someone to whom you're not married.

This permissiveness has also made you more aggressive when you see something you like. Since you can usually keep your emotions under control, you're not afraid of involvement like the Leo or the Pisces For instance, a Capricorn girl we used to know met a Sagittarian boy and began to get stomach pains. She consulted her doctor and he could find nothing wrong. It was only later that she realized those were butterflies in her stomach, not ulcers. This was a totally new feeling.

There isn't much sweet talk from Capricorns because you're not promising the romance of the century. As a point of fact, you're not promising romance at all. The other person can ask anything he wants about your profession, and you'll answer in great detail. You can discuss sports, politics, or famous people, but when it comes to your personal life, it would take the Gestapo or lighted matches under your fingernails to make you reveal intimate details when you first meet someone.

During the preliminary encounter you may seem a trifle cold, even though you're really interested in the other person. That's why they often get such a surprise once the action begins. And, oh, how you love action! You may not be terribly imaginative, but your passion makes up for what you lack in versatility. You will do everything you can to get your partner to achieve an orgasm, not so much for the pleasure it gives him or her, but the power it gives you. Power is an eminent factor in all your relationships, particularly the sexual ones, and if, by chance, you should allow yourself the luxury of involvement and you find that for some reason the object of your passion cuts you off overnight, you would be devastated.

One of the ways you wield sexual power is by keeping your body in shape. A fellow we know who runs two health clubs once did an astrological survey of his own and discovered that the sign which stayed with exercise most consistently and for the longest period of time was, for both men and women, hands down, Capricorn. There is a very impressive list of famous athletes born under your sign, not because you are naturally more athletic than other signs, but because once you set your mind to doing something, by God, you're going to do it better than anyone else. In baseball we have Dizzy Dean, Connie Mack, Steve Carlton, Early Wynn, Sandy Koufax, Hank Greenburg, Tony Conigliaro, Willie McLCovey and Nellie Fox. In boxing there is Floyd Patterson, George Foreman, Muhammed Ali, Joe Frazier and Barney Ross. In football, Bart Stahr, Patty Driscoll, Paul Hornung and Don Shula.

So much for the physical power. How about the psychological power. You will play an infinite variety of games to see how securely you can get the other person under your thumb. That may be the reason you are attracted to Sagittarians, because it takes double the effort to get a Sagittarian under anyone's thumb. But though you may be attracted to Sagittarians, you won't necessarily marry them. No, you'll more likely marry the Cancer or the Taurus who really needs you. As it is in all areas of your existence, it's *quid pro quo.* You give something, you get something. You must provide an important service to the other person, whether it be sexual, financial, social or psychological, while they in turn must provide something essential for you. Capricorns have no hesitation about using people, but are eternally wary of others using them. However, a marriage to you, and most Capricorns *do* insist on marrying, is a mutual using, to the point of keeping a mental ledger sheet.

When you are young and it comes to settling down, you don't give a tinker's dam for chemistry. You want the person who, in combination with yourself, will live up to that perfect all-American family image, which some of you picked up from Andy Hardy and others from the Donna Reed show. So carefully do you choose your mate that your marriages frequently last longer than other people's. As parents you excel. Capricorn mothers, in particular, are uniformly the best in the zodiac, because they do not smother or pamper, and their discipline is consistent.

Your marriages frequently last even after they have ceased to work, for to you, permanence is a good word, and temporary is a bad one. Later on, though, when you or your mate is established professionally and monetarily, that's when you finally reach adolescence. At last you can play, and you begin to do wo with as much concentration and energy as you used in your climb up the mountain. That's when chemistry finally becomes essential, and whereas once you were attracted to those older, you are now bedazzled by youth. The games aren't that urgent anymore either; one is not at all surprised to discover the fifty or sixty year old Capricorn divorcing his or her mate and running off with a Gemini or an Aries who is barely nineteen.

We said before that Capricorn is the sign of the Father, and all of you, whether male or female, appear to assume the paternal role from a very early age. If your parents happen to be flighty, irresponsible or unstable, you will become super-conservative and realistic as a reaction against them. We know one Pisces lady who makes up the most imaginative and fanciful stories for her little Capricorn boy. He doesn't believe a word of them.

If your parents happen to be super-conservative and realistic, you will turn out the same way. So no matter how you slice it, you start growing up with a rigid set of rules which incorporate that which is most accepted and traditional in the society in which you are raised. This leads to an inflexibility which all Capricorns have to overcome if they are to make spiritual progress. When they don't overcome it, the result is commonly frustration, because those around them do not adhere to the same code of behavior and a Capricorn's arthritis may be a physical manifestation of what is going on inside.

A fascinating thing is that no matter how rigid a Capricorn may be in his personal and professional life, dancing becomes his one form of release. You make excellent dancers, not because you're born more agile than other signs, but again, because you have the perseverance and discipline. Although Pisces and Aries are the ones most commonly associated with this field, there is an impressive number of dancers and choreographers born under the Sign of the Goat: Robert Blankshine, Jose Greco, Robert Joffrey, Mary Tyler Moore, Maurice Bejart, Yuri Grigorovich, Vera Zorina, George Balanchine, Ray Bolger, Galina Ulanova, Jose Limon, Roland Petit, Gwen Verdon, Gerald Arpino, Moira Shearer, Sheree North and Rus Tamblyn.

The same goes for music. Pisces and Taurus have been the signs traditionally noted for famous musicians, but Capricorn has the greatest number in both the popular and classical fields. From Puccini to Presley, from Renata Tebaldi and Marilyn Horn to Joan Baez and Janis Joplin, from Pablo Casals to Gene Krupa, and along the way we have Tito Schipa, Andre Kostalanetz, Jim Croce, Rod Stewart, Bobby Goldsboro, Tex Ritter, Glenn Yarborough, John Denver, David Bowie, Roger Miller and dozens of others.

The Sun in Capricorn and Venus in Scorpio is invincible. The Capricorn patience and the Scorpio monomania make for magnificent obsessions, whether they be in politics as Joseph Stalin, in sports as Sandy Koufax, in stardom as Ava Gardner or in love, as almost all of you. That obsessive kind of love doesn't happen till later in life, ususaly after you've achieved some sort of success, or your parents die and you feel free.

Earlier, your relationships are more of the pragmatic type, for even stronger than it is with most Capricorns is your reverence of wealth and fame. Since both Capricorn and Scorpio are signs that don't give up easily, whatever it is you want, you invariably get. Sometimes you get it and wonder why you wanted it. It's later in life that you throw caution to the winds and start doing things you wouldn't have dreamed of doing in high school. This position enhances psychic ability, but weakens what we mentioned before about parenthood. Often your children become a burden and you can't wait to get them out of the house so you can put on your roller skates and go out cruising.

What Capricorn wants is usually so different from what Sagittarius wants that your Sun in the former and your Venus in the latter causes an internal conflict. Part of you is after security and prestige, while the other part longs for adventure and freedom. So although you may marry, you may spend a helluva lot of time "working late at the office." You have a better sense of humor than the typical Capricorn (Victor Borge, Steve Allen and Cary Grant have this blend) and more imagination. You are the most romantic of all Capricorns, which isn't saying much, but never look a gift horse in the mouth. Also, a need for a philosophical or spiritual concept exists. With your natural sexual magnetism and your ability to woo and win, you will most likely attract a great many lovers during your lifetime. Both Kahlil Gibran and Howard Hughes had this combination. After Gibran, marriage and the family could never be the same. After Hughes, TWA and Melvin Dummar could never be the same.

The Sun and Venus both in the sign of the Goat is the Capricorn's Capricorn. You are so intent on finding a place in the sun that even other Capricorns are dazzled by your tenacity. You aren't very thoughtful with your lovers, and because you're so extremely sexual and physically dynamic, they will often complain of neglect. But what you're usually playing around with on the side is the stock market or the company's books. Elvis Presley, Aristotle Onassis, Gypsy Rose Lee and Henry Miller were all born with this blend. Children are of great importance to you and you can make superb parents. Better parents, in fact, than mates, unless you happen to be like someone else with this combination, Joan of Arc, and forego parenthood and marriage in order to save your country. Being old fashioned and conservative, you do not find it easy to accept a live-in arrangement without a legal tie. This is unfortunate, since you usually marry young and repeatedly; if you were a little more progressive in your attitudes, you could save yourself a great deal of alimony and attorney's fees.

The Capricorn with Venus in Aquarius may be just as ambitious but less convention bound and more in the swing of what's happening. There are probably more diverse and successful people born with this combination than any of the others. Robert E. Lee, Nostradamus, Paul Cezanne, Henri Matisse, Marlene Dietrich, Muhammed Ali, Janis Joplin, Mao Tse-Tung, Ethel Merman, Jacob Grimm and Robert Ripley are just a few. There is a marked stamp of individuality and a desire not to follow what everyone else is doing. You will adhere less to pleasing your folks and more to pleasing yourself. In certain instances, you will go out of your way to defy your folks, your educational background and your religious training.

Venus in Aquarius lessens the Capricorn snobbishness and class distinction. If you are not intent on a career for yourself, you will often search for someone with talent to whom you can play Pygmalion. While you want originality in your mate, you also want security and these two qualities seldom go hand in hand. But if anyone thinks that's going to stop you, they have another thing coming; a good portion of your younger days is comprised of the search, and it may lead you to some unusual places. People with this blend have been known to register with computer dating services or take their chances at a B'nai B'rith dance...even if they're not Jewish.

The Capricorn with Venus in Pisces is inclined to martyrdom, which is not a notable Capricornian trait. Those with this position seem to go to one of two extremes. If you are successful, you often choose someone socially or professionally beneath you. If you are not successful, you may latch on to someone who is. In either case, you will try to make yourselves indispensable, and frequently there will be something secretive about the relationship. The more you are mistreated, the more you will complain but the more you will enjoy the affair. Somehow you feel to love is to suffer. If you don't get the necessary masochistic stimulation from the other person, then you will often mistreat them in the style you've grown accustomed to.

This positon also gives deep sensitivity and an admirable devotion to one's family and friends. It also gives a strong desire to create. Molière, Carl Sandburg and Edgar Allen Poe are some of the geniuses who had this combination. Those with their Venuses in Pisces find it very difficult to stand alone in life and can be counted on to adopt some group or cause to feel part of.

AQUARIUS

She is 97 years old. She was born in England when Victoria was queen and came to America when Wilson was president. She was one of the great beauties of her day and a splendid, original actress. She had success and she had money, but they meant little. Affairs meant everything. She had her last one at 84. It was a 27 year old. She is an Aquarian, and her whole life has been lived for love.

The lady we have told you about proves that passion and physical allure do not end with menopause, but then you Aquarians have known that for years. And we said love, not sex. While sex is the natural culmination of love, it is almost never an end in itself as it is with so many other signs. That's why your early sexual experiences are often different from those of your friends. We don't mean they're with shoes, pantyhose or candles; we mean that what you're looking for is not necessarily what other youngsters are looking for. Oh, you will try what your pals are trying and you will attempt to be titillated by the same things that titillate them, but somehow they don't provide that ultimate satisfaction you crave.

This is not to say you Aquarians are not sexual. you can get as many kicks from wild and kinky experiences as the next person. But it is not the major thrust of your life. This may be the reason there are more famous people listed in *Who's Who* born between January 20th and February 18. If you are not a slave to your genitals, you have a helluva lot more time and energy to astound the world like Darwin, to compose a plethora of glorious music like Mozart and Schubert, to create a formidable body of literature like Dickens and Maugham, to lead your country in time of crisis like Abraham Lincoln, to invent one fantastic contraption after another like Thomas Alva Edison...or to go to court like Lee Marvin.

Aquarius is a mental sign, and mental attraction takes precedence over the physical. The Aquarian in the singles bar is there to make as much social contact as sexual. You are not the kind who says, "Let's get it on" or "What do you like in bed?" You're the ones who want to talk for a while, get to know the other person and then exchange telephone numbers. If the heroine of *Looking for Mr. Goodbar* had been an Aquarian, she'd still be alive today. For it's the courtship you love. It's the intimate conversations in the out-of-the-way restaurants. It's discovering that you both adore Neil Diamond and loathe liver. It's strolling by the sea at twilight. It's the unexpected telephone call and the spur-of-the-moment date. It's sending love poems through the mail, experiencing unusual sights together, exchanging books and records you both cherish. Sex is then the crescendo to the symphony, but it's the symphony which keeps you alive and vital at 97.

When this meeting of the minds is absent, you can be impossible. It's then you become as fussy as any Virgo and as sarcastic as any Scorpio. You don't want the out-of-the-way restaurant, you want some place where the food is great, the service impeccable, the music live and the view divine. For that stroll by the sea at twilight, you'll invite three or four friends. When the unexpected phone call comes, you let your answering machine pick it up. The love poems that come through the mail are tossed in the fireplace after the stamp is saved for your neighbor's child. The only unusual sight you want to experience with the other person is seeing him or her disappear down a crowded street. Sex a crescendo to a symphony? It's more like a bagpipe played to a tone-deaf Eskimo. You vow never again and why did I ever do it in the first place?

Whether right or wrong, you Aquarians have such decided views that it's difficult for you to pretend you feel one way when you feel another. That's why it's such a burden for you to carry on an affair for social, financial or professional reasons alone. We're sure there must be Aquarian hustlers and hookers in this world, but if there are, they probably don't rake in the profits that the Leo, Virgo or Gemini does. You have a disturbing habit of wanting to tell everyone exactly where you stand. So you're always saying things like, "Look, I want you to know I like you, but I'm not in love with you." That doesn't make for villas on the Riviera or little trinkets from Cartier's, but you often sleep easier.

Sometimes you sleep easier when you sleep alone. At any rate, you would much rather sleep alone that sleep with someone just for companionship or after they've begun to take you for granted. How you loathe this from anyone…friend or lover, because it means the magic is gone. And once that happens, there isn't much reason to continue the affair. That's why marriage is often a problem. If you marry when you are very young, as many Aquarians do, you may find yourself attempting to adjust to the ordinary concepts of what a union should be. You're much too individual for that, and if your partner's idea of wedded bliss is shoving you into a conventional pigeonhole, ultimately you'll be consulting a lawyer.

Even later on in life, marriage is still not easy. First of all, there is a curious objectivity in your love no matter how deeply involved you may be. A part of yourself is always kept in reserve, and, unlike the Cancer or Aries or Pisces, you want the other person to do the same. Love to you is as much a universal concept as it is a personal one…sometimes even more so. You can be as involved in a friendship, a group or a philosophy, and you see no reason to devote every waking moment to your mate.

Since you are not one to hide what you are feeling, you expect others to follow suit. Your emotional antenna can frequently jam, so you can't pick up or decipher someone else's unspoken sensitivities. When a conflict arises, you expect both parties to talk it out and hold no grudges. The worst thing the other person can do to you is to stop speaking. We would not recommend an affair with a Scorpio.

Then, too, you can be a queer and frustrating mixture of what is conventional and what is unorthodox. Yours is the sign ruled by two planets diametrically opposed to each other, Saturn and Uranus. Saturn represents tradition, conformity, regularity, organization and restriction. Uranus means originality, progress, individualism, eccentricity, independence. You find Aquarians who fall into one category or the other, but mostly both. The result is that you become doubly unpredictable, because just when the other person thinks you're going to react in the Saturnian way, you will do your Uranian number, and vice versa. Often you do it on purpose, just to shock. Like Sagittarians, you love to startle, because it keeps others guessing and you hate to be categorized.

The same applies in bed. Just when someone thinks he knows exactly what turns you on, you will suddenly come up with something so different and outrageous, your partner is alternately stunned and fascinated. You don't mind doing it in the same place over and over, but you do mind doing it in the same way. Lighting is terribly important to you. It must be just the right intensity and never overhead. Some Aquarians get turned on by talking about sex or looking at certain types of pornography. It's not so much out of lust as, let's say, an Aries or a Taurus; it's more out of your perpetual curiosity as to what others are doing.

Another trait that confuses lovers is your sense of responsibility for the sake of responsibility and of because of the strings attached. Your concern has that same kind of objectivity as your love, and it is not done for reasons of possession or repayment. You do not want others to become any more dependent on you than you on them. Nothing can break up an Aquarian affair quicker than a sweetheart who begins to think of you as Daddy or Mama. You don't have all that much desire to be a Daddy or Mama to start with. Many Aquarians would rather have a puppy of a kitten or a pony or a lion cub than a baby, and some Aquarians would rather have nothing. Actually, when you do have children, you are usually very good parents, because your detachment encourages individuality and freedom. You are almost never overprotective nor do you try to transfer your fears onto them.

Let an Aries choose a mate for sexual excitement and a Cancer for emotional security, you will choose one out of sheer perversity. While you abhor coddling and cosseting, you love to nurture…especially talent. You are attracted to those who are in some way original or who have a potential which often you may be the only one to see, for you must admire the person you love more than anything else; as the admiration goes, so goes the affair. This admiration can range from the individual who plays the cello to the one who plays the triangle. You can be just as attracted to the one who builds the Brooklyn Bridge as the one who sells it.

You are such born reformers, you believe no matter what the individual hang-up, you make Leonardo da Vinci out of someone who paints by numbers. You will take the alcoholic and be assured that with your love, they will soon become Brigham Young or Carrie Nation. The hardened criminal can be turned into Oral Roberts or Kathryn Kuhlman. Oh, the romance you could find in a leper colony.

One of the difficulties the Aquarian has in a long-standing love relationship is that sooner or later he starts neglecting those around him to take care of total strangers. There's a little bit of Albert Schweitzer in every Aquarian, even though Albert happened to be a Capricorn; and as far as you're concerned, charity never begins at home. Your mate is also going to have to get used to the dozens of secret contributions you will be making to the world's hundred neediest cases…secret because you almost never make your generosity known…

Another thing they have to get used to is that you'll argue at the drop of a phrase. If the mood suits you and someone says, "Isn't it a lovely day!", you will snap back with, "I don't see what's so lovely about it. What do *you* see that's so lovely about it?" As intense and convincing as you can be in an argument, there is that same marvelous detachment because it isn't necessary for you to really believe whatever point of view you have chosen to defend. The only prerequisite is it has to be the opposite of the person who opened the discussion. That's why Aquarians can shine on the high school debating team or on the floor of Parliament.

You not only love to nurture and to argue, you also love to direct. You make fine counselors no matter what the problem may be, and you fully expect others to follow your guidelines. It is interesting to note that the famous Aquarian film directors reads like a history of the cinema. These are never your schlock, commercial hacks, either. They are the ones with vision and substance. D. W. Griffith, Sergei Eisenstein, Robert Flaherty, Carl Dreyer, Ernst Lubitsch, King Vidor, Joseph L. Mankiewicz, John Ford, Francois Truffaut, Roger Vadim, Franco Zeffirelli, John Schleslinger, and possibly Fredrico Fellini. We say possibly, because he was born exactly on the Capricorn cusp and only his mother seems to know for sure.

Then there are games. All kinds of games. If your lover does not find you reading, attending classes or talking to friends, you'll usually be found at the bridge table, around a Scrabble board, or bargaining Baltic and the Electric Company for Ventnor Avenue. Although there are many noted sports figures born under your sign…Babe Ruth, Carol Heiss, Jack Nicklaus, Jackie Robinson, Ernie Banks, Nolan Ryan, Fran Tarkington, Hank Aaron, Roger Stauback, Bill Tilden, Joe Walcott, Graham Hill, Allie Reynolds, Mark Spitz, Mickey Wright, Jim Brown…you are not especially attracted to strongly competitive games. You prefer the ones that require skill and strategy rather than luck and brute force.

Opposites don't always attract, and opposite signs don't, either. Get a Virgo and a Pisces together and you could have mayhem. But, in your case, you are much drawn to your opposite sign Leo, and they to you. You like them not only as lovers, but as friends as well, and we have seen time and again very viable relationships between the two of you. As long as you let them play monarch, everything is fine. But you Aquarians, with certain exceptions like Douglas MacArthur and Tallulah Bankhead, aren't that big on playing king or queen. You would usually rather play Prime Minister.

Independence is the key to an Aquarian with Venus in Sagittarius. Although you may follow the path of least resistance when you are young, you become more definite in your view as you mature and less susceptible to the opinions of others. The lure of foreign lands is like wild geese calling, and one often meets lovers in transit. You will often find yourself doing things while traveling that you wouldn't dream of doing at home…Erica Jong's "Zipless Fuck" being one of them. Basically, however, you long for romance more than you do sex, and while others need the security of commitment, you sometimes fear that too strong a bond will take the romance away. There is not a great deal of faithfulness involved, only because as soon as you feel trapped, you want to spread your wings. Thus you will try everything in your power to inject an affair with excitement and surprise to keep it fresh and alive…from a long-stemmed rose in the morning to a carnal bombshell at night.

This position also gives a love of the occult and an uncommonly vivid imagination. Lewis Carroll, D. W. Griffith, Hans Holzer and Estelle Winwood are examples of those born with this combination.

When you find a truly horny Aquarian, chances are his Venus is in Capricorn. This is a peculiar, but not uncommon, mixture, because the progressive Aquarian nature is in conflict with the Capricorn conservatism. There is an abundance of lust, but usually within conventional boundaries so that your are not extremely venturesome in sex, at least not until later in life.

Many of you marry young and allow the Aquarian side to predominate only in your vocation or avocation. you can make excellent parents because the Capricorn in you protects and the Aquarian encourages individualism. You are impressed with fame and wealth and very ambitious for position and power. You are less fickle and more inclined to commitment. Later in life, the Aquarian side usually takes over, and you trade in your Lincoln-Continental for a crimson Ferrari and your conservative wardrobe for Gucci and Pucci, and off you go to an Esalen weekend or a rejuvenation spa in Mexico and come back with some delicious creature half your age. The tendency here is towards thrift and economy, so if that May-September affair should break up, it's not because of your lack of fascination or sexual potency, but because it might get too expensive. Some famous people born with this blend are W. C. Fields, Somerset Maugham, Virginia Woolf, Paul Newman, Sinclair Lewis and Neil Diamond.

If the average Aquarian wears a thin gauze of detachment in his love relationships, those with Venus in Aquarius seem like they're in an isolation booth. The inaccessibility is quite strong because the need for sex is always secondary to the need for friendship. Often those in love with you complain they can't get through, which isn't helped by your insistence on following your own dictates and your single mindedness about what is right and wrong for you.

Your cool exterior can serve as a challenge to others, making you tremendously appealing, so that, like John Barrymore and Lord Byron, you may develop a reputation as a Great Lover and heart-breaker, when in reality what you are doing is going through a great many people in order to find a soul mate. You have a lot of love to give, but to do so within the confines of a family is far too limiting.

Your love is of a universal nature, and you may bestow it more easily on groups or causes than individuals. Consequently, you seldom have children, and if you do, you remain psychologically removed from them. The children may feel the same about you as lovers do and attempt in every which way to win your total approval, never realizing that to do wo they would have to be Scientology or the Salvation Army. Others born with this blend are Mozart, Robert Burns, Stendhal, James Joyce, Jack Lemmon, Steve Reeves, Jack Benny and Hal Holbrook.

Folie a deux is a French term meaning "madness for two". you can take Person A who is a reasonably sane, functioning human being and put him together with Person B, who appears just as sane. Something then happens between the two of them, some peculiar alchemy which leads to what the dictionary calls "the sharing of delusional ideas by two people who are closely associated". There is the possibility of such a relationship when you're an Aquarian with your Venus in Pisces. Sometimes you must sift thorough a number of applicants before you find the right one for the job. But once you do, it's an affair that usually lasts a long time. Money, goals, flaws and addictions become interlocked, and then this happens, unlike other Aquarians, you do not have as much need for friends or social contact. You often become a paternal or maternal counselor to others without revealing your own problems or hang-ups. Whereas Venus in Capricorn is drawn to successful people, you are drawn to the underdog and those who are in some way dependent upon you. This fusion of Aquarius and Pisces gives deep sensitivity, psychic ability and artistic talent. Charles Dickens, Edith Wharton, Evangeline Adams, Arthur Rubenstein and Helen Gurley Brown are a few born with this blend.

If you're an Aquarian with your Venus in Aries, you may be the most self-sufficient people in the whole zodiac. If you have difficulty finding a total relationship with another individual, it's because you give the impression of such containment that others feel you can do perfectly well without them. In nine out of ten cases, you can. If there's any Aquarian who wants a casual kind of love, it's you. Many will have a set-up in which neither lives with the other or sometimes you will deliberately find one who resides a long distance away so you will see each other only at specified intervals.

Strong-willed yourself, you cannot bear to be directed or dominated, which may be the reason why the ordinary concept of marriage is not for you. You are inclined to be secretive about intimate things and give your confidence to very few. Real friends are treasured above lovers and maintained for years and years. Unlike Venus in Pisces, you cannot bear people who complain and complain and do nothing about their problems. Occasionally there is a curious sexual ambivalence about this position, and you seldom play the little sex games that others do.

Some famous people born with their Suns in Aquarius and their Venuses in Aries are Abraham Lincoln, Charles Darwin, Lee Marvin, and Robert Burton, who wrote *The Anatomy of Melancholy*, the title of which has a special meaning to many Aquarians.

PISCES

February 20 — March 20

PISCES

Once upon a time there was a beautiful young princess who met a frog. "Kiss me, beautiful young princess," said the frog, "and I will turn into a prince." The beautiful young princess did exactly as she was bidden, for she had raised herself on tales of bewitched frogs who were really princes, and the frog was a particularly passionate kisser. Lo and behold, before her very eyes, he did turn into the prince she had been longing for and dreaming about since she was a child. She then took him to her father, the King, and said, "Oh, sire, here is the prince of my dreams", to which her father replied, "You mean that *frog?*" Her mother, the Queen, said exactly the same thing and so did all the ladies and gentlemen of the court. But the lovely princess was not to be deterred. She took her beloved to the royal costume-maker and had a princely outfit designed for him with a little diamond crown and reintroduced him at a lavish banquet. But still they said: "Not that frog *again?!*" The princess was upset, but undaunted. she sent him to a school where they taught him to do a buck-and-wing and sing "Hello My Baby." And though he was slightly klutzy and his voice a bit flat, he toured from one court to another under the watchful proud eye of the princess. The courtiers in the other lands thought it a rousing joke when the princess introduced him as the prince of her dreams who would now entertain with his extraordinary talent. But they were rather impressed with a frog who could sing and dance, no matter how incompetently. The frog became an overnight success and soon added juggling to his act, the balls of which he would hurl at the lovely young princess at the slightest provocation. Soon he would get a sick headache every time they went to bed and in no time at all he dropped her completely and ran off with a tightrope walker with very large tits named Lola. In a while, though, his career hit the skids. A dancing, singing frog was no longer a novelty, and Lola mistreated him much in the same manner he had mistreated the lovely young princess. Broke, abandoned and on his way to becoming a lush, the frog returned to the lovely young princess. She took him back without a qualm. And even though he still threw his juggling balls at her and eternally blamed her for being the source of all his woes, they lived happily ever after.

The frog may have been a Leo and the tightrope walker a Gemini, but the princess was definitely a Pisces. You can substitute prince for princess and frogette for frog, but the story remains essentially the same true tale of a Piscean love affair. Do you detect a touch of self-sacrifice in this story? Of course you do, because isn't that what most Pisces love affairs are all about?

But let's take you back now to before the love affair starts. Let's take you back to that singles disco or that party or that Est seminar or that frog pond where first you met. One doesn't associate Pisces with being an aggressive sign. For the life of us, we can't figure out why. Like Sagittarians, you have no fear of talking to strangers and an endemic love of conquest. You go under the supposition that if you approach ten different people in an evening, one of them is bound to be interested. Most of you will search out the best looking ones first and, if rejected, you will proceed in a kind of sliding scale of beauty, but eventually you will go home with someone. When you are young, it's the physical ideal you are after, and you're willing to make almost any sacrifice to obtain it.

Let's assume that this particular night is a magical one and you find that the guy or the gal you've selected is really sensational and captivated by your charm, your humor, your understanding and your magnificent eyes. (Pisces has unquestionably the most beautiful eyes of the zodiac. One has only to look at Elizabeth Taylor, Michele Morgan or Michael Caine). You go to their place. If you're really turned on, you couldn't care less what their place looks like. It could be Twelve Oaks or Uncle Tom's cabin. All you care about is the person.

Most Pisces, because they long so for romance and love, will take their cue from someone else. You do not have the unqualified preference that a Scorpio or a Leo has. You will go along with just about anything…from doing it in the closet to caressing boots…if that's what turns the other person on. The same applies to your capacity. If the object of your passion is a Capricorn or an Aries and likes to come five or six times, then you will come five or six times, or at least pretend to come five or six times. If the person doesn't want to have sex at all, you will be extremely patient and bide your time until they do. What you want most of all is affection, tenderness and someone whispering "I love you" over and over and over again. If the other person will only say this to you as many times as you want to hear it…you're not that fussy, they can even put it on tape…you will accept just about anything they choose to do. They could like, cheat, steal or toss juggling balls at you…what difference does it make? You love them, and that's all there is to that.

While you're accepting all these things, you are also making it quite clear to the world that you *are* accepting them. Not that you necessarily go around telling everyone, but you sigh a lot. No one really knows the depth of a Piscean sigh unless he has had a Pisces for a lover, a parent or a child. There is a touch of martyrdom in almost every young Pisces affair; as with the princess in the story, no matter how you've been hurt, you will always take your lover back when he or she decides to come back. In the movies of the thirties you were always being played by Ralph Bellamy and Joan Bondell.

Probably the main reason for this long-suffering attitude is that most of you are born into this world with a feeling of inferiority. If you have brothers or sisters, you somehow decide at an early age they're better, more attractive and more popular than you, and later in life you will blame your parents for this lack of confidence. You will be encouraged by your analyst, to whom you will pay a veritable fortune, when all the time you could be saving money and energy by blaming God for having made you a Pisces to start with.

Because you are so sensitive and vulnerable, you can't bear those who criticize you or other people. If you've fallen for a Virgo, forget it. That's why the typical Pisces rarely has anything unkind to say about anyone. You ususally go in the opposite direction and try always to see the prince in the frog. It's a lovely quality in this tough old world, and it makes for many acquaintances, but unfortunately, few real friends. Any Pisces reading this will throw up his hands at this point and cry "That's not true!" but the sad fact remains that while you may consider John or Jane Doe your best friend in all this world, John or Jane may think of you…but not that often. Don't be disheartened, though. A Piscean idea of friendship is different than an Aquarian or a Scorpian, but then a Piscean idea of *anything* is different than other people's.

You see, you are ruled by two planets: Neptune and Jupiter. It's Jupiter that makes you lucky, although you may not think of yourself as such. It's Jupiter that makes you outgoing, optimistic, generous and gracious. It's Neptune, though, that makes you a Pisces. Neptune give vibrations that only you can hear and it often bathes the world in lovely shades of colors which do not exist. That's why it's so difficult for you to see either the past or the present realistically. We have experienced certain incidents with certain Pisces, only to have them years later, repeat their version of what happened and make it sound like a totally different experience. Incidentally, if you were ever to hear that lovely young princess give her interpretation of the tale we told at the beginning, you would find that her parents didn't approve of the frog, not because he was a frog, but because he was Jewish.

Thus it is when an affair is over. There used to be a remarkable young lady named Dorothy Shay, who billed herself as "The Park Avenue Hillbilly" and sang very sophisiticated lyrics to real down-home country tunes. One of these was a song that went something like "I never knew that our romance was ended until you pushed me off the roof." That, in effect, is the essence of so many endings to Piscean romances. Once again, in the princess' version of the story, the frog out of the clear blue sky one day ups and runs away with the tightrope walker. She has no recollection that he used to get those sick headaches or throw his juggling balls at her head. She only remembers that one night he suddenly tried to strangle her with her garter belt and then he was gone.

You can do the same with your children that you do with your lovers. Most Pisces have an urgent need to be parents, and children are a source of genuine satisfaction. But your discipline is erratic. When you say no on Tuesday, you could say yes to exactly the same thing on Wednesday and such inconsistency does to an obedient child make. In truth, you would rather say yes any day of the week, because you think that's love, when in actuality it's weakness. You do the same with animals, which you adore. It is the rare Pisces who does not have a veritable menagerie of pets, upon whom he heaps the same adoration as he does on the jungle of plants he has growing in every available space.

You all know that the symbol of your sign is the two fishes swimming in opposite directions, which represents the eternal Piscean conflict. But you also have an animal counterpart which may come as a surprise to many of you, and that is the parrot. There are Pisces who even resemble parrots. The parrot is raucous, extroverted, amusing and often affectionate. They are astonishingly imitative (most Pisces are wonderful mimics) and do not relate reward or punishment in learning to imitate a new sound. They are also impossible to shut up once they get going.

All the signs were given keywords years ago. Gemini's is "I communicate"; Capricorn's is "I use"; Cancer's "I feel"; and yours is "I believe." People may talk all they want to about your sign being wishy-washy, but when you believe, oh, do you believe! This is what often makes you so unique. When going through lists of famous people, you can't do what you can do with other signs. You can't say look at all the famous painters, directors, writers, boxers or what-have-you, who were born under Pisces. You can point out, however, all the really individual folk Pisces has produced. When you get an artist, you don't just get any artist, you get Michelangelo. When you get a clergyman, you get Cotton Mather. When you get a pope, you get Pius XII. When you get a scientist, you get Galileo or Copernicus or Einstein. When you get an inventor, it's Alexander Graham Bell. Consider these other absolutely unique Pisceans: Luther Burbank, Charles Goren, Buffalo Bill, Wyatt Earp, Cyrano de Bergerac, Casey Jones, Osa Johnson, Amerigo Vespucci, Edgar Cayce, Bobby Fisher, Andrew Jackson, Rudolf Nureyev, Vaslaw Nijinsky, George Plimpton, L. Ron Hubbard and Robert Baden-Powell, who founded the Boy Scouts. Whatever these people did, they did it in a manner no one else did, and when they believed, they were willing to risk everything.

It's later in life that you Pisces come into your own. You learn the hard way and often from early affairs or marriages that were disasterous. But your resiliency is amazing, and we have seen time and again Pisces who have found the perfect mate in their thirties or forties. By that time unless you've taken to the bottle, a Piscean hazard, you have usually learned that selfishness is not some hideous quality after all, but a necessity for survival. You also learn that loving is not the same as smothering and sacrifice is different from martyrdom.

Pisces is not a sign noted for its discipline or reliability. You're usually the people who call at the last minute and say you can't make it because the water heater just burst or a plane fell on the freeway and blocked the road. However, if your Venus is in Capricorn, these disasters usually don't happen to you just as you're ready to leave the house or, if they do, they don't deter you. You are more dependable and conscientious than your fellow Pisces and, therefore, make better parents. Although equally as susceptible in love, you are more concerned with money, security and career. There are strong family ties and it often takes many year before you can remove the image of your mother or father standing over your shoulder criticizing your every move.

There is the usual Piscean imagination combined with a quiet, but powerful, sense of survival. One Pisces lady we know with this blend survived four years in a concentration camp by convincing herself she was the Jewish Joan of Arc. Extremely sexual, you often do the Capricornian thing later in life and pick up with someone younger and almost as horny. Celebrities born with this blend are W. H. Auden, Robert Young, Ann Sheridan, Tom Wolfe, Zero Mostel, Paula Prentiss and Peter Fonda.

All Pisces admire talent and try to nurture it, but those with Venus in Aquarius can carry this to an extreme. You will often search for the person you think has the most creative potential and stand by him, support him, help him and love him to pieces. To a few too many pieces, perhaps, because in many cases if he should fulfill your expectation, you may be the first one he will drop. The same applies to children. Those with this blend make perfect stage mothers or fathers.

There's a deep amount of humanitarian feeling, and you will give as much time, money and effort to a cause as you will to a friend in need. Like Venus in Capricorn, you are more reliable than the typical Pisces. This is a very creative combination, and the ego is more sensitive and requires a greater amount of bolstering. As you grow older, the hurts experienced in life can make you more independent and tougher than most of your Piscean brothers. You build emotional muscles. Montaigne, Wilhelm Grimm, Rossini, Ravel, Knute Rockne, Edward Albee and Dinah Shore were all born with this mixture. This is almost as horny a position as the Capricorn Venus, but in your case, friendship becomes of equal importance. If your sex lives should become a source of too much frustration, at least you have the good sense to sublimate the energy into your work.

Everything we have said about Pisces applies in spades to those with your Venus also in Pisces. You may be the most romantic, imaginative and emotional people in the entire zodiac . . . so much so that you are often in tune with vibrations only Peruvian macaws can pick up.

To your detriment, this hypersensitivity makes you over-optimistic at the slightest success and overly depressed at the slightest setback. It can also make you confuse love with sympathy, whether it's the sympathy you are giving another person or the other person is giving you. In addition, it can lead to masturbation, a not infrequent Pisces practice. Philip Roth, who wrote the definitive book on the subject, was born with this combination, as was a friend of ours who tells a most amusing story. She was reading *Cosmopolitan,* and it gave the most effective ways to masturbate . . . one of which was with an electric toothbrush. She didn't have one, but her young son did. In true Piscean fashion, she lay down on her bed and got herself into a most romantic mood. A Pisces can't even masturbate without romance. All at once she looked down and saw the face of Snoopy staring up at her. She burst into laughter and naturally couldn't complete the ritual. This story was once repeated to Helen Gurley Brown. She was not amused.

Humor is an endemic Pisces trait, and those with their Venus in the same sign have an abundance of it. Also, it gives talent and psychic ability. All Pisces are psychic to some degree or other, but in this instance, your powers to delve into hidden mysteries are often extraordinary. If you could only do the same with your own motivations and those of others! Because you insist on seeing people not the way they are, but the way you want them to do, you set yourself up for disillusionment, particularly in love . . . unless you happen to have been Elizabeth Barrett Browning, who found what every one of you is looking for. Besides Ms. Browning and Mr. Roth, other famous personages with this combination are Galileo, George Washington, Victor Hugo, Longfellow, Grover Cleveland, Nijinsky and Joanne Woodward.

If that lovely young princess we told you about had had her Venus in Aries, the story would have been different. Once she had fallen in love with that frog and her parents told her she was a fool, she wouldn't pretend he was a prince. Instead she would have shouted back, "I know he's a frog, but I love frogs, and he's my kind of frog!" She still might have done the same things to further his career, but by damn, she'd have gotten her pound of flesh in return or he'd have been thrown out on his little frog behind. In other words, the Aries side of you gives much too strong an ego to put up with all that self-sacrifice and nobility. You are more impulsive, adventurous and aggressive in love, and considerably more demanding. Take some of those born with this position:

Michelangelo, Anna Magnani, Elizabeth Taylor, Liza Minnelli, Bobby Fisher, Rudolf Nureyev, Harry Belafonte, George Plimpton and Andrew Jackson. They are hardly prime examples of your typical retiring, martyred Pisces. As a matter of fact, if you gave most of them a choice between the safe path and the dangerous one, they'd choose the latter any day of the week, just for the sheer excitement.

As parents, you exercise more control than other Pisces, but not always in a beneficial way. We know one Pisces woman with her Venus in Aries who would remind her three children of all she had sacrificed for them, yet she consistently got confused as to which one liked what when he was a child.

There is a fetching sexual magnetism with this combination, and the sex drive invariably continues into old age.

The Sun is Pisces and Venus in Taurus is the rarest combination of all and one which brings out the gentlest qualities in each of the signs. There is a great susceptibility to love and the promises of others, so perfectly exemplified in the song "Fire and Rain" by James Taylor, who was born with this blend. Often a childlike quality exists, and even as the years progress, you hate to leave your childhood behind. There is much sensuality combined with a love of music and a singularly strong psychic ability. Which many of you may be a bit afraid to develop. You are intensely loyal and devoted to lovers, family, mates and children, and you prefer a life of ease and luxury to one in which you must struggle for recognition. That's probably why you find fewer celebrities . . . John Updike, Sabu, Howard Wilson, Irving Wallace . . . born with this combination than any of the other Sun-Venus mixtures.

PART TWO

1910-1970
Birth Tables
(Ephemerides)

BIRTH TABLES / Legend

PLANETS

SUN	☉	MARS	♂
VENUS	♀	NEPTUNE	♆

SIGNS

ARIES	♈	LIBRA	♎
TAURUS	♉	SCORPIO	♏
GEMINI	♊	SAGITTARIUS	♐
CANCER	♋	CAPRICORN	♑
LEO	♌	AQUARIUS	♒
VIRGO	♍	PISCES	♓

BIRTH TABLES - 1910

Day	JANUARY ☉	♀	♂	♆	FEBRUARY ☉	♀	♂	♆	MARCH ☉	♀	♂	♆
01	10♑	23♒	18♈	18♋	12♒	29♒	05♉	17♋	10♓	15♒	22♉	17♋
02	11	24	19		13	29	06		11	15	23	
03	12	24	19		14	28	07		12	15	23	
04	13	25	19		15	28	07		13	15	24	
05	14	26	20		16	27	08		14	15	25	
06	15	26	21	18	17	27	08	17	15	15	25	17
07	16	27	21		18	26	09		16	15	26	
08	17	27	22		19	25	10		17	15	26	
09	18	28	22		20	25	10		18	16	27	
10	19	28	23		21	24	11		19	16	28	
11	20	28	24	18	22	24	11	17	20	16	28	17
12	21	29	24		23	23	12		21	16	29	
13	22	29	25		24	22	13		22	16	30	
14	23	29	25		25	22	13		23	17	00♊	
15	24	30	26		26	21	14		24	17	01	
16	26	00♓	26	18	27	21	14	17	25	18	01	17
17	27	00	27		28	20	15		26	18	02	
18	28	01	27		29	19	16		27	18	03	
19	29	01	28		30	19	16		28	19	03	
20	30	01	29		01♓	18	17		29	19	04	
21	01♒	01	29	18	02	18	17	17	30	20	04	17
22	02	01	30		03	17	18		01♈	20	05	
23	03	01	00♉		04	17	19		02	21	06	
24	04	01	01	18	05	17	19		03	22	06	
25	05	01	01	17	06	16	20		04	22	07	
26	06	01	02	17	07	16	20	17	05	23	08	17
27	07	00	03		08	16	21		06	23	08	
28	08	00♓	03		09	16	22		07	24	09	
29	09	30♒	04						08	25	09	
30	10	30	04						09	26	10	
31	11	29	05	17					10	26	11	17

Day	APRIL ☉	♀	♂	♆	MAY ☉	♀	♂	♆	JUNE ☉	♀	♂	♆
01	11♈	27♒	11♊	17♋	10♉	24♓	30♊	17♋	10♊	28♈	19♋	18♋
02	12	28	12		11	25	00♋		11	29	20	
03	13	29	12		12	26	01		12	30	20	
04	14	29	13		13	27	02		13	01♉	21	
05	15	00♓	14		14	28	02		14	02	22	
06	16	01	14	17	15	29	03	17	15	03	22	18
07	17	02	15		16	00♈	04		16	04	23	
08	18	03	16		17	01	04		17	06	23	
09	19	03	16		18	03	05		18	07	24	
10	20	04	17		19	04	05		19	08	25	
11	21	05	17	17	20	05	06	17	20	09	25	18
12	22	06	18		21	06	07		21	10	26	
13	23	07	19		22	07	07		22	11	27	
14	24	08	19		23	08	08		23	12	27	
15	25	09	20		24	09	08		23	13	28	
16	26	10	20	17	25	10	09	17	24	15	28	18
17	27	11	21		26	11	10		25	16	29	
18	28	11	22		27	12	10		26	17	30	
19	29	12	22		28	13	11		27	18	00♌	
20	30	13	23		29	14	12		28	19	01	
21	00♉	14	24	17	30	15	12	17	29	20	01	18
22	01	15	24		01♊	17	13		00♋	22	02	
23	02	16	25		01	18	13		01	23	03	
24	03	17	25		02	19	14		02	24	03	
25	04	18	26		03	20	15		03	25	04	
26	05	19	27	17	04	21	15	17	04	26	05	18
27	06	20	27		05	22	16	18	05	27	05	19
28	07	21	28		06	23	17		06	28	06	
29	08	22	29		07	24	17		07	30	06	
30	09	23	29		08	25	18		08	01♊	07	
31					09	27	18	18				

Day	JULY				AUGUST				SEPTEMBER				OCTOBER				NOVEMBER				DECEMBER			
	☉	♀	♂	♆	☉	♀	♂	♆	☉	♀	♂	♆	☉	♀	♂	♆	☉	♀	♂	♆	☉	♀	♂	♆
01	09♋	02♊	08♌	19♋	08♌	09♋	27♌	20♋	08♍	16♌	17♍	21♋	07♎	23♍	06♎	21♋	08♏	02♏	26♎	22♋	08♐	10♐	17♏	21♋
02	10	03	08		09	10	28		09	17	17		08	24	07		09	03	27		09	11	18	
03	11	04	09		10	11	28		10	19	18		09	26	07		10	04	28		10	12	18	
04	12	05	10		11	12	29		11	20	19		10	27	08		11	06	29		11	13	19	
05	13	07	10		12	13	30		12	21	19		11	28	09		12	07	29		12	15	20	
06	14	08	11	19	13	15	00♍	20	13	22	20	21	12	29	09	21	13	08	30	22	14	16	20	21
07	14	09	11		14	16	01		14	24	21		13	01♎	10		14	09	01♏		15	17	21	
08	15	10	12		15	17	02		15	25	21		14	02	11	22	15	11	01		16	18	22	
09	16	11	13		16	18	02		16	26	22		15	03	11		16	12	02		17	20	22	
10	17	13	13		17	19	03		17	27	23		16	04	12		17	13	03		18	21	23	
11	18	14	14	19	18	21	03	20	18	28	23	21	17	06	13	22	18	15	03	22	19	22	24	21
12	19	15	15		19	22	04		19	30	24		18	07	13		19	16	04	21	20	23	24	
13	20	16	15		20	23	05		20	01♍	25		19	08	14		20	17	05		21	25	25	
14	21	17	16		21	24	05		21	02	25		20	09	15		21	18	05		22	26	26	
15	22	18	16		22	25	06		22	03	26		21	11	15		22	20	06		23	27	27	
16	23	20	17	19	23	27	07	20	23	05	26	21	22	12	16	22	23	21	07	21	24	29	27	21
17	24	21	18		24	28	07		24	06	27		23	13	17		24	22	07		25	30	28	
18	25	22	18		25	29	08		25	07	28		24	14	17		25	23	08		26	01♑	29	
19	26	23	19		26	00♌	09		26	08	28		25	16	18		26	25	09		27	02	29	
20	27	24	20		27	02	09		27	10	29		26	17	19		27	26	09		28	04	00♐	
21	28	26	20	19	28	03	10	20	28	11	30	21	27	18	19	22	28	27	10	21	29	05	01	21
22	29	27	21		28	04	10	21	29	12	00♎		28	19	20		29	28	11		30	06	01	
23	30	28	21	19	29	05	11		30	13	01		29	21	21		00♐	30	11		01♑	07	02	
24	01♌	29	22	20	00♍	06	12		01♎	15	02		00♏	22	21		01	01♐	12		02	09	03	
25	02	00♋	23		01	08	12		02	16	02		01	23	22		02	02	13		03	10	03	
26	03	01	23	20	02	09	13	21	03	17	03	21	02	24	23	22	03	03	13	21	04	11	04	21
27	04	03	24		03	10	14		03	18	04		03	26	23		04	05	14		05	12	05	
28	05	04	25		04	11	14		04	19	04		04	27	24		05	06	15		06	14	06	
29	05	05	25		05	13	15		05	21	05		05	28	25		06	07	16		07	15	06	
30	06	06	26		06	14	16		06	22	06		06	29	25		07	08	16		08	16	07	
31	07	07	27	20	07	15	16	21					07	01♏	26	22					09	17	08	20

BIRTH TABLES - 1911

Day	JANUARY				FEBRUARY				MARCH			
	☉	♀	♂	♆	☉	♀	♂	♆	☉	♀	♂	♆
01	10♑	19♑	08♐	20♋	12♒	28♒	00♑	20♋	10♓	02♈	21♑	19♋
02	11	20	09		13	29	01		11	04	22	
03	12	21	10		14	00♓	02		12	05	22	
04	13	22	11		15	01	03		13	06	23	
05	14	24	11		16	03	03		14	07	24	
06	15	25	12	20	17	04	04	19	15	09	24	19
07	16	26	12		18	05	05		16	10	25	
08	17	27	13		19	06	06		17	11	26	
09	18	29	14		20	08	06		18	12	27	
10	19	30	15		21	09	07		19	13	27	
11	20	01♒	15	20	22	10	08	19	20	15	28	19
12	21	02	16		23	11	08		21	16	29	
13	22	04	17		24	12	09		22	17	30	
14	23	05	18		25	14	10		23	18	00♒	
15	24	06	18		26	15	11		24	20	01	
16	25	07	19	20	27	16	11	19	25	21	02	19
17	26	09	20		28	17	12		26	22	03	
18	27	10	20		29	19	13		27	23	03	
19	28	11	21		30	20	13		28	25	04	
20	29	12	22		01♓	21	14		29	26	05	
21	00♒	14	23	20	02	22	15	19	30	27	06	19
22	01	15	23		03	24	16		01♈	28	06	
23	02	16	24		04	25	16		02	29	07	
24	03	18	25		05	26	17		03	01♉	08	
25	04	19	25		06	27	18		04	02	09	
26	05	20	26	20	07	29	19	19	05	03	09	19
27	06	21	27		08	30	19		06	04	10	
28	07	23	28		09	01♈	20		07	06	11	
29	08	24	28						08	07	12	
30	09	25	29						09	08	12	
31	11	26	30	20					10	09	13	19

Day	APRIL				MAY				JUNE			
	☉	♀	♂	♆	☉	♀	♂	♆	☉	♀	♂	♆
01	11♈	10♉	14♒	19♋	10♉	16♊	06♓	19♋	10♊	22♋	29♓	20♋
02	12	12	14		11	17	07		11	23	30	
03	13	13	15		12	19	08		12	24	00♈	
04	14	14	16		13	20	08		13	25	01	
05	15	15	17		14	21	09		14	26	02	
06	16	16	17	19	15	22	10	19	15	28	02	20
07	17	18	18		16	23	11		16	29	03	
08	18	19	19		17	25	11		17	30	04	
09	19	20	20		18	26	12		18	01♌	05	
10	20	21	20		19	27	13		18	02	05	
11	20	22	21	19	20	28	14	19	19	03	06	20
12	21	24	22		21	29	14		20	04	07	
13	22	25	23		22	00♋	15		21	05	08	
14	23	26	23		23	01	16		22	06	08	
15	24	27	24		24	03	16		23	07	09	
16	25	28	25	19	24	04	17	19	24	08	10	20
17	26	30	26		25	05	18		25	09	11	
18	27	01♊	26		26	06	19		26	10	11	
19	28	02	27		27	07	19		27	12	12	
20	29	03	28		28	08	20		28	13	13	
21	00♉	04	29	19	29	10	21	19	29	14	13	20
22	01	06	29		00♊	11	22	20	30	15	14	
23	02	07	00♓		01	12	22		01♋	16	15	21
24	03	08	01		02	13	23		02	17	15	
25	04	09	02		03	14	24		03	18	16	
26	05	10	02	19	04	15	25	20	04	19	17	21
27	06	12	03		05	16	25		05	20	18	
28	07	13	04		06	17	26		06	21	18	
29	08	14	05		07	19	27		07	22	19	
30	09	15	05		08	20	28		08	23	20	
31					09	21	28	20				

Day	JULY				AUGUST				SEPTEMBER				OCTOBER				NOVEMBER				DECEMBER			
	☉	♀	♂	♆	☉	♀	♂	♆	☉	♀	♂	♆	☉	♀	♂	♆	☉	♀	♂	♆	☉	♀	♂	♆
01	09♋	24♌	20♈	21♋	08♌	21♍	11♉	22♋	08♍	28♍	28♉	23♋	07♎	14♍	09♊	24♋	08♏	24♍	09♊	24♋	08♐	22♎	30♉	23♋
02	09	25	21		09	21	11		09	28	29		08	14	09		09	25	09		09	23	29	
03	10	26	22		10	22	12		10	28	29		09	14	09		10	26	09		10	24	29	
04	11	27	22		11	22	13		11	27	29		10	13	10		11	26	09		11	25	28	
05	12	28	23		12	23	13		12	27	30		11	13	10		12	27	09		12	26	28	
06	13	29	24	21	13	24	14	22	13	27	00♊	23	12	13	10	24	13	28	08	24	13	27	28	23
07	14	30	25		14	24	14		14	26	01		13	13	10		14	29	08		14	28	28	
08	15	01♍	25		15	25	15		15	26	01		14	13	10		15	30	08		15	29	27	
09	16	02	26		16	25	16		16	25	02		15	14	10		16	00♎	07		16	00♏	27	
10	17	03	27		17	26	16		17	25	02		16	14	11		17	01	07		17	01	27	
11	18	03	27	21	18	26	17	22	18	24	03	23	17	14	11	24	18	02	07	24	18	02	27	23
12	19	04	28		19	27	17		19	23	03		18	14	11		19	03	06		19	03	26	
13	20	05	29		20	27	18		20	23	03		19	14	11		20	04	06		20	05	26	
14	21	06	29		21	27	19		21	22	04		20	15	11		21	05	06		21	06	26	
15	22	07	30		22	28	19		22	22	04		21	15	11		22	06	05		22	07	26	
16	23	08	01♉	21	22	28	20	22	22	21	05	23	22	15	11	24	23	07	05	24	23	08	26	23
17	24	09	01		23	28	20		23	20	05		23	16	11		24	08	05		24	09	25	
18	25	10	02		24	29	21		24	20	05		24	16	11		25	09	04		25	10	25	
19	26	11	02		25	29	21		25	19	06		25	16	11		26	09	04		26	11	25	
20	27	11	03		26	29	22		26	19	06		26	17	11		27	10	04		27	12	25	
21	28	12	04	22	27	29	22	23	27	18	06	23	27	17	11	24	28	11	03	24	29	14	25	23
22	29	13	04		28	29	23		28	17	07		28	18	11		29	12	03		30	15	25	
23	30	14	05		29	29	24		29	17	07		29	18	11		00♐	13	02		01♑	16	25	
24	00♌	15	06		00♍	29	24		00♎	16	07		30	19	11		01	14	02		02	17	24	
25	01	15	06		01	29	25		01	16	07	24	01♏	19	11		02	15	02		03	18	24	
26	02	16	07	22	02	29	25	23	02	16	08	24	02	20	10	24	03	16	01	24	04	19	24	23
27	03	17	08		03	29	26		03	15	08		03	21	10		04	17	01		05	20	24	
28	04	17	08		04	29	26		04	15	08		04	21	10		05	18	01		06	22	24	
29	05	18	09		05	29	27		05	14	09		05	22	10		06	19	00		07	23	24	
30	06	19	10		06	29	27		06	14	09		06	23	10		07	21	30♉		08	24	24	
31	07	20	10	22	07	29	28	23					07	23	10	24					09	25	24	23

BIRTH TABLES - 1912

Day	JAN ☉	JAN ♀	JAN ♂	JAN ♆	FEB ☉	FEB ♀	FEB ♂	FEB ♆	MAR ☉	MAR ♀	MAR ♂	MAR ♆
01	10♑	26♏	24♉	23♋	11♒	03♑	01♊	22♋	11♓	08♒	12♊	21♋
02	11	27	24		12	04	01		12	10	13	
03	12	29	24		13	06	01		13	11	13	
04	13	30	25		14	07	02		14	12	14	
05	14	01♐	25		15	08	02		15	13	14	
06	15	02	25	23	16	09	02	22	16	15	15	21
07	16	03	25		17	10	03		17	16	15	
08	17	04	25		18	12	03		18	17	16	
09	18	06	25		19	13	03		19	18	16	
10	19	07	25		20	14	04		20	19	17	
11	20	08	25	22	21	15	04	22	21	21	17	21
12	21	09	25		22	16	05		22	22	18	
13	22	10	26		23	18	05		23	23	18	
14	23	12	26		24	19	05		24	24	19	
15	24	13	26		25	20	06		25	26	19	
16	25	14	26	22	26	21	06	22	26	27	20	21
17	26	15	26		27	23	07		27	28	20	
18	27	16	27		28	24	07	21	28	29	21	
19	28	17	27		29	25	07		29	00♓	21	
20	29	19	27		01♓	26	08		30	02	22	
21	00♒	20	27	22	02	27	08	21	01♈	03	22	21
22	01	21	28		03	29	09		02	04	23	
23	02	22	28		04	30	09		03	05	23	
24	03	23	28		05	01♒	10		03	07	24	
25	04	25	28		06	02	10		04	08	24	
26	05	26	29	22	07	04	10	21	05	09	25	21
27	06	27	29		08	05	11		06	10	25	
28	07	28	29		09	06	11		07	11	26	
29	08	29	30		10	07	12		08	13	26	
30	09	01♑	30						09	14	27	
31	10	02	00♊	22					10	15	27	21

Day	APR ☉	APR ♀	APR ♂	APR ♆	MAY ☉	MAY ♀	MAY ♂	MAY ♆	JUN ☉	JUN ♀	JUN ♂	JUN ♆
01	11♈	16♓	28♊	21♋	11♉	23♈	14♋	21♋	11♊	01♊	02♌	22♋
02	12	18	28		12	24	15		12	02	03	
03	13	19	29		13	26	16		13	04	04	
04	14	20	29		14	27	16		13	05	04	
05	15	21	00♋		15	28	17		14	06	05	
06	16	23	01	21	16	29	17	21	15	07	05	22
07	17	24	01		17	01♉	18		16	09	06	
08	18	25	02		18	02	18		17	10	07	
09	19	26	02		18	03	19		18	11	07	
10	20	27	03		19	04	20		19	12	08	
11	21	29	03	21	20	05	20	21	20	13	08	22
12	22	30	04		21	07	21		21	15	09	
13	23	01♈	04		22	08	21		22	16	10	
14	24	02	05		23	09	22		23	17	10	
15	25	04	05		24	10	23	22	24	18	11	
16	26	05	06	21	25	12	23	22	25	20	11	22
17	27	06	07		26	13	24		26	21	12	
18	28	07	07		27	14	24		27	22	13	23
19	29	08	08		28	15	25		28	23	13	
20	00♉	10	08		29	16	25		29	24	14	
21	01	11	09	21	00♊	18	26	22	30	26	14	23
22	02	12	09		01	19	27		01♋	27	15	
23	03	13	10		02	20	27		02	28	16	
24	04	15	11		03	21	28		03	29	16	
25	05	16	11		04	23	28		04	01♋	17	
26	06	17	12	21	05	24	29	22	04	02	17	23
27	07	18	12		06	25	30		05	03	18	
28	08	20	13		07	26	00♌		06	04	19	
29	09	21	13		08	28	01		07	06	19	
30	10	22	14		09	29	01		08	07	20	
31					10	30	02	22				

Day	JULY ☉	♀	♂	♆	AUGUST ☉	♀	♂	♆	SEPTEMBER ☉	♀	♂	♆
01	09♋	08♋	20♌	23♋	09♌	16♌	10	24♋	09♍	24♍	29♍	25♋
02	10	09	21		10	17	10		10	26	30	
03	11	10	22		11	19	11		11	27	01♎	
04	12	12	22		12	20	11		12	28	01	
05	13	13	23		13	21	12		13	29	02	
06	14	14	24	23	14	22	13	24	13	01♎	02	25
07	15	15	24		15	24	13		14	02	03	
08	16	17	25		16	25	14		15	03	04	
09	17	18	25		16	26	15		16	04	04	
10	18	19	26		17	27	15		17	06	05	
11	19	20	27	23	18	28	16	24	18	07	06	25
12	20	22	27		19	30	16	25	19	08	06	
13	21	23	28		20	01♍	17		20	09	07	
14	22	24	28		21	02	18		21	10	08	
15	23	25	29		22	03	18		22	12	08	
16	24	26	30	24	23	05	19	25	23	13	09	26
17	25	28	00♍		24	06	20		24	14	10	
18	25	29	01		25	07	20		25	15	10	
19	26	00♌	01		26	08	21		26	17	11	
20	27	01	02		27	10	22		27	18	12	
21	28	03	03	24	28	11	22	25	28	19	12	26
22	29	04	03		29	12	23		29	20	13	
23	00♌	05	04		30	13	23		00♎	22	14	
24	01	06	05		01♍	15	24		01	23	14	
25	02	08	05		02	16	25		02	24	15	
26	03	09	06	24	03	17	25	25	03	25	16	26
27	04	10	06		04	18	26		04	27	16	
28	05	11	07		05	19	27		05	28	17	
29	06	12	08		06	21	27		06	29	18	
30	07	14	08		07	22	28		07	00♏	18	
31	08	15	09	24	08	23	29	25				

Day	OCTOBER ☉	♀	♂	♆	NOVEMBER ☉	♀	♂	♆	DECEMBER ☉	♀	♂	♆
01	08♎	01♏	19♎	26♋	09♏	10♐	10♏	26♋	09♐	16♑	01♐	26♋
02	09	03	20		10	11	11		10	17	02	
03	10	04	20		11	12	11		11	19	02	
04	11	05	21		12	13	12		12	20	03	
05	12	06	22		13	14	13		13	21	04	
06	13	08	22	26	14	16	13	26	14	22	04	26
07	14	09	23		15	17	14		15	23	05	
08	15	10	24		16	18	15		16	25	06	
09	16	11	24		17	19	15		17	26	07	
10	17	13	25		18	21	16		18	27	07	
11	18	14	26	26	19	22	17	26	19	28	08	26
12	19	15	26		20	23	17		20	29	09	
13	20	16	27		21	24	18		21	01♒	09	25
14	21	17	28		22	25	19		22	02	10	
15	22	19	28		23	27	20		23	03	11	
16	23	20	29	26	24	28	20	26	24	04	12	25
17	24	21	30		25	29	21		25	06	12	
18	25	22	00♏		26	00♑	22		26	07	13	
19	26	24	01		27	02	22		27	08	14	
20	27	25	02		28	03	23		28	09	15	
21	28	26	02	26	29	04	24	26	29	10	15	25
22	29	27	03		30	05	24		00♑	11	16	
23	30	29	04		01♐	06	25		01	13	17	
24	01♏	30	04		02	08	26		02	14	17	
25	02	01♐	05		03	09	27		03	15	18	
26	03	02	06	26	04	10	27	26	04	16	19	25
27	04	03	06		05	11	28		05	17	20	
28	05	05	07		06	13	29		06	19	20	
29	06	06	08		07	14	29		07	20	21	
30	07	07	08		08	15	00♐		08	21	22	
31	08	08	09	26					09	22	23	25

BIRTH TABLES - 1913

JANUARY

Day	☉	♀	♂	♆
01	10♑	23♒	23♐	25♋
02	12	24	24	
03	13	26	25	
04	14	27	26	
05	15	28	26	
06	16	00♓	27	25
07	17	01	28	
08	18	03	28	
09	19	04	29	
10	20	05	00♑	
11	21	05	01	25
12	22	06	02	
13	23	07	03	
14	24	08	04	
15	25	10	04	
16	26	11	05	25
17	27	12	05	
18	28	13	06	
19	29	14	07	
20	00♒	15	07	24
21	01	16	08	24
22	02	17	09	
23	03	19	10	
24	04	20	10	
25	05	21	11	
26	06	22	12	24
27	07	23	13	
28	08	24	13	
29	09	25	14	
30	10	26	15	
31	11	27	16	24

FEBRUARY

Day	☉	♀	♂	♆
01	12♒	28♓	16♑	24♋
02	13	00♈	17	
03	14	01	18	
04	15	02	19	
05	16	03	19	
06	17	04	20	24
07	18	05	21	
08	19	06	22	
09	20	07	22	
10	21	08	23	
11	22	09	24	24
12	23	10	25	
13	24	11	26	
14	25	12	26	
15	26	13	27	
16	27	14	28	24
17	28	15	29	
18	29	16	29	
19	00♓	17	00♒	
20	01	18	01	
21	02	19	02	24
22	03	20	02	
23	04	21	03	
24	05	21	04	
25	06	22	05	
26	07	23	06	24
27	08	24	06	
28	09	25	07	24

MARCH

Day	☉	♀	♂	♆
01	10♓	26♈	08♒	24♋
02	11	27	09	
03	12	27	09	23
04	13	28	10	
05	14	29	11	
06	15	00♉	12	23
07	16	01	12	
08	17	01	13	
09	18	02	14	
10	19	03	15	
11	20	04	16	23
12	21	04	16	
13	22	05	17	
14	23	05	18	
15	24	06	19	
16	25	07	19	23
17	26	07	20	
18	27	08	21	
19	28	08	22	
20	29	09	22	
21	00♈	09	23	23
22	01	10	24	
23	02	10	25	
24	03	11	26	
25	04	11	26	
26	05	11	27	23
27	06	12	28	
28	07	12	29	
29	08	12	29	
30	09	12	00♓	
31	10	12	01	23

APRIL

Day	☉	♀	♂	♆
01	11♈	12♉	02♓	23♋
02	12	12	03	
03	13	13	03	
04	41	12	04	23
05	51	12	05	23
06	16	12	06	23
07	17	12	06	
08	18	12	07	
09	19	12	08	
10	20	12	09	
11	21	11	10	23
12	22	11	10	
13	23	11	11	
14	24	10	12	
15	25	10	13	
16	26	09	13	23
17	27	09	14	
18	28	08	15	
19	29	08	16	
20	00♉	07	16	
21	01	06	17	23
22	02	06	18	
23	03	05	19	
24	04	05	20	
25	05	04	20	
26	06	03	21	23
27	07	03	22	
28	08	02	23	
29	09	02	23	
30	10	01	24	23

MAY

Day	☉	♀	♂	♆
01	10♉	00♉	25♓	23♋
02	11	00	26	
03	12	29♈	26	
04	13	29	27	
05	14	28	28	
06	15	28	29	23
07	16	28	00♈	24
08	17	27	00	
09	18	27	01	
10	19	27	02	
11	20	27	03	24
12	21	26	03	
13	22	26	04	
14	23	26	05	
15	24	26	06	
16	25	26	06	24
17	26	26	07	
18	27	26	08	
19	28	26	09	
20	29	26	09	
21	00♊	27	10	24
22	01	27	11	
23	02	27	12	
24	03	27	12	
25	04	28	13	
26	05	28	14	24
27	06	28	15	
28	06	29	15	
29	07	29	16	
30	08	00♉	17	
31	09	00	18	24

JUNE

Day	☉	♀	♂	♆
01	10♊	01♉	18♈	24♋
02	11	01	19	
03	12	02	20	
04	13	02	21	
05	14	03	21	
06	15	03	22	24
07	16	04	23	
08	17	05	24	
09	18	05	24	
10	19	06	25	
11	20	07	26	24
12	21	07	27	
13	22	08	27	
14	23	09	28	25
15	24	10	29	
16	25	10	00♉	25
17	26	11	00	
18	27	12	01	
19	28	13	02	
20	29	14	03	
21	29	15	03	25
22	00♋	15	04	
23	01	16	05	
24	02	17	05	
25	03	18	06	
26	04	19	07	25
27	05	20	08	
28	06	21	08	
29	07	22	09	
30	08	22	10	25

The table gives, for each day (01–31), the degree and sign of four bodies in each month: ☉ (Sun), ♀ (Venus), ♂ (Mars) and ♆ (Neptune, printed only on the days it advances). Sign glyphs: ♉ Taurus, ♊ Gemini, ♋ Cancer, ♌ Leo, ♍ Virgo, ♎ Libra, ♏ Scorpio, ♐ Sagittarius, ♑ Capricorn.

July – September

Day	Jul ☉	Jul ♀	Jul ♂	Jul ♆	Aug ☉	Aug ♀	Aug ♂	Aug ♆	Sep ☉	Sep ♀	Sep ♂	Sep ♆
01	09♋	23♉	11♉	25♋	09♌	25♊	02♊	26♋	08♍	00♌	22♊	27♋
02	10	24	11		10	26	03		09	01	22	
03	11	25	12		11	27	03		10	02	23	
04	12	26	13		11	28	04		11	04	24	
05	13	27	13		12	29	05		12	05	24	
06	14	28	14		13	00♋	05		13	06	25	27
07	15	29	15		14	02	06		14	07	25	
08	16	00♊	16		15	03	07		15	08	26	
09	17	01	16		16	04	07		16	10	26	
10	18	02	17		17	05	08		17	11	27	
11	19	03	18		18	06	09		18	12	28	28♋
12	20	04	18		19	07	09		19	13	28	
13	20	05	19		20	08	10		20	14	29	
14	21	06	20		21	10	11		21	15	29	
15	22	07	20		22	11	11		22	17	00♋	
16	23	08	21	25	23	12	12	26♋	23	19	01	28
17	24	09	22		24	13	13		24	20	02	
18	25	10	23		25	14	13		25	21	02	
19	26	11	23		26	15	14		26	23	03	
20	27	12	24		27	16	14		27	24	03	
21	28	13	25	26	28	17	15		28	25	04	28
22	29	14	25		29	19	16		29	26	04	
23	30	15	26		30	20	16		30	27	05	
24	01♌	16	27		01♍	21	17		01♎	28	05	
25	02	18	27		02	22	17		02	29	06	
26	03	19	28		03	23	18		03	30	06	28
27	04	20	29		04	24	19		04	01♍	07	
28	05	21	30		05	25	19		05	02	07	
29	06	22	00♊		06	27	20		06	03	08	
30	07	23	01		06	28	21		07	05	08	
31	08	24	01		07	29	21					

October – December

Day	Oct ☉	Oct ♀	Oct ♂	Oct ♆	Nov ☉	Nov ♀	Nov ♂	Nov ♆	Dec ☉	Dec ♀	Dec ♂	Dec ♆
01	08♎	06♍	08♋	28♋	09♏	14♎	21♋	28♋	09♐	21♏	24♋	28♋
02	09	07	09		10	15	21		10	23	24	
03	10	08	09		11	16	21		11	24	24	
04	11	09	10		12	18	21		12	25	24	
05	12	11	10		13	19	22		13	26	24	
06	13	12	11		14	20	22		14	28	24	28
07	14	13	11		15	22	22		15	29	24	
08	15	14	12		15	23	22		16	00♐	24	
09	16	16	12		16	24	23		17	01	23	
10	17	17	12		17	25	23		18	03	23	
11	18	18	13	28	18	26	23	28	19	04	23	28
12	19	19	13		19	28	23		20	05	23	
13	20	20	14		20	29	23		21	06	23	
14	21	22	14		21	00♏	24		22	08	22	
15	22	23	15		22	01	24		23	09	22	
16	23	24	15		23	03	24		24	10	22	28
17	24	25	16		24	04	24		25	11	22	
18	25	27	16		25	05	24		26	13	21	
19	25	28	16		26	06	24		27	14	21	
20	26	29	17		27	08	24		28	15	21	
21	27	00♎	17	28	28	09	24	28	29	16	20	28
22	28	02	17		29	10	24		00♑	18	20	
23	29	03	18		00♐	11	24		01	19	20	
24	30	04	18		01	13	25		02	20	19	
25	01♏	05	18		02	14	25		03	22	19	
26	02	06	19		03	15	25		04	23	19	27
27	03	08	19		04	16	25		05	24	18	
28	04	09	19		05	18	25		06	25	18	
29	05	10	20		06	19	25		07	27	18	
30	06	11	20		07	20	24		08	28	17	
31	07	13	20						09	29	17	27

BIRTH TABLES - 1914

Day	JAN ☉	JAN ♀	JAN ♂	JAN ♆	FEB ☉	FEB ♀	FEB ♂	FEB ♆	MAR ☉	MAR ♀	MAR ♂	MAR ♆
01	10♑	00♑	16♋	27♋	12♒	09♒	07♋	26♋	10♓	14♓	07♋	26♋
02	11	02	16		13	11	06		11	16	07	
03	12	03	16		14	12	06		12	17	08	
04	13	04	15		15	13	06		13	18	08	
05	14	05	15		16	14	06		14	19	08	
06	15	07	14	27	17	16	06	26	15	21	08	26
07	16	08	14		18	17	06		16	22	08	
08	17	09	14		19	18	06		17	23	09	
09	18	10	13		20	19	06		18	24	09	
10	19	12	13		21	21	06		19	26	09	
11	20	13	12	27	22	22	06	26	20	27	09	26
12	21	14	12		23	23	06		21	28	10	
13	22	15	12		24	24	06		22	29	10	
14	24	17	11		25	26	06		23	01♈	10	
15	25	18	11		26	27	06		24	02	11	
16	26	19	11	27	27	28	06	26	25	03	11	26
17	27	20	10		28	29	06		26	04	11	
18	28	22	10		29	01♓	06		27	06	12	
19	29	23	10		00♓	02	06		28	07	12	
20	30	24	09		01	03	06		29	08	12	
21	01♒	25	09	27	02	04	06	26	00♈	09	12	26
22	02	27	09		03	06	06		01	11	13	
23	03	28	08		04	07	06		02	12	14	25
24	04	29	08		05	08	06		03	13	14	
25	05	01♒	08		06	09	07		04	14	14	
26	06	02	08	27	07	11	07	26	05	16	14	25
27	07	03	07		08	12	07		06	17	14	
28	08	04	07		09	13	07		07	18	14	
29	09	06	07						08	19	14	
30	10	07	07	26					09	20	16	
31	11	08	07	26					10	22	16	25

Day	APR ☉	APR ♀	APR ♂	APR ♆	MAY ☉	MAY ♀	MAY ♂	MAY ♆	JUN ☉	JUN ♀	JUN ♂	JUN ♆
01	11♈	23♈	16♋	25♋	10♉	30♉	30♋	26♋	10♊	08♋	16♌	26♋
02	12	24	17		11	01♊	00♌		11	09	17	
03	13	26	17		12	02	01		12	10	17	
04	14	27	18		13	04	01		13	11	18	
05	15	28	19		14	05	02		14	12	18	
06	16	29	18	25	15	06	02	26	15	14	19	26
07	17	00♉	19		16	07	03		16	15	19	
08	18	02	19		17	08	03		17	16	20	
09	19	03	20		18	10	04		18	17	20	
10	20	04	20		19	11	04		19	18	21	27
11	21	05	21	25	20	12	05	26	20	20	22	27
12	22	07	21		21	13	05		21	21	22	
13	23	08	21		22	15	06		22	22	23	
14	24	09	22		23	16	06		23	23	23	
15	25	10	22		24	17	07		24	24	24	
16	26	11	23	25	25	18	07	26	26	26	24	27
17	27	13	23		26	19	08		27	27	25	
18	28	14	24		27	21	08		28	28	26	
19	29	15	24		28	22	09		29	29	26	
20	30	16	25		29	23	10		00♋	00♌	27	
21	01♉	18	25	26	30	24	10	26	02	02	27	27
22	02	19	26		01♊	25	11		03	03	28	
23	02	20	26	25	01	27	11		04	04	28	
24	03	21	26		02	28	12		05	05	29	
25	04	23	27		03	29	12		06	06	30	
26	05	24	27	26	04	00♋	12	26	08	08	00♍	27
27	06	25	28		05	02	13		09	09	01	
28	07	26	28		06	03	14		10	10	01	
29	08	27	29		07	04	14		11	11	02	
30	09	29	29		08	05	15		12	12	03	
31					09	06	15	26				

Day	JULY				AUGUST				SEPTEMBER				OCTOBER				NOVEMBER				DECEMBER			
	☉	♀	♂	♆	☉	♀	♂	♆	☉	♀	♂	♆	☉	♀	♂	♆	☉	♀	♂	♆	☉	♀	♂	♆
01	09♋	13♌	03♍	27♋	08♌	20♍	22♍	28♋	08♍	24♎	11♎	29♋	07♎	23♏	01♏	00♌	08♏	12♐	23♏	00♌	08♐	02♐	15♐	00♌
02	10	15	04		09	21	23		09	25	12		08	24	02		09	12	23		09	02	15	
03	11	16	04		10	22	23		10	26	13		09	25	03		10	12	24		10	01	16	
04	12	17	05		11	23	24		11	27	13		10	26	03		11	12	25		12	01	17	
05	13	18	05		12	24	24		12	28	14		11	26	04		12	12	26		13	00	18	
06	14	19	06	27	13	25	25	29	13	29	15	30	12	27	05	00	13	12	26	00	14	30♍	18	00
07	15	21	07		14	26	26		14	00♏	15		13	28	05		14	12	27		15	29	19	
08	15	22	07		15	27	26		15	01	16		14	29	06		15	12	28		16	29	20	
09	16	23	08		16	29	27		16	02	17		15	30	07		16	12	29		17	29	21	
10	17	24	08		17	30	27		17	03	17		16	00♐	08		17	12	29		18	28	21	
11	18	25	09	28	18	01♎	28	29	18	04	18	30	17	01	08	00	18	12	00♐	00	19	28	22	00
12	19	26	10		19	02	29		19	05	19		18	02	09		19	12	01		20	28	23	
13	20	28	10		20	03	29		20	06	19		19	02	10		20	11	01		21	27	24	
14	21	29	11		21	04	30		21	07	20		20	03	10		21	11	02		22	27	24	
15	22	30	11		22	05	01♎		22	08	21		21	04	11		22	11	03		23	27	25	
16	23	01♍	12	28	23	06	01	29	23	09	21	30	22	05	12	00	23	11	04	00	24	27	26	30♋
17	24	02	13		24	08	02		24	10	22		23	05	12		24	10	04		25	27	27	
18	25	03	13		25	09	03		25	11	23		24	06	13		25	09	05		26	27	27	
19	26	05	14		26	10	03		26	12	23		25	06	14		26	09	06		27	27	28	
20	27	06	14		27	11	04		27	13	24		26	07	14		27	09	07		28	27	29	
21	28	07	15	28	28	12	04	29	28	14	25	30	27	07	15	00	28	08	07	00	29	27	30	30
22	29	08	16		29	13	05		29	15	25		28	08	16		29	08	08		30	27	00♑	
23	30	09	16		30	14	06		30	16	26		29	08	17		00♐	07	09		01♑	28	01	
24	01♌	10	17		00♍	15	06		01♎	17	27		00♏	09	17		01	07	09		02	28	02	
25	02	12	18		01	16	07		02	18	27		01	09	18		02	06	10		03	28	03	
26	03	13	18	28	02	17	08	29	03	19	28	00♌	02	10	19	00	03	05	11	00	04	28	03	30
27	04	14	19		03	18	08		04	20	29		03	10	19		04	05	12		05	29	04	
28	05	15	19		04	20	09		05	20	29		04	11	20		05	04	12		06	29	05	
29	06	16	20		05	21	10		05	21	00♏		05	11	21		06	04	13		07	29	06	
30	06	17	21		06	22	10		06	22	01		06	11	21		07	03	14		08	30	06	
31	07	18	21	28	07	23	11	29					07	11	22	00					09	00♐	07	30

BIRTH TABLES - 1915

	JANUARY				FEBRUARY				MARCH			
Day	☉	♀	♂	♆	☉	♀	♂	♆	☉	♀	♂	♆
01	10♑	01♐	08♑	30♋	12♒	25♐	02♒	29♋	10♓	24♑	24♒	28♋
02	11	01	09		13	26	03		11	25	24	
03	12	02	09		14	27	03		12	27	25	
04	13	02	10		15	28	04		13	28	26	
05	14	03	11	29	16	29	05		14	29	27	
06	15	03	12	29	17	30	06	29	15	30	28	28
07	16	04	12		18	01♑	06		16	01♒	28	
08	17	05	13		19	02	07		17	02	29	
09	18	05	14		20	03	08		18	03	30	
10	19	06	15		21	04	09	28	19	04	01♓	
11	20	07	15	29	22	05	10	28	20	06	02	28
12	21	08	16		23	06	10		21	07	02	
13	22	08	17		24	07	11		22	08	03	
14	23	09	18		25	08	12		23	09	04	
15	24	10	19		26	09	13		24	10	05	
16	25	11	19	29	27	10	13	28	25	11	05	28
17	26	11	20		28	11	14		26	12	06	
18	27	12	21		29	12	15		27	14	07	
19	28	13	22		30	13	16		28	15	08	
20	29	14	22		01♓	14	17		29	16	09	
21	01♒	15	23	29	02	16	17	28	30	17	09	28
22	02	16	24		03	17	18		01♈	18	10	
23	02	17	25		04	18	19		02	19	11	
24	03	17	26		05	19	20		03	21	12	
25	04	18	26		06	20	21		04	22	13	
26	05	19	27	29	07	21	21	28	05	23	13	28
27	06	20	28		08	22	22		06	24	14	
28	07	21	29		09	23	23		07	25	15	
29	09	22	29						08	26	16	
30	10	23	00♒						09	28	16	
31	11	24	01	29					10	29	17	28

	APRIL				MAY				JUNE			
Day	☉	♀	♂	♆	☉	♀	♂	♆	☉	♀	♂	♆
01	11♈	30♒	18♓	28♋	10♉	05♈	11♈	28♋	10♊	12♉	05♉	28♋
02	12	01♓	19		11	07	12		11	14	06	
03	13	02	20		12	08	13		12	15	06	
04	14	03	20		13	09	14		13	16	07	
05	15	05	21		14	10	14		14	17	08	29
06	16	06	22	28	15	11	15	28	15	19	08	29
07	17	07	23		16	12	16		16	20	09	
08	18	08	23		17	14	17		17	21	10	
09	19	09	24		18	15	17		18	22	11	
10	20	10	25		19	16	18		19	23	11	
11	21	12	26	28	20	17	19	28	19	25	12	29
12	22	13	27		21	18	20		20	26	13	
13	22	14	27		22	20	20		21	27	14	
14	23	15	28		23	21	21		22	28	14	
15	24	16	29		24	22	22		23	29	15	
16	25	18	30	28	25	23	23	28	24	01♊	16	29
17	26	19	01♈		26	24	24		25	02	17	
18	27	20	01		26	26	24		26	03	17	
19	28	21	02		27	27	25		27	04	18	
20	29	22	03		28	28	26		28	05	19	
21	00♉	23	04	28	29	29	27	28	29	07	19	29
22	01	25	04		00♊	00♉	27		30	08	20	
23	02	26	05		01	02	28		01♋	09	21	
24	03	27	06		02	03	29		02	10	22	
25	04	28	07		03	04	30		03	11	22	
26	05	29	08	28	04	05	00♉	28	04	13	23	29
27	06	01♈	08		05	06	01		05	14	24	
28	07	02	09		06	08	02		06	15	24	
29	08	03	10		07	09	03		07	16	25	
30	09	04	11		08	10	03		08	18	26	
31					09	11	04	28				

Day	JULY				AUGUST				SEPTEMBER			
	☉	♀	♂	♆	☉	♀	♂	♆	☉	♀	♂	♆
01	09♋	19♓	27♉	29♋	08♌	27♋	18♊	01♌	08♍	05♍	08♋	02♌
02	10	20	27		09	28	19		09	06	09	
03	10	21	28		10	29	20		10	07	10	
04	11	22	29		11	00♌	20		11	09	10	
05	12	24	29		12	02	21		12	10	11	
06	13	25	00♊	30	13	03	22	01	13	11	12	02
07	14	26	01		14	04	22		14	12	12	
08	15	27	02		15	05	23		15	14	13	
09	16	29	02		16	06	24		16	15	13	
10	17	30	03		17	08	24		17	16	14	
11	18	01♋	04	30	18	09	25	01	18	17	15	02
12	19	02	04		19	10	26		19	19	15	
13	20	03	05		20	11	26		20	20	16	
14	21	05	06		21	12	27		21	21	16	
15	22	06	06		22	14	27		22	22	17	
16	23	07	07	30	23	15	28	01	23	24	18	02
17	24	08	08		23	16	29		24	25	18	
18	25	09	09		24	18	29		24	26	19	
19	26	11	09	00♌	25	19	00♋		25	27	19	
20	27	12	10		26	20	01		26	29	20	
21	28	13	11	00	27	21	01	01	27	30	21	02
22	29	14	11		28	23	02		28	01♎	21	
23	30	16	12		29	24	03		29	02	22	
24	00♌	17	13		00♍	25	03		00♎	04	22	
25	01	18	13		01	26	04		01	05	23	
26	02	19	14	00	02	27	05	01	02	06	24	02
27	03	21	15		03	29	05		03	07	24	
28	04	22	15		04	30	06		04	08	25	
29	05	23	16		05	01♍	07		05	10	25	
30	06	24	17		06	02	07		06	11	26	
31	07	25	17	00	07	04	08	02				

Day	OCTOBER				NOVEMBER				DECEMBER			
	☉	♀	♂	♆	☉	♀	♂	♆	☉	♀	♂	♆
01	07♎	12♎	26♋	02♌	08♏	21♏	13♌	03♌	08♐	28♐	25♌	03♌
02	08	13	27		09	22	13		09	30	25	02
03	09	15	28		10	23	14		10	01♑	25	
04	10	16	28		11	25	14		11	02	26	
05	11	17	29		12	26	15		12	03	26	
06	12	18	29	02	13	27	15	03	13	05	26	02
07	13	20	30		14	28	15		14	06	26	
08	14	21	00♌		15	30	16		15	07	27	
09	15	22	01		16	01♐	16		16	08	27	
10	16	23	01		17	02	17		17	10	27	
11	17	25	02	02	18	03	17	03	18	11	27	02
12	18	26	03	03	19	05	18		19	12	28	
13	19	27	03		20	06	18		20	13	28	
14	20	28	04		21	07	19		21	15	28	
15	21	30	04		22	08	19		22	16	28	
16	22	01♏	05	03	23	10	19	03	23	17	28	02
17	23	02	05		24	11	20		24	18	29	
18	24	03	06		25	12	20		25	20	29	
19	25	05	06		26	13	21		27	21	29	
20	26	06	07		27	15	21		28	22	29	
21	27	07	07	03	28	16	21	03	29	23	29	02
22	28	08	08		29	17	22		30	25	29	
23	29	10	08		00♐	18	22		01♑	26	29	
24	30	11	09		01	20	22		02	27	20	
25	01♏	12	09		02	21	23		03	28	30	
26	02	13	10	03	03	22	23	03	04	30	30	02
27	03	15	10		04	23	23		05	01♒	30	
28	04	16	11		05	25	24		06	02	30	
29	05	17	11		06	26	24		07	03	30	
30	06	18	12		07	27	24		08	05	30	
31	07	20	12	03					09	06	30	02

BIRTH TABLES - 1916

	JANUARY				FEBRUARY				MARCH				APRIL				MAY				JUNE			
	☉	♀	♂	♆	☉	♀	♂	♆	☉	♀	♂	♆	☉	♀	♂	♆	☉	♀	♂	♆	☉	♀	♂	♆
01	10♑	07♒	30♌	02♌	11♒	15♓	23♌	01♌	11♓	20♈	13♌	00♌	11♈	26♉	11♌	30♋	11♉	26♊	19♌	30♋	11♊	18♋	02♍	01♌
02	11	08	30		12	16	23		12	21	13		12	27	11		12	27	19	00♌	12	18	02	
03	12	10	30		13	18	23		13	23	12		13	28	11		13	28	19		13	18	03	
04	13	11	30		14	19	22		14	24	12		14	29	11		14	29	20		14	19	03	
05	14	12	30		15	20	22		15	25	12		15	30	12		15	30	20		14	19	04	
06	15	13	30	02	16	21	21	01	16	26	12	00	16	01♊	12	30	16	01♋	20	00	15	19	04	01
07	16	14	30		17	23	21		17	27	12		17	02	12		17	01	21		16	19	05	
08	17	16	29		18	24	21		18	28	11		18	03	12		18	02	21		17	19	05	
09	18	17	29		19	25	20		19	30	11		19	04	12		19	03	22		18	20	06	
10	19	18	29		20	26	20		20	01♉	11		20	05	13		19	04	22		19	20	06	
11	20	19	29	02	21	27	19	01	21	02	11	00	21	06	13	30	20	05	22	00	20	20	07	01
12	21	21	29		22	29	19		22	03	11		22	07	13		21	06	23		21	20	07	
13	22	22	29		23	30	19		23	04	11		23	08	13		22	06	23		22	20	08	
14	23	23	29		24	01♈	18		24	05	11		24	09	13		23	07	24		23	20	08	
15	24	24	28	01	25	02	18		25	06	11		25	11	14		24	08	24		24	20	09	
16	25	26	28	01	26	03	18	01	26	08	10	00	26	12	14	30	25	09	24	00	25	19	09	01
17	26	27	28		28	05	17		27	09	10		27	13	14		26	09	25		26	19	10	
18	27	28	28		29	06	17		28	10	10		28	14	14		27	10	25		27	19	10	
19	28	29	28		30	07	16		29	11	10	00	29	15	14		28	11	26		28	19	11	
20	29	01♓	27		01♓	08	16		30	12	10	30♋	00♉	16	15		29	11	26		29	18	11	
21	00♒	02	27	01	02	09	16	01	01♈	13	10	30	01	17	15	30	00♊	12	27	00	30	18	12	01
22	01	03	27		03	11	15	00	02	14	10	00	02	18	16		01	13	27		01♋	18	13	
23	02	04	26		04	12	15		03	16	10		03	19	16		02	13	28		02	17	13	
24	03	05	26		05	13	15		04	17	10		04	20	16		03	14	28		03	17	14	
25	04	07	26		06	14	14		05	18	10		05	20	17		04	14	28		04	16	14	
26	05	08	26	01	07	15	14	00	06	19	10	30	06	21	17	30	05	15	29	00	05	16	15	01
27	06	09	25		08	17	14		06	20	11		07	22	17		06	15	29		05	15	15	
28	07	10	25		09	18	13		07	21	11		08	23	18		07	16	30		06	14	16	
29	08	12	25		10	19	13		08	22	11		09	24	18		08	16	00♍	01	07	14	16	
30	09	13	24						09	23	11		10	25	18		09	17	01		08	14	17	
31	10	14	24	01					10	24	11	30					10	17	01	01				

DAYS AND NIGHTS FOR MAKING LOVE
c. Paul Rosner and Joyce Nunn 1979
Published by Vulcan Books

DATE	JULY				AUGUST				SEPTEMBER				OCTOBER				NOVEMBER			
	☉	♀	♂	♆	☉	♀	♂	♆	☉	♀	♂	♆	☉	♀	♂	♆	☉	♀	♂	♆
01	09♋	05♊	08♎	15♎	09♌	12♋	25♎	15♎	08♍	19♌	14♍	16♎	08♎	27♍	04♐	17♎	08♏	05♏	26♐	18♎
02	10	06	09		10	13	25		09	21	14		09	28	05		09	07	27	
03	11	07	09		11	14	26		10	22	15		10	29	05		10	08	28	
04	12	08	10		12	15	26		11	23	16		11	00♎	06		11	09	29	
05	13	10	10		12	17	27		12	24	16		12	02	07		13	10	29	
06	14	11	11	15	13	18	28	15	13	26	17	16	13	03	08	17	14	12	00♑	18
07	15	12	11		14	19	28		14	27	18		14	04	08		15	13	01	
08	16	13	12		15	20	29		15	28	18		15	05	09		16	14	02	
09	17	14	12		16	21	29		16	29	19		16	07	10		17	15	02	
10	18	15	13		17	23	30		17	01♍	20		17	08	10		18	17	03	
11	19	17	13	15	18	24	00♏	15	18	02	20	16	18	09	11	17	19	18	04	18
12	20	18	14		19	25	01		19	03	21		19	10	12		20	19	05	
13	21	19	14		20	26	02		20	04	22		20	12	13		21	20	05	
14	21	20	15		21	27	02		21	05	22		21	13	13		22	22	06	
15	22	21	15		22	29	03		22	07	23		22	14	14		23	23	07	
16	23	23	16	15	23	30	04	15	23	08	24	16	23	15	15	17	24	24	08	18
17	24	24	16		24	01♌	04		24	09	24		24	17	15		25	25	08	
18	25	25	17		25	02	05		25	10	25		25	18	16		26	27	09	
19	26	26	17		26	04	05		26	12	26		26	19	17		27	28	10	
20	27	27	18		27	05	06		27	13	26		27	20	18		28	29	11	
21	28	29	18	15	28	06	07	15	28	14	27	16	28	22	18	17	29	00♐	12	19
22	29	30	19		29	07	07		29	15	28		29	23	19	18	30	02	12	
23	00♌	01♋	20		30	08	08		30	17	28		30	24	20		01♐	03	13	
24	01	02	20		01♍	10	09		01♎	18	29		01♏	25	21		02	04	14	
25	02	03	21		02	11	09	16	02	19	30	17	02	27	21		03	06	15	
26	03	05	21	15	03	12	10	16	03	20	00♐	17	03	28	22	18	04	07	15	19
27	04	06	22		04	13	10		04	22	01		03	29	23		05	08	16	
28	05	07	22		05	15	11		05	23	02		04	00♏	23		06	09	17	
29	06	08	23		06	16	12		06	24	03		05	02	24		07	11	18	
30	07	09	23		07	17	12		07	25	03		06	03	25		08	12	18	
31	08	11	24	15	08	18	13	16					07	04	26	18				

HOW TO USE THIS BOOK

1. Read the Introduction on page 7.

2. On the back of this sheet is a reproduction of a birth table on page 209 which contains the example used in the Introduction for a person born on 9/29/50. See number 2 on the back of this sheet.

3. Please note on the above example that the extreme left hand column of this page and every page of the birth tables are the numbers of the days of the month. We have inadvertently omitted the word "DATE". See number 3 on the back of this sheet.

4. Please also note that throughout the birth tables whenever you see "30" (degrees) of an sign, subtract 1 (one) making it 29 degrees of that sign.

30 Aries	= 29 Aries	30 Libra	= 29 Libra
30 Taurus	= 29 Taurus	30 Scorpio	= 29 Scorpio
30 Gemini	= 29 Gemini	30 Sag.	= 29 Sag.
30 Cancer	= 29 Cancer	30 Capricorn	= 29 Cap.
30 Leo	= 29 Leo	30 Aquarius	=29 Aquarius
30 Virgo	= 29 Virgo	30 Pisces	= 29 Pisces

See number 4 on the back of this sheet.

5. Please note that you will always have four (4) planets and four (4) signs. If you think you are "missing" a planet, look up the column of that planet and note the last number (degree) and sign listed. That is your "missing" planet. See number 5 on the back of this sheet.

6. Remember that the names of the astrological symbols (glyphs) are listed on page 127.

7. Part Four. Venus and Mars. Please remember that the signs these planets are in are not always the same sign your Sun is in. Please refer back to the Birth Tables on your birthday for the sign and degree of your Venus and Mars.

DAYS AND NIGHTS FOR MAKING LOVE
c. Paul Rosner & Joyce Nunn 1979
Published by Vulcan Books

Day	JULY ☉	♀	♂	♆	AUGUST ☉	♀	♂	♆	SEPTEMBER ☉	♀	♂	♆
01	09♋	13♋	17♍	02♌	09♌	04♋	06♎	03♌	09♍	23♋	25♎	04♌
02	10	12	18		10	04	06		10	24	26	
03	11	12	19		11	05	07		11	25	27	
04	12	11	19		12	05	07		12	26	27	
05	13	10	20		13	05	08		13	27	28	
06	14	10	20	02	14	06	09	03	14	28	29	04
07	15	09	21		15	06	09		15	29	29	
08	16	09	21		16	07	10		15	30	30	
09	17	08	22		17	07	11		16	01♌	01♏	
10	18	08	23		17	08	11		17	01	01	
11	19	07	23	02	18	08	12	03	18	02	02	04
12	20	06	24		19	09	12		19	03	03	
13	21	06	24		20	09	13		20	04	03	
14	22	06	25		21	10	14		21	05	04	
15	23	05	25		22	10	14		22	06	05	
16	24	05	26	02	23	11	15	03	23	07	05	04
17	25	04	27		24	12	16		24	08	06	
18	25	04	27		25	12	16		25	09	07	
19	26	04	28		26	13	17		26	10	07	
20	27	04	28		27	14	17		27	11	08	
21	28	04	29	02	28	14	18	03	28	12	09	04
22	29	03	30		29	15	19		29	13	09	
23	00♌	03	00♎		30	16	19		00♎	14	10	
24	01	03	01		01♍	17	20		01	16	11	
25	02	03	01		02	17	21		02	17	11	
26	03	03	02	02	03	18	21	04	03	18	12	04
27	04	03	03		04	19	22		04	19	13	
28	05	03	03		05	20	23		05	20	13	
29	06	04	04		06	21	23		06	21	14	
30	07	04	04		07	22	24		07	22	15	05
31	08	04	05	03	08	22	25	04				

Day	OCTOBER ☉	♀	♂	♆	NOVEMBER ☉	♀	♂	♆	DECEMBER ☉	♀	♂	♆
01	08♎	23♌	15♏	05♌	09♏	28♍	08♐	05♌	09♐	04♏	30♐	05♌
02	09	24	16		10	29	08		10	06	01♑	
03	10	25	17		11	01♎	09		11	07	01	
04	11	26	18		12	02	10		12	08	02	
05	12	27	18		13	03	10		13	09	03	
06	13	28	19	05	14	04	11	05	14	10	04	05
07	14	30	20		15	05	12		15	12	04	
08	15	01♍	20		16	06	13		16	13	05	
09	16	02	21		17	08	13		17	14	06	
10	17	03	22		18	09	14		18	15	07	
11	18	04	22	05	19	10	15	05	19	17	07	05
12	19	05	23		20	11	16		20	18	08	
13	20	06	24		21	12	16		21	19	09	
14	21	07	25		22	14	17		22	20	10	
15	22	09	25		23	15	18		23	22	11	
16	23	10	26	05	24	16	19	05	24	23	11	04
17	24	11	27		25	17	19		25	24	12	
18	25	12	27		26	19	20		26	25	13	
19	26	13	28		27	20	21		27	27	14	
20	27	14	29		28	21	22		28	28	15	
21	28	15	30	05	29	22	22	05	29	29	15	04
22	29	17	00♐		30	23	23		00♑	00♐	16	
23	30	18	01		01♐	25	24		01	01	17	
24	01♏	19	02		02	26	25		02	03	18	
25	02	20	02		03	27	25		03	04	18	
26	03	21	03	05	04	28	26	05	04	05	19	04
27	04	22	04		05	29	27		05	06	20	
28	05	23	05		06	01♏	28		06	08	21	
29	06	25	05		07	02	28		07	09	21	
30	07	26	06		08	03	29		08	10	22	
31	08	27	07	05					10	11	23	04

BIRTH TABLES - 1917

JANUARY

Day	☉	♀	♂	♆
01	11♑	13♐	24♑	04♌
02	12	14	25	
03	13	15	25	
04	14	16	26	
05	15	18	27	
06	16	19	28	04
07	17	20	28	
08	18	21	29	
09	19	23	30	
10	20	24	01♒	
11	21	25	02	04
12	22	26	02	
13	23	28	03	
14	24	29	04	
15	25	00♑	05	
16	26	01	05	04
17	27	03	06	
18	28	04	07	
19	29	05	08	
20	30	06	09	
21	01♒	08	09	04
22	02	09	10	
23	03	10	11	
24	04	11	12	03
25	05	13	13	
26	06	14	13	03
27	07	15	14	
28	08	16	15	
29	09	18	16	
30	10	19	17	
31	11	20	17	03

FEBRUARY

Day	☉	♀	♂	♆
01	12♒	21♑	18♒	03♌
02	13	23	19	
03	14	24	20	
04	15	25	20	
05	16	26	21	
06	17	28	22	03
07	18	29	23	
08	19	00♒	24	
09	20	01	24	
10	21	03	25	
11	22	04	26	03
12	23	05	27	
13	24	06	28	
14	25	08	28	
15	26	09	29	
16	27	10	30	03
17	28	11	01♓	
18	29	13	02	
19	00♓	14	02	
20	01	15	03	
21	02	16	04	03
22	03	17	05	
23	04	19	06	
24	05	20	06	
25	06	21	07	
26	07	22	08	03
27	08	24	09	
28	09	25	09	

MARCH

Day	☉	♀	♂	♆
01	10♓	26♒	10♓	03♌
02	11	27	11	
03	12	29	12	
04	13	30	13	
05	14	01♓	13	02
06	15	02	14	02
07	16	04	15	
08	17	05	16	
09	18	06	17	
10	19	07	17	
11	20	09	18	02
12	21	10	19	
13	22	11	20	
14	23	12	20	
15	24	14	21	
16	25	15	22	02
17	26	16	23	
18	27	17	24	
19	28	19	24	
20	29	20	25	
21	00♈	21	26	02
22	01	22	27	
23	02	24	27	
24	03	25	28	
25	04	26	29	
26	05	27	30	02
27	06	29	01♈	
28	07	30	01	
29	08	01♈	02	
30	09	02	03	
31	10	04	04	02

APRIL

Day	☉	♀	♂	♆
01	11♈	05♈	04♈	02♌
02	12	06	05	
03	13	07	06	
04	14	08	07	
05	15	10	08	
06	16	11	08	02
07	17	12	09	
08	18	13	10	
09	19	15	11	
10	20	16	11	
11	21	17	12	02
12	22	18	13	
13	23	20	14	
14	24	21	15	
15	25	22	15	
16	26	23	16	02
17	27	25	17	
18	28	26	18	
19	29	27	18	
20	30	28	19	
21	01♉	30	20	02
22	02	01♉	21	
23	03	02	21	
24	04	03	22	
25	05	04	23	
26	06	06	24	02
27	07	07	24	
28	08	08	25	
29	09	09	26	
30	10	11	27	

MAY

Day	☉	♀	♂	♆
01	11♉	12♉	27♈	02♌
02	11	13	28	
03	12	14	29	
04	13	16	30	
05	14	17	00♉	
06	15	18	01	02
07	16	19	02	
08	17	21	03	
09	18	22	03	
10	19	23	04	
11	20	24	05	02
12	21	25	06	
13	22	27	06	
14	23	28	07	
15	24	29	08	
16	25	00♊	09	02
17	26	02	09	
18	27	03	10	
19	28	04	11	
20	29	05	12	
21	30	07	12	02
22	01♊	08	13	03
23	02	09	14	
24	03	10	15	
25	04	11	15	
26	05	13	16	03
27	06	14	17	
28	07	15	17	
29	08	16	18	
30	09	18	19	
31	10	19	20	03

JUNE

Day	☉	♀	♂	♆
01	10♊	20♊	20♉	03♌
02	11	21	21	
03	12	22	22	
04	13	24	23	
05	14	25	23	
06	15	26	24	03
07	16	27	25	
08	17	29	25	
09	18	30	26	
10	19	01♋	27	
11	20	02	28	03
12	21	04	28	
13	22	05	29	
14	23	06	30	
15	24	07	00♊	
16	25	08	01♊	03
17	26	10	02	
18	27	11	03	
19	28	12	03	
20	29	13	04	
21	30	15	05	03
22	00♋	16	05	
23	01	17	06	
24	02	18	07	
25	03	19	08	
26	04	21	08	03
27	05	22	09	04
28	06	23	10	
29	07	24	10	
30	08	26	11	

	JULY				AUGUST				SEPTEMBER				OCTOBER				NOVEMBER				DECEMBER			
	☉	♀	♂	♆	☉	♀	♂	♆	☉	♀	♂	♆	☉	♀	♂	♆	☉	♀	♂	♆	☉	♀	♂	♆
01	09♋	27♋	12♊	04♌	09♌	05♍	03♋	05♌	09♍	12♎	23♋	06♌	08♎	18♏	12♌	07♌	08♏	24♐	29♌	07♌	09♐	26♑	15♍	07♌
02	10	28	12		10	06	04		09	13	24		09	19	12		09	25	00♍		09	27	15	
03	11	29	13		11	07	04		10	14	24		10	20	13		11	26	01		11	28	16	
04	12	00♌	14		12	08	05		11	16	25		11	21	13		12	27	01		12	29	16	
05	13	02	15		12	09	06		12	17	26		12	22	14		13	28	02		13	30	17	
06	14	03	15	04	13	11	06	05	13	18	26	06	13	24	15	07	14	29	02	07	14	01♒	17	07
07	15	04	16		14	12	07		14	19	27		14	25	15		15	00♑	03		15	02	18	
08	16	05	17		15	13	08		15	20	28		15	26	16		16	01	03		16	03	18	
09	17	07	17		16	14	08		16	22	28		16	27	16		17	03	04		17	04	18	
10	18	08	18		17	15	09		17	23	29		17	28	17		18	04	04		18	05	19	
11	19	09	19	04	18	17	10	05	18	24	29	06	18	29	18	07	19	05	05	07	19	06	19	07
12	20	10	19		19	18	10		19	25	00♌		19	01♐	18		20	06	05		20	07	20	
13	20	11	20		20	19	11		20	26	01		20	02	19		21	07	06		21	08	20	
14	21	13	21		21	20	12		21	28	01		21	03	19		22	08	06		22	08	21	
15	22	14	21		22	22	12		22	29	02		22	04	20		23	09	07		23	09	21	
16	23	15	22	04	23	23	13	05	23	30	03	06	23	05	20	07	24	10	07	07	24	10	21	07
17	24	16	23		24	24	13		24	01♏	03		24	06	21		25	11	08		25	11	22	
18	25	18	23		25	25	14		25	02	04		25	08	22		26	12	08		26	12	22	
19	26	19	24		26	26	15		26	04	04		26	09	22		27	13	09		27	13	23	
20	27	20	25		27	28	15		27	05	05		27	10	23		28	15	09		28	14	23	
21	28	21	26	04	28	29	16	06	28	06	06	06	28	11	23	07	29	16	10	07	29	14	23	07
22	29	22	26		29	00♎	17		29	07	06		29	12	24		30	17	10		00♑	15	24	
23	00♌	24	27		30	01	17		30	08	07		30	13	24		01♐	18	11		01	16	24	
24	01	25	28		01♍	02	18		01♎	09	07	07	01♏	14	25		02	19	11		02	17	24	
25	02	26	28	05	02	04	19		02	11	08		02	15	26		03	20	12		03	18	25	
26	03	27	29	05	03	05	19	06	03	12	09	07	03	17	26	07	04	21	12	07	04	18	25	07
27	04	29	30		04	06	20		04	13	09		04	18	27		05	22	13		05	19	25	
28	05	30	00♋		05	07	21		05	14	10		05	19	27		06	23	13		06	20	26	06
29	06	01♍	01		06	08	21		06	15	10		05	20	28		07	24	14		07	20	26	
30	07	02	02		07	10	22		07	17	11		06	21	28		08	25	14		08	21	26	
31	08	03	02	05	07	11	22	06					07	22	29	07					09	22	27	06

BIRTH TABLES - 1918

Day	Jan ☉	Jan ♀	Jan ♂	Jan ♇	Feb ☉	Feb ♀	Feb ♂	Feb ♇	Mar ☉	Mar ♀	Mar ♂	Mar ♇
01	10♑	22♒	27♍	06♌	12♒	25♒	03♎	06♌	10♓	13♒	29♍	05♌
02	11	23	28		13	25	03		11	13	29	
03	12	23	28		14	24	03		12	13	28	
04	13	24	28		15	24	03		13	13	28	
05	14	24	28		16	23	03		14	13	28	
06	15	25	29	06	17	23	03	05	15	13	27	05
07	16	25	29		18	22	03		16	13	27	
08	17	26	29		19	22	03		17	13	26	
09	18	26	30		20	21	03		18	14	26	
10	19	27	30		21	20	03		19	14	26	
11	20	27	00♎	06	22	20	03	05	20	14	25	05
12	21	27	00		23	19	03		21	15	25	
13	23	28	01		24	18	02		22	15	25	
14	24	28	01		25	18	02		23	15	24	
15	25	28	01		26	17	02		24	16	24	
16	26	28	01	06	27	17	02	05	25	16	23	05
17	27	28	01		28	16	02		26	17	23	
18	28	28	02		29	16	02		27	17	23	
19	29	29	02		00♓	15	02		28	18	22	
20	30	29	02		01	15	01		29	18	22	
21	01♒	28	02	06	02	14	01	05	00♈	19	21	05
22	02	28	02		03	14	01		01	19	21	
23	03	28	02		04	14	01		02	20	21	
24	04	28	02		05	14	00		03	21	20	
25	05	28	03		06	13	00♎		04	21	20	
26	06	28	03	06	07	13	30♍	05	05	22	20	04
27	07	27	03		08	13	30		06	23	19	
28	08	27	03		09	13	29		07	23	19	
29	09	27	03						08	24	19	
30	10	26	03						09	25	18	
31	11	26	03	06					10	26	18	04

Day	Apr ☉	Apr ♀	Apr ♂	Apr ♇	May ☉	May ♀	May ♂	May ♇	Jun ☉	Jun ♀	Jun ♂	Jun ♇
01	11♈	26♒	18♍	04♌	10♉	24♓	14♍	04♌	10♊	28♈	21♍	05♌
02	12	27	17		11	25	14		11	29	21	
03	13	28	17		12	26	14		12	00♉	22	
04	14	29	17		13	28	14		13	01	22	
05	15	30	16		14	29	14		14	03	22	
06	16	01♓	16	04	15	30	14	04	15	04	23	05
07	17	01	16		16	01♈	15		16	05	23	
08	18	02	16		17	02	15		17	06	23	
09	19	03	16		18	03	15		18	07	24	
10	20	04	15		19	04	15		19	08	24	
11	21	05	15	04	20	05	15	04	20	09	25	05
12	22	06	15		21	06	15		21	11	25	
13	23	07	15		22	07	16		22	12	25	
14	24	08	15		23	08	16		23	13	26	
15	25	09	15		24	09	16		24	14	26	
16	26	10	14	04	25	10	16	05	25	15	27	05
17	27	10	14		26	11	17		25	16	27	
18	28	11	14		27	13	17		26	17	28	
19	29	12	14		28	14	17		27	19	28	
20	30	13	14		29	15	17		28	20	29	
21	01♉	14	14	04	30	16	18	05	29	21	29	05
22	02	15	14		01♊	17	18		00♋	22	29	
23	02	16	14		02	18	18		01	23	30	
24	03	17	14		02	19	18		02	24	00♎	
25	04	18	14		03	20	19		03	25	01	
26	05	19	14	04	04	21	19	05	04	27	01	06
27	06	20	14		05	22	19		05	28	02	
28	07	21	14		06	24	20		06	29	02	
29	08	22	14		07	25	20		07	00♊	03	
30	09	23	14		08	26	20		08	01	03	
31					09	27	21	05				

	JULY				AUGUST				SEPTEMBER				OCTOBER				NOVEMBER				DECEMBER			
	☉	♀	♂	♆	☉	♀	♂	♆	☉	♀	♂	♆	☉	♀	♂	♆	☉	♀	♂	♆	☉	♀	♂	♆
01	09♋	03♊	04♎	06♌	08♌	09♋	21♎	07♌	09♍	17♌	10♏	08♌	07♎	24♍	00♐	09♌	08♏	03♏	23♐	09♌	08♐	10♐	15♑	09♌
02	10	04	04		09	10	21		09	18	10		08	25	01		09	04	23		10	12	16	
03	11	05	05		10	12	22		10	19	11		09	26	02		10	05	24		11	13	17	
04	12	06	05		11	13	22		11	21	12		10	28	02		11	06	25		12	14	18	
05	13	07	06		12	14	23		12	22	12		11	29	03		12	08	26		13	15	18	
06	14	08	06	06	13	15	23	07	13	23	13	08	12	00♎	04	09	13	09	26	09	14	17	19	09
07	15	10	07		14	16	24		14	24	14		13	01	04		14	10	27		15	18	20	
08	15	11	07		15	18	25		15	25	14		14	03	05		15	11	28		16	19	21	
09	16	12	08		16	19	25		16	27	15		15	04	06		16	13	29		17	20	22	
10	17	13	08		17	20	26		17	28	16		16	05	07		17	14	29		18	22	22	
11	18	14	09	06	18	21	27	07	18	29	16	08	17	06	07	09	18	15	00♑	09	19	23	23	09
12	19	15	09		19	22	27		19	00♍	17		18	08	08		19	16	01		20	24	24	
13	20	17	10		20	24	28		20	02	18		19	09	09		20	18	02		21	25	25	
14	21	18	10		21	25	28		21	03	18		20	10	09		21	19	02		22	27	25	
15	22	19	11		22	26	29		22	04	19		21	11	10		22	20	03		23	28	26	
16	23	20	11	06	23	27	30	07	23	05	20	08	22	13	11	09	23	21	04	09	24	29	27	09
17	24	21	12		24	29	00♏		24	07	20		23	14	12		24	23	05		25	00♑	28	
18	25	23	13		25	30	01		25	08	21		24	15	12		25	24	05		26	02	29	
19	26	24	13		26	01♌	01		26	09	22		25	16	13		26	25	06		27	03	29	
20	27	25	14		27	02	02		27	10	23		26	18	14		27	27	07		28	04	00♒	
21	28	26	14	06	28	03	03	08	28	11	23	09	27	19	14	09	28	28	08	09	29	05	01	09
22	29	27	15		29	05	03		29	13	24		28	20	15		29	29	08		30	07	02	
23	30	28	15		30	06	04		30	14	25		29	21	16		00♐	00♐	09		01♑	08	02	
24	01♌	30	16		00♍	07	05		01♎	15	25		00♏	23	17		01	02	10		02	09	03	
25	02	01♋	16		01	08	05		02	16	26		01	24	17		02	03	11		03	11	04	
26	03	02	17	07	02	09	06	08	03	18	27	09	02	25	18	09	03	04	11	09	04	12	05	09
27	04	03	18		03	11	07		04	19	27		03	26	19		04	05	12		05	13	06	
28	05	04	18		04	12	07		05	20	28		04	28	20		05	07	13		06	14	06	
29	06	06	19		05	13	08		06	21	29		05	29	20		06	08	14		07	16	07	
30	07	07	19		06	14	08		07	23	29		06	00♏	21		07	09	15		08	17	08	
31	08	08	20	07	07	16	09	08					07	01	22	09					09	18	09	09

BIRTH TABLES - 1919

Day	JANUARY ☉	♀	♂	♆	FEBRUARY ☉	♀	♂	♆	MARCH ☉	♀	♂	♆
01	10♑	19♑	10♒	09♌	12♒	28♒	04♓	08♌	10♓	03♈	26♓	07♌
02	11	21	10		13	29	05		11	04	27	
03	12	22	11		14	01♓	06		12	05	27	
04	13	23	12		15	02	06		13	07	28	
05	14	24	13		16	03	07		14	08	29	
06	15	26	13	09	17	04	08	08	15	09	30	07
07	16	27	14		18	06	09		16	10	01♈	
08	17	28	15		19	07	09		17	12	01	
09	18	29	16		20	08	10		18	13	02	
10	19	01♒	17		21	09	11		19	14	03	
11	20	02	17	08	22	11	12	08	20	15	04	07
12	21	03	18		23	12	13		21	17	04	
13	22	04	19		24	13	13		22	18	05	
14	23	06	20		25	14	14		23	19	06	
15	24	07	21		26	16	15		24	20	07	
16	25	08	21	08	27	17	16	07	25	22	08	07
17	26	09	22		28	18	17		26	23	08	
18	27	11	23		29	19	17		27	24	09	
19	28	12	24		30	21	18		28	25	10	
20	29	13	25		01♓	22	19		29	26	11	
21	00♒	14	25	08	02	23	20	07	30	28	11	07
22	01	16	26		03	24	21		01♈	29	12	
23	02	17	27		04	26	21		02	00♉	13	
24	03	18	28		05	27	22		03	01	14	
25	04	19	28		06	28	23		04	03	14	
26	05	21	29	08	07	29	24	07	05	04	15	07
27	07	22	00♓		08	01♈	24		06	05	16	
28	08	23	01		09	02	25		07	06	17	
29	09	24	02						08	07	17	
30	10	26	02						09	09	18	
31	11	27	03	08					10	10	19	07

Day	APRIL ☉	♀	♂	♆	MAY ☉	♀	♂	♆	JUNE ☉	♀	♂	♆
01	11♈	11♉	20♈	07♌	10♉	17♊	12♉	07♌	10♊	22♋	04♊	07♌
02	12	12	20		11	18	13		11	23	05	
03	13	13	21		12	19	14		12	25	06	
04	14	15	22		13	20	14		13	26	06	
05	15	16	23		14	22	15		14	27	07	
06	16	17	23	07	15	23	16	07	15	28	08	07
07	17	18	24		16	24	16		16	29	09	
08	18	19	25		17	25	17		17	00♌	09	
09	19	21	26		18	26	18		18	01	10	
10	20	22	26		19	27	19		19	02	11	
11	21	23	27	07	20	29	19	07	20	03	11	07
12	22	24	28		21	30	20		20	04	12	
13	23	25	29		22	01♋	21		21	05	13	
14	23	27	29		23	02	22		22	07	13	
15	24	28	00♉		24	03	22		23	08	14	
16	25	29	01	07	25	04	23	07	24	09	15	07
17	26	00♊	02		26	05	24		25	10	16	
18	27	01	02		26	07	24		26	11	16	
19	28	03	03		27	08	25		27	12	17	
20	29	04	04		28	09	26		28	13	18	
21	00♉	05	05	07	29	10	27	07	29	14	18	08
22	01	06	05		00♊	11	27		00♋	15	19	
23	02	07	06		01	12	28		01	16	20	
24	03	09	07		02	13	29		02	17	20	
25	04	10	08		03	15	29		03	18	21	
26	05	11	08	07	04	16	00♊	07	04	19	22	08
27	06	12	09		05	17	01		05	20	23	
28	07	13	10		06	18	02		06	21	23	
29	08	14	11		07	19	02		07	22	24	
30	09	16	11		08	20	03		08	23	25	
31					09	21	04	07				

JULY

Day	☉	♀	♂	♆
01	09♋	24♌	25♊	08♌
02	10	25	26	
03	10	26	26	
04	11	27	27	
05	12	28	28	
06	13	29	28	08
07	14	30	29	
08	15	01♍	30	
09	16	02	01♋	
10	17	03	01	
11	17	03	02	08
12	18	04	03	
13	20	05	03	
14	21	06	04	
15	22	07	05	
16	23	08	05	08
17	24	09	06	
18	25	10	07	
19	26	10	07	
20	27	11	08	
21	28	12	09	09
22	29	13	09	
23	30	14	10	
24	01♌	14	11	
25	01	15	11	
26	02	16	12	09
27	03	17	13	
28	04	17	13	
29	05	18	14	
30	06	19	15	
31	07	19	15	09

AUGUST

Day	☉	♀	♂	♆
01	08♌	20♍	16♋	09♌
02	09	20	17	
03	10	21	17	
04	11	22	18	
05	12	22	18	
06	13	23	19	09
07	14	23	20	
08	15	24	20	
09	16	24	21	
10	17	25	22	
11	18	25	22	09
12	19	25	23	
13	20	26	24	
14	21	26	24	
15	22	26	25	
16	23	26	26	10
17	24	27	26	
18	24	27	27	
19	25	27	28	
20	26	27	28	
21	27	27	29	10
22	28	27	30	
23	29	27	00♌	
24	00♍	27	01	
25	01	27	01	
26	02	27	02	10
27	03	27	03	
28	04	27	03	
29	05	26	04	
30	06	26	05	
31	07	26	05	10

SEPTEMBER

Day	☉	♀	♂	♆
01	08♍	25♍	06♌	10♌
02	09	25	06	
03	10	25	07	
04	11	24	08	
05	12	24	08	
06	13	23	09	10
07	14	23	10	
08	15	22	10	
09	16	21	11	
10	17	21	12	
11	18	20	12	10
12	19	20	13	
13	20	19	14	
14	21	18	14	
15	22	18	15	
16	23	17	15	11
17	24	17	16	
18	25	16	17	
19	25	15	17	
20	26	15	18	
21	27	14	19	11
22	28	14	19	
23	39	14	20	
24	00♎	13	20	
25	01	13	21	
26	02	12	22	11
27	03	12	22	
28	04	12	23	
29	05	12	23	
30	06	11	24	

OCTOBER

Day	☉	♀	♂	♆
01	07♎	11♍	25♌	11♌
02	08	11	25	
03	09	11	26	
04	10	11	26	
05	11	11	27	
06	12	11	27	11
07	13	11	28	
08	14	11	29	
09	15	12	30	
10	16	12	00♍	
11	17	12	01	11
12	18	12	01	
13	19	13	02	
14	20	13	03	
15	21	13	03	
16	22	14	04	11
17	23	14	04	
18	24	15	05	
19	25	15	06	
20	26	16	06	
21	27	16	07	11
22	28	17	07	
23	29	17	08	
24	00♏	18	09	
25	01	19	09	
26	02	19	10	11
27	03	20	10	
28	04	21	11	
29	05	21	12	
30	06	22	12	
31	07	23	13	11

NOVEMBER

Day	☉	♀	♂	♆
01	08♏	24♍	13♍	12♌
02	09	24	14	
03	10	25	14	
04	11	26	15	
05	12	27	16	
06	13	28	16	12
07	14	28	17	
08	15	29	18	
09	16	00♎	18	
10	17	01	19	
11	18	02	19	12
12	19	03	20	
13	20	04	20	
14	21	05	21	
15	22	06	22	
16	23	07	22	12
17	24	08	23	
18	25	09	23	
19	26	09	24	
20	27	10	24	
21	28	11	25	12
22	29	12	26	
23	00♐	13	26	
24	01	14	27	
25	02	15	27	
26	03	17	28	12
27	04	18	28	
28	05	19	29	
29	06	20	29	
30	07	21	00♎	

DECEMBER

Day	☉	♀	♂	♆
01	08♐	22♎	01♎	11♌
02	09	23	01	
03	10	24	02	
04	11	25	02	
05	12	26	03	
06	13	27	03	11
07	14	28	04	
08	15	29	04	
09	16	00♏	05	
10	17	02	05	
11	18	03	06	11
12	19	04	07	
13	20	05	07	
14	21	06	08	
15	22	07	08	
16	23	08	09	11
17	25	09	09	
18	26	10	10	
19	27	12	10	
20	28	13	11	
21	29	14	11	11
22	30	15	12	
23	01♑	16	12	
24	02	17	13	
25	03	18	13	
26	04	20	14	11
27	05	21	14	
28	06	22	15	
29	07	23	15	
30	08	24	16	
31	09	25	16	11

BIRTH TABLES - 1920

Day	JANUARY				FEBRUARY			
	☉	♀	♂	Ψ	☉	♀	♂	Ψ
01	10♑	27♏	17♎	11♌	11♒	04♑	00♏	10♌
02	11	28	17		12	05	01	
03	12	29	18		13	06	01	
04	13	00♐	18		14	07	01	
05	14	01	19		15	08	02	
06	15	03	19	11	16	10	02	10
07	16	04	20		17	11	02	
08	17	05	20		18	12	03	
09	18	06	21		19	13	03	
10	19	07	21		20	15	03	
11	20	08	21	11	21	16	04	10
12	21	10	22		22	17	04	
13	22	11	22		24	18	04	
14	23	12	23		25	19	04	
15	24	13	23		26	21	05	
16	25	14	24	11	27	22	05	10
17	26	16	24		28	23	05	
18	27	17	25		29	24	06	
19	28	18	25		30	26	06	
20	29	19	25		01♓	27	06	
21	00♒	20	26	10	02	28	06	10
22	01	22	26		03	29	07	
23	02	23	27		04	00♒	07	
24	03	24	27		05	02	07	
25	04	25	28		06	03	07	
26	05	26	28	10	07	04	07	09
27	06	28	28		08	05	08	
28	07	29	29		09	07	08	
29	08	00♑	29		10	08	08	
30	09	01	29					
31	10	02	30	10				

Day	MARCH				APRIL			
	☉	♀	♂	Ψ	☉	♀	♂	Ψ
01	11♓	09♒	08♏	09♌	11♈	17♓	07♏	09♌
02	12	10	08		12	18	07	
03	13	11	08		13	19	07	
04	14	13	08		14	21	06	
05	15	14	09		15	22	06	
06	16	15	09	09	16	23	06	09
07	17	16	09		17	24	06	
08	18	18	09		18	26	05	
09	19	19	09		19	27	05	
10	20	20	09		20	28	05	
11	21	21	09	09	21	29	04	09
12	22	22	09		22	01♈	04	
13	23	24	09		23	02	04	
14	24	25	09		24	03	03	
15	25	26	09		25	04	03	
16	26	27	09	09	26	05	03	09
17	27	29	09		27	07	02	
18	28	30	09		28	08	02	
19	29	01♓	09		29	09	02	
20	30	02	09		00♉	10	01	
21	01♈	04	09	09	01	12	01	09
22	02	05	09		02	13	01	
23	03	06	09		03	14	00♏	
24	04	07	09		04	15	30♎	
25	05	08	08		05	16	29	
26	06	10	08	09	06	18	29	09
27	07	11	08		07	19	29	
28	08	12	08		08	20	28	
29	09	13	08		09	21	28	
30	09	15	08		10	23	28	
31	10	16	07	09				

Day	MAY				JUNE			
	☉	♀	♂	Ψ	☉	♀	♂	Ψ
01	11♉	24♈	27♎	09♌	11♊	02♊	21♎	09♌
02	12	25	27		12	03	21	
03	13	26	26		13	04	21	
04	14	28	26		14	06	21	
05	15	29	26		14	07	21	
06	16	30	26	09	15	08	21	09
07	17	01♉	25		16	09	22	
08	18	02	25		17	10	22	
09	19	04	25		18	12	22	
10	20	05	24		19	13	22	
11	20	06	24	09	20	14	22	10
12	21	07	24		21	15	22	
13	22	09	24		22	17	22	
14	23	10	23		23	18	22	
15	24	11	23		24	19	23	
16	25	12	23	09	25	20	23	10
17	26	13	23		26	21	23	
18	27	15	22		27	23	23	
19	28	16	22		28	24	23	
20	29	17	22		29	25	24	
21	00♊	18	22	09	30	26	24	10
22	01	20	22		01♋	28	24	
23	02	21	22		02	29	24	
24	03	22	22		03	00♋	25	
25	04	23	22		04	01	25	
26	05	24	21	09	05	03	25	10
27	06	26	21		05	04	25	
28	07	27	21		06	05	26	
29	08	28	21		07	06	26	
30	09	29	21		08	07	26	
31	10	01♊	21	09				

JULY

Day	⊙	♀	♂	♆
01	09♋	09♋	27♎	10♌
02	10	10	27	
03	11	11	27	
04	12	12	28	
05	13	14	28	
06	14	15	28	10
07	15	16	29	
08	16	17	29	
09	17	19	30	
10	18	20	30	
11	19	21	00♏	10
12	20	22	01	
13	21	23	01	
14	22	25	02	
15	23	26	02	
16	24	27	02	11
17	25	28	03	
18	26	30	03	
19	26	01♌	04	
20	27	02	04	
21	28	03	05	11
22	29	05	05	
23	00♌	06	06	
24	01	07	06	
25	02	08	07	
26	03	09	07	11
27	04	11	07	
28	05	12	08	
29	06	13	08	
30	07	14	09	
31	08	16	09	11

AUGUST

Day	⊙	♀	♂	♆
01	09♌	17♌	10♏	11♌
02	10	18	11	
03	11	19	11	
04	12	21	12	
05	13	22	12	
06	14	23	13	11
07	15	24	13	
08	16	25	14	
09	17	27	14	
10	18	28	15	
11	18	29	15	12
12	19	00♍	16	
13	20	02	17	
14	21	03	17	
15	22	04	18	
16	23	05	18	12
17	24	07	19	
18	25	08	19	
19	26	09	20	
20	27	10	21	
21	28	12	21	12
22	29	13	22	
23	00♍	14	22	
24	01	15	23	
25	02	16	24	
26	03	18	24	12
27	04	19	25	
28	05	20	25	
29	06	21	26	
30	07	23	27	
31	08	24	27	12

SEPTEMBER

Day	⊙	♀	♂	♆
01	09♍	25♍	28♏	12♌
02	10	26	29	
03	11	28	29	
04	12	29	30	
05	13	00♎	00♐	
06	14	01	01	12
07	15	02	02	
08	16	04	02	
09	16	05	03	
10	17	06	04	
11	18	07	04	13
12	19	09	05	
13	20	10	06	
14	21	11	06	
15	22	12	07	
16	23	14	08	13
17	24	15	08	
18	25	16	09	
19	26	17	10	
20	27	19	10	
21	28	20	11	13
22	29	21	12	
23	00♎	22	12	
24	01	23	13	
25	02	25	14	
26	03	26	14	13
27	04	27	15	
28	05	28	16	
29	06	30	16	
30	07	01♏	17	

OCTOBER

Day	⊙	♀	♂	♆
01	08♎	02♏	18♐	13♌
02	09	03	19	
03	10	05	19	
04	11	06	20	
05	12	07	21	
06	13	08	21	13
07	14	09	22	
08	15	11	23	
09	16	12	23	
10	17	13	24	
11	18	14	25	13
12	19	16	26	
13	20	17	26	
14	21	18	27	
15	22	19	28	
16	23	21	29	14
17	24	22	29	
18	25	23	30	
19	26	24	01♑	
20	27	25	01	
21	28	27	02	14
22	29	28	03	
23	30	29	04	
24	01♏	00♐	04	
25	02	02	05	
26	03	03	06	14
27	04	04	07	
28	05	05	07	
29	06	06	08	
30	07	08	09	
31	08	09	10	14

NOVEMBER

Day	⊙	♀	♂	♆
01	09♏	10♐	10♑	14♌
02	10	11	11	
03	11	13	12	
04	12	14	13	
05	13	15	13	
06	14	16	14	14
07	15	18	15	
08	16	19	16	
09	17	20	16	
10	18	21	17	
11	19	22	18	14
12	20	24	19	
13	21	25	19	
14	22	26	20	
15	23	27	21	
16	24	29	22	14
17	25	30	22	
18	26	01♑	23	
19	27	02	24	
20	28	03	25	
21	29	05	25	14
22	30	06	26	
23	01♐	07	27	
24	02	08	28	
25	03	09	28	
26	04	11	29	14
27	05	12	30	
28	06	13	01♒	
29	07	14	01	
30	08	16	02	

DECEMBER

Day	⊙	♀	♂	♆
01	09♐	17♑	03♒	14♌
02	10	18	04	
03	11	19	05	
04	12	20	05	
05	13	22	06	
06	14	23	07	14
07	15	24	08	
08	16	25	08	
09	17	26	09	
10	18	28	10	
11	19	29	11	14
12	20	00♒	12	
13	21	01	12	
14	22	02	13	
15	23	04	14	
16	24	05	15	14
17	25	06	15	
18	26	07	16	
19	27	08	17	
20	28	10	18	
21	29	11	19	13
22	00♑	12	19	
23	01	13	20	
24	02	14	21	
25	03	16	22	
26	04	17	22	13
27	05	18	23	
28	06	19	24	
29	08	20	25	
30	09	21	25	
31	10	23	26	13

BIRTH TABLES - 1921

JANUARY

Day	☉	♀	♂	♆
01	11♑	24♒	27♒	13♌
02	12	25	28	
03	13	26	29	
04	14	27	29	
05	15	28	00♓	
06	16	30	01	13
07	17	01♓	02	
08	18	02	02	
09	19	03	03	
10	20	04	04	
11	21	05	05	13
12	22	07	06	
13	23	08	06	
14	24	09	07	
15	25	10	08	
16	26	11	09	13
17	27	12	09	
18	28	13	10	
19	29	14	11	
20	30	16	12	
21	01♒	17	13	13
22	02	18	13	
23	03	19	14	
24	04	20	15	
25	05	21	16	
26	06	22	16	13
27	07	23	17	
28	08	24	18	
29	09	26	19	
30	10	27	20	
31	11	28	20	12

FEBRUARY

Day	☉	♀	♂	♆
01	12♒	29♓	21♓	12♌
02	13	30	22	
03	14	01♈	23	
04	15	02	23	
05	16	03	24	
06	17	04	25	12
07	18	05	26	
08	19	06	26	
09	20	07	27	
10	21	08	28	
11	22	09	29	12
12	23	10	29	
13	24	11	00♈	
14	25	12	01	
15	26	13	02	
16	27	14	03	12
17	28	15	03	
18	29	16	04	
19	00♓	17	05	
20	01	18	06	
21	02	19	06	12
22	03	19	07	
23	04	20	08	
24	05	21	09	
25	06	22	09	
26	07	23	10	12
27	08	24	11	
28	09	25	12	

MARCH

Day	☉	♀	♂	♆
01	10♓	25♈	12♈	12♌
02	11	26	13	
03	12	27	14	
04	13	28	15	
05	14	29	15	
06	15	29	16	12
07	16	00♉	17	
08	17	01	18	
09	18	01	18	
10	19	02	19	
11	20	03	20	11
12	21	03	21	
13	22	04	21	
14	23	05	22	
15	24	05	23	
16	25	06	24	11
17	26	06	24	
18	27	07	25	
19	28	07	26	
20	29	08	27	
21	00♈	08	27	11
22	01	08	28	
23	02	09	29	
24	03	09	29	
25	04	09	00♉	
26	05	10	01	11
27	06	10	02	
28	07	10	02	
29	08	10	03	
30	09	10	04	
31	10	10	05	11

APRIL

Day	☉	♀	♂	♆
01	11♈	10♉	05♉	11♌
02	12	10	06	
03	13	10	07	
04	14	10	07	
05	15	10	08	
06	16	10	09	11
07	17	09	10	
08	18	09	10	
09	19	09	11	
10	20	09	12	
11	21	08	13	11
12	22	08	13	
13	23	07	14	
14	24	07	15	
15	25	06	15	
16	26	06	16	11
17	27	05	17	
18	28	05	18	
19	29	04	18	
20	30	03	19	
21	01♉	03	20	11
22	02	02	20	
23	03	02	21	
24	04	01	22	
25	05	00♉	23	
26	06	30♈	23	11
27	07	29	24	
28	08	28	25	
29	09	28	25	
30	10	27	26	

MAY

Day	☉	♀	♂	♆
01	11♉	27♈	27♉	11♌
02	12	27	28	
03	12	26	28	
04	13	26	29	
05	14	25	30	
06	15	25	00♊	11
07	16	25	01	
08	17	24	02	
09	18	24	02	
10	19	24	03	
11	20	24	04	11
12	21	24	05	
13	22	24	05	
14	23	24	06	
15	24	24	07	
16	25	24	07	11
17	26	24	08	
18	27	24	09	
19	28	24	09	
20	29	25	10	
21	30	25	11	11
22	01♊	25	11	
23	02	26	12	
24	03	26	13	
25	04	26	13	
26	05	27	14	11
27	06	27	15	
28	07	28	16	
29	08	28	16	
30	09	29	17	
31	09	29	18	11

JUNE

Day	☉	♀	♂	♆
01	10♊	30♈	18♊	11♌
02	11	00♉	19	
03	12	01	20	
04	13	01	20	
05	14	02	21	
06	15	03	22	12
07	16	03	22	
08	17	04	23	
09	18	05	24	
10	19	05	24	
11	20	06	25	12
12	21	07	26	
13	22	08	26	
14	23	09	27	
15	24	09	28	
16	25	10	28	12
17	26	11	29	
18	27	12	30	
19	28	13	00♋	
20	29	13	01	
21	30	14	02	12
22	00♋	15	02	
23	01	16	03	
24	02	17	04	
25	03	18	04	
26	04	19	05	12
27	05	19	06	
28	06	21	06	
29	07	22	07	
30	08	22	08	

JULY

Day	☉	♀	♂	♆
01	09♋	23♉	08♋	12♌
02	10	24	09	
03	11	25	10	
04	12	26	10	
05	13	27	11	
06	14	28	12	12
07	15	29	12	
08	16	00♊	13	
09	17	01	14	
10	18	02	14	
11	19	03	15	13
12	20	04	16	
13	21	05	16	
14	21	06	17	
15	22	07	18	
16	23	08	18	13
17	24	09	19	
18	25	10	20	
19	26	12	20	
20	27	13	21	
21	28	14	22	13
22	29	15	22	
23	00♌	16	23	
24	01	17	24	
25	02	18	24	
26	03	19	25	13
27	04	20	26	
28	05	21	26	
29	06	22	27	
30	07	23	27	
31	08	24	28	13

AUGUST

Day	☉	♀	♂	♆
01	09♌	25♊	29♋	13♌
02	10	27	29	
03	11	28	00♌	
04	12	29	01	
05	12	30	01	
06	13	01♋	02	13
07	14	02	03	
08	15	03	03	
09	16	04	04	
10	17	05	05	
11	18	07	05	14
12	19	08	05	
13	20	09	06	
14	21	10	07	
15	22	11	08	
16	23	12	08	14
17	24	13	09	
18	25	15	10	
19	26	16	10	
20	27	17	11	
21	28	18	12	14
22	29	19	12	
23	30	20	13	
24	01♍	21	13	
25	02	23	14	
26	03	24	14	14
27	04	25	15	
28	05	26	16	
29	06	27	17	
30	07	28	17	
31	08	30	18	14

SEPTEMBER

Day	☉	♀	♂	♆
01	08♍	01♌	19♌	14♌
02	09	02	19	
03	10	03	20	
04	11	04	21	
05	12	05	21	
06	13	07	22	14
07	14	08	22	
08	15	09	23	
09	16	11	24	
10	17	11	24	
11	18	12	25	15
12	19	14	26	
13	20	15	26	
14	21	16	27	
15	22	17	28	
16	23	18	28	15
17	24	20	29	
18	25	21	29	
19	26	22	00♍	
20	27	23	01	
21	28	24	01	15
22	29	26	02	
23	30	27	03	
24	01♎	28	03	
25	02	29	04	
26	03	00♍	04	15
27	04	02	05	
28	05	03	06	
29	06	04	06	
30	07	05	07	

OCTOBER

Day	☉	♀	♂	♆
01	08♎	06♍	08♍	15♌
02	09	08	08	
03	10	09	09	
04	11	10	09	
05	12	11	10	
06	13	13	11	15
07	14	14	11	
08	15	15	12	
09	16	16	13	
10	17	17	13	
11	18	19	14	16
12	19	20	14	
13	20	21	15	
14	21	22	16	
15	22	24	16	
16	23	25	17	16
17	24	26	18	
18	25	27	18	
19	26	28	19	
20	27	30	19	
21	28	01♎	20	16
22	29	02	21	
23	30	03	21	
24	01♏	05	22	
25	02	06	23	
26	03	07	23	16
27	04	08	24	
28	05	10	24	
29	06	11	25	
30	07	12	26	
31	08	13	26	16

NOVEMBER

Day	☉	♀	♂	♆
01	09♏	15♎	27♍	16♌
02	10	16	27	
03	11	17	28	
04	12	18	29	
05	13	20	29	
06	14	21	30	16
07	15	22	01♎	
08	16	23	01	
09	17	25	02	
10	18	26	02	
11	19	27	03	16
12	20	28	04	
13	21	30	04	
14	22	01♏	05	
15	23	02	05	
16	24	03	06	16
17	25	05	07	
18	26	06	07	
19	27	07	08	
20	28	08	08	
21	29	10	09	16
22	30	11	10	
23	01♐	12	10	
24	02	13	11	
25	03	15	11	
26	04	16	12	16
27	05	17	13	
28	06	18	13	
29	07	20	14	
30	08	21	15	

DECEMBER

Day	☉	♀	♂	♆
01	09♐	22♏	15♎	16♌
02	10	23	16	
03	11	25	16	
04	12	26	17	
05	13	27	18	
06	14	28	18	16
07	15	30	19	
08	16	01♐	19	
09	17	02	20	
10	18	03	21	
11	19	05	21	16
12	20	06	22	
13	21	07	22	
14	22	08	23	
15	23	10	24	
16	24	11	24	16
17	25	12	25	
18	26	13	25	
19	27	15	26	
20	28	16	26	
21	29	17	27	16
22	00♑	18	28	
23	01	20	28	
24	02	21	29	
25	03	22	29	
26	04	23	00♏	16
27	05	25	01	
28	06	26	01	
29	07	27	02	
30	08	29	02	
31	09	30	03	15

BIRTH TABLES - 1922

Day	JANUARY ☉	♀	♂	Ψ	FEBRUARY ☉	♀	♂	Ψ	MARCH ☉	♀	♂	Ψ	APRIL ☉	♀	♂	Ψ	MAY ☉	♀	♂	Ψ	JUNE ☉	♀	♂	Ψ
01	10♑	01♑	04♏	15♌	12♒	10♒	21♏	15♌	10♓	15♓	05♐	14♌	11♈	24♈	18♐	13♌	10♉	01♊	25♐	13♌	10♊	08♋	22♐	14♌
02	11	02	04		13	11	22		11	16	06		12	25	19		11	02	25		11	09	21	
03	12	04	05		14	13	22		12	18	06		13	26	19		12	03	25		12	11	21	
04	13	05	05		15	14	23		13	19	07		14	27	19		13	04	25		13	12	21	
05	14	06	06		16	15	23		14	20	07		15	29	20		14	05	25		14	13	21	
06	15	07	06	15	17	16	24	15	15	21	08	14	16	30	20	13	15	07	25	13	15	14	20	14
07	16	09	07		18	18	24		16	23	08		17	01♉	20		16	08	25		16	15	20	
08	17	10	08		19	19	25		17	24	09		18	02	21		17	09	25		17	17	20	
09	18	11	08		20	20	25		18	25	09		19	04	21		18	10	25		18	18	19	
10	19	12	09		21	21	26		19	26	10		20	05	21		19	12	25		19	19	19	
11	21	14	09	15	22	23	26	14	20	28	10	14	21	06	21	13	20	13	25	13	20	20	19	14
12	22	15	10		23	24	27		21	29	10		22	07	22		21	14	25		21	21	18	
13	23	16	10		24	25	27		22	00♈	11		23	08	22		22	15	25		22	23	18	
14	24	17	11		25	26	28		23	01	11		24	10	22		23	16	25		23	24	18	
15	25	19	12		26	28	28		24	03	12		25	11	22		24	18	25		24	25	17	
16	26	20	12	15	27	29	29	14	25	04	12	14	26	12	23	13	25	19	25	13	25	26	17	14
17	27	21	13		28	00♓	29		26	05	13		27	13	23		26	20	25		25	27	17	
18	28	22	13		29	01	30		27	06	13		28	15	23		27	21	25		26	29	16	
19	29	24	14		00♓	03	00♐		28	08	13		29	16	23		28	22	24		27	30	16	
20	30	25	14		01	04	01		29	09	14		30	17	23		29	24	24		28	01♌	16	
21	01♒	26	15	15	02	05	01	14	00♈	10	14	14	01♉	18	24	13	30	25	24	13	29	02	15	14
22	02	27	15		03	06	02		01	11	15		02	20	24		01♊	26	24		00♋	03	15	
23	03	29	16		04	08	02		02	12	15		03	21	24		02	27	24		01	05	15	
24	04	30	17		05	09	03		03	14	15		04	22	24		03	29	24		02	06	15	
25	05	01♒	17		06	10	03		04	15	16		04	23	24		03	30	23		03	07	14	
26	06	02	18	15	07	11	04	14	05	16	16	13	05	24	24	13	04	01♋	23	13	04	08	14	14
27	07	04	18		08	13	04		06	17	17		06	26	25		05	02	23		05	09	14	
28	08	05	19		09	14	05		07	19	17		07	27	25		06	03	23		06	11	13	
29	09	06	19						08	20	17		08	28	25		07	05	22		07	12	13	
30	10	07	20						09	21	18		09	29	25		08	06	22		08	13	13	
31	11	09	20	15					10	22	18	13					09	07	22	14				

Day	JULY ☉	♀	♂	♆	AUGUST ☉	♀	♂	♆	SEPTEMBER ☉	♀	♂	♆	OCTOBER ☉	♀	♂	♆	NOVEMBER ☉	♀	♂	♆	DECEMBER ☉	♀	♂	♆
01	09♋	14♌	13♐	14♌	08♌	20♍	13♐	15♌	09♍	24♎	24♐	17♌	08♎	23♏	11♑	17♌	09♏	10♐	01♒	18♌	09♐	29♏	23♒	18♌
02	10	15	13		09	21	13		09	25	24		09	24	11		09	10	02		10	28	23	
03	11	16	12		10	22	13		10	26	25		09	24	12		10	10	03		11	28	24	
04	12	18	12		11	23	13		11	27	25		10	25	12		11	10	03		12	27	25	
05	13	19	12		12	25	14		12	28	26		11	26	13		12	10	04		13	27	26	
06	14	20	12	14	13	26	14	16	13	29	26	17	12	27	14	18	13	10	05	18	14	26	26	18
07	15	21	12		14	27	14		14	00♏	27		13	28	14		14	10	05		15	26	27	
08	16	22	12		15	28	14		15	01	27		14	28	15		15	10	06		16	26	28	
09	16	23	12		16	29	15		16	02	28		15	29	16		16	09	07		17	25	29	
10	17	25	11		17	00♎	15		17	03	28		16	30	16		17	09	08		18	25	29	
11	18	26	11	15	18	01	15	16	18	04	29	17	17	00♐	17	18	18	09	08	18	19	25	30	18
12	19	27	11		19	02	16		19	05	29		18	01	18		19	09	09		20	25	01♓	
13	20	28	11		20	03	16		20	06	30		19	02	18		20	08	10		21	25	01	
14	21	29	11		21	05	16		21	07	01♑		20	02	19		21	08	10		22	25	02	
15	22	00♍	11		22	06	17		22	08	01		21	03	20		22	07	11		23	25	03	
16	23	02	11	15	23	07	17	16	23	09	02	17	22	04	20	18	23	07	12	18	24	25	04	18
17	24	03	11		24	08	17		24	10	02		23	04	21		24	07	13		25	25	04	
18	25	04	11		25	09	18		25	11	03		24	05	22		25	06	13		26	25	05	
19	26	05	11		26	10	18		26	12	03		25	05	22		26	06	14		27	25	06	
20	27	06	11		27	11	19		27	13	04		26	06	23		27	05	15		28	25	07	
21	28	07	11	15	28	12	19	16	28	14	05	17	27	06	24	18	28	04	15	18	29	25	07	18
22	29	09	11		29	13	19		29	15	05		28	07	24		29	04	16		30	25	08	
23	30	10	11		30	14	20		30	16	06		29	07	25		00♐	03	17		01♑	26	09	
24	01♌	11	11		01♍	16	20		01♎	17	06		00♏	08	26		01	03	18		02	26	10	
25	02	12	12		01	17	21		02	18	07		01	08	26		02	02	18		03	26	10	
26	03	13	12	15	02	18	21	16	03	18	08	17	02	08	27	18	03	02	19	18	04	27	11	18
27	04	14	12		03	19	21		04	19	08		03	09	28		04	01	20		05	27	12	
28	05	15	12		04	20	22		05	20	09		04	09	28		05	00♐	20		06	28	12	
29	06	17	12		05	21	22		06	21	09		05	09	29		06	30♏	21		07	28	13	
30	07	18	12		06	22	23		07	22	10		06	09	30		08	29	22		08	28	14	
31	07	19	13	15	07	23	23	17					07	10	01♒	18					09	29	15	18

BIRTH TABLES - 1923

	JANUARY ☉	♀	♂	♆	FEBRUARY ☉	♀	♂	♆	MARCH ☉	♀	♂	♆	APRIL ☉	♀	♂	♆	MAY ☉	♀	♂	♆	JUNE ☉	♀	♂	♆
01	10♑	30♍	15♓	18♌	12♒	25♐	08♈	17♌	10♓	25♑	28♈	16♌	11♈	00♓	20♉	16♌	10♉	06♈	10♊	15♌	10♊	13♉	01♋	16♌
02	11	00♐	16		13	26	09		11	26	29		12	02	21		11	07	11		11	14	02	
03	12	01	17		14	27	10		12	27	30		13	03	21		12	08	12		12	16	02	
04	13	01	18		15	28	10		13	28	00♉		14	04	22		13	09	12		13	17	03	
05	14	02	18		16	29	11		14	29	01		15	05	23		14	11	13		14	18	04	
06	15	03	19	18	17	30	12	17	15	00♒	02	16	16	06	23	15	15	12	14	15	15	19	04	16
07	16	03	20		18	01♑	12		16	01	02		17	07	24		16	13	14		16	20	05	
08	17	04	21		19	02	13		17	03	03		18	09	25		17	14	15		17	22	06	
09	18	05	21		20	03	14		18	04	04		19	10	25		18	15	16		18	23	06	
10	19	05	22		21	04	15		19	05	05		20	11	26		19	17	16		19	24	07	
11	20	06	23	17	22	05	15	17	20	06	05	16	21	12	27	15	20	18	17	15	20	25	08	16
12	21	07	23		23	06	16		21	07	06		22	13	28		21	19	18		20	26	08	
13	22	08	24		24	07	17		22	08	07		23	14	28		22	20	18		21	28	09	
14	23	09	25		25	08	17		23	09	07		24	16	29		23	21	19		22	29	10	
15	24	09	26		26	09	18		24	11	08		24	17	30		24	23	20		23	00♊	10	
16	25	10	26	17	27	10	19	17	25	12	09	16	25	18	00♊	15	25	24	20	15	24	01	11	16
17	26	11	27		28	11	20		26	13	10		26	19	01		26	25	21		25	02	12	
18	27	12	28		29	13	20		27	14	10		27	20	02		27	26	22		26	04	12	
19	28	13	29		30	14	21		28	15	11		28	22	02		27	27	22		27	05	13	
20	29	14	29		01♓	15	22		29	16	12		39	23	03		28	29	23		28	06	14	
21	00♒	14	00♈	17	02	16	23	16	30	18	12	16	00♉	24	04	15	29	30	24	16	29	07	14	16
22	01	15	01		03	17	23		01♈	19	13		01	25	C4		00♊	01♉	24		00♋	09	15	
23	02	16	02		04	18	24		02	20	14		02	26	05		01	02	25		01	10	15	
24	03	17	02		05	19	25		03	21	14		03	28	06		02	03	26		02	11	16	
25	05	18	03		06	20	25		04	22	15		04	29	06		03	05	26		03	12	17	
26	06	19	04	17	07	21	26	16	05	23	16	16	05	30	07	15	04	06	27	16	04	13	17	16
27	07	20	04		08	22	27		06	24	17		06	01♈	08		05	07	28		05	15	18	
28	08	21	05		09	24	28		07	26	17		07	02	08		06	08	28		06	16	19	
29	09	22	06						08	27	18		08	04	09		07	09	29		07	17	19	
30	10	23	07						C9	28	19		09	05	10		08	11	30		08	18	20	
31	11	24	07						10	29	19	16					09	12	00♋	16				

	JULY				AUGUST				SEPTEMBER			
	☉	♀	♂	♆	☉	♀	♂	♆	☉	♀	♂	♆
01	09♋	19♊	20♋	16♌	08♌	27♋	11♌	18♌	08♍	06♍	00♍	19♌
02	10	21	21		09	29	11		09	07	01	
03	11	22	22		10	30	12		10	08	02	
04	11	23	23		11	01♌	12		11	09	02	
05	12	24	23		12	02	13		12	11	03	
06	13	26	24	17	13	03	14	18	13	12	03	19
07	14	27	25		14	05	14		14	13	04	
08	15	28	25		15	06	15		15	14	05	
09	16	29	26		16	07	16		16	16	05	
10	17	00♋	26		17	08	16		17	17	06	
11	18	02	27	17	18	10	17	18	18	18	07	19
12	19	03	28		19	11	18		19	19	07	
13	20	04	28		20	12	18		20	21	08	
14	21	05	29		21	13	19		21	22	09	
15	22	06	30		22	15	19		22	23	09	
16	23	08	00♌	17	23	16	20	18	23	24	10	19
17	24	09	01		24	17	21		24	25	10	
18	25	10	02		25	18	21		25	27	11	
19	26	11	02		25	20	22		26	28	12	
20	27	13	03		26	21	23		26	29	12	
21	28	14	04	17	27	22	23	18	27	00♎	13	19
22	29	15	04		28	23	24		28	02	14	
23	30	16	05		29	25	25		29	03	14	
24	01♌	18	05		00♍	26	25		00♎	04	15	
25	02	19	06		01	27	26		01	05	16	
26	02	20	07	17	02	28	26	18	02	07	16	19
27	03	21	07		03	29	27		03	08	17	
28	04	22	08		04	01♍	28		04	09	17	
29	05	24	09		05	02	28		05	10	18	
30	06	25	09		06	03	29		06	12	19	
31	07	26	10	17	07	04	30	19				

	OCTOBER				NOVEMBER				DECEMBER			
	☉	♀	♂	♆	☉	♀	♂	♆	☉	♀	♂	♆
01	07♎	13♎	19♍	20♌	09♏	22♏	09♎	20♌	08♐	29♐	28♎	20♌
02	08	14	20		09	23	10		09	00♑	29	
03	09	15	21		10	24	10		10	02	30	
04	10	17	21		11	25	11		11	03	00♏	
05	11	18	22		12	27	12		12	04	01	
06	12	19	23	20	13	28	12	20	13	05	02	20
07	13	20	23		14	29	13		14	07	02	
08	14	22	24		15	00♐	14		15	08	03	
09	15	23	24		16	02	14		16	09	03	
10	16	24	25		17	03	15		17	10	04	
11	17	25	26	20	18	04	16	20	18	12	05	20
12	18	27	26		19	05	16		19	13	05	
13	19	28	27		20	07	17		20	14	06	
14	20	29	28		21	08	17		21	15	07	
15	21	00♏	28		22	09	18		22	17	07	
16	22	02	29	20	23	10	19	20	24	18	08	20
17	23	03	30		24	12	19		25	19	09	
18	24	04	00♎		25	13	20		26	20	09	
19	25	05	01		26	14	21		27	22	10	
20	26	07	01		27	15	21		28	23	11	
21	27	08	02	20	28	17	22	20	29	24	11	20
22	28	09	03		29	18	23		30	25	12	
23	29	10	03		00♐	19	23		01♑	26	12	
24	00♏	12	04		01	20	24		02	28	13	
25	01	13	05		02	22	25		03	29	14	
26	02	14	05	20	03	23	25	20	04	00♒	14	20
27	03	15	06		04	24	26		05	01	15	
28	04	17	07		05	25	26		06	03	16	
29	05	18	07		06	27	27		07	04	16	
30	06	19	08		07	28	28		08	05	17	
31	07	20	09	20					09	06	18	20

BIRTH TABLES - 1924

Day	JANUARY ☉	♀	♂	Ψ	FEBRUARY ☉	♀	♂	Ψ	MARCH ☉	♀	♂	Ψ
01	10♑	08♒	18♏	20♌	11♒	16♓	08♐	19♌	11♓	21♈	27♐	18♌
02	11	09	19		12	17	09		12	22	27	
03	12	10	20		13	18	09		13	23	28	
04	13	11	20		14	20	10		14	24	29	
05	14	13	21		15	21	11		15	25	29	
06	15	14	21	20	16	22	11	19	16	27	30	18
07	16	15	22		17	23	12		17	28	00♑	
08	17	16	23		18	24	13		18	29	01	
09	18	18	23		19	26	13		19	00♉	02	
10	19	19	24		20	27	14		20	01	02	
11	20	20	25	20	22	28	15	19	21	02	03	18
12	21	21	25		23	29	15		22	03	04	
13	22	23	26		24	00♈	16		23	05	04	
14	23	24	27		25	02	16		24	06	05	
15	24	25	27		26	03	17		25	07	05	
16	25	26	28	20	27	04	18	19	26	08	06	18
17	26	27	29		28	05	18		27	09	07	
18	27	29	29		29	06	19		28	10	07	
19	28	30	30		30	08	20		29	11	08	
20	29	01♓	00♐		01♓	09	20		30	13	09	
21	00♒	02	01	20	02	10	21	19	01♈	14	09	18
22	01	04	02		03	11	21		02	15	10	
23	02	05	03		04	12	22		03	16	10	
24	03	06	03		05	14	23		04	17	11	
25	04	07	04		06	15	23		05	18	12	
26	05	09	04	19	07	16	24	19	06	19	12	18
27	06	10	05		08	17	25		07	20	13	
28	07	11	06		09	18	25		08	22	14	
29	08	12	06		10	19	26		09	23	14	
30	09	13	07						10	24	15	
31	10	15	08	19					11	25	15	18

Day	APRIL ☉	♀	♂	Ψ	MAY ☉	♀	♂	Ψ	JUNE ☉	♀	♂	Ψ
01	11♈	26♉	16♑	18♌	11♉	26♊	04♒	18♌	11♊	16♋	20♒	18♌
02	12	27	17		12	27	05		12	17	21	
03	13	28	17		13	28	05		13	17	21	
04	14	29	18		14	29	06		14	17	22	
05	15	00♊	19		15	30	06		15	17	22	
06	16	01	19	18	16	00♋	07	18	15	17	23	18
07	17	02	20		17	01	07		16	17	23	
08	18	03	20		18	02	08		17	18	24	
09	19	04	21		19	03	09		18	18	24	
10	20	06	22		20	04	09		19	18	25	
11	21	07	22	18	21	05	10	18	20	18	25	18
12	22	08	23		21	05	10		21	17	25	
13	23	09	23		22	06	11		22	17	26	
14	24	10	24		23	07	11		23	17	26	
15	25	11	25		24	07	12		24	17	27	
16	26	12	25	18	25	08	12	18	25	17	27	18
17	27	13	26		26	09	13		26	16	27	
18	28	14	26		27	09	13		27	16	28	
19	29	15	27		28	10	14		28	16	28	
20	00♉	16	28		29	11	14		29	15	29	
21	01	17	28	18	00♊	11	15	18	30	15	29	18
22	02	18	29		01	12	15		01♋	15	29	
23	03	19	29		02	12	16		02	14	30	
24	04	20	30		03	13	17		03	14	30	
25	05	21	00♒		04	13	17		04	13	00♓	
26	06	21	01	18	05	14	18	18	05	12	01	18
27	07	22	02		06	14	18		06	12	01	
28	08	23	02		07	15	19		06	11	01	
29	09	24	03		08	15	19		07	11	02	
30	10	25	03		09	16	20		08	10	02	
31					10	16	20	18				

Day	JUL ☉	JUL ♀	JUL ♂	JUL ♆	AUG ☉	AUG ♀	AUG ♂	AUG ♆	SEP ☉	SEP ♀	SEP ♂	SEP ♆
01	09♋	09♋	02♓	19♌	09♌	03♋	05♓	20♌	09♍	23♋	28♒	21♌
02	10	09	02		10	03	05		10	24	28	
03	11	08	03		11	03	05		11	25	28	
04	12	08	03		12	04	05		12	26	27	
05	13	07	03		13	04	04		13	27	27	
06	14	06	03	19	14	05	04	20	14	28	27	21
07	15	06	03		15	05	04		15	29	27	
08	16	05	04		16	06	04		16	30	27	
09	17	05	04		17	06	04		17	01♌	26	
10	18	04	04		18	07	03		17	02	26	
11	19	04	04	19	19	07	03	20	18	03	26	21
12	20	03	04		19	08	03		19	04	26	
13	21	03	05		20	08	03		20	04	26	
14	22	03	05		21	09	03		21	05	26	
15	23	02	05		22	10	02		22	06	26	
16	24	02	05	19	23	10	02	20	23	07	26	21
17	25	02	05		24	11	02		24	09	25	
18	26	01	05		25	12	02		25	10	25	
19	27	01	05		26	13	01		26	11	25	
20	27	01	05		27	13	01		27	12	25	
21	28	01	05	19	28	14	01	20	28	13	25	22
22	29	01	05		29	15	01		29	14	25	
23	00♌	01	05		00♍	15	00		00♎	15	25	
24	01	01	05		01	16	00		01	16	25	
25	02	01	05		02	17	30♒		02	17	25	
26	03	01	05	19	03	18	30	21	03	18	25	22
27	04	01	05		04	19	29		04	19	26	
28	05	02	05		05	20	29		05	20	26	
29	06	02	05		06	21	29		06	21	26	
30	07	02	05		07	21	28		07	22	26	
31	07	02	05	20	08	22	28	21				

Day	OCT ☉	OCT ♀	OCT ♂	OCT ♆	NOV ☉	NOV ♀	NOV ♂	NOV ♆	DEC ☉	DEC ♀	DEC ♂	DEC ♆
01	08♎	23♌	26♒	22♌	09♏	29♍	05♓	22♌	09♐	05♏	20♓	23♌
02	09	24	26		10	30	05		10	06	20	
03	10	25	26		11	01♎	06		11	07	21	
04	11	27	26		12	02	06		12	09	21	
05	12	28	26		13	03	06		13	10	22	
06	13	29	27	22	14	05	07	22	14	11	22	23
07	14	30	27		15	06	07		15	12	23	
08	15	01♍	27		16	07	08		16	14	24	
09	16	02	27		17	08	08		17	15	24	
10	17	03	27		18	09	09		18	16	25	
11	18	04	28	22	19	11	09	23	19	17	25	23
12	19	06	28		20	12	10		20	18	26	
13	20	07	28		21	13	10		21	20	26	
14	21	08	28		22	14	11		22	21	27	
15	22	09	29		23	15	11		23	22	28	
16	23	10	29	22	24	17	12	23	24	23	28	22
17	24	11	29		25	18	12		25	25	29	
18	25	12	30		26	19	13		26	26	29	
19	26	14	30		27	20	13		27	27	00♈	
20	27	15	00♓		28	21	14		28	28	01	
21	28	16	01	22	29	23	14	23	29	30	01	22
22	29	17	01		30	24	15		00♑	01♐	02	
23	30	18	01		01♐	25	15		01	02	02	
24	01♏	19	02		02	26	16		02	03	03	
25	02	20	02		03	28	16		03	05	04	
26	03	22	02	22	04	29	17	23	04	06	04	22
27	04	23	03		05	00♏	17		06	07	05	
28	05	24	03		06	01	18		07	08	05	
29	06	25	04		07	02	19		08	10	06	
30	07	26	04		08	04	19		09	11	07	
31	08	28	04	22					10	12	07	22

BIRTH TABLES - 1925

Day	JAN ☉	JAN ♀	JAN ♂	JAN ♆	FEB ☉	FEB ♀	FEB ♂	FEB ♆	MAR ☉	MAR ♀	MAR ♂	MAR ♆
01	11♑	13♐	08♈	22♌	12♒	22♑	27♈	21♌	10♓	27♒	16♉	21♌
02	12	15	09		13	23	28		11	28	16	
03	13	16	09		14	24	29		12	29	17	
04	14	17	10		15	26	29		13	01♓	17	
05	15	18	10		16	27	00♉		14	02	18	
06	16	20	11	22	17	28	01	21	15	03	19	21
07	17	21	12		18	29	02		16	04	19	
08	18	22	12		19	01♒	02		17	06	20	
09	19	23	13		20	02	03		18	07	21	
10	20	24	14		21	03	03		19	08	21	
11	21	26	14	22	22	04	04	21	20	09	22	20
12	22	27	15		23	06	05		21	10	23	
13	23	28	15		24	07	05		22	12	23	
14	24	29	16		25	08	06		23	13	24	
15	25	01♑	17		26	09	06		24	14	25	
16	26	02	17	22	27	11	07	21	25	16	25	20
17	27	03	18		28	12	08		26	17	26	
18	28	04	19		29	13	08		27	18	26	
19	29	06	19		00♓	14	09		28	19	27	
20	30	07	20		01	16	10		29	21	28	
21	01♒	08	20	22	02	17	10	21	00♈	22	28	20
22	02	09	21		03	18	11		01	23	29	
23	03	11	22		04	19	12		02	24	30	
24	04	12	22		05	21	12		03	26	00♊	
25	05	13	23		06	22	13		04	27	01	
26	06	14	23	22	07	23	14	21	05	28	02	20
27	07	16	24		08	24	14		06	29	02	
28	08	17	25		09	26	15		07	00♈	03	
29	09	18	26						08	02	04	
30	10	19	26						09	03	04	
31	11	21	27	21					10	04	05	20

Day	APR ☉	APR ♀	APR ♂	APR ♆	MAY ☉	MAY ♀	MAY ♂	MAY ♆	JUN ☉	JUN ♀	JUN ♂	JUN ♆
01	11♈	06♈	05♊	20♌	11♉	13♉	25♊	20♌	10♊	21♊	14♋	20♌
02	12	07	06		12	14	25		11	22	15	
03	13	08	07		13	15	26		12	23	16	
04	14	09	07		13	16	27		13	24	16	
05	15	10	08		14	17	27		14	26	17	
06	16	12	09	20	15	19	28	20	15	27	17	20
07	17	13	09		16	20	28		16	28	18	
08	18	14	10		17	21	29		17	29	19	
09	19	15	11		18	22	30		18	01♋	19	
10	20	17	11		19	24	00♋		19	02	20	
11	21	18	12	20	20	25	01	20	20	03	21	20
12	22	19	13		21	26	02		21	04	21	
13	23	20	13		22	27	02		22	05	22	
14	24	22	14		23	29	03		23	07	23	
15	25	23	14		24	30	04		24	08	23	
16	26	24	15	20	25	01♊	04	20	25	09	24	20
17	27	25	16		26	02	05		26	10	24	
18	28	27	16		27	04	05		27	12	25	
19	29	28	17		28	05	06		28	13	26	
20	30	29	18		29	06	07		29	14	26	
21	01♉	00♉	18	20	30	07	07	20	30	15	27	20
22	02	01	19		01♊	08	08		01♋	16	28	
23	03	03	20		02	10	09		01	18	28	
24	04	04	20		03	11	09		02	19	29	
25	05	05	21		04	12	10		03	20	29	
26	06	06	21	20	05	13	11	20	04	21	00♌	21
27	07	08	22		06	15	11		05	23	01	
28	08	09	23		07	16	12		06	24	01	
29	09	10	23		08	17	13		09	25	02	
30	10	11	24		09	18	13		08	26	03	
31					09	19	14	20				

JULY

Day	☉	♀	♂	♆
01	09♋	27♋	03♌	21♌
02	10	29	04	
03	11	30	05	
04	12	01♌	05	
05	13	02	06	
06	14	04	06	21
07	15	05	07	
08	16	06	08	
09	17	07	08	
10	18	08	09	
11	19	10	10	21
12	20	11	10	
13	21	12	11	
14	21	13	11	
15	22	15	12	
16	23	16	13	21
17	24	17	13	
18	25	18	14	
19	26	19	15	
20	27	21	15	
21	28	22	16	21
22	29	23	16	
23	00♌	24	17	
24	01	25	18	
25	02	26	18	
26	03	28	19	21
27	04	29	20	
28	05	00♍	20	
29	06	02	21	
30	07	03	22	
31	08	04	22	21

AUGUST

Day	☉	♀	♂	♆
01	09♌	05♍	23♌	22♌
02	10	06	23	
03	11	08	24	
04	12	09	25	
05	13	10	25	
06	13	11	26	22
07	14	12	27	
08	15	14	27	
09	16	15	28	
10	17	16	29	
11	18	17	29	22
12	19	19	30	
13	20	20	00♍	
14	21	21	01	
15	22	22	02	
16	23	23	02	22
17	24	25	03	
18	25	26	04	
19	26	27	04	
20	27	28	05	
21	28	29	05	22
22	29	01≏	06	
23	30	02	07	
24	01♍	03	07	
25	02	04	08	
26	03	05	09	22
27	04	07	09	
28	05	08	10	
29	06	09	11	
30	07	10	11	
31	08	11	12	22

SEPTEMBER

Day	☉	♀	♂	♆
01	09♍	13≏	12♍	23♌
02	10	14	13	
03	11	15	14	
04	12	16	14	
05	13	17	15	
06	14	19	16	23
07	15	20	16	
08	16	21	17	
09	17	22	18	
10	18	23	18	
11	19	25	19	23
12	20	26	20	
13	21	27	20	
14	22	28	21	
15	23	29	21	
16	24	01♏	22	23
17	25	02	23	
18	26	03	23	
19	27	04	24	
20	28	05	25	
21	29	06	25	23
22	30	08	26	
23	01≏	09	27	
24	02	10	27	
25	03	11	28	
26	04	12	29	23
27	05	14	29	
28	06	15	30	
29	07	16	00≏	
30	08	17	01	

OCTOBER

Day	☉	♀	♂	♆
01	08≏	18♏	02≏	24♌
02	09	19	02	
03	10	21	03	
04	11	22	04	
05	12	23	04	
06	13	24	05	24
07	14	25	06	
08	15	26	06	
09	16	28	07	
10	17	29	08	
11	18	30	08	24
12	19	01♐	09	
13	20	02	10	
14	21	03	10	
15	22	05	11	
16	23	06	12	24
17	24	07	12	
18	25	08	13	
19	26	09	13	
20	27	10	14	
21	28	11	15	24
22	29	13	15	
23	30	14	16	
24	01♏	15	17	
25	02	16	17	
26	03	17	18	25
27	04	18	19	
28	05	19	19	
29	06	21	20	
30	07	22	21	
31	08	23	21	25

NOVEMBER

Day	☉	♀	♂	♆
01	09♏	24♐	22≏	25♌
02	10	25	23	
03	11	26	23	
04	12	27	24	
05	13	28	25	
06	14	30	25	25
07	15	01♑	26	
08	16	02	27	
09	17	03	27	
10	18	04	28	
11	19	05	29	25
12	20	06	29	
13	21	07	30	
14	22	08	01♏	
15	23	09	01	
16	24	10	02	25
17	25	12	03	
18	26	13	03	
19	27	14	04	
20	28	15	05	
21	29	16	05	25
22	30	17	06	
23	01♐	18	07	
24	02	19	08	
25	03	20	08	
26	04	21	09	25
27	05	22	09	
28	06	23	10	
29	07	24	11	
30	08	25	11	

DECEMBER

Day	☉	♀	♂	♆
01	09♐	26♑	12♏	25♌
02	10	27	13	
03	11	28	13	
04	12	29	14	
05	13	30	15	
06	14	01♒	15	25
07	15	02	16	
08	16	03	17	
09	17	04	17	
10	18	05	18	
11	19	05	19	25
12	20	06	19	
13	21	07	20	
14	22	08	21	
15	23	09	21	
16	24	10	22	25
17	25	11	23	
18	26	11	24	
19	27	12	24	
20	28	13	25	
21	29	14	26	25
22	00♑	15	26	
23	01	15	27	
24	02	16	28	
25	03	17	28	
26	04	18	29	25
27	05	18	30	
28	06	19	00♐	
29	07	19	01	
30	08	20	02	
31	09	21	02	24

BIRTH TABLES - 1926

	JANUARY				FEBRUARY				MARCH			
	☉	♀	♂	Ψ	☉	♀	♂	Ψ	☉	♀	♂	Ψ
01	10♑	21♒	03♐	24♌	12♒	22♒	25♐	24♌	10♓	10♒	14♑	23♌
02	11	22	04		13	21	25		11	10	15	
03	12	22	04		14	21	26		12	11	16	
04	13	23	05		15	20	27		13	11	17	
05	14	23	06		16	20	27		14	11	17	
06	15	24	07	25	17	19	28	24	15	11	18	23
07	16	24	07		18	18	29		16	11	19	
08	17	24	08		19	18	30		17	12	19	
09	18	25	09		20	17	00♑		18	12	20	
10	20	25	09		21	16	01		19	12	21	
11	21	25	10	24	22	16	02	23	20	13	22	23
12	22	25	11		23	15	02		21	13	22	
13	23	26	11		24	15	03		22	14	23	
14	24	26	12		25	14	04		23	14	24	
15	25	26	13		26	14	05		24	15	24	
16	26	26	13	24	27	13	05	23	25	15	25	23
17	27	26	14		28	13	06		26	16	26	
18	28	26	15		29	12	07		27	16	26	
19	29	26	16		00♓	12	07		28	17	27	
20	30	26	16		01	12	08		29	17	28	
21	01♒	26	17	24	02	11	09	23	00♈	18	29	22
22	02	26	18		03	11	09		01	19	30	
23	03	25	18		04	11	10		02	19	00♒	
24	04	25	19		05	11	11		03	20	01	
25	05	25	20		06	10	12		04	21	02	
26	06	25	20	24	07	10	12	23	05	21	02	22
27	07	24	21		08	10	13		06	22	03	
28	08	24	22		09	10	14		07	23	04	
29	09	23	23						08	24	05	
30	10	23	23						09	24	05	
31	11	22	24	24					10	25	06	22

	APRIL				MAY				JUNE			
	☉	♀	♂	Ψ	☉	♀	♂	Ψ	☉	♀	♂	Ψ
01	11♈	26♒	07♒	22♌	10♉	25♓	28♒	22♌	10♊	29♈	1♓	22♌
02	12	27	07		11	26	29		11	30	21	
03	13	28	08		12	27	30		12	01♉	22	
04	14	29	09		13	28	01♓		13	02	23	
05	15	29	10		14	29	01		14	03	23	
06	16	00♓	10	22	15	30	02	22	15	04	24	22
07	17	01	11		16	01♈	03		16	05	25	
08	18	02	12		17	02	03		17	06	25	
09	19	03	13		18	03	04		18	08	26	
10	20	04	13		19	04	05		19	09	27	
11	21	05	14	22	20	05	06	22	20	10	28	22
12	22	06	15		21	06	06		21	11	28	
13	23	07	15		22	07	07		22	12	29	
14	24	08	16		23	08	08		23	13	30	
15	25	09	17		24	10	08		24	14	00♈	
16	26	10	18	22	25	11	09	22	25	16	01	23
17	27	10	18		26	12	10		26	17	02	
18	28	11	19		27	13	11		26	18	02	
19	29	12	20		28	14	11		27	19	03	
20	30	13	20		29	15	12		28	20	04	
21	01♉	14	21	22	30	16	13	22	29	21	04	23
22	02	15	22		01♊	17	13		00♋	23	05	
23	03	16	23		02	18	14		01	24	06	
24	04	17	23		03	20	15		02	25	06	
25	05	18	24		04	21	16		03	26	07	
26	05	19	25	22	04	22	16	22	04	27	08	23
27	06	20	26		05	23	17		05	28	08	
28	07	21	26		06	24	18		06	30	09	
29	08	23	27		07	25	18		07	01♊	10	
30	09	24	28		08	26	19		08	02	10	
31					09	27	20	22				

Day	Jul ☉	Jul ♀	Jul ♂	Jul ♆	Aug ☉	Aug ♀	Aug ♂	Aug ♆	Sep ☉	Sep ♀	Sep ♂	Sep ♆
01	09♋	03♊	11♈	23♌	08♌	10♋	00♉	24♌	08♍	17♌	14♉	25♌
02	10	04	12		09	11	01		09	19	15	
03	11	05	12		10	12	01		10	20	15	
04	12	07	13		11	13	02		11	21	15	
05	13	08	14		12	15	02		12	22	16	
06	14	09	14	23	13	16	03	24	13	24	16	25
07	15	10	15		14	17	03		14	25	16	
08	16	11	16		15	18	04		15	26	17	
09	17	12	16		16	19	04		16	27	17	
10	17	14	17		17	21	05		17	29	17	
11	18	15	18	23	18	22	05	24	18	30	17	25
12	19	16	18		19	23	06		19	01♍	18	
13	20	17	19		20	24	06		20	02	18	
14	21	18	19		21	26	07		21	03	18	
15	22	20	20		22	27	07		22	05	18	
16	23	21	21	23	23	28	08	24	23	06	18	26
17	24	22	21		24	29	08		24	07	18	
18	25	23	22		25	00♌	09		25	08	19	
19	26	24	23		26	02	09		26	10	19	
20	27	26	23		27	03	10		27	11	19	
21	28	27	24	23	28	04	10	25	28	12	19	26
22	29	28	24		29	05	10		29	13	19	
23	30	29	25		30	06	11		30	15	19	
24	01♌	00♋	25		01♍	08	11		01♎	16	19	
25	02	01	26		02	09	12		02	17	19	
26	03	03	27	24	02	10	12	25	03	18	19	26
27	04	04	27		03	11	13		04	20	19	
28	05	05	28		04	13	13		05	21	19	
29	06	06	28		05	14	13		06	22	19	
30	07	07	29		06	15	14		07	23	19	
31	08	09	30	24	07	16	14	25				

Day	Oct ☉	Oct ♀	Oct ♂	Oct ♆	Nov ☉	Nov ♀	Nov ♂	Nov ♆	Dec ☉	Dec ♀	Dec ♂	Dec ♆
01	08♎	25♍	19♉	26♌	08♏	03♏	12♉	27♌	09♐	11♐	05♉	27♌
02	09	26	19		09	05	12		10	12	05	
03	10	27	19		10	06	12		11	14	05	
04	11	28	19		11	07	11		12	15	05	
05	11	30	19		12	08	11		13	16	05	
06	12	01♎	19	26	13	10	10	27	14	17	05	27
07	13	02	19		14	11	10		15	19	05	
08	14	03	19		15	12	10		16	20	05	
09	15	05	19		16	13	09		17	21	05	
10	16	06	19		17	15	09		18	22	05	
11	17	07	18	26	18	16	09	27	19	24	05	27
12	18	08	18		19	17	09		20	25	05	
13	19	10	18		20	18	08		21	26	05	
14	20	11	18		21	20	08		22	27	05	
15	21	12	18		22	21	08		23	29	05	
16	22	13	17	26	23	22	07	27	24	30	05	27
17	23	15	17		24	23	07		25	01♑	05	
18	24	16	17		25	25	07		26	02	05	
19	25	17	16		26	26	07		27	04	06	
20	26	18	16		27	27	06		28	05	06	
21	27	20	16	26	28	28	06	27	29	06	06	27
22	28	21	16		29	30	06		30	07	06	
23	29	22	15		00♐	01♐	06		01♑	09	06	
24	00♏	23	15		01	02	06		02	10	06	
25	01	25	15		02	03	05		03	11	07	
26	02	26	14	27	03	05	05	27	04	12	07	27
27	03	27	14		04	06	05		05	14	07	
28	04	28	14		06	07	05		06	15	07	
29	05	30	13		07	08	05		07	16	08	
30	06	01♏	13		08	10	05		08	17	08	
31	07	02	13	27					09	19	08	27

BIRTH TABLES - 1927

Day	JAN ☉	JAN ♀	JAN ♂	JAN ♆	FEB ☉	FEB ♀	FEB ♂	FEB ♆	MAR ☉	MAR ♀	MAR ♂	MAR ♆
01	10♑	20♑	08♉	27♌	12♒	29♒	20♉	26♌	10♓	04♈	04♊	25♌
02	11	21	09		13	00♓	21		11	05	04	
03	12	22	09		14	01	21		12	06	05	
04	13	24	09		15	04	21		13	07	06	
05	14	25	09		16	04	22		14	09	06	
06	15	26	10	27	17	05	22	26	15	10	07	25
07	16	28	10		18	06	23		16	11	07	
08	17	29	10		19	08	23		17	12	08	
09	18	00♒	11		20	09	24		18	14	08	
10	19	01	11		21	10	24		19	15	09	
11	20	03	11	27	22	11	25	26	20	16	09	25
12	21	04	12		23	13	25		21	17	10	
13	22	05	12		24	14	26		22	18	10	
14	23	06	13		25	15	26		23	20	11	
15	24	08	13		26	16	27		24	21	11	
16	25	09	13	26	27	18	27	26	25	22	12	25
17	26	10	14		28	19	28		26	23	13	
18	27	11	14		29	20	28		27	25	13	
19	28	13	14		30	21	29		28	26	14	
20	29	14	15		01♓	23	29		29	27	14	
21	00♒	15	15	26	02	24	30	25	30	28	15	25
22	01	16	16		03	25	00♊		01♈	29	15	
23	02	18	16		04	26	01		02	01♉	16	
24	04	19	17		05	27	01		03	02	17	
25	05	20	17		06	29	02		04	03	17	
26	06	21	17	26	07	30	02	25	05	04	18	25
27	07	23	18		08	01♈	03		06	06	18	
28	08	24	18		09	02	03		07	07	19	
29	09	25	19						08	08	19	
30	10	26	19						09	09	20	
31	11	28	20	26					10	10	20	25

Day	APR ☉	APR ♀	APR ♂	APR ♆	MAY ☉	MAY ♀	MAY ♂	MAY ♆	JUN ☉	JUN ♀	JUN ♂	JUN ♆
01	11♈	12♉	21♊	25♌	10♉	17♊	08♋	24♌	10♊	23♋	27♋	24♌
02	12	13	22		11	19	09		11	24	28	
03	13	14	22		12	20	10		12	25	28	
04	14	15	23		13	21	10		13	26	29	
05	15	16	23		14	22	11		14	27	29	
06	16	18	24	24	15	23	11	24	15	28	00♌	24
07	17	19	24		16	24	12		16	29	01	
08	18	20	25		17	26	13		17	00♌	01	
09	19	21	26		18	27	13		18	02	02	
10	20	22	26		19	28	14		19	03	02	
11	21	24	27	24	20	29	14	24	20	04	03	25
12	22	25	27		21	00♋	15		21	05	04	
13	23	26	28		22	01	16		21	06	04	
14	24	27	29		23	02	16		22	07	05	
15	25	28	29		24	04	17		23	08	05	
16	26	30	30	24	25	05	17	24	24	09	06	25
17	26	01♊	00♋		26	06	18		25	10	07	
18	27	02	01		27	07	19		26	11	07	
19	28	03	01		28	08	19		27	12	08	
20	29	04	02		28	09	20		28	13	09	
21	00♉	06	03	24	29	10	20	24	29	14	09	25
22	01	07	03		00♊	12	21		00♋	15	10	
23	02	08	04		01	13	22		01	16	10	
24	03	09	04		02	14	22		02	17	11	
25	04	10	05		03	15	23		03	18	12	
26	05	12	06	24	04	16	23	24	04	19	12	25
27	06	13	06		05	17	24		05	20	13	
28	07	14	07		06	18	25		06	21	13	
29	08	15	07		07	19	25		07	22	14	
30	09	16	08		08	21	26		08	23	15	
31					09	22	26	24				

Day	JULY				AUGUST				SEPTEMBER			
	☉	♀	♂	♆	☉	♀	♂	♆	☉	♀	♂	♆
01	09♋	24♌	15♌	25♌	08♌	19♍	05♍	26♌	08♍	22♍	24♍	27♌
02	10	25	16		09	20	05		09	22	25	
03	10	26	17		10	20	06		10	21	25	
04	12	27	17		11	21	06		11	21	26	
05	12	28	18		12	21	07		12	20	27	
06	13	29	18	25	13	22	08	26	13	20	27	27
07	14	30	19		14	22	08		14	19	28	
08	15	01♍	20		15	22	09		15	18	29	
09	16	02	20		16	23	10		16	18	29	
10	17	02	21		16	23	10		16	17	30	
11	18	03	21	25	17	24	11	26	17	17	01♎	28
12	19	04	22		18	24	11		18	16	01	
13	20	05	23		20	24	12		20	15	02	
14	21	06	23		21	24	13		21	15	03	
15	22	07	24		22	25	13		22	14	03	
16	23	08	25	25	23	25	14	27	23	14	04	28
17	24	08	25		24	25	15		24	13	04	
18	25	09	26		25	25	15		25	12	05	
19	26	10	26		26	25	16		25	12	06	
20	27	11	27		26	25	16		27	12	06	
21	28	12	28	26	27	25	17	27	28	11	07	28
22	29	12	28		28	25	18		28	11	08	
23	30	13	29		29	25	18		29	10	08	
24	01♌	14	30		00♍	25	19		00♎	10	09	
25	02	15	00♍		01	25	20		01	10	10	
26	02	15	01	26	02	24	20	27	02	09	10	28
27	03	16	01		03	24	21		03	09	11	
28	04	17	02		04	24	22		04	09	12	
29	05	17	03		05	23	22		05	09	12	
30	06	18	03		06	23	23		06	09	13	
31	07	18	04	26	07	23	24	27				

Day	OCTOBER				NOVEMBER				DECEMBER			
	☉	♀	♂	♆	☉	♀	♂	♆	☉	♀	♂	♆
01	07♎	09♍	14♎	28♌	08♏	23♍	04♏	29♌	08♐	22♎	25♏	29♌
02	08	09	14		09	24	05		09	23	26	
03	09	09	15		10	25	06		10	24	27	
04	10	09	16		11	26	06		11	25	27	
05	11	09	16		12	26	07		12	26	28	
06	12	09	17	28	13	27	08	29	13	27	29	29
07	13	09	18		14	28	09		14	28	29	
08	14	10	18		15	29	09		15	30	00♐	
09	15	10	19		16	30	10		16	01♏	01	
10	16	10	20		17	01♎	11		17	02	01	
11	17	11	20	28	18	02	11	29	18	03	02	29
12	18	11	21		19	03	12		19	04	03	
13	19	11	22		20	04	13		20	05	04	
14	20	12	22		21	05	13		22	06	04	
15	21	12	23		22	06	14		23	07	05	
16	22	13	24	29	23	07	15	29	24	09	06	29
17	23	13	24		24	08	15		25	10	06	
18	24	14	25		25	09	16		26	11	07	
19	25	14	26		26	09	17		27	12	08	
20	26	15	26		27	10	17		28	13	09	
21	27	15	27	29	28	12	18	29	29	14	09	29
22	28	16	28		29	13	19		30	15	10	
23	29	17	28		00♐	14	20		01♑	17	11	
24	00♏	17	29		01	15	20		02	18	11	
25	01	18	30		02	16	21		03	19	12	
26	02	19	00♏	29	03	17	22	29	04	20	13	29
27	03	19	01		04	18	22		05	21	14	
28	04	20	02		05	19	23		06	22	14	
29	05	21	02		06	20	24		07	24	15	
30	06	22	03		07	21	24		08	25	16	
31	07	22	04	29					09	26	16	29

BIRTH TABLES · 1928

Day	JANUARY ☉	♀	♂	♆	FEBRUARY ☉	♀	♂	♆	MARCH ☉	♀	♂	♆	APRIL ☉	♀	♂	♆	MAY ☉	♀	♂	♆	JUNE ☉	♀	♂	♆
01	10♑	27♏	17♐	29♌	11♒	04♑	10♑	28♌	11♓	10♒	02♒	27♌	12♈	18♓	25♒	27♌	11♉	24♈	18♓	26♌	11♊	03♊	12♈	27♌
02	11	28	18		12	05	11		12	11	02		13	19	26		12	26	19		12	04	12	
03	12	29	19		13	07	11		13	12	03		13	20	27		13	27	20		13	05	13	
04	13	01♐	19		14	08	12		14	13	04		14	21	28		14	28	21		14	06	14	
05	14	02	20		15	09	13		15	15	05		15	23	28		15	29	21		15	07	15	
06	15	03	21	29	16	10	14	28	16	16	05	27	16	24	29	27	16	01♉	22	26	16	09	15	27
07	16	04	22		17	11	14		17	17	06		17	25	30		17	02	23		16	10	16	
08	17	05	22		18	13	15		18	18	07		18	26	01♓		18	03	24		17	11	17	
09	18	07	23		20	14	16		19	19	08		19	27	01		19	04	24		18	12	18	
10	19	08	24		21	15	16		20	21	09		20	29	02		20	06	25		19	14	18	
11	20	09	24	29	22	16	17	28	21	22	09	27	21	30	03	27	21	07	26	26	20	15	19	27
12	21	10	25		23	18	18		22	23	10		22	01♈	04		21	08	27		21	16	20	
13	22	11	26		24	19	19		23	24	11		23	02	05		22	09	27		22	17	21	
14	23	12	27		25	20	20		24	26	12		24	04	05		23	10	28		23	18	21	
15	24	14	27		26	21	20		25	27	12		25	05	06		24	12	29		24	20	22	
16	25	15	28	29	27	22	21	28	26	28	13	27	26	06	07	27	25	13	30	26	25	21	23	27
17	26	16	29		28	24	22		27	29	14		27	07	08		26	14	00♈		26	22	24	
18	27	17	30		29	25	23		28	00♓	15		28	09	08		27	15	01		27	23	24	
19	28	18	00♑		30	26	23		29	02	15		29	10	09		28	17	02		28	25	25	
20	29	20	01		01♓	27	24		30	03	16		00♉	11	10		29	18	03		29	26	26	
21	00♒	21	02	29	02	29	25	28	01♈	04	17	27	01	12	11	26	00♊	19	03	26	30	27	26	27
22	01	22	03		03	30	26		02	05	18		02	13	11		01	20	04		01♋	28	27	
23	02	23	03		04	01♒	26		03	07	18		03	15	12		02	21	05		02	30	28	
24	03	25	04		05	02	27		04	08	19		04	16	13		03	23	06		03	01♋	29	
25	04	26	05		06	03	28		05	09	20		05	17	14		04	24	07		04	02	29	
26	05	27	05	28	07	05	29	28	06	10	21	27	06	18	14	26	05	25	07	26	05	03	00♉	27
27	06	28	06		08	06	29		07	12	22		07	20	15		06	26	08		06	04	01	
28	07	29	07		09	07	00♒		08	13	22		08	21	16		07	28	09		07	05	02	
29	08	01♑	08		10	08	01		09	14	23		09	22	17		08	29	10		07	07	02	
30	09	02	08						10	15	24		10	23	18		09	00♊	10		08	08	03	
31	10	03	09	28					11	16	25	27					10	01	11	27				

Day	JULY ☉	♀	♂	♆	AUGUST ☉	♀	♂	♆	SEPTEMBER ☉	♀	♂	♆
01	09♋	09♋	04♉	27♌	09♌	18♌	25♉	28♌	09♍	26♍	14♊	29♌
02	10	11	04		10	19	26		10	27	15	
03	11	12	05		11	20	26		11	28	15	
04	12	13	06		12	21	27		12	29	16	
05	13	14	07		13	22	28		13	01♎	16	
06	14	15	07	27	14	24	28	28	14	02	17	29
07	15	17	08		15	25	29		15	03	18	
08	16	18	09		16	26	30		16	04	18	
09	17	19	09		17	27	00♊		17	06	19	
10	18	20	10		18	29	01		18	07	19	
11	19	22	11	27	19	30	01	29	18	08	20	30
12	20	23	11		19	01♍	02		19	09	20	
13	21	24	12		20	02	03		20	11	21	
14	22	25	13		21	04	03		21	12	21	
15	23	27	14		22	05	04		22	13	22	
16	24	28	14	28	23	06	05	29	23	14	22	30
17	25	29	15		24	07	05		24	15	23	
18	26	00♌	16		25	08	06		25	17	23	
19	27	01	16		26	10	06		26	18	24	
20	27	03	17		27	11	07		27	19	25	
21	28	04	18	28	28	12	08	29	28	20	25	30
22	29	05	18		29	13	09		29	22	25	
23	00♌	06	19		00♍	15	09		00♎	23	26	
24	01	08	20		01	16	10		01	24	26	
25	02	09	20		02	17	10		02	25	27	
26	03	10	21	28	03	18	11	29	03	27	27	00♍
27	04	11	22		04	20	11		04	28	28	
28	05	13	22		05	21	12		05	29	28	
29	06	14	23		06	22	13		06	00♏	29	
30	07	15	24		07	23	13		07	01	29	
31	08	16	24	28	08	25	14	29				

Day	OCTOBER ☉	♀	♂	♆	NOVEMBER ☉	♀	♂	♆	DECEMBER ☉	♀	♂	♆
01	09♎	03♏	29♊	00♍	09♏	11♐	09♋	01♍	09♐	17♑	07♋	01♍
02	09	04	30		10	12	09		10	19	06	
03	10	05	00♋		11	13	09		11	20	06	
04	11	06	01		12	14	09		12	21	06	
05	12	08	01		13	16	09		13	22	05	
06	13	09	01	00	14	17	09	01	14	23	05	01
07	14	10	02		15	18	09		15	25	05	
08	15	11	02		16	19	09		16	26	04	
09	16	13	02		17	21	09		17	27	04	
10	17	14	03		18	22	09		18	28	04	
11	18	15	03	01	19	23	09	01	19	29	03	01
12	19	16	03		20	24	09		20	01♒	03	
13	20	17	04		21	25	09		21	02	03	
14	21	19	04		22	27	09		22	03	02	
15	22	20	05		23	28	09		23	04	02	
16	23	21	05	01	24	29	09	01	24	05	01	01
17	24	22	05		25	00♑	09		25	07	01	
18	25	24	05		26	02	09		26	08	01	
19	26	25	06		27	03	09		27	09	00	
20	27	26	06		28	04	09		28	10	30♊	
21	28	27	06	01	29	05	09	01	29	11	30	01
22	29	29	07		30	06	09		00♑	12	29	
23	30	30	07		01♐	08	08		01	14	29	
24	01♏	01♐	07		02	09	08		02	15	28	
25	02	02	07		03	10	08		03	16	28	
26	03	03	07	01	04	11	08	01	04	17	28	01
27	04	05	08		05	12	08		06	18	27	
28	05	06	08		06	14	07		07	20	27	
29	06	07	08		07	15	07		08	21	26	
30	07	08	08		08	16	07		09	22	26	
31	08	10	08	01					10	23	26	01

BIRTH TABLES - 1929

Day	JAN ☉	JAN ♀	JAN ♂	JAN ♆	FEB ☉	FEB ♀	FEB ♂	FEB ♆	MAR ☉	MAR ♀	MAR ♂	MAR ♆
01	11♑	24♒	25♊	01♍	12♒	29♓	21♊	00♍	10♓	25♈	27♊	30♌
02	12	25	25		13	30	21		11	26	27	
03	13	27	25		14	01♈	21		12	27	27	
04	14	28	25		15	02	21		13	27	28	
05	15	29	24		16	03	21		14	28	28	
06	16	00♓	24	01	17	04	22	00	15	29	28	30
07	17	01	24		18	05	22		16	29	29	
08	18	02	23		19	06	22		17	00♉	29	
09	19	03	23		20	07	22		18	01	29	
10	20	05	23		21	08	22		19	01	30	
11	21	06	23	01	22	09	22	00	20	02	00♋	29
12	22	07	22		23	10	23		21	03	01	
13	23	08	22		24	11	23		22	03	01	
14	24	09	22		25	12	23		23	04	01	
15	25	10	22		26	13	23		24	04	02	
16	26	11	22	01	27	14	23	00	25	05	02	29
17	27	13	22		28	15	24		26	05	03	
18	28	14	22		29	16	24		27	06	03	
19	29	15	21		00♓	17	24		28	06	03	
20	30	16	21		01	18	24		29	06	04	
21	01♒	17	21	01	02	18	24	30♌	00♈	07	04	29
22	02	18	21		03	19	25		01	07	5	
23	03	19	21		04	20	25		02	07	05	
24	04	20	21		05	21	25		03	07	05	
25	05	21	21		06	22	26		04	08	06	
26	06	22	21	01	07	23	26	30	05	08	06	29
27	07	24	21		08	24	26		06	08	07	
28	08	25	21		09	24	26		07	08	07	
29	09	26	21						08	08	08	
30	10	27	21						09	08	08	
31	11	28	21	01					10	08	09	29

Day	APR ☉	APR ♀	APR ♂	APR ♆	MAY ☉	MAY ♀	MAY ♂	MAY ♆	JUN ☉	JUN ♀	JUN ♂	JUN ♆
01	11♈	08♉	09♋	29♌	11♉	24♈	24♋	29♌	10♊	29♈	11♌	29♌
02	12	08	09		12	23	24		11	29	11	
03	13	08	10		13	23	25		12	00♉	12	
04	14	07	10		14	23	25		13	01	13	
05	15	07	11		14	22	26		14	01	13	
06	16	07	11	29	15	22	26	29	15	02	14	29
07	17	07	12		16	22	27		16	03	14	
08	18	06	12		17	22	28		17	04	15	
09	19	06	13		18	22	28		18	04	15	
10	20	05	13		19	22	29		19	05	16	
11	21	05	14	29	20	22	29	29	20	06	17	29
12	22	04	14		21	22	30		21	07	17	
13	23	04	15		22	22	00♌		22	07	18	
14	24	03	15		23	22	01		23	08	18	
15	25	03	16		24	22	01		24	09	19	
16	26	02	16	29	25	22	02	29	25	10	19	29
17	27	02	17		26	22	02		26	11	20	
18	28	01	17		27	23	03		27	12	21	
19	29	00♉	18		28	23	04		28	12	21	
20	30	30♈	18		29	23	04		29	13	22	
21	01♉	29	19	29	30	23	05	29	30	14	22	29
22	02	28	19		01♊	24	05		01♋	15	23	
23	03	28	20		02	24	06		02	16	24	
24	04	27	20		03	25	06		02	17	24	
25	05	27	21		04	25	07		03	18	25	
26	06	26	21	29	05	25	07	29	04	19	25	29
27	07	26	22		06	26	08		05	20	26	
28	08	25	22		07	27	09		06	21	26	
29	09	25	23		08	27	09		07	22	27	
30	10	24	23		09	28	10		08	23	28	
31					10	28	10	29				

Day	JULY ☉	♀	♂	♆	AUGUST ☉	♀	♂	♆	SEPTEMBER ☉	♀	♂	♆
01	09♋	24♉	28♌	29♌	09♌	26♊	17♍	00♍	09♍	01♌	07♎	01♍
02	10	24	29		10	27	18		10	02	07	
03	11	25	29		11	28	18		10	04	08	
04	12	26	00♍		12	29	19		11	05	09	
05	13	27	00		13	00♋	20		12	06	09	
06	14	28	01	29	14	01	20	00	13	07	10	02
07	15	29	02		14	03	21		14	08	11	
08	16	00♊	02		15	04	22		15	09	11	
09	17	01	03		16	05	22		16	11	12	
10	18	02	04		17	06	23		17	12	13	
11	19	03	04	30	18	07	23	01	18	13	13	02
12	20	05	05		19	08	24		19	14	14	
13	21	06	05		20	09	25		20	15	15	
14	22	07	06		21	10	25		21	17	15	
15	22	08	07		22	12	26		22	18	16	
16	23	09	07	30	23	13	27	01	23	19	17	02
17	24	10	08		24	14	27		24	20	17	
18	25	11	09		25	15	28		25	21	18	
19	26	12	09		26	16	28		26	23	19	
20	27	13	10		27	17	29		27	24	19	
21	28	14	10	30♌	28	18	30	01	28	25	20	02
22	29	15	11		29	20	00♎		29	26	21	
23	00♌	16	12		30	21	01		30	27	21	
24	01	17	12		01♍	22	02		01♎	29	22	
25	02	18	13		02	23	02		02	30	23	
26	03	19	13	00♍	03	24	03	01	03	01♍	23	02
27	04	20	14		04	25	04		04	02	24	
28	05	21	15		05	27	04		05	03	25	
29	06	23	15		06	28	05		06	05	25	
30	07	24	16		07	29	06		07	06	26	
31	08	25	17	00	08	00♌	06	01				

Day	OCTOBER ☉	♀	♂	♆	NOVEMBER ☉	♀	♂	♆	DECEMBER ☉	♀	♂	♆
01	08♎	07♍	27♎	02♍	09♏	15♎	18♏	03♍	09♐	22♏	09♐	04♍
02	09	08	27		10	16	19		10	24	10	
03	10	10	28		11	18	19		11	25	11	
04	11	11	29		12	19	20		12	27	12	
05	12	12	29		13	20	21		13	28	12	
06	13	13	00♏	03	14	21	21	03	14	29	13	04
07	14	14	01		15	23	22		15	00♐	14	
08	15	16	01		16	24	23		16	02	14	
09	16	17	02		17	25	24		17	03	15	
10	17	18	03		18	26	24		18	04	16	
11	18	19	03	03	19	28	25	03	19	05	17	04
12	19	21	04		20	29	26		20	07	17	
13	20	22	05		21	00♏	26		21	08	18	
14	21	23	05		22	01	27		22	09	19	
15	22	24	06		23	03	28		23	10	20	
16	23	25	07	03	24	04	29	03	24	12	20	04
17	24	27	08		25	05	29		25	13	21	
18	25	28	08		26	06	30		26	14	22	
19	26	29	09		27	08	01♐		27	15	23	
20	27	00♎	09		28	09	01		28	17	23	
21	28	02	10	03	29	10	02	04	29	18	24	04
22	29	03	11		30	11	03		00♑	19	25	
23	30	04	12		01♐	13	04		01	20	26	
24	01♏	05	12		02	14	04		02	22	26	
25	02	07	13		03	15	05		03	23	27	
26	03	08	14	03	04	16	06	04	04	24	28	03
27	04	09	14		05	18	06		05	25	29	
28	05	10	15		06	19	07		06	27	29	
29	06	12	16		07	20	08		07	28	00♑	
30	07	13	17		08	21	09		08	29	01	
31	08	14	17	03					09	00♑	02	03

BIRTH TABLES - 1930

Day	JANUARY ☉	♀	♂	♆	FEBRUARY ☉	♀	♂	♆	MARCH ☉	♀	♂	♆
01	10♑	02♑	02♑	03♍	12♒	11♒	26♑	03♍	10♓	16♓	18♒	02♍
02	11	03	03		13	12	27		11	17	18	
03	12	04	04		14	13	27		12	18	19	
04	13	05	05		15	14	28		13	19	20	
05	14	07	05		16	16	29		14	21	21	
06	15	08	06	03	17	17	30	03	15	22	22	02
07	16	09	07		18	18	01♒		16	23	22	
08	18	11	08		19	19	01		17	24	23	
09	19	12	08		20	21	02		18	26	24	
10	20	13	09		21	22	03		19	27	25	
11	21	14	10	03	22	23	04	03	20	28	26	02
12	22	16	11		23	24	04		21	29	26	
13	23	17	11		24	26	05		22	01♈	27	
14	24	18	12		25	27	06		23	02	28	
15	25	19	13		26	28	07		24	03	29	
16	26	21	14	03	27	29	08	02	25	04	29	02
17	27	22	14		28	01♓	08		26	06	00♓	
18	28	23	15		29	02	09		27	07	01	
19	29	24	16		00♓	03	10		28	08	02	
20	30	26	17		01	04	11		29	09	03	
21	01♒	27	17	03	02	06	11	02	00♈	11	03	01
22	02	28	18		03	07	12		01	12	04	
23	03	29	19		04	08	13		02	13	05	
24	04	01♒	20		05	10	14		03	14	06	
25	05	02	21		06	11	15		04	16	06	
26	06	03	21	03	07	12	15	02	05	17	07	01
27	07	04	22		08	13	16		06	18	08	
28	08	06	23		09	15	17		07	19	09	
29	09	07	24						08	21	10	
30	10	08	24						09	22	10	
31	11	09	25	03					10	23	11	01

Day	APRIL ☉	♀	♂	♆	MAY ☉	♀	♂	♆	JUNE ☉	♀	♂	♆
01	11♈	24♈	12♓	01♍	10♉	01♊	05♈	01♍	10♊	09♋	29♈	01♍
02	12	26	13		11	02	06		11	10	30	
03	13	27	14		12	04	07		12	11	00♉	
04	14	28	14		13	05	08		13	12	01	
05	15	29	15		14	06	08		14	14	02	
06	16	00♉	16	01	15	07	09	01	15	15	03	01
07	17	02	17		16	09	10		16	16	03	
08	18	03	17		17	10	11		17	17	04	
09	19	04	18		18	11	11		18	18	05	
10	20	05	19		19	12	12		19	20	05	
11	21	07	20	01	20	13	13	01	20	21	06	01
12	22	08	21		21	15	14		21	22	07	
13	23	09	21		22	16	14		22	23	08	
14	24	10	22		23	17	15		23	24	08	
15	25	12	23		24	18	16		24	26	09	
16	26	13	24	01	25	19	17	01	25	27	10	01
17	27	14	24		26	21	17		26	28	11	
18	28	15	25		27	22	18		27	29	11	
19	29	17	26		28	23	19		27	00♌	12	
20	30	18	27		29	24	20		28	02	13	
21	01♉	19	28	01	30	26	21	01	29	03	13	01
22	02	20	28		01♊	27	21		00♋	04	14	
23	03	21	29		02	28	22		01	05	15	
24	04	23	30		03	29	23		02	06	16	
25	05	24	01♈		04	00♋	24		03	08	16	
26	06	25	01	01	04	02	24	01	04	09	17	01
27	06	26	02		05	03	25		05	10	18	
28	07	28	03		06	04	26		06	11	19	
29	08	29	04		07	05	27		07	12	19	
30	09	30	04		08	06	27		08	13	20	
31					09	08	28	01				

Part Two / **BIRTH TABLES 1930**   169

	JULY ☉	♀	♂	Ψ	AUGUST ☉	♀	♂	Ψ	SEPTEMBER ☉	♀	♂	Ψ	OCTOBER ☉	♀	♂	Ψ	NOVEMBER ☉	♀	♂	Ψ	DECEMBER ☉	♀	♂	Ψ
01	09♋	15♌	21♉	01♍	08♌	20♍	12♊	02♍	08♍	24♎	03♋	04♍	08♎	22♏	20♋	05♍	08♏	07♐	05♌	05♍	09♐	25♏	15♌	06♍
02	10	16	21		09	22	13		09	25	03		09	23	21		09	07	06		10	24	15	
03	11	17	22		10	23	14		10	26	04		10	24	21		10	07	06		11	24	15	
04	12	18	23		11	24	14		11	27	04		11	25	22		11	07	07		12	24	16	
05	13	19	24		12	25	15		12	28	05		12	25	22		12	07	07		13	23	16	
06	14	20	24	02	13	26	16	03	13	29	06	04	13	26	23	05	13	07	07	05	14	23	16	06
07	15	22	25		14	27	16		14	00♏	06		13	27	23		14	07	08		15	23	16	
08	16	23	26		15	28	17		15	01	07		14	28	24		15	07	08		16	23	16	
09	17	24	26		16	29	18		16	02	07		15	28	24		16	06	09		17	22	16	
10	17	25	27		17	01♎	18		17	03	08		16	29	25		17	06	09		18	22	16	
11	18	26	28	02	18	02	19	03	18	04	09	04	17	30	25	05	18	06	09	06	19	22	16	06
12	19	27	29		19	03	20		19	05	09		18	00♐	26		19	05	10		20	22	17	
13	20	29	29		20	04	20		20	06	10		19	01	26		20	05	10		21	22	17	
14	21	30	30		21	05	21		21	07	10		20	01	27		21	04	10		22	22	17	
15	22	01♍	01♊		22	06	22		22	08	11		21	02	28		22	04	11		23	22	17	
16	23	02	01	02	23	07	22	03	23	09	12	04	22	03	28	05	23	03	11	06	24	22	17	06
17	24	03	02		24	08	23		24	10	12		23	03	28		24	03	11		25	22	17	
18	25	04	03		25	09	24		25	11	13		24	04	29		25	02	12		26	23	17	
19	26	06	03		26	10	24		26	12	13		25	04	29		26	02	12		27	23	17	
20	27	07	04		27	11	25		27	13	14		26	04	30		27	01	12		28	23	17	
21	28	08	05	02	28	13	26	03	28	14	15	04	27	05	00♌	05	28	01	13	06	29	23	17	06
22	29	09	06		29	14	26		29	15	15		28	05	01		29	30	13		30	24	17	
23	30	10	06		30	15	27		30	16	16		29	06	01		00♐	29♏	13		01♑	24	17	
24	01♌	11	07		01♍	16	27		01♎	16	16		00♏	06	02		01	29	13		02	24	17	
25	02	12	08		02	17	28		02	17	17		01	06	02		03	28	14		03	25	16	
26	03	14	08	02	03	18	29	03	03	18	17	04	02	07	03	05	04	28	14	06	04	25	16	06
27	04	15	09		03	19	29		04	19	18		03	07	03		05	27	14		05	26	16	
28	05	16	10		04	20	00♋		05	20	18		04	07	04		06	26	14		06	26	16	
29	06	17	10		05	21	01		06	21	19		05	07	04		07	26	15		07	27	16	
30	07	18	11		06	22	01		07	22	20		06	07	05		08	25	15		08	27	16	
31	08	19	12	02	07	23	02	03					07	07	05	05					09	28	16	06

BIRTH TABLES - 1931

Day	JAN ☉	JAN ♀	JAN ♂	JAN ♆	FEB ☉	FEB ♀	FEB ♂	FEB ♆	MAR ☉	MAR ♀	MAR ♂	MAR ♆	APR ☉	APR ♀	APR ♂	APR ♆	MAY ☉	MAY ♀	MAY ♂	MAY ♆	JUN ☉	JUN ♀	JUN ♂	JUN ♆
01	10♑	29♏	16♌	06♍	12♒	25♐	05♌	05♍	10♓	25♑	28♋	04♍	11♈	01♓	01♌	03♍	10♉	06♈	11♌	03♍	10♊	14♉	25♌	03♍
02	11	29	15		13	26	05		11	26	28		12	02	01		11	08	11		11	15	26	
03	12	30	15		14	27	04		12	27	28		13	03	01		12	09	12		12	16	26	
04	13	00♐	15		15	28	04		13	28	28		14	04	01		13	10	12		13	17	27	
05	14	01	15		16	29	04		14	30	27		15	06	02		14	11	12		14	19	27	
06	15	02	14	06	17	30	03	05	15	01♒	27	04	16	07	02	03	15	12	13	03	15	20	28	03
07	16	03	14		18	01♑	03		16	02	27		17	08	02		16	14	13		16	21	28	
08	17	03	14		19	02	02		17	03	27		18	09	02		17	15	14		17	22	29	
09	18	04	14		20	03	02		18	04	27		19	10	03		18	16	14		18	23	29	
10	19	05	13		21	04	02		19	05	27		20	11	03		19	17	15		19	25	30	
11	20	06	13	05	22	05	01	05	20	06	27	04	21	13	03	03	20	18	15	03	20	26	00♍	03
12	21	06	13		23	06	01		21	08	28		22	14	04		21	20	16		21	27	01	
13	22	07	12		24	07	01		22	09	28		23	15	04		22	21	16		22	28	02	
14	23	08	12		25	08	01		23	10	28		24	16	04		23	22	16		22	29	02	
15	24	09	12		26	10	00		24	11	28		25	17	05		24	23	17		23	01♊	03	
16	25	10	11	05	27	11	00	05	25	12	28	04	26	19	05	03	25	24	17	03	24	02	03	03
17	26	11	11		28	12	30♋		26	13	28		27	20	05		26	26	18		25	03	04	
18	27	12	11		29	13	30		27	14	28		27	21	06		27	27	18		26	04	04	
19	28	12	10		30	14	29		28	16	28		28	22	06		28	28	19		27	06	05	
20	29	13	10		01♓	15	29		29	17	28		29	23	06		29	29	19		28	07	05	
21	00♒	14	09	05	02	16	29	04	30	18	28	04	00♉	25	07	03	29	00♉	20	03	29	08	06	03
22	02	15	09		03	17	29		01♈	19	29		01	26	07		00♊	02	20		00♋	09	06	
23	03	16	09		04	18	29		02	20	29		02	27	08		01	03	21		01	10	07	
24	04	17	08		05	19	28		03	21	29		03	28	08		02	04	21		02	12	08	
25	05	18	08		06	21	28		04	23	29		04	29	08		03	05	22		03	13	08	
26	06	19	07	05	07	22	28	04	05	24	29	04	05	01♈	09	03	04	07	22	03	04	14	09	03
27	07	20	07		08	23	28		06	25	29		06	02	09		05	08	23		05	15	09	
28	08	21	07		09	24	28		07	26	30		07	03	09		06	09	23		06	16	10	
29	09	22	06						08	27	30		08	04	10		07	10	24		07	18	10	
30	10	23	06						09	28	00♌		09	05	10		08	11	24		08	19	11	
31	11	24	05	05					10	30	00	04					09	13	25	03				

Day	☉	♀	♂	♆	☉	♀	♂	♆	☉	♀	♂	♆
	JULY				**AUGUST**				**SEPTEMBER**			
01	09♋	20♊	12♍	04♍	08♌	28♋	30	05♍	08♍	06♍	20♎	06♍
02	10	21	12		09	29	01♎		09	08	20	
03	11	23	13		10	00♌	01		10	09	21	
04	12	24	13		11	02	02		11	10	21	
05	13	25	14		12	03	02		12	11	22	
06	13	26	14	04	13	04	03	05	13	12	23	06
07	14	27	15		14	05	04		14	14	23	
08	15	29	16		15	07	04		15	15	24	
09	16	30	16		16	08	05		16	16	25	
10	17	01♋	17		17	09	05		17	17	25	
11	18	02	17	04	18	10	06	05	18	19	26	06
12	19	03	18		19	12	07		19	20	27	
13	20	05	18		20	13	07		20	21	27	
14	21	06	19		21	14	08		21	22	28	
15	22	07	20		22	15	09		22	24	29	
16	23	08	20	04	23	16	09	05	23	25	29	06
17	24	10	21		24	18	10		24	26	00♏	
18	25	11	21		25	19	11		25	27	01	
19	26	12	22		26	20	11		26	29	01	
20	27	13	23		27	21	12		27	30	02	
21	28	14	23	04	27	23	12	05	28	01♎	03	06
22	29	16	24		28	24	13		29	02	03	
23	30	17	24		29	25	14		30	04	04	
24	01♌	18	25		00♍	26	14		00♎	05	05	
25	02	19	26		01	28	15		01	06	06	
26	03	21	26	04	02	29	16	05	02	07	06	07
27	03	22	27		03	00♍	16		03	09	07	
28	04	23	27		04	01	17		04	10	08	
29	05	24	28		05	03	18	06	05	11	08	
30	06	26	29		06	04	18		06	12	09	
31	07	27	29	04	07	05	19	06				

Day	☉	♀	♂	♆	☉	♀	♂	♆	☉	♀	♂	♆
	OCTOBER				**NOVEMBER**				**DECEMBER**			
01	07♎	14♎	10♏	07♍	08♏	22♏	01♐	08♍	08♐	30♐	24♐	08♍
02	08	15	10		09	24	02		09	01♑	24	
03	09	16	11		10	25	03		10	02	25	
04	10	17	12		11	26	04		11	03	26	
05	11	19	12		12	27	04		12	05	27	
06	12	20	13	07	13	29	05	08	13	06	27	08
07	13	21	14		14	30	06		14	07	28	
08	14	22	14		15	01♐	07		15	08	29	
09	15	24	15		16	02	07		16	10	30	
10	16	25	16		17	04	08		17	11	00♑	
11	17	26	17	07	18	05	09	08	18	12	01	08
12	18	27	17		19	06	09		20	13	02	
13	19	29	18		20	07	10		21	15	03	
14	20	30	18		21	09	11		22	16	03	
15	21	01♏	19		22	10	12		23	17	04	
16	22	02	20	07	23	11	12	08	24	18	05	08
17	23	04	21		24	12	13		25	20	06	
18	24	05	21		25	14	14		26	21	06	
19	25	06	22		26	15	15		27	22	07	
20	26	07	23		27	16	15		28	23	08	
21	27	09	24	07	28	17	16	08	29	25	09	08
22	28	10	24		29	19	17		30	26	09	
23	29	11	25		00♐	20	18		01♑	27	10	
24	00♏	12	26		01	21	18		02	28	11	
25	01	14	26		02	22	19		03	30	12	
26	02	15	27	07	03	23	20	08	04	01♒	13	08
27	03	16	28		04	25	21		05	02	13	
28	04	17	29		05	26	21		06	03	14	
29	05	19	29		06	27	22		07	05	15	
30	06	20	30		07	28	23		08	06	16	
31	07	21	01♐	08					09	07	16	08

BIRTH TABLES - 1932

Day	JANUARY ☉	♀	♂	♆	FEBRUARY ☉	♀	♂	♆	MARCH ☉	♀	♂	♆
01	10♑	08♒	17♑	08♍	11♒	16♓	11♒	07♍	11♓	21♈	04♓	07♍
02	11	10	18		12	18	12		12	22	05	06
03	12	11	19		13	19	13		13	24	06	
04	13	12	19		14	20	14		14	25	07	
05	14	13	20		15	21	15		15	26	07	
06	15	14	21	08	17	23	15	07	16	27	08	06
07	16	16	22		18	24	16		17	28	09	
08	17	17	23		19	25	17		18	29	10	
09	18	18	23		20	26	18		19	00♉	11	
10	19	19	24		21	27	18		20	02	11	
11	20	21	25	08	22	29	19	07	21	03	12	06
12	21	22	26		23	30	20		22	04	13	
13	22	23	26		24	01♈	21		23	05	14	
14	23	24	27	07	25	02	22		24	06	15	
15	24	26	28		26	03	22		25	07	15	
16	25	27	29	07	27	05	23	07	26	09	16	06
17	26	28	30		28	06	24		27	10	17	
18	27	29	00♒		29	07	25		28	11	18	
19	28	01♓	01		30	08	26		29	12	18	
20	29	02	02		01♓	09	26		30	13	19	
21	00♒	03	03	07	02	11	27	07	01♈	14	20	06
22	01	04	04		03	12	28		02	15	21	
23	02	06	04		04	13	29		03	16	22	
24	03	07	05		05	14	30		04	17	22	
25	04	08	06		06	15	00♓		05	19	23	
26	05	09	07	07	07	16	01	07	06	20	24	06
27	06	10	07		08	18	02		07	21	25	
28	07	12	08		09	19	03		08	22	26	
29	08	13	09		10	20	03		09	23	26	
30	09	14	10						10	24	27	
31	10	15	11	07					11	25	28	06

Day	APRIL ☉	♀	♂	♆	MAY ☉	♀	♂	♆	JUNE ☉	♀	♂	♆
01	12♈	26♉	29♓	06♍	11♉	26♊	22♈	05♍	11♊	14♋	15♉	05♍
02	13	27	29		12	27	22		12	15	16	
03	14	28	00♈		13	28	23		13	15	16	
04	15	29	01		14	28	24		14	15	17	
05	15	01♊	02		15	29	25		15	15	18	
06	16	02	03	06	16	00♋	26	05	16	15	19	05
07	17	03	03		17	01	26		17	15	19	
08	18	04	04		18	02	27		17	15	20	
09	19	05	05		19	02	28		18	15	21	
10	20	06	06		20	03	29		19	15	21	
11	21	07	06	06	21	04	29	05	20	15	22	05
12	22	08	07		22	05	00♉		21	15	23	
13	23	09	08	05	22	05	01		22	15	24	
14	24	10	09		23	06	02		23	15	24	
15	25	11	09		24	07	02		24	14	25	
16	26	12	10	05	25	07	03	05	25	14	26	05
17	27	13	11		26	08	04		26	14	27	
18	28	14	12		27	09	05		27	13	27	06
19	29	15	13		28	09	05		28	13	28	
20	00♉	16	13		29	10	06		29	12	29	
21	01	17	14	05	00♊	10	07	05	30	12	29	06
22	02	18	15		01	11	08		01♋	11	00♊	
23	03	19	16	05	02	11	09		02	11	01	
24	04	20	16		03	12	09		03	10	02	
25	05	21	17		04	12	10		04	09	02	
26	06	21	18	05	05	13	10	05	05	09	03	06
27	07	22	19		06	13	11		06	08	04	
28	08	23	19		07	14	12		07	08	04	
29	09	24	20		08	14	13		07	07	05	
30	10	25	21		09	14	13		08	06	06	
31					10	14	14	05				

Day	JULY ☉	♀	♂	♆	AUGUST ☉	♀	♂	♆	SEPTEMBER ☉	♀	♂	♆	OCTOBER ☉	♀	♂	♆	NOVEMBER ☉	♀	♂	♆	DECEMBER ☉	♀	♂	♆
01	09♋	06♋	06♊	06♍	09♌	01♋	28♊	06♍	09♍	23♋	18♋	08♍	08♎	24♌	07♌	09♍	09♏	29♍	24♌	10♍	09♐	06♏	08♍	10♍
02	10	05	07		10	02	29		10	24	19		09	25	07		10	00♎	24		10	07	08	
03	11	05	08		11	02	29		11	25	19		10	26	08		11	02	25		11	08	09	
04	12	04	09		12	03	30		12	26	20		11	27	08		12	03	25		12	09	09	
05	13	03	09		13	03	00♋		13	27	21		12	28	09		13	04	26		13	10	10	
06	14	04	10	06	14	04	01	06	14	28	21	08	13	29	09	09	14	05	26	10	14	12	10	10
07	15	02	11		15	04	02		15	29	22		14	00♍	10		15	06	27		15	13	10	
08	16	02	11		16	05	03		16	30	22		15	01	10		16	08	27		16	14	11	
09	17	01	12		17	05	03		17	01♌	23		16	03	11		17	09	28		17	15	11	
10	18	01	13		18	06	04		18	02	24		17	04	12		18	10	28		18	17	12	
11	19	01	13	06	19	07	04	06	19	03	24	08	18	05	12	09	19	11	29	10	19	18	12	10
12	20	00	14		20	07	05		19	04	25		19	06	13		20	12	29		20	19	12	
13	21	30♊	15		21	08	06		20	05	26		20	07	13		21	14	30		21	20	13	
14	22	30	16		21	08	06		21	06	26		21	08	14		22	15	00♍		22	22	13	
15	23	29	16		22	09	07		22	07	27		22	09	14		23	16	01		23	23	13	
16	24	29	17	06	23	10	08	06	23	08	27	08	23	11	15	09	24	17	01	10	24	24	14	10
17	25	29	18		24	11	08		24	09	28		24	12	16		25	18	02		25	25	14	
18	26	29	18		25	11	09		25	10	29		25	13	16		26	20	02		26	27	14	
19	27	29	19		26	12	10		26	11	29		26	14	17		27	21	03		27	28	15	
20	28	29	20		27	13	10		27	12	30		27	15	17		28	22	03		28	29	15	
21	28	29	20	06	28	14	11	06	28	13	00♌	09	28	16	18	09	29	23	04	10	29	00♐	15	10
22	29	29	21		29	14	12		29	14	01		29	17	18		30	25	04		00♑	01	16	
23	00♌	29	22		00♍	15	12		00♎	15	02		30	19	19	10	01♐	26	05		01	03	16	
24	01	29	22		01	16	13		01	16	02		01♏	20	19		02	27	05		02	04	16	
25	02	29	23		02	17	14		02	17	03		02	21	20		03	28	05		04	05	16	
26	03	30	24	06	03	18	14	06	03	18	03	09	03	22	21	10	04	29	06	10	05	06	17	10
27	04	30	24	07	04	19	15	07	04	19	04		04	23	21		05	01♏	06		06	08	17	
28	05	00♋	25		05	20	15		05	20	05		05	24	22		06	02	07		07	09	17	
29	06	00	26		06	20	16		06	21	05		06	26	22		07	03	07		08	10	17	
30	07	01	26		07	21	17		07	23	06		07	27	23		08	04	08		09	11	18	
31	08	01	27	07	08	22	17	07					08	28	23	10					10	13	18	10

BIRTH TABLES · 1933

	JANUARY				FEBRUARY				MARCH			
	☉	♀	♂	♆	☉	♀	♂	♆	☉	♀	♂	♆
01	11♑	14♐	18♍	10♍	12♒	23♑	19♍	10♍	10♓	28♒	11♍	09♍
02	12	15	18		13	24	19	09	11	29	11	
03	13	16	19		14	25	19		12	00♓	10	
04	14	18	19		15	26	19		13	01	10	
05	15	19	19		16	28	19		14	03	09	
06	16	20	19	10	17	29	19	09	14	04	09	09
07	17	21	19		18	00♒	18		16	05	09	
08	18	23	19		19	01	18		17	06	08	
09	19	24	19		20	03	18		18	08	08	
10	20	25	20		21	04	18		19	09	07	
11	21	26	20	10	22	05	17	09	20	10	07	09
12	22	28	20		23	06	17		21	11	07	08
13	23	29	20		24	08	17		22	13	06	
14	24	00♑	20		25	09	16		23	14	06	
15	25	01	20		26	10	16		24	15	06	
16	26	03	20	10	27	11	16	09	25	16	05	08
17	27	04	20		28	13	15		26	17	05	
18	28	05	20		29	14	15		27	19	05	
19	29	06	20		00♓	15	15		28	20	04	
20	00♒	08	20		01	16	14		29	21	04	
21	01	09	20	10	02	18	14	09	00♈	22	04	08
22	02	10	20		03	19	14		01	24	04	
23	03	11	20		04	20	13		02	25	03	
24	04	13	20		05	21	13		03	26	03	
25	05	14	20		06	23	13		04	27	03	
26	06	15	20	10	07	24	12	09	05	29	03	08
27	07	16	20		08	25	12		06	30	02	
28	08	18	20		09	26	11		07	01♈	02	
29	09	19	20						08	02	02	
30	10	20	20						09	04	02	
31	11	21	20	10					10	05	02	08

	APRIL				MAY				JUNE			
	☉	♀	♂	♆	☉	♀	♂	♆	☉	♀	♂	♆
01	11♈	06♈	02♍	08♍	11♉	13♉	03♍	07♍	11♊	21♊	13♍	07♍
02	12	07	01		12	14	03		11	23	13	
03	13	09	01		13	16	03		12	24	14	
04	14	10	01		14	17	04		13	25	14	
05	15	11	01		15	18	04		14	26	15	
06	16	12	01	08	15	19	04	07	15	28	15	07
07	17	14	01		16	21	04		16	29	15	
08	18	15	01		17	22	05		17	30	16	
09	19	16	01		18	23	05		18	01♋	16	
10	20	17	01		19	24	05		19	02	17	
11	21	19	01	08	20	26	05	07	20	04	17	08
12	22	20	01		21	27	06		21	05	18	
13	23	21	01		22	28	06		22	06	18	
14	24	22	01		23	29	06		23	07	19	
15	25	23	01		24	00♊	07		24	09	19	
16	26	25	01	08	25	02	07	07	25	10	20	08
17	27	26	01		26	03	07		26	11	20	
18	28	27	01		27	04	08		27	12	21	
19	29	28	01		28	05	08		28	13	21	
20	30	30	01		29	07	08		29	15	22	
21	01♉	01♉	01	08	30	08	09	07	30	16	22	08
22	02	02	02		01♊	09	09		01♋	17	23	
23	03	03	02		02	10	09		02	18	23	
24	04	05	02		03	12	10		02	20	24	
25	05	06	02		04	13	10		03	21	24	
26	06	07	02	08	05	14	11	07	04	22	25	08
27	07	08	02		06	15	11		05	23	25	
28	08	10	02		07	16	11		06	25	26	
29	09	11	03		08	18	12		07	26	26	
30	10	12	03	07	09	19	12		08	27	27	
31					10	20	13	07				

	JULY				AUGUST				SEPTEMBER				OCTOBER				NOVEMBER				DECEMBER			
	☉	♀	♂	♆	☉	♀	♂	♆	☉	♀	♂	♆	☉	♀	♂	♆	☉	♀	♂	♆	☉	♀	♂	♆
01	09♋	28♋	27♍	08♍	09♌	06♍	15♎	09♍	09♍	13♎	04♏	10♍	08♎	19♏	24♏	11♍	09♏	24♐	17♐	11♍	09♐	26♑	09♑	12♍
02	10	29	28		10	07	15		10	14	05		09	20	25		10	25	17		10	27	10	
03	11	01♌	28		11	08	16		11	16	05		10	21	26		11	27	18		11	28	11	
04	12	02	29		12	09	16		11	17	06		11	22	26		12	28	19		12	29	12	
05	13	03	29		13	11	17		12	18	07		12	23	27		13	29	20		13	30	12	
06	14	04	30	08	14	12	18	09	13	19	07	10	13	25	28	11	14	30	20	11	14	01♒	13	12
07	15	05	00♎		15	13	18		14	20	08		14	26	29		15	01♑	21	12	15	02	14	
08	16	07	01		15	14	19		15	21	09		15	27	29		16	02	22		16	03	15	
09	17	08	01		16	16	19		16	23	09		16	28	00♐		17	03	23		17	03	15	
10	18	09	02		17	17	20		17	24	10		17	29	01		18	04	23		18	04	16	
11	19	10	03	08	18	18	21	09	18	25	11	10	18	00♐	01	11	19	05	24	12	19	05	17	12
12	20	12	03		19	19	21		19	26	11		19	02	02		20	06	25		20	06	18	
13	21	13	04		20	20	22		20	27	12		20	03	03		21	07	26		21	07	19	
14	22	14	04		21	22	23		21	29	13		21	04	04		22	09	26		22	08	19	
15	23	15	05		22	23	23		22	30	13		22	05	04		23	10	27		23	09	20	
16	23	16	05	08	23	24	24	09	23	01♏	14	10	23	06	05	11	24	11	28	12	24	09	21	12
17	24	18	06		24	25	24		24	02	15		24	07	06		25	12	29		25	10	22	
18	25	19	06		25	26	25		25	03	15	11	25	08	06	12	26	13	29		26	11	22	
19	26	20	07		26	28	26		26	05	16		26	10	07		27	14	00♑		27	12	23	
20	27	21	08		27	29	26		27	06	17		27	11	08		28	15	01		28	13	24	
21	28	22	08	08	28	30	27	09	28	07	17	11	28	12	09	12	29	16	02	12	29	13	25	12
22	29	24	09		29	01♎	28	10	29	08	18		29	13	09		30	17	02		00♑	14	26	
23	00♌	25	09	09	30	02	28	09	30	09	19		30	14	10		01♐	18	03		01	15	26	
24	01	26	10		01♍	04	29		01♎	11	20		01♏	15	11		02	19	04		02	15	27	
25	02	27	10		02	05	30		02	12	20		02	16	12		03	20	05		03	16	28	
26	03	29	11	09	03	06	00♏	10	03	13	21	11	03	18	12	12	04	21	05	12	04	17	29	12
27	04	30	12		04	07	01		04	14	22		04	19	13		05	22	06		05	17	30	
28	05	01♍	12		05	08	01		05	15	22		05	20	14		06	23	07		06	18	00♒	
29	06	02	13		06	10	02		06	16	23		06	21	14		07	24	08		07	18	01	
30	07	03	13		07	11	03		07	18	24		07	22	15		08	25	09		08	19	02	
31	08	05	14	09	08	12	03	10				11	08	23	16	12					09	20	03	12

BIRTH TABLES - 1934

Day	JANUARY ☉	♀	♂	♆	FEBRUARY ☉	♀	♂	♆	MARCH ☉	♀	♂	♆
01	10♑	20♒	03♒	12♍	12♒	18♒	28♒	12♍	10♓	08♒	20♓	11♍
02	11	21	04		13	17	29		11	08	21	
03	12	21	05		14	17	29		12	09	22	
04	13	21	06		15	16	00♓		13	09	22	
05	14	22	07		16	15	01		14	09	23	
06	16	22	07	12	17	15	02	12	15	09	24	11
07	17	22	08		18	14	03		16	10	25	
08	18	23	09		19	14	03		17	10	25	
09	19	23	10		20	13	04		18	11	26	
10	20	23	11		21	13	05		19	11	27	
11	21	23	11	12	22	12	06	12	20	11	28	11
12	22	23	12		23	11	07	11	21	12	29	
13	23	24	13		24	11	07		22	12	29	
14	24	24	14		25	10	08		23	13	00♈	
15	25	24	14		26	10	09		24	13	01	
16	26	24	15	12	27	10	10	11	25	14	02	11
17	27	24	16		28	09	11		26	15	02	
18	28	23	17		29	09	11		27	15	03	
19	29	23	18		00♓	09	12		28	16	04	
20	30	23	18		01	09	13		29	17	05	
21	01♒	23	19	12	02	08	14	11	00♈	17	06	11
22	02	23	20		03	08	14		01	18	06	10
23	03	22	21		04	08	15		02	19	07	
24	04	22	22		05	08	16		03	19	08	
25	05	22	22		06	08	17		04	20	09	
26	06	21	23	12	07	08	18	11	05	21	09	10
27	07	21	24		08	08	18		06	22	10	
28	08	20	25		09	08	19		07	22	11	
29	09	20	26						08	23	12	
30	10	19	26						09	24	12	
31	11	19	27	12					10	25	13	10

Day	APRIL ☉	♀	♂	♆	MAY ☉	♀	♂	♆	JUNE ☉	♀	♂	♆
01	11♈	26♒	14♈	10♍	10♉	25♓	07♉	10♍	10♊	29♈	29♉	10♍
02	12	27	15		11	26	07		11	00♉	30	
03	13	27	16		12	27	08		12	01	01♊	
04	14	28	17		13	28	09		13	02	01	
05	15	29	17		14	29	10		14	04	02	
06	16	00♓	18	10	15	00♈	10	10	15	05	03	10
07	17	01	19		16	01	11		16	06	03	
08	18	02	19		17	02	12		17	07	04	
09	19	03	20		18	03	13		18	08	05	
10	20	04	21		19	04	13		19	09	06	
11	21	05	22	10	20	06	14	10	20	10	06	10
12	22	06	22		21	07	15		21	12	07	
13	23	07	23		22	08	15		22	13	08	
14	24	08	24		23	09	16		23	14	08	
15	25	09	25		24	10	17		24	15	09	
16	26	10	25	10	25	11	18	10	25	16	10	10
17	27	11	26		26	12	18		26	17	10	
18	28	11	27		27	13	19		27	18	11	
19	29	12	28		28	14	20		28	20	12	
20	30	13	28		29	15	21		28	21	13	
21	01♉	14	29	10	30	17	21	10	29	22	13	10
22	02	16	30		01♊	18	22		00♋	23	14	
23	03	17	01♉		02	19	23		01	24	15	
24	04	18	01		03	20	23		02	25	15	
25	05	19	02		04	21	24		03	27	16	
26	06	20	03	10	04	22	25	10	04	28	17	10
27	07	21	04		05	23	26		05	29	17	
28	08	22	04		06	24	26		06	00♊	18	
29	08	23	05		07	26	27		07	01	19	
30	09	24	06		08	27	28		08	02	20	
31					09	28	28	10				

	JULY				AUGUST				SEPTEMBER				OCTOBER				NOVEMBER				DECEMBER			
	☉	♀	♂	♆	☉	♀	♂	♆	☉	♀	♂	♆	☉	♀	♂	♆	☉	♀	♂	♆	☉	♀	♂	♆
01	09♋	04♊	20♊	10♍	09♌	10♋	11♋	11♍	08♍	18♌	01♌	12♍	08♎	25♍	20♌	13♍	08♏	04♏	08♍	14♍	09♐	12♐	25♍	15♍
02	10	05	21		09	12	12		09	19	02		09	26	21		09	05	09		10	13	25	
03	11	06	22		10	13	12		10	21	03		10	28	21		10	07	10		11	14	26	
04	12	07	22		11	14	13		11	22	03		11	29	22		11	08	10		12	15	26	
05	13	08	23		12	15	14		12	23	04		12	00♎	22		12	09	11		13	17	27	
06	14	10	24	10	13	17	14	11	13	24	04	12	13	01	23	13	13	10	11	14	14	18	28	15
07	15	11	24		14	18	15		14	26	05		14	03	24		14	12	12		15	19	28	
08	16	12	25		15	19	16		15	27	06		15	04	24		15	13	12		16	21	29	
09	17	13	26		16	20	16		16	28	06		16	05	25		16	14	13		17	22	29	
10	18	14	26		17	21	17		17	29	07		16	06	25		17	15	13		18	23	30	
11	18	15	27	10	18	23	18	11	18	00♍	08	12	17	08	26	13	18	17	14	14	19	24	00♎	15
12	19	17	28		19	24	18		19	02	08		18	09	27		19	18	15		20	26	01	
13	20	18	28		20	25	19		20	03	09		19	10	27		20	19	15		21	27	01	
14	21	19	29		21	26	20		21	04	09		20	11	28	14	21	20	16		22	28	02	
15	22	20	30		22	27	20		22	05	10		21	13	28		22	22	16		23	29	02	
16	23	21	00♋	10	23	29	21	11	23	07	11	13	22	14	29	14	23	23	17	14	24	01♑	03	15
17	24	23	01		24	30	22		24	08	11		23	15	30		24	24	17		25	02	03	
18	25	24	02		25	01♌	22		25	09	12		24	16	00♍		25	25	18		26	03	04	
19	26	25	03		26	02	23	12	26	10	13		25	18	01		26	27	18		27	04	04	
20	27	26	03	11	27	03	24		27	12	13		26	19	01		27	28	19		28	06	04	
21	28	27	04	11	28	05	24	12	28	13	14	13	27	20	02	14	28	29	20	14	29	07	05	15
22	29	29	04		29	06	25		29	14	14		28	21	03		30	00♐	20		30	08	05	
23	30	30	05		30	07	25		30	15	15		29	23	03		01♐	02	21		01♑	09	06	
24	01♌	01♋	06		01♍	08	26		01♎	17	16		00♏	24	04		02	03	21		02	11	06	
25	02	02	06		02	10	27		02	18	16		01	25	04		03	04	22		03	12	07	
26	03	03	07	11	03	11	27	12	03	19	17	13	02	26	05	14	04	05	22	14	04	13	07	15
27	04	04	08		03	12	28		04	20	18		03	28	05		05	07	23		05	14	08	
28	05	06	08		04	13	29		05	22	18		04	29	06		06	08	23		06	16	08	
29	06	07	09		05	14	29		06	23	19		05	00♏	07		07	09	24		07	17	09	
30	07	08	10		06	16	30		07	24	19		06	02	07		08	10	24	15	08	18	09	
31	08	09	10	11	07	17	01♌	12					07	03	08	14					09	19	09	15

BIRTH TABLES - 1935

	JANUARY				FEBRUARY				MARCH				APRIL				MAY				JUNE			
Day	☉	♀	♂	♆	☉	♀	♂	♆	☉	♀	♂	♆	☉	♀	♂	♆	☉	♀	♂	♆	☉	♀	♂	♆
01	10♑	21♑	10♎	15♍	12♒	30♒	21♎	14♍	10♓	04♈	25♎	13♍	11♈	12♉	18♎	12♍	10♉	18♊	08♎	12♍	10♊	23♋	07♎	12♍
02	11	22	10		13	01♓	21		11	06	25		12	13	18		11	19	08		11	24	08	
03	12	23	11		14	02	21		12	07	25		13	15	17		12	20	07		12	25	08	
04	13	24	11		15	03	22		13	08	24		14	16	17		13	21	07		13	26	08	
05	14	26	12		16	05	22		14	09	24		15	17	16		14	23	07		14	28	08	
06	15	27	12	14	17	06	22	14	15	11	24	13	16	18	16	12	15	24	07	12	15	29	08	12
07	16	28	12		18	07	22		16	12	24		17	19	16		16	25	07		16	30	09	
08	17	29	13		19	08	23		17	13	24		18	21	15		17	26	07		17	01♌	09	
09	18	01♒	13		20	10	23		18	14	24		19	22	15		18	27	07		18	02	09	
10	19	02	14		21	11	23		19	15	24		20	23	15		19	28	06		19	03	09	
11	20	03	14	14	22	12	23	14	20	17	24	13	21	24	14	12	20	30	06	12	20	04	10	12
12	21	04	14		23	13	23		21	18	24		22	25	14		21	01♋	06		21	05	10	
13	22	06	15		24	14	23		22	19	23		23	27	13		22	02	06		22	06	10	
14	23	07	15		25	16	24		23	20	23		24	28	13		23	03	06		22	07	10	
15	24	08	16		26	17	24		24	22	23		25	29	13		24	04	06		23	08	11	
16	25	09	16	14	27	18	24	14	25	23	23	13	26	00♊	12	12	25	05	06	12	24	09	11	12
17	26	11	16		28	19	24		26	24	23		27	01	12		26	06	06		25	10	11	
18	27	12	17		29	21	24		27	25	22		28	03	12		27	08	06		26	11	12	
19	28	13	17		30	22	24		28	26	22		29	04	11		28	09	06		27	12	12	
20	30	15	17		01♓	23	24		29	28	22		29	05	11		29	10	06		28	13	12	
21	01♒	16	18	14	02	24	24	14	30	29	22	13	00♉	06	11	12	30	11	06	12	29	14	13	12
22	02	17	18		03	26	24		01♈	00♉	21		01	07	10		00♊	12	06		00♋	15	13	
23	03	18	18		04	27	25	13	02	01	21		02	09	10		01	13	06		01	16	13	
24	04	20	19		05	28	25		03	03	21		03	10	10		02	14	06		02	17	14	
25	05	21	19		06	29	25		04	04	20		04	11	09		03	15	06		03	18	14	
26	06	22	19	14	07	01♈	25	13	05	05	20	13	05	12	09	12	04	17	07	12	04	19	14	12
27	07	23	20		08	02	25		06	06	20		06	13	09		05	18	07		05	20	15	
28	08	25	20		09	03	25		07	07	19		07	14	09		06	19	07		06	21	15	
29	09	26	20						08	09	19		08	16	08		07	20	07		07	22	16	
30	10	27	20						09	10	19		09	17	08		08	21	07		08	23	16	
31	11	28	21	14					10	11	18	13					09	22	07	12				

Day	JULY ☉	♀	♂	Ψ	AUGUST ☉	♀	♂	Ψ	SEPTEMBER ☉	♀	♂	Ψ
01	09♋	24♌	16♎	12♍	08♌	18♍	02♏	13♍	08♍	19♍	20♏	14♍
02	10	25	17		09	19	02		09	18	21	
03	11	26	17		10	19	03		10	18	21	
04	12	27	18		11	20	03		11	17	22	
05	13	28	18		12	20	04		12	17	23	
06	13	29	19	12	13	20	04	13	13	16	23	14
07	14	30	19		14	21	05		14	15	24	
08	15	01♍	19		15	21	05		15	15	25	
09	16	01	20		16	21	06		16	14	25	
10	17	02	20		17	22	07		17	14	26	
11	18	03	21	12	18	22	07	13	18	13	27	14
12	19	04	21		19	22	08		19	13	27	15
13	20	05	22		20	22	08		20	12	28	
14	21	06	22		21	23	09		21	11	29	
15	22	07	23	13	22	23	10		22	11	29	
16	23	07	23	13	23	23	10	14	23	10	30	15
17	24	08	24		24	23	11		24	10	01♐	
18	25	09	24		25	23	11		25	09	01	
19	26	10	25		26	23	12		26	09	02	
20	27	10	25		27	23	13		27	08	03	
21	28	11	26	13	27	23	13	14	28	08	03	15
22	29	12	26		28	22	14		29	08	04	
23	30	13	27		29	22	14		30	07	05	
24	01♌	13	27		00♍	22	15		01♎	07	05	
25	02	14	28		01	22	16		01	07	06	
26	03	15	28	13	02	21	16	14	02	07	07	15
27	04	15	29		03	21	17		03	07	08	
28	04	16	29		04	21	18		04	07	08	
29	05	16	30		05	20	18		05	07	09	
30	06	17	00♏		06	20	19		06	07	10	
31	07	18	01	13	07	19	19	14				

Day	OCTOBER ☉	♀	♂	Ψ	NOVEMBER ☉	♀	♂	Ψ	DECEMBER ☉	♀	♂	Ψ
01	07♎	07♍	10♐	15♍	08♏	23♍	03♑	16♍	08♐	22♎	26♑	17♍
02	08	07	11		09	24	04		09	23	26	
03	09	07	12		10	24	04		10	24	27	
04	10	07	12		11	25	05		11	25	28	
05	11	07	13		12	26	06		12	27	29	
06	12	07	14	15	13	27	07	16	13	28	29	17
07	13	08	15		14	28	07		14	29	00♒	
08	14	08	15		15	29	08		15	30	01	
09	15	08	16		16	30	09		16	01♏	02	
10	16	09	17	16	17	01♎	10		18	02	03	
11	17	09	17	16	18	02	10	16	19	03	03	17
12	18	10	18		19	03	11		20	04	04	
13	19	10	19		20	04	12		21	06	05	
14	20	11	20		21	05	13		22	07	06	
15	21	11	20		22	06	13		23	08	06	
16	22	12	21	16	23	07	14	16	24	09	07	17
17	23	12	22		24	08	15		25	10	08	
18	24	13	22		25	09	16	17	26	11	09	
19	25	13	23		26	10	16		27	12	10	
20	26	14	24		27	11	17		28	14	10	
21	27	15	25	16	28	12	18	17	29	15	11	17
22	28	15	25		29	13	19		30	16	12	
23	29	16	26		00♐	14	19		01♑	17	13	
24	00♏	17	27		01	15	20		02	18	14	
25	01	17	28		02	16	21		03	19	14	
26	02	18	28	16	03	17	22	17	04	20	15	17
27	03	19	29		04	18	23		05	22	16	
28	04	20	30		05	19	23		06	23	17	
29	05	20	01♑		06	20	24		07	24	17	
30	06	21	01		07	21	25		08	25	18	
31	07	22	02	16					09	26	19	17

BIRTH TABLES - 1936

	JANUARY				FEBRUARY				MARCH				APRIL				MAY				JUNE			
	☉	♀	♂	♆	☉	♀	♂	♆	☉	♀	♂	♆	☉	♀	♂	♆	☉	♀	♂	♆	☉	♀	♂	♆
01	10♑	28♏	20♒	17♍	11♒	05♑	14♓	16♍	11♓	10♒	06♈	16♍	12♈	18♓	30♈	15♍	11♉	25♈	22♉	14♍	11♊	03♊	13♊	14♍
02	11	29	21		12	06	15		12	11	07		13	20	00♉		12	26	22		12	04	14	
03	12	30	21		14	07	16		13	13	08	15	14	21	01		13	28	23		13	06	15	
04	13	01♐	22		15	08	16		14	14	09		15	22	02		14	29	24		14	07	15	
05	14	02	23		16	10	17		15	15	09		16	23	03		15	00	24		15	08	16	
06	15	03	24	17	17	11	18	16	16	16	10	15	17	24	03	15	16	01♉	25	14	16	09	17	14
07	16	05	24		18	12	19		17	18	11		17	26	04		17	03	26		17	11	18	
08	17	06	25		19	13	19		18	19	12		18	27	05		18	04	27		17	12	18	
09	18	07	26		20	15	20		19	20	12		19	28	06		19	05	27		18	13	19	
10	19	08	27		21	16	21		20	21	13		20	29	06		20	06	28		19	14	20	
11	20	09	28	17	22	17	22	16	21	22	14	15	21	01♈	07	14	21	07	29	14	20	15	20	14
12	21	11	28		23	18	23		22	24	15		22	02	08		22	09	29		21	17	21	
13	22	12	29		24	19	23		23	25	16		23	03	09		23	10	00♊		22	18	22	
14	23	13	30		25	21	24		24	26	16		24	04	09		23	11	01		23	19	22	
15	24	14	01♓		26	22	25		25	27	17		25	06	10		24	12	02		24	20	23	
16	25	15	02	17	27	23	26	16	26	29	18	15	26	07	11	14	25	14	02	14	25	22	24	14
17	26	17	02		28	24	26		27	30	19		27	08	11		26	15	03		26	23	24	
18	27	18	03		29	26	27		28	01♓	19		28	09	12		27	16	04		27	24	25	
19	28	19	04		30	27	28		29	02	20		29	10	13		28	17	04		28	25	26	
20	29	20	05		01♓	28	29		30	04	21		00♉	12	14		29	18	05		29	27	26	
21	30	21	05	17	02	29	30	16	01♈	05	22	15	01	13	14	14	00♊	20	06	14	30	28	27	14
22	01♒	23	06	16	03	00♒	00♈		02	06	22		02	14	15		01	21	06		01♋	29	28	
23	02	24	07		04	02	01		03	07	23		03	15	16		02	22	07		02	00♋	28	
24	03	25	08		05	03	02		04	08	24		04	17	17		03	23	08		03	01	29	
25	04	26	09		06	04	03		05	10	25		05	18	17		04	25	09		04	03	30	
26	05	27	09	16	07	05	03	16	06	11	25	15	06	19	18	14	05	26	09	14	05	04	00♋	14
27	06	29	10		08	07	04		07	12	26		07	20	19		06	27	10		06	05	01	
28	07	30	11		09	08	05		08	13	27		08	21	19		07	29	11		07	06	02	
29	08	01♑	12		10	09	06		09	15	28		09	23	20		08	30	11		08	08	02	
30	09	02	12						10	16	28		10	24	21		09	01♊	12		08	09	03	
31	10	04	13	16					11	17	29	15					10	02	13	14				

JULY

Day	☉	♀	♂	♆
01	09♋	11♋	04♋	14♍
02	10	12	04	
03	11	13	05	
04	12	14	06	
05	13	16	06	
06	14	17	07	
07	15	18	08	
08	16	19	08	
09	17	21	09	
10	18	22	10	
11	19	23	10	
12	20	24	11	
13	21	26	12	
14	22	27	13	
15	23	28	13	
16	24	29	14	
17	25	00♌	15	
18	26	02	15	
19	27	03	16	
20	28	04	17	
21	29	05	18	
22	29	07	18	
23	00♌	08	19	
24	01	09	20	
25	02	10	20	
26	03	11	21	
27	04	13	22	
28	05	14	22	
29	06	15	23	
30	07	16	24	
31	08	17	24	

AUGUST

Day	☉	♀	♂	♆
01	09♌	18♌	24♋	15♍
02	10	19	24	
03	11	21	25	
04	12	22	26	
05	13	23	26	
06	14	24	27	
07	15	26	28	
08	16	27	29	
09	17	28	29	
10	18	29	00♌	
11	19	00♍	01	
12	20	02	02	
13	21	03	02	
14	22	04	03	
15	23	05	04	
16	24	06	04	
17	25	08	05	
18	26	09	06	
19	27	10	07	
20	28	11	07	
21	29	13	08	
22	29	14	09	
23	00♍	15	09	
24	01	16	10	
25	02	18	11	
26	03	19	12	
27	04	20	12	
28	05	21	13	
29	06	22	13	
30	07	24	14	
31	08	25	14	

SEPTEMBER

Day	☉	♀	♂	♆
01	09♍	26♍	14♌	16♍
02	10	28	15	
03	11	29	15	
04	12	00♎	16	
05	13	01	17	
06	14	03	17	
07	15	04	18	
08	16	05	19	
09	17	06	20	
10	18	08	20	
11	19	09	21	
12	20	10	22	
13	21	11	22	
14	22	13	23	
15	23	14	24	
16	24	15	25	
17	25	16	25	
18	26	18	26	
19	27	19	27	
20	28	20	28	
21	29	21	28	
22	29	23	29	
23	00♎	24	00♍	
24	01	25	01	
25	02	26	01	
26	03	28	02	
27	04	29	03	
28	05	00♏	04	
29	06	01	04	
30	07	02	05	

OCTOBER

Day	☉	♀	♂	♆
01	08♎	03♏	06♍	17♍
02	09	05	06	
03	10	06	07	
04	11	07	07	
05	12	08	08	
06	13	09	08	
07	14	11	09	
08	15	12	10	
09	16	13	10	
10	17	14	11	
11	18	16	11	
12	19	17	12	
13	20	18	12	
14	21	19	13	
15	22	21	14	
16	23	22	14	
17	24	23	15	
18	25	24	15	
19	26	25	16	
20	27	27	16	
21	28	28	17	
22	29	29	17	
23	00♏	00♐	18	
24	01	01	19	
25	02	02	19	
26	03	04	20	
27	04	05	20	
28	05	06	21	
29	06	07	21	
30	07	08	22	
31	08	10	22	

NOVEMBER

Day	☉	♀	♂	♆
01	09♏	11♐	22♍	18♍
02	10	13	23	
03	11	14	23	
04	12	15	24	
05	13	16	24	
06	14	17	25	
07	15	19	26	
08	16	20	26	
09	17	21	27	
10	18	22	28	
11	19	24	28	
12	20	25	29	
13	21	26	00♎	
14	22	27	00	
15	23	29	01	
16	24	00♑	02	
17	25	01	02	
18	26	02	03	
19	27	03	04	
20	28	05	04	
21	29	06	05	
22	00♐	07	06	
23	01	08	06	
24	02	09	07	
25	03	11	08	
26	04	12	08	
27	05	13	09	
28	06	14	09	
29	07	15	10	
30	08	17	10	

DECEMBER

Day	☉	♀	♂	♆
01	09♐	18♑	10♎	19♍
02	10	19	11	
03	11	20	11	
04	12	21	12	
05	13	23	12	
06	14	24	13	
07	15	25	13	
08	16	26	14	
09	17	27	15	
10	18	29	15	
11	19	00♒	16	
12	20	01	16	
13	21	02	17	
14	22	03	18	
15	23	05	18	
16	24	06	19	
17	25	07	19	
18	26	08	20	
19	27	09	20	
20	28	11	21	
21	29	12	22	
22	00♑	13	22	
23	01	14	23	
24	02	15	23	
25	03	16	24	
26	04	18	24	
27	05	19	25	
28	06	20	25	
29	07	21	26	
30	08	22	27	
31	09	24	27	

BIRTH TABLES - 1937

Day	JAN ☉	JAN ♀	JAN ♂	JAN ♆	FEB ☉	FEB ♀	FEB ♂	FEB ♆	MAR ☉	MAR ♀	MAR ♂	MAR ♆	APR ☉	APR ♀	APR ♂	APR ♆	MAY ☉	MAY ♀	MAY ♂	MAY ♆	JUN ☉	JUN ♀	JUN ♂	JUN ♆
01	11♑	25♒	28♎	19♍	12♒	29♓	14♏	18♍	11♓	25♈	26♏	18♍	11♈	05♉	05♐	17♍	11♉	21♈	04♐	16♍	11♊	28♈	24♏	16♍
02	12	26	28		13	00♈	14		12	25	26		12	05	05		12	20	04		12	29	24	
03	13	27	29		14	01	15		13	26	27		13	05	05		13	20	03		12	29	23	
04	14	28	29		15	02	15		14	27	27		14	05	05		14	20	03		13	00♉	23	
05	15	29	30		16	03	16		15	27	27		15	04	05		15	20	03		14	01	23	
06	16	00♓	00♏	19	17	04	16	18	16	28	28	18	16	04	05	17	16	20	03	16	15	02	23	16
07	17	02	01		18	05	17		17	29	28		17	04	05		16	20	02		16	02	22	
08	18	03	01		19	06	17		18	29	29		18	03	05		17	19	02		17	03	22	
09	19	04	02		20	07	18		19	30	29		19	03	05		18	19	02		18	04	22	
10	20	05	03		21	08	18		20	01♉	29		20	02	05		19	19	01		19	05	22	
11	21	06	03	19	22	09	18	18	21	01	29	18	21	02	05	17	20	20	01	16	20	06	21	16
12	22	07	04		23	10	19		22	02	30		22	01	06		21	20	01		21	06	21	
13	23	08	04		24	11	19		23	02	00♐		23	00	06		22	20	00		22	07	21	
14	24	10	05		25	12	20		24	03	00		24	30♈	06		23	20	00		23	08	21	
15	25	11	05		26	13	20		24	03	01		25	29	06		24	20	30♏		24	09	21	
16	26	12	06	19	27	14	21	18	25	03	01	17	26	28	06	17	25	20	29	16	25	10	20	16
17	27	13	06		28	15	21		26	04	01		27	28	05		26	21	29		26	11	20	
18	28	14	07		29	16	22		27	04	02		28	27	05		27	21	29		27	11	20	
19	29	15	07		00♓	16	22		28	05	02		29	27	05		28	21	28		28	12	20	
20	00♒	16	08		01	17	23		29	05	02		30	26	05		29	22	28		29	13	20	
21	01	17	08	19	02	18	23	18	00♈	05	02	17	01♉	25	05	17	00♊	22	28	16	30	14	20	16
22	02	18	09		03	19	23		01	05	03		02	25	05		01	23	27		01♋	15	20	
23	03	19	09		04	20	24		02	05	03		03	24	05	16	02	23	27		02	16	20	
24	04	21	10		05	21	24		03	06	03		04	24	05		03	23	27		03	17	20	
25	05	22	10		06	22	24		04	06	03		05	23	05		04	24	26		03	18	20	
26	06	23	11	19	07	22	25	18	05	06	03	17	06	23	05	16	05	24	26	16	04	19	20	16
27	07	24	11		08	23	25		06	06	04		07	22	05		06	25	26		05	20	20	
28	08	25	12		09	24	26		07	06	04		08	22	04		07	26	25		06	21	20	
29	09	26	12						08	06	04		09	21	04		08	26	25		07	22	20	
30	10	27	13						09	06	04		10	21	04		09	27	25		08	23	20	
31	11	28	13	19					10	06	04	17					10	27	24	16				

Day	JULY				AUGUST				SEPTEMBER				OCTOBER				NOVEMBER				DECEMBER			
	☉	♀	♂	♆	☉	♀	♂	♆	☉	♀	♂	♆	☉	♀	♂	♆	☉	♀	♂	♆	☉	♀	♂	♆
01	09♋	24♉	20♏	17♍	09♌	26♊	27♏	17♍	09♍	02♌	12♐	18♍	08♎	08♍	01♑	19♍	09♏	16♎	22♑	20♍	09♐	23♏	15♒	21♍
02	10	25	20		10	27	27		10	03	13		09	09	01		10	17	23		10	25	15	
03	11	26	20		11	29	28		11	04	13		10	10	02	20	11	18	24		11	26	16	
04	12	27	20		12	30	28		12	05	14		11	11	03		12	20	25	21	12	27	17	
05	13	28	20		13	01♋	29		12	06	14		12	13	03		13	21	25		13	28	18	
06	14	29	20	17	14	02	29	17	13	08	15	19.	13	14	04	20	14	22	26	21	14	30	18	21
07	15	30	20		15	03	29		14	09	16		14	15	05		15	23	27		15	01♐	19	
08	16	01♊	20		16	04	30		15	10	16		15	16	06		16	25	28		16	02	20	
09	17	02	21		16	05	00♐	18	16	11	17		16	17	06		17	26	28		17	03	21	
10	18	03	21		17	06	01		17	12	17		17	19	07		18	27	29		18	05	22	
11	19	04	21	17	18	08	01	18	18	14	18	19	18	20	08	20	19	28	30	21	19	06	22	21
12	20	05	21		19	09	02		19	15	19		19	21	08		20	30	01♒		20	07	23	
13	21	06	21		20	10	02		20	16	19		20	22	09		21	01♏	01		21	08	24	
14	22	07	21		21	11	03		21	17	20		21	24	10		22	02	02		22	10	25	
15	23	08	22		22	12	03		22	18	20		22	25	10		23	03	03		23	11	25	
16	24	09	22	17	23	13	04	18	23	20	21	19	23	26	11	20	24	05	04	21	24	12	26	21
17	24	10	22		24	14	04		24	21	22		24	27	12		25	06	04		25	14	27	
18	25	11	22		25	15	05		25	22	22		25	29	12		26	07	05		26	15	28	
19	26	12	23		26	17	05		26	23	23		26	30	13		27	08	06		27	16	28	
20	27	13	23		27	18	06		27	24	24		27	01♎	14		28	10	06		28	17	29	
21	28	14	23	17	28	19	06	18	28	26	24	19	28	02	15	20	29	11	07	21	29	19	30	21
22	29	15	24		29	20	07		29	27	25		29	03	15		30	12	08		00♑	20	01♓	
23	00♌	16	24		30	21	07		00♎	28	25		30	05	16		01♐	13	09		01	21	01	
24	01	18	24		01♍	22	08		01	29	26		01♏	06	17		02	15	09		02	22	02	
25	02	19	24		02	24	08		02	00♍	27		02	07	17		03	16	10		03	24	03	
26	03	20	25	17	03	25	09	18	03	02	27	19	03	08	18	20	04	17	11	21	04	25	04	21
27	04	21	25		04	26	09		04	03	28		04	10	19		05	18	12		05	26	04	
28	05	22	25		05	27	10		05	04	29		05	11	20		06	20	12		06	27	05	
29	06	23	26		06	28	10		06	05	29		06	12	20		07	21	13		07	29	06	
30	07	24	26		07	29	11		07	06	00♑		07	13	21		08	22	14		08	30	07	
31	08	25	27	17	08	01♌	11	18					08	15	22	20					09	01♑	07	21

BIRTH TABLES - 1938

Day	☉ Jan	♀ Jan	♂ Jan	♆ Jan	☉ Feb	♀ Feb	♂ Feb	♆ Feb	☉ Mar	♀ Mar	♂ Mar	♆ Mar
01	10♑	02♑	08♓	21♍	12♒	11♒	01♈	21♍	10♓	16♓	22♈	20♍
02	11	04	09		13	13	02		11	18	23	
03	12	05	10		14	14	03		12	19	24	
04	13	06	10		15	15	04		13	20	24	
05	15	07	11		16	16	04		14	21	25	
06	16	09	12	21	17	18	05	21	15	23	26	20
07	17	10	13		18	19	06		16	24	27	
08	18	11	13		19	20	07		17	25	27	
09	19	12	14		20	21	07		18	26	28	
10	20	14	15		21	23	08		19	28	29	
11	21	15	16	21	22	24	09	21	20	29	29	20
12	22	16	16		23	25	10		21	00♈	00♉	
13	23	17	17		24	26	10		22	01	01	
14	24	18	18		25	28	11		23	03	02	
15	25	20	19		26	29	12		24	04	02	
16	26	21	19	21	27	00♓	13	20	25	05	03	20
17	27	23	20		28	01	13		26	06	04	
18	28	24	21		29	03	14		27	08	04	
19	29	25	22		00♓	04	15		28	09	05	
20	30	26	22		01	05	16		29	10	06	
21	01♒	28	23	21	02	06	16	20	00♈	11	07	19
22	02	29	24		03	08	17		01	13	07	
23	03	00♒	25		04	09	18		02	14	08	
24	04	01	26		05	10	19		03	15	09	
25	05	03	26		06	11	19		04	16	09	
26	06	04	27	21	07	13	20	20	05	18	10	19
27	07	05	28		08	14	21		06	19	11	
28	08	06	28		09	15	21		07	20	12	
29	09	08	29						08	21	12	
30	10	09	30						09	23	13	
31	11	10	01♈	21					10	24	14	19

Day	☉ Apr	♀ Apr	♂ Apr	♆ Apr	☉ May	♀ May	♂ May	♆ May	☉ Jun	♀ Jun	♂ Jun	♆ Jun
01	11♈	25♈	14♉	19♍	10♉	02♊	05♊	19♍	10♊	10♋	26♊	18♍
02	12	26	15		11	03	06		11	11	27	
03	13	27	16		12	04	07		12	12	27	
04	14	29	17		13	06	07		13	13	28	
05	15	30	17		14	07	08		14	14	29	
06	16	01♉	18	19	15	08	09	19	15	15	30	18
07	17	02	19		16	09	09		16	17	00♋	
08	18	04	19		17	10	10	18	17	18	01	
09	19	05	20		18	12	11		18	19	02	
10	20	06	21		19	13	11		19	20	02	
11	21	07	21	19	20	14	12	18	20	21	03	18
12	22	09	22		21	15	13		21	23	04	
13	23	10	23		22	16	14		22	24	04	
14	24	11	24		23	18	14		23	25	05	
15	25	12	24		24	19	15		24	26	06	
16	26	13	25	19	25	20	16	18	25	27	06	18
17	27	15	26		26	21	16		26	29	07	
18	28	16	26		27	23	17		27	30	08	
19	29	17	27		28	24	17		28	01♌	08	
20	30	18	28		29	25	18		28	02	09	
21	01♉	20	28	19	30	26	19	18	29	03	10	19
22	02	21	29		01♊	27	20		00♋	05	10	
23	03	22	30		02	29	20		01	06	11	
24	04	23	01♊		03	30	21		02	07	12	
25	05	25	01		04	01♋	22		03	08	12	
26	06	26	02	19	05	02	22	18	04	09	13	19
27	07	27	03		06	03	23		05	10	13	
28	08	28	03		06	05	23		06	12	14	
29	09	29	04		07	06	24		07	13	15	
30	09	01♊	05		08	07	25		08	14	15	
31					09	08	26	18				

Day	JULY				AUGUST				SEPTEMBER			
	☉	♀	♂	Ψ	☉	♀	♂	Ψ	☉	♀	♂	Ψ
01	09♋	15♌	16♋	19♍	09♌	21♍	06♌	19♍	08♍	24♎	26♌	20♍
02	10	16	17		10	22	07		09	25	27	
03	11	18	17		10	23	07		10	26	27	
04	12	19	18		11	24	08		11	27	28	21
05	13	20	19		12	25	09	20	12	28	29	
06	14	21	19	19	13	26	09	20	13	29	29	21
07	15	22	20		14	28	10		14	00♏	30	
08	16	23	21		15	29	11		15	01	00♍	
09	17	25	21		16	30	11		16	02	01	
10	18	26	22		17	01♎	12		17	03	02	
11	19	27	23	19	18	02	13	20	18	04	02	21
12	19	28	23		19	03	13		19	05	03	
13	20	29	24		20	04	14		20	06	04	
14	21	00♍	25		21	05	15		21	07	04	
15	22	01	25		22	06	15		22	08	05	
16	23	03	26	19	23	07	16	20	23	09	06	21
17	24	04	27		24	09	16		24	10	06	
18	25	05	27		25	10	17		25	11	07	
19	26	06	28		26	11	18		26	12	07	
20	27	07	28		27	12	18		27	13	08	
21	28	08	29	19	28	13	19	20	28	13	09	21
22	29	10	30		29	14	20		29	14	09	
23	30	11	00♌		30	15	20		30	15	10	
24	01♌	12	01		01♍	16	21		01♎	16	11	
25	02	13	02		02	17	22		02	17	11	
26	03	14	02	19	03	18	22	20	03	18	12	21
27	04	15	03		04	19	23		04	19	12	
28	05	16	04		05	20	23		05	20	13	
29	06	17	04		05	21	24		06	20	14	
30	07	19	05		06	22	25		07	21	14	
31	08	20	06	19	07	23	25	20				

Day	OCTOBER				NOVEMBER				DECEMBER			
	☉	♀	♂	Ψ	☉	♀	♂	Ψ	☉	♀	♂	Ψ
01	08♎	22♏	15♍	22♍	08♏	05♐	05♎	23♍	09♐	21♏	24♎	23♍
02	09	23	16		09	05	05		10	21	24	
03	10	23	16		10	05	06		11	21	25	
04	11	24	17		11	04	06		12	20	25	
05	12	25	18		12	04	07		13	20	26	
06	13	26	18	22	13	04	08	23	14	20	27	23
07	14	26	19		14	04	08		15	20	27	
08	15	27	19		15	03	09		16	20	28	
09	16	28	20		16	03	10		17	20	28	
10	17	28	21		17	03	10		18	20	29	
11	18	29	21	22	18	02	11	23	19	20	30	23
12	18	29	22		19	02	12		20	20	00♏	
13	19	30	23		20	01	12		21	20	01	
14	20	00♐	23		21	01	13		22	20	02	
15	21	01	24		22	00	13		23	20	02	
16	22	01	24	22	23	30♏	14	23	24	20	03	23
17	23	02	25		24	29	15		25	20	03	
18	24	02	26		25	28	15		26	21	04	
19	25	03	26		27	28	16		27	21	05	
20	26	03	27		28	27	17		28	21	05	
21	27	03	28	22	29	27	17	23	29	22	06	23
22	28	04	28		30	26	18		30	22	07	
23	29	04	29		01♐	25	18		01♑	23	07	
24	00♏	04	30		02	25	19		02	23	08	
25	01	04	00♎		03	24	20		03	24	08	
26	02	05	01	22	04	24	20	23	04	24	09	23
27	03	05	01		05	23	21		05	25	10	
28	04	05	02		06	23	22		06	25	10	
29	05	05	03		07	22	22		07	26	11	
30	06	05	03		08	22	23		08	26	12	
31	07	05	04	23					09	27	12	23

BIRTH TABLES - 1939

JANUARY · FEBRUARY · MARCH

Day	JAN ☉	JAN ♀	JAN ♂	JAN ♆	FEB ☉	FEB ♀	FEB ♂	FEB ♆	MAR ☉	MAR ♀	MAR ♂	MAR ♆
01	10♑	28♏	13♏	23♍	12♒	25♐	02♐	23♍	10♓	25♑	18♐	22♍
02	11	28	13		13	26	03		11	27	19	
03	12	29	14		14	27	04		12	28	20	
04	13	30	15		15	28	04		13	29	20	
05	14	00♐	15		16	29	05		14	30	21	
06	15	01	16	23	17	00♑	05	23	15	01♒	22	22
07	16	02	17		18	01	06		16	02	22	
08	17	03	17		19	02	06		17	03	23	
09	18	04	18		20	03	07		18	05	23	
10	19	04	18		21	04	07		19	06	24	
11	20	05	19	23	22	05	08	23	20	07	24	22
12	21	06	20		23	07	09		21	08	25	
13	22	07	20		24	08	09		22	09	26	
14	23	08	21		25	09	10		23	10	26	
15	24	09	21		26	10	10		24	11	27	
16	25	09	22	23	27	11	11	23	25	13	27	22
17	26	10	23		28	12	12		26	14	28	
18	28	11	23		29	13	12		27	15	28	
19	29	12	24		30	14	13		28	16	29	
20	30	13	25		01♓	15	13		29	17	30	
21	01♒	14	25	23	02	16	14	23	30	18	00♑	22
22	02	15	26		03	18	15	22	01♈	20	01	
23	03	16	26		04	19	15		02	21	01	
24	04	17	27		05	20	16		03	22	02	
25	05	18	28		06	21	16		04	23	02	
26	06	19	28	23	07	22	17	22	05	24	03	22
27	07	20	29		08	23	17		06	25	03	
28	08	21	29		09	24	18		07	27	04	
29	09	22	00♐						08	28	05	
30	10	23	01						09	29	05	
31	11	24	01	23					10	00♓	06	21

APRIL · MAY · JUNE

Day	APR ☉	APR ♀	APR ♂	APR ♆	MAY ☉	MAY ♀	MAY ♂	MAY ♆	JUN ☉	JUN ♀	JUN ♂	JUN ♆
01	11♈	01♓	06♑	21♍	10♉	07♈	21♑	21♍	10♊	14♉	02♒	21♍
02	12	03	07		11	08	22		11	16	02	
03	13	04	07		12	09	22		12	17	02	
04	14	05	08		13	11	22		13	18	03	
05	15	06	08		14	12	23		14	19	03	
06	16	07	09	21	15	13	23	21	15	20	03	21
07	17	08	09		16	14	24		16	22	03	
08	18	10	10		17	15	24		17	23	03	
09	19	11	10		18	17	24		18	24	04	
10	20	12	11		19	18	25		19	25	04	
11	21	13	11	21	20	19	25	21	20	26	04	21
12	22	14	12		21	20	26		21	28	04	
13	23	16	12		22	21	26		22	29	04	
14	24	17	13		23	23	26		23	00♊	04	
15	25	18	13		24	24	27		23	01	04	
16	26	19	14	21	25	25	27	21	24	03	04	21
17	27	20	14		26	26	28		25	04	05	
18	28	22	15		27	27	28		26	05	05	
19	29	23	15		28	29	28		27	06	05	
20	30	24	16		29	30	29		28	07	05	
21	00♉	25	16	21	30	01♉	29	21	29	09	05	21
22	01	26	17		01♊	02	29		00♋	10	05	
23	02	28	17		01	04	30		01	11	05	
24	03	29	18		02	05	30		02	12	05	
25	04	30	18		03	06	00♒		03	13	05	
26	05	01♈	19	21	04	07	00	21	04	15	05	21
27	06	02	19		05	08	01		05	16	05	
28	07	03	20		06	10	01		06	17	05	
29	08	05	20		07	11	01		07	18	04	
30	09	06	21		08	12	02		08	20	04	
31					09	13	02	21				

	JULY ☉	JULY ♀	JULY ♂	JULY ♆	AUGUST ☉	AUGUST ♀	AUGUST ♂	AUGUST ♆	SEPTEMBER ☉	SEPTEMBER ♀	SEPTEMBER ♂	SEPTEMBER ♆	OCTOBER ☉	OCTOBER ♀	OCTOBER ♂	OCTOBER ♆	NOVEMBER ☉	NOVEMBER ♀	NOVEMBER ♂	NOVEMBER ♆	DECEMBER ☉	DECEMBER ♀	DECEMBER ♂	DECEMBER ♆
01	09♋	21♊	04♒	21♍	08♌	29♋	27♑	21♍	08♍	07♍	24♑	23♍	07♎	14♎	03♒	24♍	09♏	23♏	19♒	25♍	08♐	00♑	08♓	25♍
02	10	22	04		09	30	27	22	09	08	25		08	16	03		09	24	20		09	02	08	
03	11	23	04		10	01♌	27		10	09	25		09	17	04		10	25	20		10	03	09	
04	12	24	04		11	02	26		11	11	25		10	18	04		11	27	21		11	04	10	
05	13	26	04		12	04	26		12	12	25		11	19	05		12	28	21		12	05	10	
06	14	27	04	21	13	05	26	22	13	13	25	23	12	21	05	24	13	29	22	25	13	07	11	25
07	14	28	03		14	06	26		14	14	25		13	22	06		14	00♐	22		14	08	12	
08	15	29	03		15	07	26		15	16	26		14	23	06		15	02	23		15	09	12	
09	16	01♋	03		16	09	25		16	17	26		15	24	07		16	03	24		17	10	13	
10	17	02	03		17	10	25		17	18	26		16	26	07		17	04	24		18	12	14	
11	18	03	03	21	18	11	25	22	18	19	26	23	17	27	08	24	18	05	25	25	19	13	14	25
12	19	04	02		19	12	25		19	21	26		18	28	08		19	07	26		20	14	15	
13	20	05	02		20	13	25		20	22	27		19	29	09		20	08	26		21	15	16	
14	21	07	02		21	15	25		21	23	27		20	01♏	09		21	09	27		22	17	16	
15	22	08	02		22	16	24		22	24	27		21	02	10		22	10	27		23	18	17	
16	23	09	01	21	23	17	24	22	23	26	28	23	22	03	10	24	23	12	28	25	24	19	18	25
17	24	11	01		24	18	24		24	27	28		23	04	11		24	13	29		25	20	18	
18	25	12	01		25	20	24		25	28	28		24	05	11		25	14	29		26	22	19	
19	26	13	01		26	21	24		26	29	28		25	07	12		26	15	30		27	23	20	26
20	27	14	00		27	22	24		27	01♎	29		26	08	12		27	17	01♓		28	24	20	
21	28	15	00	21	28	23	24	22	28	02	29	23	27	09	13	24	28	18	01	25	29	25	21	26
22	29	16	30♑		28	25	24		29	03	29		28	10	13		29	19	02		30	27	22	
23	30	18	30		29	26	24		30	04	30		29	12	14		00♐	20	02		01♑	28	22	
24	01♌	19	29		00♍	27	24		01♎	06	00♒		00♏	13	14		01	22	03		02	29	23	
25	02	20	29		01	28	24		02	07	01		01	14	15		02	23	04		03	00♒	24	
26	03	21	29	21	02	30	24	22	02	08	01	23	02	15	15	24	03	24	04	25	04	01	24	26
27	04	23	28		03	01♍	24		03	09	01		03	17	16	25	04	25	05		05	03	25	
28	05	24	28		04	02	24		04	11	02	24	04	18	17		05	27	06		06	04	26	
29	05	25	28		05	03	24		05	12	02		05	19	17		06	28	06		07	05	26	
30	06	26	28		06	04	24		06	13	03		06	20	18		07	29	07		08	06	27	
31	07	27	27	21	07	06	24	22					07	22	18	25					09	08	28	26

BIRTH TABLES - 1940

	JANUARY				FEBRUARY				MARCH				APRIL				MAY				JUNE			
	☉	♀	♂	♆	☉	♀	♂	♆	☉	♀	♂	♆	☉	♀	♂	♆	☉	♀	♂	♆	☉	♀	♂	♆
01	10♑	09♒	28♓	26♍	11♒	17♓	19♈	25♍	11♓	22♈	09♉	25♍	12♈	27♉	30♉	24♍	11♉	26♊	20♊	23♍	11♊	13♋	10♋	23♍
02	11	10	29		13	18	20		12	23	10	24	13	28	00♊		12	27	20		12	13	10	
03	12	11	30		14	19	21		13	24	10		14	29	01		13	27	21		13	13	11	
04	13	13	00♈		15	21	21		14	25	11		15	30	02		14	28	22		14	13	12	
05	14	14	01		16	22	22		15	26	12		16	01♊	02		15	29	22		15	13	12	
06	15	15	02	26	17	23	23	25	16	27	12	24	17	02	03	24	16	30	23	23	16	13	13	23
07	16	16	03	25	18	24	24		17	29	13		18	03	04		17	01♋	23		17	13	13	
08	17	18	03		19	26	24		18	30	14		19	04	04	23	18	01	24		18	13	14	
09	18	19	04		20	27	25		19	01♉	14		19	05	05		19	02	25		18	13	15	
10	19	20	04		21	28	26		20	02	15		20	06	06		20	03	25		19	13	15	
11	20	21	05	25	22	29	26	25	21	03	16	24	21	07	06	23	21	03	26	23	20	13	16	23
12	21	23	06		23	00♈	27		22	04	16		22	08	07		22	04	27		21	12	17	
13	22	24	06		24	02	28		23	06	17		23	09	08		23	05	27		22	12	17	
14	23	25	07		25	03	28		24	07	18		24	10	08		24	05	28		23	12	18	
15	24	26	08		26	04	29		25	08	19		25	11	09		24	06	29		24	11	19	
16	25	27	09	25	27	05	30	25	26	09	19	24	26	12	10	23	25	07	29	23	25	11	19	23
17	26	29	09		28	06	00♉		27	10	20		27	13	10		26	07	30		26	10	20	
18	27	30	10		29	08	01		28	11	21		28	14	11		27	08	01♋		27	10	20	
19	28	01♓	11		30	09	02		29	12	21		29	15	12		28	08	01		28	09	21	
20	29	02	11		01♓	10	02		30	13	22		00♉	16	12		29	09	02		29	09	22	
21	00♒	04	12	25	02	11	03	25	01♈	15	23	24	01	17	13	23	00♊	09	03	23	30	08	23	23
22	01	05	13		03	12	04		02	16	23		02	18	14		01	10	03		01♋	08	23	
23	02	06	13		04	13	04		03	17	24		03	19	14		02	10	04		02	07	24	
24	03	07	14		05	15	05		04	18	25		04	20	15		03	11	04		03	07	24	
25	04	08	15		06	16	06		05	19	25		05	21	16		04	11	05		04	06	25	
26	05	10	15	25	07	17	06	25	06	20	26	24	06	21	16	23	05	12	06	23	05	05	26	23
27	06	11	16		08	18	07		07	21	27		07	22	17		06	12	06		06	05	26	
28	07	12	17		09	19	08		08	22	27		08	23	18		07	12	07		07	04	27	
29	08	13	17		10	21	08		09	23	28		09	24	18		08	12	08		08	03	28	
30	09	15	18						10	24	29		10	25	19		09	13	08		09	03	28	
31	10	16	19	25					11	25	29	24					10	13	09	23				

	JULY				AUGUST				SEPTEMBER			
Day	☉	♀	♂	♆	☉	♀	♂	♆	☉	♀	♂	♆
01	09♋	02♋	29♋	23♍	09♌	00♋	18♌	24♍	09♍	23♋	08♍	25♍
02	10	02	29		10	01	19		10	24	09	
03	11	01	00♌		11	01	20		11	25	09	
04	12	01	01		12	02	20		12	26	10	
05	13	00	01		13	02	21		13	27	11	
06	14	30♊	02	23	14	03	22	24	14	28	11	25
07	15	29	03		15	03	22		15	29	12	
08	16	29	03		16	04	23		16	30	13	
09	17	28	04		17	04	24		17	01♌	13	
10	18	28	05		18	05	24		18	02	14	
11	19	28	05	23	19	06	25	24	19	03	15	25
12	20	28	06		20	07	25		20	04	15	
13	21	27	06		21	07	26		21	05	16	
14	22	27	07		22	08	27		22	06	16	
15	23	27	08		22	09	27		22	07	17	
16	24	27	08	23	23	09	28	24	23	08	18	25
17	25	27	09		24	10	29		24	09	18	
18	26	27	10		25	11	29		25	10	19	
19	27	27	10		26	12	30		26	11	20	
20	28	27	11		27	13	01♍		27	12	20	
21	29	27	11	23	28	13	01	24	28	13	21	25
22	30	27	12		29	14	02		29	14	22	
23	00♌	27	13		00♍	15	02		00♎	15	22	
24	01	27	13		01	16	03		01	16	23	
25	02	28	14		02	17	04		02	17	24	26
26	03	28	15	23	03	18	04	24	03	19	24	26
27	04	28	15		04	19	05		04	20	25	
28	05	29	16	24	05	19	06	25	05	21	25	
29	06	29	17		06	20	06		06	22	26	
30	07	29	17		07	21	07		07	23	27	
31	08	30♊	18	24	08	22	08	25				

	OCTOBER				NOVEMBER				DECEMBER			
Day	☉	♀	♂	♆	☉	♀	♂	♆	☉	♀	♂	♆
01	08♎	24♌	27♍	26♍	09♏	30	17♎	27♍	09♐	06♏	07♏	27♍
02	09	25	28		10	01♎	18		10	07	08	
03	10	26	29		11	02	19		11	09	08	28
04	11	27	29		12	03	19		12	10	09	
05	12	28	30		13	05	20		13	11	10	
06	13	30	01♎	26	14	06	21	27	14	12	10	28
07	14	01♍	01		15	07	21		15	14	11	
08	15	02	02		16	08	22		16	15	12	
09	16	03	02		17	09	23		17	16	12	
10	17	04	03		18	11	23		18	17	13	
11	18	05	04	26	19	12	24	27	19	18	14	28
12	19	06	04		20	13	25		20	20	14	
13	20	08	05		21	14	25		21	21	15	
14	21	09	06		22	15	26		22	22	16	
15	22	10	06		23	17	27		23	23	16	
16	23	11	07	26	24	18	27	27	24	25	17	28
17	24	12	08		25	19	28		25	26	18	
18	25	13	08		26	20	29		26	27	18	
19	26	14	09		27	21	29		27	28	19	
20	27	16	10		28	23	30		28	30	20	
21	28	17	10	26	29	24	01♏	27	29	01♐	20	28
22	29	18	11		00♐	25	01		01♑	02	21	
23	30	19	12	27	01	26	02		02	03	22	
24	01♏	20	12		02	28	03		03	05	22	
25	02	21	13		03	29	03		04	06	23	
26	03	23	14	27	04	30	04	27	05	07	24	28
27	04	24	14		05	01♏	05		06	08	24	
28	05	25	15		06	02	05		07	10	25	
29	06	26	15		07	04	06		08	11	26	
30	07	27	16		08	05	06		09	12	26	
31	08	29	17	27					10	13	27	28

BIRTH TABLES - 1941

	JANUARY				FEBRUARY				MARCH				APRIL				MAY				JUNE			
	☉	♀	♂	♆	☉	♀	♂	♆	☉	♀	♂	♆	☉	♀	♂	♆	☉	♀	♂	♆	☉	♀	♂	♆
01	11♑	15♐	28♏	28♍	12♒	23♑	19♐	27♍	11♓	28♒	08♑	27♍	11♈	07♈	29♑	26♍	11♉	14♉	20♒	25♍	11♊	22♊	11♓	25♍
02	12	16	28		13	25	19		12	29	09		12	08	00♒		12	15	21		12	23	12	
03	13	17	29		14	26	20		13	01♓	09		13	09	01		13	16	21		13	25	12	
04	14	18	30		15	27	21		14	02	10		14	11	01		14	18	22		13	26	13	
05	15	20	00♐		16	28	21		15	03	11		15	12	02		15	19	23		14	27	13	
06	16	21	01	28	17	30	22	27	16	04	11	27	16	13	03	26	16	20	23	25	15	28	14	25
07	17	22	02		18	01♒	23		17	06	12		17	14	03		17	21	24		16	29	15	
08	18	23	02		19	02	24		18	07	13		18	15	04		17	23	25		17	01♋	15	
09	19	25	03		20	03	24		19	08	13		19	17	05		18	24	25		18	02	16	
10	20	26	04		21	05	25		20	09	14		20	18	06		19	25	26		19	03	17	
11	21	27	05	28	22	06	26	27	21	11	15	26	21	19	06	26	20	26	27	25	20	04	17	25
12	22	28	05		23	07	26		22	12	16		22	20	07		21	27	28		21	06	18	
13	23	30	06		24	08	27		23	13	16		23	22	08		22	29	28		22	07	19	
14	24	01♑	07		25	10	28		24	14	17		24	23	08		23	30	29		23	08	19	
15	25	02	07		26	11	28		25	16	18		25	24	09		24	01♊	30		24	09	20	
16	26	03	08	28	27	12	29	27	26	17	18	26	26	25	10	26	25	02	00♓	25	25	10	20	25
17	27	05	09		28	13	30		27	18	19		27	27	10		26	04	01		26	12	21	
18	28	06	09		29	14	00♑		28	19	20		28	28	11		27	05	02		27	13	22	
19	29	07	10		00♓	16	01		28	21	20		29	29	12	25	28	06	02		28	14	22	
20	00♒	08	11		01	17	02		29	22	21		00♉	00♉	12		29	07	03		29	15	23	
21	01	10	11	28	02	18	02	27	00♈	23	22	26	01	02	13	25	00♊	09	04	25	30	17	24	25
22	02	11	12		03	19	03		01	24	22		02	03	14		01	10	04		01♋	18	24	
23	03	12	13		04	21	04		02	26	23		03	04	15		02	11	05		02	19	25	
24	04	13	13		05	22	04		03	27	24		04	05	15		03	12	06		03	20	25	
25	05	15	14		07	23	05		04	28	24		05	07	16		04	13	06		04	21	26	
26	06	16	15	27	08	24	06	27	05	29	25	26	06	08	17	25	05	15	07	25	04	23	27	25
27	07	17	15		09	26	07		06	01♈	26		07	09	17		06	16	08		05	24	27	
28	08	18	16		10	27	07		07	02	27		08	10	18		07	17	08		06	25	28	
29	09	20	17						08	03	27		09	11	19		08	18	09		07	26	28	
30	10	21	17						09	04	28		10	13	19		09	20	10		08	28	29	
31	11	22	18	27					10	06	29	26					10	21	10	25				

Day	JUL ☉	JUL ♀	JUL ♂	JUL Ψ	AUG ☉	AUG ♀	AUG ♂	AUG Ψ	SEP ☉	SEP ♀	SEP ♂	SEP Ψ
01	09♋	29♋	30♓	25♍	09♌	06♍	15♈	26♍	09♍	14♎	24♈	27♍
02	10	30♌	00♈		10	08	16		10	15	24	
03	11	01	01		11	09	16		11	16	24	
04	12	02	01		12	10	17		12	17	24	
05	13	03	02		13	11	17		13	19	24	
06	14	05	02	25	14	13	17	26	13	20	24	27
07	15	06	03		15	14	18		14	21	24	
08	16	07	04		16	15	18		15	22	24	
09	17	09	04		16	16	18		16	23	24	
10	18	10	05		17	17	19		17	24	24	
11	19	11	05	25	18	19	19	26	18	26	24	27
12	20	12	06		19	20	19		19	27	23	
13	21	13	06		20	21	20		20	28	23	
14	22	15	07		21	22	20		21	29	23	
15	23	16	07		22	23	20		22	00♏	23	
16	24	17	08	25	23	25	21	26	23	02	23	27
17	24	18	08		24	26	21		24	03	23	
18	25	19	09		25	27	21		25	04	23	
19	26	21	09		26	28	21		26	05	23	
20	27	22	10		27	29	22		27	06	22	
21	28	23	10	25	28	01♎	22	26	28	07	22	27
22	29	24	11		29	02	22		29	09	22	28
23	00♌	26	11	26	30	03	22		00♎	10	22	
24	01	27	12		01♍	04	23		01	11	22	
25	02	28	12		02	05	23		02	12	21	
26	03	29	13	26	03	07	23	27	03	13	21	28
27	04	00♍	13		04	08	23		04	15	21	
28	05	02	14		05	09	23		05	16	21	
29	06	03	14		06	10	23		06	17	20	
30	07	04	15		07	11	23		07	18	20	
31	08	05	15	26	08	13	23	27				

Day	OCT ☉	OCT ♀	OCT ♂	OCT Ψ	NOV ☉	NOV ♀	NOV ♂	NOV Ψ	DEC ☉	DEC ♀	DEC ♂	DEC Ψ
01	08♎	19♏	20♈	28♍	09♏	25♐	12♈	29♍	09♐	26♑	14♈	30♍
02	09	20	19		10	26	11		10	27	14	
03	10	22	19		11	27	11		11	28	14	
04	11	23	19		12	28	11		12	29	15	
05	12	25	18		13	29	11		13	30	15	
06	13	25	18	28	14	00♑	11	29	14	00♒	15	30
07	14	26	18		15	01	11		15	01	15	
08	15	27	17		16	02	11		16	02	16	
09	16	29	17		17	03	11		17	03	16	
10	17	30	17		18	04	11		18	04	16	
11	18	01♐	17	28	19	05	11	29	19	05	17	30
12	19	02	16		20	07	11		20	06	17	
13	20	03	16		21	08	11		21	07	17	
14	21	04	16		22	09	11		22	07	18	
15	22	05	15		23	10	11		23	08	18	
16	23	07	15	28	24	11	11	29	24	09	18	30
17	24	08	15		25	12	11		25	10	19	
18	25	09	14		26	13	12		26	10	19	
19	26	10	14		27	14	12		27	11	20	
20	27	11	14		28	15	12		28	12	20	
21	28	12	14	29	29	16	12	29	29	13	20	30
22	29	13	13		30	17	12		00♑	13	21	
23	30	15	13		01♐	18	12		01	14	21	
24	01♏	16	13		02	19	12		02	15	22	
25	02	17	13		03	20	13		03	16	22	
26	03	18	13	29	04	21	13	30	04	16	22	30
27	04	19	12		05	22	13		05	16	23	
28	05	20	12		06	23	13		06	17	23	
29	06	21	12		07	24	13		07	17	24	
30	07	22	12		08	25	14	30	08	18	24	
31	08	23	12	29					09	18	25	30

BIRTH TABLES - 1942

Day	JANUARY				FEBRUARY				MARCH			
	☉	♀	♂	♆	☉	♀	♂	♆	☉	♀	♂	♆
01	10♑	19♒	25♈	30♍	12♒	14♒	11♉	30♍	10♓	06♒	27♉	29♍
02	11	19	26		13	13	11		11	07	27	
03	12	19	26		14	13	12		12	07	28	
04	14	20	26		15	12	12		13	07	28	
05	15	20	27		16	12	13		14	07	29	
06	16	20	27	30	17	11	13	30	15	08	30	29
07	17	21	28		18	10	14		16	08	00♊	
08	18	21	28		19	10	15		17	09	01	
09	19	21	29		20	09	15		18	09	01	
10	20	21	29		21	09	16		19	10	02	
11	21	21	30	30	22	08	16	29	20	10	02	29
12	22	21	00♉		23	08	17		21	11	03	
13	23	21	01		24	07	17		22	11	04	
14	24	21	01		25	07	18		23	12	04	
15	25	21	02		26	07	19		24	13	05	
16	26	21	02	30	27	06	19	29	25	13	05	29
17	27	21	03		28	06	20		26	14	06	
18	28	21	03		29	06	20		27	14	07	
19	29	20	04		00♓	06	21		28	15	07	
20	30	20	04		01	06	21		29	16	08	28
21	01♒	20	05	30	02	06	22	29	00♈	17	08	28
22	02	19	05		03	06	23		01	17	09	
23	03	19	06		04	06	23		02	18	10	
24	04	18	06		05	06	24		03	19	10	
25	05	18	07		06	06	24		04	20	11	
26	06	18	07	30	07	06	25	29	05	20	11	28
27	07	17	08		08	06	25		06	21	12	
28	08	16	09		09	06	26		07	22	13	
29	09	16	09						08	23	13	
30	10	15	10						09	24	14	
31	11	15	10	30					10	25	14	28

Day	APRIL				MAY				JUNE			
	☉	♀	♂	♆	☉	♀	♂	♆	☉	♀	♂	♆
01	11♈	25♒	15♊	28♍	10♉	25♓	03♋	27♍	10♊	29♈	22♋	27♍
02	12	26	16		11	26	04		11	01♉	23	
03	13	27	16		12	27	04		12	02	23	
04	14	28	17		13	28	05		13	03	24	
05	15	29	17		14	29	06		14	04	25	
06	16	30	18	28	15	00♈	06	27	15	05	25	27
07	17	01♓	19		16	02	07		16	06	26	
08	18	02	19		17	03	07		17	07	27	
09	19	03	20		18	04	08		18	09	27	
10	20	04	20		19	05	09		19	10	28	
11	21	05	21	28	20	06	09	27	20	11	28	27
12	22	06	22		21	07	10		21	12	29	
13	23	07	22		22	08	11		22	13	30	
14	24	08	23		23	09	11		23	14	00♌	
15	25	09	23		24	10	12		24	16	01	
16	26	10	24	28	25	11	12	27	25	17	01	27
17	27	11	25		26	13	13		26	18	02	
18	28	12	25		27	14	14		27	19	03	
19	29	13	26		28	15	14		28	20	03	
20	30	14	27		29	16	15		29	21	04	
21	01♉	15	27	28	30	17	15	27	00♋	22	05	27
22	02	16	28		01♊	18	16		01	24	05	
23	03	17	28		02	19	17		01	25	06	
24	04	18	29		03	20	17		02	26	06	
25	05	19	30		04	21	18		03	27	07	
26	06	20	00♋	28	05	23	19	27	04	28	08	27
27	07	21	01		06	24	19		05	30	08	
28	08	22	01		07	25	20		06	01♊	09	
29	09	23	02		07	26	20		07	02	10	
30	10	24	03	27	08	27	21		08	03	10	
31					09	28	22	27				

Day	JULY ☉	JULY ♀	JULY ♂	JULY ♆	AUGUST ☉	AUGUST ♀	AUGUST ♂	AUGUST ♆	SEPTEMBER ☉	SEPTEMBER ♀	SEPTEMBER ♂	SEPTEMBER ♆
01	09♋	04♊	11♌	27♍	09♌	11♋	00♍	28	08♍	19♌	20♍	29♍
02	10	05	11		10	12	01		09	20	20	
03	11	06	12		11	14	01		10	21	21	
04	12	08	13		11	15	02		11	22	22	
05	13	09	13		12	16	02		12	24	22	
06	14	10	14	27	13	17	03	28	13	25	23	29
07	15	11	15		14	18	04		14	26	24	
08	16	12	15		15	20	05		15	27	24	
09	17	14	16		16	21	05		16	29	25	
10	18	15	16		17	22	06		17	30	26	
11	19	16	17	27	18	23	06	28	18	01♍	26	29
12	19	17	18		19	24	07		19	02	27	
13	20	18	18		20	26	08		20	04	27	
14	21	20	19		21	27	08		21	05	28	
15	22	21	19		22	28	09		22	06	29	
16	23	22	20	27	23	29	10	28	23	07	29	29
17	24	23	21	28	24	00♌	10		24	09	00≏	
18	25	24	21		25	02	11		25	10	01	
19	26	26	22		26	03	11		26	11	01	
20	27	27	23		27	04	12		27	12	02	30
21	28	28	23	28	28	05	13	28	28	13	02	
22	29	29	24		29	07	13		29	15	03	
23	30	00♋	24		30	08	14	29	30	16	04	
24	01♌	02	25		01♍	09	15		01≏	17	05	
25	02	03	26		02	10	15		02	18	05	30
26	03	04	26	28	03	11	16	29	03	20	06	
27	04	05	27		04	13	17		04	21	07	
28	05	06	28		05	14	17		05	22	07	
29	06	07	28		06	15	18		06	23	08	
30	07	09	29		06	16	18		07	25	09	30
31	08	10	29	28	07	18	19	29				

Day	OCTOBER ☉	OCTOBER ♀	OCTOBER ♂	OCTOBER ♆	NOVEMBER ☉	NOVEMBER ♀	NOVEMBER ♂	NOVEMBER ♆	DECEMBER ☉	DECEMBER ♀	DECEMBER ♂	DECEMBER ♆
01	08≏	26♍	09≏	30♍	08♏	05♏	30≏	01≏	09♐	12♐	20♏	02≏
02	09	27	10		09	06	00♏		10	14	21	
03	10	28	10	00≏	10	07	01		11	15	22	
04	11	30	11		11	08	02		12	16	22	
05	12	01≏	12		12	10	02		13	17	23	
06	13	02	12	00	13	11	03	01	14	19	24	02
07	14	03	13		14	12	04		15	20	24	
08	15	05	14		15	13	04		16	21	25	
09	16	06	14		16	15	05		17	22	26	
10	17	07	15		17	16	06		18	24	26	
11	18	08	16	00	18	17	06	01	19	25	27	02
12	19	10	16		19	18	07		20	26	28	
13	20	11	17		20	20	08		21	27	28	
14	21	12	18		21	21	09		22	29	29	
15	22	13	18		22	22	09		23	30	30	
16	22	15	19	00	24	24	10	01	24	01♑	01♐	02
17	23	16	20	01	25	25	11		25	02	01	
18	24	17	20		26	26	11		26	04	02	
19	25	18	21		27	27	12	02	27	05	03	
20	26	20	22		28	29	13		28	06	03	
21	27	21	22	01	29	30	13	02	29	08	04	02
22	28	22	23		30	01♐	14		00♑	09	05	
23	29	23	24		01♐	02	15		01	10	05	
24	00♏	25	24		02	04	15		02	11	06	
25	01	26	25		03	05	16		03	13	07	
26	02	27	26	01	04	06	17	02	04	14	08	02
27	03	28	26		05	07	17		05	15	08	
28	04	30	27		06	09	18		06	16	09	
29	05	01♏	28		07	10	19		07	18	10	
30	06	02	28		08	11	19		08	19	10	
31	07	03	29	01					09	20	11	02

BIRTH TABLES - 1943

	JANUARY				FEBRUARY				MARCH				APRIL				MAY				JUNE			
	☉	♀	♂	♇	☉	♀	♂	♇	☉	♀	♂	♇	☉	♀	♂	♇	☉	♀	♂	♇	☉	♀	♂	♇
01	10♑	21♑	12♐	02♎	12♒	00♓	04♑	02♎	10♓	05♈	25♑	01♎	11♈	13♉	18♒	00♎	10♉	18♊	11♓	30♍	10♊	24♋	04♈	29♍
02	11	23	13		13	01	05		11	06	26		12	14	19		11	20	11		11	25	05	
03	12	24	13		14	03	06		12	07	26		13	15	20		12	21	12		12	26	05	
04	13	25	14		15	04	06		13	09	27		14	16	20		13	22	13		13	27	06	
05	14	26	14		16	05	07		14	10	28		15	18	21		14	23	14		14	28	07	
06	15	28	15	02	17	06	08	02	15	11	29	01	16	19	22	00	15	24	14	30	15	29	07	29
07	16	29	16		18	08	09		16	12	29		17	20	23		16	25	15		16	00♌	08	
08	17	00♒	17		19	09	09		17	14	30		18	21	23		17	27	16		17	01	09	
09	18	01	18		20	10	10		18	15	01♒		19	22	24		18	28	17		18	02	10	
10	19	03	18		21	11	11		19	16	01		20	24	25		19	29	17		19	03	10	
11	20	04	19	02	22	13	11	02	20	17	02	30	21	25	26	00	20	00♋	18	30	20	04	11	29
12	21	05	20		23	14	12		21	18	03		22	26	26		21	01	19		21	05	12	
13	22	06	20		24	15	13		22	20	04		23	27	27		22	02	20	29	22	06	13	
14	23	08	21		25	16	14		23	21	04		24	28	28		23	03	20		23	07	13	
15	24	09	22		26	18	14		24	22	05		25	30	29		24	05	21		24	08	14	
16	25	10	23	02	27	19	15	02	25	23	06	30	26	01♊	29	00♎	25	06	22	29	24	09	15	29
17	27	11	23		28	20	16		26	25	07		27	02	00♓		26	07	23		25	10	15	
18	28	13	24		29	21	17		27	26	07		28	03	01	30♍	27	08	23		26	11	16	
19	29	14	25		30	23	17	01	28	27	08		29	04	02		28	09	24		27	12	17	
20	30	15	25		01♓	24	18		29	28	09		30	06	02		29	10	25		28	14	18	
21	01♒	16	26	02	02	25	19	01	30	29	10	30	01♉	07	03	30	30	11	26	29	29	15	18	29
22	02	18	27		03	26	20		01♈	01♉	10		01	08	04		01♊	12	26		00♋	15	19	
23	03	19	28		04	28	20		02	02	11		02	09	05		01	14	27		01	16	20	
24	04	20	28		05	29	21		03	03	12		03	10	05		02	15	28		02	17	21	
25	05	21	29		06	00♈	22		04	04	13		04	11	06		03	16	29		03	18	21	
26	06	23	30	02	07	01	23	01	05	06	13	30	05	13	07	30	04	17	29	29	04	19	22	29
27	07	24	01♑		08	02	23		06	07	14		06	14	08		05	18	00♈		05	20	23	
28	09	25	01		09	04	24		07	08	15		07	15	08		06	19	01		06	21	23	
29	09	26	02						08	09	16	00	08	16	09		07	20	02		07	22	24	
30	10	28	03						09	10	16		09	17	10		08	21	02		08	23	25	
31	11	29	03	02					10	12	17	00					09	22	03	29				

JULY

Day	☉	♀	♂	♆
01	09♋	24♌	25♈	29♍
02	10	25	26	
03	11	26	27	
04	12	27	28	
05	13	28	28	
06	14	29	29	29
07	14	30	30	
08	15	00♍	00♉	
09	16	01	01	30
10	17	02	02	
11	18	03	02	30
12	19	04	03	
13	20	05	04	
14	21	05	05	
15	22	06	05	
16	23	07	06	30
17	24	08	07	
18	25	08	07	
19	26	09	08	
20	27	10	09	
21	28	11	09	30
22	29	11	10	
23	30	12	11	
24	01♌	13	11	
25	02	13	12	
26	03	14	13	30
27	04	14	13	
28	05	15	14	
29	05	16	14	
30	06	16	15	
31	07	17	16	30

AUGUST

Day	☉	♀	♂	♆
01	08♌	17♍	17♉	30♍
02	09	18	17	00♎
03	10	18	18	
04	11	18	18	
05	12	19	19	
06	13	19	20	00
07	14	19	20	
08	15	20	21	
09	16	20	21	
10	17	20	22	
11	18	20	23	00
12	19	20	23	
13	20	20	24	
14	21	21	24	
15	22	21	25	
16	23	21	26	00
17	24	20	26	
18	25	20	27	
19	26	20	27	
20	27	20	28	01
21	28	20	29	01
22	29	20	29	
23	29	19	30	
24	00♍	19	00♊	
25	01	19	01	
26	02	18	01	01
27	03	18	02	
28	04	17	03	
29	05	17	03	
30	06	16	04	
31	07	16	04	01

SEPTEMBER

Day	☉	♀	♂	♆
01	08♍	15♍	05♊	01♎
02	09	15	05	
03	10	14	06	
04	11	13	06	
05	12	13	07	
06	13	12	07	01
07	14	12	08	
08	15	11	08	
09	16	10	09	
10	17	10	09	
11	18	09	10	01
12	19	09	10	
13	20	08	11	
14	21	08	11	
15	22	07	11	
16	23	07	12	01
17	24	06	12	02
18	25	06	13	
19	26	06	13	
20	27	05	14	
21	28	05	14	02
22	29	05	14	
23	30	05	15	
24	01♎	05	15	
25	02	04	16	
26	03	04	16	02
27	04	04	16	
28	04	04	17	
29	05	04	17	
30	06	05	17	

OCTOBER

Day	☉	♀	♂	♆
01	07♎	05♍	18♊	02♎
02	08	05	18	
03	09	05	18	
04	10	05	19	
05	11	06	19	
06	12	06	19	02
07	13	06	19	
08	14	07	20	
09	15	07	20	
10	16	07	20	
11	17	08	20	02
12	18	08	21	
13	19	09	21	
14	20	09	21	03
15	21	10	21	
16	22	11	21	03
17	23	11	21	
18	24	12	22	
19	25	12	22	
20	26	13	22	
21	27	14	22	03
22	28	15	22	
23	29	15	22	
24	00♏	16	22	
25	01	17	22	
26	02	18	22	03
27	03	18	22	
28	04	19	22	
29	05	20	22	
30	06	21	22	
31	07	22	22	03

NOVEMBER

Day	☉	♀	♂	♆
01	08♏	22♍	22♊	03♎
02	09	23	22	
03	10	24	22	
04	11	25	22	
05	12	26	22	
06	13	27	22	03
07	14	28	21	
08	15	29	21	
09	16	30	21	
10	17	01♎	21	
11	18	02	21	03
12	19	03	21	
13	20	04	20	
14	21	05	20	
15	22	06	20	04
16	23	07	20	04
17	24	08	19	
18	25	09	19	
19	26	10	19	
20	27	11	18	
21	28	12	18	04
22	29	13	18	
23	00♐	14	17	
24	01	15	17	
25	02	16	17	
26	03	17	16	04
27	04	18	16	
28	05	19	16	
29	06	20	15	
30	07	21	15	

DECEMBER

Day	☉	♀	♂	♆
01	08♐	22♎	14♊	04♎
02	09	24	14	
03	10	25	14	
04	11	26	13	
05	12	27	13	
06	13	28	12	04
07	15	29	12	
08	16	00♏	12	
09	17	01	11	
10	18	02	11	
11	19	04	11	04
12	20	05	10	
13	21	06	10	
14	22	07	10	
15	23	08	09	
16	24	09	09	04
17	25	10	09	
18	26	12	08	
19	27	13	08	
20	28	14	08	
21	29	15	07	04
22	30	16	07	
23	01♑	17	07	
24	02	19	07	
25	03	20	07	
26	04	21	06	04
27	05	22	06	
28	06	23	06	
29	07	24	06	
30	08	26	06	
31	09	27	05	04

BIRTH TABLES - 1944

Day	JAN ☉	JAN ♀	JAN ♂	JAN Ψ	FEB ☉	FEB ♀	FEB ♂	FEB Ψ	MAR ☉	MAR ♀	MAR ♂	MAR Ψ
01	10♑	28♏	05♊	04♎	12♒	05♑	08♊	04♎	11♓	11♒	18♊	03♎
02	11	29	05		13	07	08		12	12	18	
03	12	00♐	05		14	08	08		13	13	18	
04	13	02	05		15	09	08		14	15	19	
05	14	03	05		16	10	09		15	16	19	
06	15	04	05	04	17	11	09	04	16	17	20	03
07	16	05	05		18	13	09		17	18	20	
08	17	06	05		19	14	10		18	19	21	
09	18	08	05		20	15	10		19	21	21	
10	19	09	05		21	16	10		20	22	21	
11	20	10	05	04	22	18	11	04	21	23	22	03
12	21	11	05		23	19	11		22	24	22	
13	22	12	05		24	20	11		23	26	23	
14	23	14	05		25	21	12		24	27	23	
15	24	15	05		26	22	12		25	28	24	
16	25	16	05	04	27	24	12	04	26	29	24	03
17	26	17	05		28	25	13		27	00♓	25	
18	27	18	05		29	26	13		28	02	25	
19	28	20	05		30	27	13		29	03	26	
20	29	21	06		01♓	29	14		30	04	26	
21	00♒	22	06	04	02	30	14	04	01♈	05	27	03
22	01	23	06		03	01♒	14		02	07	27	
23	02	24	06		04	02	15		03	08	28	
24	03	26	06		05	03	15		04	09	28	
25	04	27	06		06	05	16		05	10	29	
26	05	28	06	04	07	06	16	04	06	12	29	03
27	06	29	07		08	07	16		07	13	30	
28	07	00♑	07		09	08	17		08	14	00♋	
29	08	02	07		10	10	17		09	15	01	
30	09	03	07						10	16	01	
31	11	04	07	04					11	18	02	03

Day	APR ☉	APR ♀	APR ♂	APR Ψ	MAY ☉	MAY ♀	MAY ♂	MAY Ψ	JUN ☉	JUN ♀	JUN ♂	JUN Ψ
01	12♈	19♓	02♋	03♎	11♉	26♈	18♋	02♎	11♊	04♊	06♌	02♎
02	13	20	03		12	27	19		12	05	06	
03	14	21	03		13	28	19		13	06	07	01
04	15	23	04		14	30	20		14	08	08	
05	16	24	04		15	01♉	20		15	09	08	
06	17	25	05	03	16	02	21	02	16	10	09	01
07	18	26	05		17	03	21		17	11	09	
08	19	28	06		18	04	22		18	12	10	
09	20	29	06		19	06	23		18	14	10	
10	20	00♈	07		20	07	23		19	15	11	
11	21	01	07	02	21	08	24	02	20	16	12	01
12	22	02	08		22	09	24		21	17	12	
13	23	04	08		23	11	25		22	19	13	
14	24	05	09		24	12	25		23	20	13	
15	25	06	09		25	13	26		24	21	14	
16	26	07	10	02	25	14	27	02	25	22	15	01
17	27	09	10		26	15	27		26	24	15	
18	28	10	11		27	17	28		27	25	16	02
19	29	11	12		28	18	28		28	26	16	
20	00♉	12	12		29	19	29		29	27	17	
21	01	14	13	02	00♊	20	29	02	30	28	18	02
22	02	15	13		01	22	30		01♋	30	18	
23	03	16	14		02	23	01♌		02	01♋	19	
24	04	17	14		03	24	01		03	02	19	
25	05	18	15		04	25	02		04	03	20	
26	06	20	15	02	05	27	02	02	05	05	21	02
27	07	21	16		06	28	03		06	06	21	
28	08	22	16		07	29	03		07	07	22	
29	09	23	17		08	00♊	04		08	08	22	
30	10	25	18		09	01	05		09	09	23	
31					10	03	05	02				

Day	JULY ☉	♀	♂	♆	AUGUST ☉	♀	♂	♆	SEPTEMBER ☉	♀	♂	♆
01	09♋	11♋	24♌	02♎	09♌	19♌	13♍	02♎	09♍	27♍	02♎	03♎
02	10	12	24		10	20	13		10	28	03	
03	11	13	25		11	21	14		11	30	04	
04	12	14	25		12	23	14		12	01♎	04	
05	13	16	26		13	24	15		13	02	05	
06	14	17	27	02	14	25	16	02	14	03	05	03
07	15	18	27		15	26	16		15	04	06	
08	16	19	28		16	27	17		16	06	07	
09	17	21	28		17	29	18		17	07	07	
10	18	22	29		18	30	18		18	08	08	
11	19	23	30	02	19	01♍	19	02	19	09	09	03
12	20	24	00♍		20	02	19		20	11	09	
13	21	25	01		21	04	20		21	12	10	
14	22	27	01		22	05	21		22	13	11	04
15	23	28	02		23	06	21	03	23	14	11	
16	24	29	03	02	23	07	22	03	23	16	12	04
17	25	00♌	03		24	09	23		24	17	13	
18	26	02	04		25	10	23		25	18	13	
19	27	03	05		26	11	24		26	19	14	
20	28	04	05		27	12	25		27	20	15	
21	29	05	06	02	28	14	25	03	28	22	15	04
22	30	07	06		29	15	26		29	23	16	
23	00♌	08	07		00♍	16	26		00♎	24	17	
24	01	09	08		01	17	27		01	25	17	
25	02	10	08		02	18	28		02	27	18	
26	03	11	09	02	03	20	28	03	03	28	19	04
27	04	13	09		04	21	29		04	29	19	
28	05	14	10		05	22	30		05	00♏	20	
29	06	15	11		06	23	00♎		06	02	21	
30	07	16	11		07	25	01		07	03	21	
31	08	18	12	02	08	26	02	03				

Day	OCTOBER ☉	♀	♂	♆	NOVEMBER ☉	♀	♂	♆	DECEMBER ☉	♀	♂	♆
01	08♎	04♏	22♎	04♎	09♏	12♐	13♏	05♎	09♐	18♑	04♐	06♎
02	09	05	23		10	13	14		10	20	05	
03	10	06	24		11	14	14		11	21	06	
04	11	08	24		12	16	15		12	22	06	
05	12	09	25		13	17	16		13	23	07	
06	13	10	25	04	14	18	17	05	14	24	08	06
07	14	11	26		15	19	17		15	25	09	
08	15	13	27		16	21	18		16	27	09	
09	16	14	27		17	22	18	06	17	28	10	
10	17	15	28		18	23	19		18	29	11	
11	18	16	29	05	19	24	20	06	19	00♒	11	06
12	19	18	29		20	25	21		20	02	12	
13	20	19	00♏		21	27	21		21	03	13	
14	21	20	01		22	28	22		22	04	14	
15	22	21	01		23	29	23		23	05	14	
16	23	22	02	05	24	00♑	24	06	24	06	15	06
17	24	24	03		25	01	24		25	08	16	
18	25	25	03		26	03	25		26	09	17	
19	26	26	04		27	04	26		27	10	17	
20	27	27	05		28	05	26		29	11	18	
21	28	29	05	05	29	07	27	06	30	12	19	06
22	29	30	06		00♐	08	28		01♑	13	19	
23	30	01♐	07		01	09	28		02	15	20	
24	01♏	02	08		02	10	29		03	16	21	
25	02	03	08		03	11	30		04	17	22	
26	03	05	09	05	04	12	01♐	06	05	18	22	06
27	04	06	10		05	13	01		06	19	23	
28	05	07	10		06	15	02		07	20	24	
29	06	08	11		07	16	03		09	22	25	
30	07	10	12		08	17	03		09	23	25	
31	08	11	12	05					10	24	26	06

BIRTH TABLES - 1945

Day	JAN ☉	JAN ♀	JAN ♂	JAN ♆	FEB ☉	FEB ♀	FEB ♂	FEB ♆	MAR ☉	MAR ♀	MAR ♂	MAR ♆
01	11♑	25♒	27♐	06♎	12♒	29♓	20♑	06♎	11♓	24♈	12♒	06♎
02	12	26	28		13	00♈	21		12	25	12	
03	13	27	28		14	01	22		13	25	13	
04	14	29	29		15	02	22		14	26	14	
05	15	30	30		16	03	23		15	27	15	
06	16	01♓	01♑	06	17	04	24	06	16	27	16	06
07	17	02	01		18	05	25		17	28	16	
08	18	03	02		19	06	25		18	28	17	
09	19	04	03		20	07	26		19	29	18	
10	20	05	04		21	08	27		20	30	19	
11	21	06	04	06	22	09	28	06	21	01♉	19	05
12	22	08	05		23	10	29		22	01	20	
13	23	09	06		24	11	29		23	01	21	
14	24	10	07		25	12	00♒		24	01	22	
15	25	11	07		26	13	01		25	02	23	
16	26	12	08	06	27	14	02	06	26	02	23	05
17	27	13	09		28	14	02		27	02	24	
18	28	14	10		29	15	03		28	03	25	
19	29	15	10		00♓	16	04		29	03	26	
20	00♒	16	11		02	17	05		30	03	26	
21	01	18	12	06	03	18	05	06	01♈	03	27	05
22	02	19	13		04	19	06		02	03	28	
23	03	20	13		05	20	07		02	04	29	
24	04	21	14		06	20	08		03	04	30	
25	05	22	15		07	21	09		04	04	00♓	
26	06	23	16	06	08	22	09	06	05	04	01	05
27	07	24	16		09	23	10		06	04	02	
28	08	25	17		10	23	11		07	03	03	
29	09	26	18						08	03	03	
30	10	27	19						09	03	04	
31	11	28	19	06					10	03	05	05

Day	APR ☉	APR ♀	APR ♂	APR ♆	MAY ☉	MAY ♀	MAY ♂	MAY ♆	JUN ☉	JUN ♀	JUN ♂	JUN ♆
01	11♈	03♉	06♓	05♎	11♉	18♈	29♓	04♎	11♊	27♈	23♈	04♎
02	12	02	07		12	18	30		12	28	23	
03	13	02	07		13	17	01♈		13	29	24	
04	14	02	08		14	17	01		13	30	25	
05	15	01	09		15	17	02		14	00♉	26	
06	16	01	10	05	16	17	03	04	15	01	26	04
07	17	00♉	10		17	17	04		16	02	27	
08	18	30♈	11		18	17	04		17	03	28	
09	19	29	12		18	17	05		18	04	29	
10	20	29	13		19	17	06		19	04	29	
11	21	28	14	05	20	18	07	04	20	05	00♉	04
12	22	27	14		21	18	07		21	06	01	
13	23	27	15		22	18	08		22	07	02	
14	24	26	16		23	18	09		23	08	02	
15	25	25	17		24	19	10		24	09	03	
16	26	25	17	05	25	19	10	04	25	10	04	04
17	27	24	18	04	26	19	11		26	11	04	
18	28	24	19		27	20	12		27	11	05	
19	29	23	20		28	20	13		28	12	06	
20	00♉	22	20		29	20	14		29	13	07	
21	01	22	21	04	00♊	21	14	04	30	14	07	04
22	02	21	22		01	21	15		01♋	15	08	
23	03	21	23		02	22	16		02	16	09	
24	04	20	24		03	22	17		03	17	10	
25	05	20	24		04	23	17		04	18	10	
26	06	20	25	04	05	24	18	04	04	19	11	04
27	07	19	26		06	24	19		05	20	12	
28	08	19	26		07	25	20		06	21	12	
29	09	18	27		08	25	20		07	22	13	
30	10	18	28		09	26	21		08	23	14	
31					10	27	22	04				

JULY

Day	☉	♀	♂	♆
01	09♋	24♉	15♉	04♎
02	10	25	15	
03	11	26	16	
04	12	26	17	
05	13	27	17	
06	14	29	18	04
07	15	30	19	
08	16	01♊	20	
09	17	02	20	
10	18	03	21	
11	19	04	22	04
12	20	05	22	
13	21	06	23	
14	22	07	24	
15	23	08	25	
16	24	09	25	04
17	25	10	26	
18	25	11	27	
19	26	12	27	
20	27	14	28	
21	28	15	29	04
22	29	16	29	
23	00♌	17	00♊	
24	01	18	01	
25	02	19	01	
26	03	20	02	04
27	04	21	03	
28	05	22	04	
29	06	23	04	
30	07	24	05	
31	08	26	06	04

AUGUST

Day	☉	♀	♂	♆
01	09♌	27♊	06♊	04♎
02	10	28	07	
03	11	29	08	
04	12	00♋	08	
05	13	01	09	
06	14	02	10	04
07	15	03	10	
08	16	05	11	
09	17	06	12	
10	17	07	12	
11	18	08	13	05
12	19	09	14	
13	20	10	14	
14	21	11	15	
15	22	13	15	
16	23	14	16	05
17	24	15	17	
18	25	16	17	
19	26	17	18	
20	27	18	19	
21	28	19	19	05
22	29	21	20	
23	30	22	21	
24	01♍	23	21	
25	02	24	22	
26	03	25	22	05
27	04	26	23	
28	05	28	24	
29	06	29	24	
30	07	30	25	
31	08	01♌	26	05

SEPTEMBER

Day	☉	♀	♂	♆
01	09	02♌	26♊	05♎
02	10	03	27	
03	11	05	27	
04	12	06	28	
05	13	07	29	
06	14	08	29	05
07	14	09	30	
08	15	11	00♋	
09	16	12	01	
10	17	13	02	
11	18	14	02	06
12	19	15	03	
13	20	17	03	
14	21	18	04	
15	22	19	04	
16	23	20	05	06
17	24	21	06	
18	25	23	06	
19	26	24	07	
20	27	25	07	
21	28	26	08	06
22	29	27	08	
23	00♎	29	09	
24	01	30	09	
25	02	01♍	10	
26	03	02	11	06
27	04	03	11	
28	05	05	12	
29	06	06	12	
30	07	07	13	

OCTOBER

Day	☉	♀	♂	♆
01	08♎	08♍	13♋	06♎
02	09	10	14	
03	10	11	14	
04	11	12	15	
05	12	13	15	
06	13	14	16	06
07	14	16	16	
08	15	17	17	
09	16	18	17	
10	17	19	18	
11	18	21	18	07
12	19	22	19	
13	20	23	19	
14	21	24	20	
15	22	25	20	
16	23	27	20	07
17	24	28	21	
18	25	29	21	
19	26	00♎	22	
20	27	02	22	
21	28	03	23	07
22	29	04	23	
23	30	05	23	
24	01♏	07	24	
25	02	08	24	
26	03	09	25	07
27	04	10	25	
28	05	12	25	
29	06	13	26	
30	07	14	26	
31	08	15	26	07

NOVEMBER

Day	☉	♀	♂	♆
01	09♏	17♎	27♋	07♎
02	10	18	27	
03	11	19	28	
04	12	20	28	
05	13	22	28	
06	14	23	28	08
07	15	24	29	
08	16	25	29	
09	17	27	29	
10	18	28	30	
11	19	29	30	08
12	20	00♏	00♌	
13	21	02	00	
14	22	03	01	
15	23	04	01	
16	24	05	01	08
17	25	07	01	
18	26	08	02	
19	27	09	02	
20	28	10	02	
21	29	12	02	08
22	30	13	02	
23	01♐	14	02	
24	02	15	03	
25	03	17	03	
26	04	18	03	08
27	05	19	03	
28	06	20	03	
29	07	22	03	
30	08	23	03	

DECEMBER

Day	☉	♀	♂	♆
01	09♐	24♏	03♌	08♎
02	10	25	03	
03	11	26	03	
04	12	28	03	
05	13	29	03	
06	14	00♐	03	08
07	15	02	03	
08	16	03	03	
09	17	04	03	
10	18	05	03	
11	19	07	03	08
12	20	08	03	
13	21	09	03	
14	22	10	03	
15	23	12	02	
16	24	13	02	08
17	25	14	02	
18	26	15	02	
19	27	17	02	
20	28	18	02	
21	29	19	01	09
22	00♑	20	01	
23	01	22	01	
24	02	23	01	
25	03	24	00	
26	04	26	00♌	09
27	05	27	30♋	
28	06	28	29	
29	07	29	29	
30	08	01♑	29	
31	09	02	28	09

BIRTH TABLES - 1946

JANUARY

Day	☉	♀	♂	♆
01	10♑	03♑	28♋	09♎
02	12	04	28	
03	13	06	27	
04	14	07	27	
05	15	08	27	
06	16	09	26	09
07	17	11	26	
08	18	12	25	
09	19	13	25	
10	20	14	25	
11	21	16	24	09
12	22	17	24	
13	23	18	23	
14	24	19	23	
15	25	21	23	
16	26	22	22	09
17	27	23	22	
18	28	24	22	
19	29	26	21	
20	30	27	21	
21	01♒	28	20	09
22	02	29	20	
23	03	01♒	20	
24	04	02	19	
25	05	03	19	
26	06	04	19	09
27	07	06	18	
28	08	07	18	
29	09	08	18	
30	10	10	17	
31	11	11	17	09

FEBRUARY

Day	☉	♀	♂	♆
01	12♒	12♒	17♋	08♎
02	13	13	17	
03	14	15	16	
04	15	16	16	
05	16	17	16	
06	17	18	16	08
07	18	20	15	
08	19	21	15	
09	20	22	15	
10	21	23	15	
11	22	25	15	08
12	23	26	15	
13	24	27	15	
14	25	28	14	
15	26	30	14	
16	27	01♓	14	08
17	28	02	14	
18	29	03	14	
19	00♓	05	14	
20	01	06	14	
21	02	07	14	08
22	03	08	14	
23	04	10	14	
24	05	11	14	
25	06	12	14	
26	07	13	14	08
27	08	15	14	
28	09	16	14	

MARCH

Day	☉	♀	♂	♆
01	10♓	17♓	14♋	08♎
02	11	18	15	
03	12	20	15	
04	13	21	15	
05	14	22	15	
06	15	23	15	08
07	16	25	15	
08	17	26	15	
09	18	27	16	
10	19	28	16	
11	20	30	16	08
12	21	01♈	16	
13	22	02	16	
14	23	03	16	
15	24	05	17	
16	25	06	17	08
17	26	07	17	
18	27	08	17	
19	28	10	18	
20	29	11	18	07
21	00♈	12	18	07
22	01	13	18	
23	02	14	19	
24	03	16	19	
25	04	17	19	
26	05	18	20	07
27	06	19	20	
28	07	21	20	
29	08	22	21	
30	09	23	21	
31	10	24	21	07

APRIL

Day	☉	♀	♂	♆
01	11♈	26♈	22♋	07♎
02	12	27	22	
03	13	28	22	
04	14	29	23	
05	15	01♉	23	
06	16	02	23	07
07	17	03	24	
08	18	04	24	
09	19	06	25	
10	20	07	25	
11	21	08	25	07
12	22	09	26	
13	23	10	26	
14	24	12	26	
15	25	13	27	
16	26	14	27	07
17	27	15	28	
18	28	17	28	
19	29	18	29	
20	30	19	29	
21	01♉	20	29	07
22	02	22	30	
23	03	23	00♌	
24	04	24	01	
25	05	25	01	
26	06	26	02	07
27	07	28	02	06
28	08	29	03	
29	09	00♊	03	
30	10	01	03	

MAY

Day	☉	♀	♂	♆
01	11♉	03♊	04♌	06♎
02	11	04	04	
03	12	05	05	
04	13	06	05	
05	14	07	06	
06	15	09	06	06
07	16	10	07	
08	17	11	07	
09	18	12	08	
10	19	13	08	
11	20	15	09	06
12	21	16	09	
13	22	17	10	
14	23	18	10	
15	24	20	11	
16	25	21	11	06
17	26	22	12	
18	27	23	12	
19	28	24	13	
20	29	26	13	
21	30	27	14	06
22	01♊	28	14	
23	02	29	15	
24	03	00♋	15	
25	04	02	16	
26	05	03	16	06
27	06	04	17	
28	07	05	17	
29	08	06	18	
30	08	08	19	
31	09	09	19	06

JUNE

Day	☉	♀	♂	♆
01	10♊	11	20♌	06♎
02	11	11	20	
03	12	12	21	
04	13	14	21	
05	14	15	22	
06	15	16	22	06
07	16	17	23	
08	17	18	23	
09	18	20	24	
10	19	21	25	
11	20	22	25	06
12	21	23	26	
13	22	24	26	
14	23	26	27	
15	24	27	27	
16	25	28	28	06
17	26	29	28	
18	27	00♌	29	
19	28	02	30	
20	29	03	00♍	
21	29	04	01	06
22	00♋	05	01	
23	01	06	02	
24	02	07	02	
25	03	09	03	
26	04	10	04	06
27	05	11	04	
28	06	12	05	
29	07	13	05	
30	08	15	06	

	JULY				AUGUST				SEPTEMBER				OCTOBER				NOVEMBER				DECEMBER			
	☉	♀	♂	♆	☉	♀	♂	♆	☉	♀	♂	♆	☉	♀	♂	♆	☉	♀	♂	♆	☉	♀	♂	♆
01	09♋	16♌	06♍	06♎	09♌	21♍	25♍	06♎	08♍	25♎	15♎	07♎	08♎	21♏	05♏	08♎	08♏	02♐	26♏	09♎	09♐	18♏	18♐	10♎
02	10	17	07		10	22	26		09	26	15		09	22	05		09	02	27	10	10	18	19	
03	11	18	08		11	24	26		10	27	16		10	23	06		10	02	28		11	18	20	
04	12	19	08		11	25	27		10	28	17		11	23	07		11	01	28		12	17	20	
05	13	20	09		12	26	27		11	29	17		12	24	07	09	12	01	29		13	17	21	
06	14	21	09	06	13	27	28	07	12	30	18	07	13	25	08	09	13	01	30	10	14	17	22	10
07	15	23	10		14	28	29		13	00♏	19		14	25	09		14	00♐	01♐		15	17	23	
08	16	24	11		15	29	29		14	01	19	08	15	26	09		15	30♏	01		16	17	23	
09	17	25	11		16	00♎	30		15	02	20		16	27	10		16	29	02		17	17	24	
10	18	26	12		17	01	01♎		16	03	21		17	27	11		17	29	03		18	17	25	
11	19	27	12	06	18	02	01	07	17	04	21	08	18	28	12	09	18	28	03	10	19	17	26	11
12	20	29	13		19	03	02		18	05	22		19	28	12		20	28	04		20	17	26	
13	20	30	13		20	05	02		19	06	23		20	29	13		21	27	05		21	18	27	
14	21	01♍	14		21	06	03		20	07	23		21	29	14		22	27	06		22	18	28	
15	22	02	15		22	07	04		21	08	24		22	30	14		23	26	06		23	18	29	
16	23	03	15	06	23	08	04	07	22	09	25	08	23	01♐	15	09	24	26	07	10	24	18	29	11
17	24	04	16		24	09	05		23	10	25		24	01	16		25	25	08		25	19	00♑	
18	25	05	16		25	10	06		24	11	26		25	01	16		26	24	09		26	19	01	
19	26	07	17		26	11	06		25	12	27		25	01	17		27	24	09		27	19	02	
20	27	08	18		27	12	07		26	13	27		26	01	18		28	23	10		28	20	02	
21	28	09	18	06	28	13	08	07	27	13	28	08	27	02	18	09	29	23	11	10	29	20	03	11
22	29	10	19		29	14	08		28	14	29		28	02	19		30	22	11		00♑	21	04	
23	00♌	11	19		30	15	09		29	15	29		29	02	20		01♐	21	12		01	21	05	
24	01	12	20		01♍	16	09		30	16	30		00♏	02	21		02	21	13		02	22	05	
25	02	13	21		02	17	10		01♎	17	01♏		01	02	21		03	20	14		03	22	06	
26	03	15	21	06	03	18	11	07	02	18	01	08	02	02	22	09	04	20	14	10	04	23	07	11
27	04	16	22		04	19	11		03	18	02		03	02	23		05	20	15		05	24	08	
28	05	17	23		05	20	12		04	19	03		04	03	23		06	19	16		06	24	08	
29	06	18	23		06	21	13		05	20	03		05	02	24		07	19	17		07	25	09	
30	07	19	24		07	23	13		06	21	04		06	02	25		08	18	17		08	25	10	
31	08	20	24	06	07	24	14	07					07	02	26	09					09	26	11	11

BIRTH TABLES - 1947

Day	JAN ⊙	♀	♂	Ψ	FEB ⊙	♀	♂	Ψ	MAR ⊙	♀	♂	Ψ	APR ⊙	♀	♂	Ψ	MAY ⊙	♀	♂	Ψ	JUN ⊙	♀	♂	Ψ
01	10♑	27♍	11♑	11♎	12♒	25♐	05♒	11♎	10♓	26♑	27♒	10♎	11♈	02♓	22♓	09♎	10♉	08♈	15♈	09♎	10♊	15♉	08♉	08♎
02	11	28	12		13	26	06		11	27	28		12	03	23		11	09	16		11	16	09	
03	12	28	13		14	27	07		12	28	29		13	04	23		12	10	17		12	17	10	
04	13	29	14		15	28	08		13	29	30		14	05	24		13	11	17		13	19	11	
05	14	30	15		16	29	09		14	00♒	01♓		15	07	25		14	12	18		14	20	11	
06	15	01♐	15	11	17	00♑	09	11	15	01	01	10	16	08	26	09	15	14	19	09	15	21	12	08
07	16	01	16		18	01	10		16	03	02		17	09	27		16	15	20		16	22	13	
08	17	02	17		19	02	11		17	04	03		18	10	27		17	16	20	08	17	23	14	
09	18	03	18		20	04	12		18	05	04		19	11	28		18	17	21		18	25	14	
10	19	04	18		21	05	13		19	06	05		20	13	29		19	18	22		19	26	15	
11	20	05	19	11	22	06	13	11	20	07	05	10	21	14	30	09	20	20	23	08	20	27	16	08
12	21	06	20		23	07	14		21	08	06		22	15	00♈		21	21	23		21	28	17	
13	22	07	21		24	08	15		22	10	07		23	16	01		22	22	24		22	30	17	
14	23	07	21		25	09	16		23	11	08		24	17	02		23	23	25		23	01♊	18	
15	25	08	22		26	10	16		24	12	09		25	19	03		24	24	26		24	02	19	
16	26	09	23	11	27	11	17	10	25	13	09	10	26	20	04	09	25	25	27	08	24	03	19	08
17	27	10	24		28	12	18		26	14	10		27	21	04		26	27	27		25	04	20	
18	28	11	25		29	13	19		27	15	11		28	22	05		27	28	28		26	06	21	
19	29	12	25		00♓	14	20		28	17	12		29	23	06		28	29	29		27	07	22	
20	30	13	26		01	16	20		29	18	12		30	24	07		29	01♉	30		28	08	23	
21	01♒	14	27	11	02	17	21	10	00♈	19	13	10	01♉	26	07	09	30	02	00♉	08	29	09	23	08
22	02	15	28		03	18	22		01	20	14		02	27	08		01♊	03	01		00♋	10	24	
23	03	16	28		04	19	23		02	21	15		02	28	09		02	04	02		01	12	25	
24	04	17	29		05	20	24		03	22	16		03	29	10		02	05	03		02	13	25	
25	05	18	00♒		06	21	24		04	24	16		04	00♈	10		03	07	03		03	14	26	
26	06	19	01	11	07	22	25	10	05	25	17	10	05	02	11	09	04	08	04	08	04	15	27	08
27	07	20	02		08	23	26		06	26	18		06	03	12		05	09	05		05	17	27	
28	08	21	02		09	25	27		07	27	19		07	04	13		06	10	06		06	18	28	
29	09	22	03						08	28	20	09	08	05	14		07	11	06		07	19	29	
30	10	23	04						09	30	20		09	06	14		08	13	07		08	20	30	
31	11	24	05	11					10	01♓	21	09					09	14	08	08				

Day	JULY ☉	JULY ♀	JULY ♂	JULY ♆	AUGUST ☉	AUGUST ♀	AUGUST ♂	AUGUST ♆	SEPTEMBER ☉	SEPTEMBER ♀	SEPTEMBER ♂	SEPTEMBER ♆
01	09♋	21♊	00♊	08♎	08♌	29	22♊	09♎	08♍	08♍	12♋	09♎
02	10	23	01		09	01♌	22		09	09	13	
03	11	24	02		10	02	23		10	10	13	
04	12	25	02		11	03	24		11	11	14	
05	13	26	03		12	04	24		12	13	15	10
06	14	28	04	08	13	06	25	09	13	14	15	10
07	15	29	05		14	07	26		14	15	16	
08	15	30	05		15	08	26		15	16	16	
09	16	01♋	06		16	09	27		16	18	17	
10	17	02	07		17	10	28		17	19	18	
11	18	04	07	08	18	12	28	09	18	20	18	10
12	19	05	08		19	13	29		19	21	19	
13	20	06	09		20	14	30		20	23	20	
14	21	07	09		21	15	00♋		21	24	20	
15	22	08	10		22	17	01		22	25	21	
16	23	10	11	08	23	18	02	09	23	26	21	10
17	24	11	11		24	19	02		24	28	22	
18	25	12	12		25	20	03		25	29	23	
19	26	13	13		26	22	04		26	00♎	23	
20	27	15	14		27	23	04		27	01	24	
21	28	16	14	08	28	24	05	09	28	03	24	10
22	29	17	15		29	25	06		29	04	25	
23	30	18	16		30	26	06		30	05	26	
24	01♌	20	16		00♍	28	07		01♎	06	26	
25	02	21	17		01	29	08		02	07	27	
26	03	22	18	08	02	00♍	08	09	03	09	27	10
27	04	23	18		03	01	09		04	10	28	
28	05	24	19		04	03	10		05	11	28	
29	06	26	20		05	04	10		05	12	29	
30	06	27	20		06	05	11		06	14	30	
31	07	28	21	08	07	06	11	09				

Day	OCTOBER ☉	OCTOBER ♀	OCTOBER ♂	OCTOBER ♆	NOVEMBER ☉	NOVEMBER ♀	NOVEMBER ♂	NOVEMBER ♆	DECEMBER ☉	DECEMBER ♀	DECEMBER ♂	DECEMBER ♆
01	07♎	15♎	00♌	10♎	08♏	24♏	17♌	12♎	08♐	01♑	00♍	12♎
02	08	16	01		09	25	18		09	02	00	
03	09	17	01	11	10	26	18		10	04	01	13
04	10	19	02		11	27	18		11	05	01	
05	11	20	03		12	29	19		13	06	01	
06	12	21	03	11	13	30	19	12	14	07	02	13
07	13	22	04		14	01♐	20		15	09	02	
08	14	24	04		15	02	20		16	10	02	
09	15	25	05		16	04	21		17	11	03	
10	16	26	05		17	05	21		18	12	03	
11	17	27	06	11	18	06	22	12	19	13	03	13
12	18	29	06		19	07	22		20	15	04	
13	19	30	07		20	09	23		21	16	04	
14	20	01♏	08		21	10	23		22	17	04	
15	21	02	08		22	11	24		23	18	04	
16	22	04	09	11	23	12	24	12	24	20	05	13
17	23	05	09		24	14	24		25	21	05	
18	24	06	10		25	15	25		26	22	05	
19	25	07	10		26	16	25		27	23	05	
20	26	09	11		27	17	26		28	25	05	
21	27	10	11	11	28	19	26	12	29	26	06	13
22	28	11	12		29	20	27		30	27	06	
23	29	12	12		00♐	21	27		01♑	28	06	
24	00♏	14	13		01	22	27		02	30	06	
25	01	15	13		02	24	28		03	01♒	06	
26	02	16	14	11	03	25	28	12	04	02	07	13
27	03	17	14		04	26	29		05	03	07	
28	04	19	15		05	27	29		06	05	07	
29	05	20	16		06	29	29		07	06	07	
30	06	21	16	12	07	30	30		08	07	07	
31	07	22	17	12					09	08	07	13

BIRTH TABLES - 1948

Day	JANUARY				FEBRUARY				MARCH				APRIL				MAY				JUNE			
	☉	♀	♂	♆	☉	♀	♂	♆	☉	♀	♂	♆	☉	♀	♂	♆	☉	♀	♂	♆	☉	♀	♂	♆
01	10♑	10♒	07♍	13≏	12♒	18♓	04♍	13≏	11♓	22♈	23♌	12≏	12♈	27♉	18♌	12≏	11♉	25♊	24♌	11≏	11♊	11♋	06♍	10≏
02	11	11	07		13	19	04		12	23	23		13	28	18		12	26	24		12	11	06	
03	12	12	07		14	20	04		13	24	22		14	29	18		13	27	24		13	11	07	
04	13	13	08		15	21	03		14	26	22		15	30	18		14	28	25		14	11	07	
05	14	15	08		16	22	03		15	27	22		16	01♊	18		15	29	25		15	11	08	
06	15	16	08	13	17	24	02	13	16	28	21	12	17	02	18	12	16	29	25	11	16	11	08	10
07	16	17	08		18	25	02		17	29	21		18	03	19	11	17	00♋	26		17	11	09	
08	17	18	08		19	26	01		18	00♉	21		19	04	19		18	01	26		18	11	09	
09	18	19	08		20	27	01		19	01	21		20	05	19		19	02	26		19	10	10	
10	19	21	08		21	28	01		20	03	20		21	06	19		20	02	27		19	10	10	
11	20	22	08	13	22	30	00	13	21	04	20	12	22	07	19	11	21	03	27	11	20	10	11	10
12	21	23	08		23	01♈	30♌		22	05	20		22	08	19		22	04	28		21	09	11	
13	22	24	07		24	02	30		23	06	20		23	09	19		23	04	28		22	09	12	
14	23	26	07		25	03	29		24	07	20		24	10	20		24	05	28		23	09	12	
15	24	27	07		26	04	29		25	08	19		25	11	20		25	05	29		24	08	13	
16	25	28	07	13	27	06	28	13	26	09	19	12	26	12	20	11	26	06	29	11	25	08	13	10
17	26	29	07		28	07	28		27	10	19		27	13	20		26	06	29		26	07	14	
18	27	01♓	07		29	08	28		28	12	19		28	14	20		27	07	30	10	27	07	14	
19	28	02	07		30	09	27		29	13	19		29	15	21		28	07	00♍		28	06	15	
20	29	03	07		01♓	10	27		30	14	19		00♉	16	21		29	08	01		29	05	15	
21	00♒	04	07	13	02	12	26	13	01♈	15	19	12	01	17	21	11	00♊	08	01	10	30	05	16	10
22	01	05	06		03	13	26		02	16	18		02	18	21		01	09	02		01♋	04	16	
23	02	07	06		04	14	26		03	17	18		03	19	21		02	09	02		02	04	17	
24	03	08	06		05	15	25		04	18	18		04	20	22		03	09	02		03	03	17	
25	04	09	06		06	16	25		05	19	18		05	20	22		04	10	03		04	02	18	
26	05	10	05	13	07	17	25	13	06	20	18	12	06	21	22	11	05	10	03	10	05	02	18	10
27	06	12	05		08	19	24		07	21	18		07	22	23		06	10	04		06	01	19	
28	07	13	05		09	20	24	12	08	23	18		08	23	23		07	11	04		07	00	20	
29	09	14	05		10	21	23		09	24	18		09	24	23		08	11	05		08	30♊	20	
30	10	15	04						10	25	18		10	25	23		09	11	05		09	29	21	
31	11	16	04	13					11	26	18	12					10	11	05	10				

	JULY				AUGUST				SEPTEMBER			
	☉	♀	♂	♆	☉	♀	♂	♆	☉	♀	♂	♆
01	10♋	29♊	21♍	10♎	09♌	29♊	09♎	11♎	09♍	23♋	29♎	12♎
02	10	28	22		10	30	10		10	24	29	
03	11	28	22		11	00♋	10		11	25	30	
04	12	27	23		12	01	11		12	26	01♏	
05	13	27	23		13	01	12		13	27	01	
06	14	26	24	10	14	02	12	11	14	28	02	12
07	15	26	24		15	03	13		15	29	03	
08	16	26	25		16	03	13		16	30	03	
09	17	26	26		17	04	14		17	01♌	04	
10	18	25	26		18	05	15		18	02	05	
11	19	25	27	10	19	05	15	11	19	03	05	12
12	20	25	27		20	06	16		20	04	06	
13	21	25	28		21	07	16		21	05	07	
14	22	25	28		22	07	17		22	06	07	
15	23	25	29		23	08	18		23	07	08	
16	24	25	30	10	24	09	18	11	24	08	09	12
17	25	25	00♎		24	10	19		24	09	09	
18	26	25	01		25	11	20		25	10	10	
19	27	25	01		26	11	20		26	11	11	
20	28	25	02		27	12	21		27	12	11	
21	29	25	03	10	28	13	22	11	28	13	12	12
22	30	25	03		29	14	22		29	15	13	
23	01♌	26	04	11	00♍	15	23		00♎	16	13	
24	01	26	04		01	16	23		01	17	14	
25	02	26	05		02	17	24		02	18	15	
26	03	27	05	11	03	18	25	11	03	19	15	12
27	04	27	06		04	18	25		04	20	16	
28	05	27	07		05	19	26		05	21	17	
29	06	28	07		06	20	27		06	22	18	13
30	07	28	08		07	21	27		07	23	18	
31	08	29	08	11	08	22	28	11				

	OCTOBER				NOVEMBER				DECEMBER			
	☉	♀	♂	♆	☉	♀	♂	♆	☉	♀	♂	♆
01	08♎	24♌	19♏	13♎	09♏	00♎	11♐	14♎	09♐	07♏	04♑	15♎
02	09	26	20		10	01	12		10	08	04	
03	10	27	20		10	03	13		11	09	05	
04	11	28	21		12	04	13		12	10	06	
05	12	29	22		13	05	14		13	12	07	
06	13	30	22	13	14	06	15	14	14	13	07	15
07	14	01♍	23		15	07	15		15	14	08	
08	15	02	24		16	09	16		16	15	09	
09	16	03	25		17	10	17		17	17	10	
10	17	05	25		18	11	18		18	18	10	
11	18	06	26	13	19	12	18	14	19	19	11	15
12	19	07	26		20	14	19		20	20	12	
13	20	08	27		21	15	20		21	22	13	
14	21	09	28		22	16	21		22	23	13	
15	22	10	29		23	17	21		23	24	14	
16	23	11	29	13	24	18	22	14	24	25	15	15
17	24	13	00♐		25	20	23		25	27	16	
18	25	14	01		26	21	24		26	28	17	
19	26	15	02		27	22	24		28	29	17	
20	27	16	02		28	23	25		29	00♐	18	
21	28	17	03	13	29	24	26	14	30	01	19	15
22	29	18	04		00♐	26	27		01♑	03	20	
23	30	20	05		01	27	27		02	04	20	
24	01♏	21	05		02	28	28		03	05	21	
25	02	22	06		03	29	29		04	06	22	
26	03	23	07	13	04	01♏	30	14	05	08	23	15
27	04	24	07	14	05	02	00♑		06	09	24	
28	05	26	08		06	03	01	15	07	10	24	
29	06	27	09		07	04	02		08	11	25	
30	07	28	10		08	06	03		09	13	26	
31	08	29	10	14					10	14	27	15

BIRTH TABLES - 1949

JANUARY

Day	☉	♀	♂	♆
01	11♑	15♐	27♑	15♎
02	12	16	28	
03	13	18	29	
04	14	19	30	
05	15	20	01♒	
06	16	21	01	15
07	17	23	02	
08	18	24	03	
09	19	25	04	
10	20	26	05	
11	21	28	05	15
12	22	29	06	
13	23	00♑	07	
14	24	01	08	
15	25	03	08	
16	26	04	09	15
17	27	05	10	
18	28	06	11	
19	29	08	12	
20	00♒	09	12	
21	01	10	13	15
22	02	11	14	
23	03	13	15	
24	04	14	16	
25	05	15	16	
26	06	16	17	15
27	07	18	18	
28	08	19	19	
29	09	20	20	
30	10	21	20	
31	11	23	21	15

FEBRUARY

Day	☉	♀	♂	♆
01	12♒	24♑	22♒	15♎
02	13	25	23	
03	14	26	23	
04	15	28	24	
05	16	29	25	
06	17	00♒	26	15
07	18	01	27	
08	19	03	27	
09	20	04	28	
10	21	05	29	
11	22	06	30	15
12	23	08	01♓	
13	24	09	01	
14	25	10	02	
15	26	11	03	
16	28	13	04	15
17	29	14	05	
18	30	15	05	
19	01♓	16	06	
20	02	18	07	
21	03	19	08	15
22	04	20	09	
23	05	21	09	
24	06	23	10	
25	07	24	11	
26	08	25	12	15
27	09	26	12	
28	10	28	13	

MARCH

Day	☉	♀	♂	♆
01	11♓	29♒	14♓	15♎
02	12	00♓	15	
03	13	01	15	
04	14	03	16	
05	15	04	17	
06	16	05	18	15
07	17	06	19	
08	18	08	20	
09	19	09	20	
10	20	10	21	
11	21	11	22	14
12	22	13	23	
13	23	14	23	
14	24	15	24	
15	25	16	25	
16	26	18	26	14
17	27	19	27	
18	28	20	27	
19	29	21	28	
20	30	22	29	
21	01♈	24	30	14
22	02	25	00♈	
23	03	26	01	
24	04	28	02	
25	05	29	03	
26	06	00♈	04	14
27	06	01	04	
28	07	03	05	
29	08	04	06	
30	09	05	07	
31	10	06	07	14

APRIL

Day	☉	♀	♂	♆
01	11♈	07♈	08♈	14♎
02	12	09	09	
03	13	10	10	
04	14	11	11	
05	15	12	11	
06	16	14	12	14
07	17	15	13	
08	18	16	14	
09	19	17	14	
10	20	19	15	
11	21	20	16	14
12	22	21	17	
13	23	22	17	
14	24	24	18	
15	25	25	19	
16	26	26	20	13
17	27	27	20	
18	28	29	21	
19	29	30	22	
20	00♉	01♉	23	
21	01	02	24	13
22	02	04	24	
23	03	05	25	
24	04	06	26	
25	05	07	27	
26	06	08	27	13
27	07	10	28	
28	08	11	29	
29	09	12	30	
30	10	13	00♉	

MAY

Day	☉	♀	♂	♆
01	11♉	15♉	01♉	13♎
02	12	16	02	
03	13	17	03	
04	14	18	03	
05	15	20	04	
06	16	21	05	13
07	17	22	06	
08	18	23	06	
09	19	24	07	
10	19	26	08	
11	20	27	09	13
12	21	28	09	
13	22	29	10	
14	23	01♊	11	
15	24	02	11	
16	25	03	12	13
17	26	04	13	
18	27	06	14	
19	28	07	14	
20	29	08	15	
21	00♊	09	16	13
22	01	10	17	
23	02	12	17	
24	03	13	18	
25	04	14	19	
26	05	15	20	13
27	06	17	20	
28	07	18	21	
29	08	19	22	
30	09	20	22	
31	10	22	23	13

JUNE

Day	☉	♀	♂	♆
01	11♊	23♊	24♉	13♎
02	12	24	25	
03	13	25	25	
04	14	26	26	
05	14	28	27	
06	15	29	27	12
07	16	00♋	28	
08	17	01	29	
09	18	03	30	
10	19	04	00♊	
11	20	05	01	12
12	21	06	02	
13	22	07	02	
14	23	09	03	
15	24	10	04	
16	25	11	05	12
17	26	12	05	
18	27	14	06	
19	28	15	07	
20	29	16	07	
21	30	17	08	12
22	01♋	18	09	
23	02	20	10	
24	03	21	10	
25	04	22	11	
26	05	23	11	12
27	05	25	12	
28	06	26	13	
29	07	27	14	
30	08	28	14	

Day	JULY ☉	♀	♂	♆	AUGUST ☉	♀	♂	♆	SEPTEMBER ☉	♀	♂	♆	OCTOBER ☉	♀	♂	♆	NOVEMBER ☉	♀	♂	♆	DECEMBER ☉	♀	♂	♆
01	09♋	29♋	15♊	12♎	09♌	07♍	06♋	13♎	09♍	14♎	26♋	14♎	08♎	20♏	15♌	15♎	09♏	25♐	03♍	16♎	09♐	26♑	19♍	17♎
02	10	01♌	16		10	08	07		10	16	27		09	21	16		10	26	04		10	27	19	
03	11	02	17		11	10	08		11	17	28		10	22	16		11	27	04		11	28	20	
04	12	03	17		12	11	08		12	18	28		11	23	17		12	28	05		12	28	20	
05	13	04	18		13	12	09		13	19	29		12	24	17		13	29	05		13	29	21	
06	14	06	19	12	14	13	10	13	14	20	30	14	13	25	18	15	14	00♑	06	16	14	00♒	21	17
07	15	07	19		15	14	10		15	21	00♌		14	27	19		15	01	06		15	01	22	
08	16	08	20		16	16	11		15	23	01		15	28	19		16	02	07		16	02	22	
09	17	09	21		17	17	12		16	24	01		16	29	20		17	04	08		17	03	23	
10	18	10	21		18	18	12		17	25	02		17	00♐	20		18	05	08		18	04	23	
11	19	12	22	12	18	19	13	13	18	26	03	14	18	01	21	15	19	06	09	16	19	04	24	17
12	20	13	23		19	20	13		19	27	03		19	02	22		20	07	09		20	05	24	
13	21	14	23	13	20	22	14		20	29	04		20	04	22		21	08	10		21	06	25	
14	22	15	24		21	23	15		21	30	05		21	05	23		22	09	10		22	07	25	
15	23	16	25		22	24	15		22	01♏	05		22	06	23		23	10	11		23	08	25	
16	24	18	25	13	23	25	16	13	23	02	06	14	23	07	24	15	24	11	11	16	24	08	26	17
17	25	19	26		24	26	17		24	03	06		24	08	25		25	12	12		25	09	26	
18	26	20	27		25	28	17		25	04	07		25	09	25		26	13	12		26	10	27	
19	26	21	27		26	29	18		26	06	08		26	10	26		27	14	13		27	10	27	
20	27	23	28		27	30	19		27	07	08		27	11	26		28	15	13		28	11	28	
21	28	24	29	13	28	01♎	19	13	28	08	09	14	28	13	27	15	29	16	14	16	29	12	28	17
22	29	25	30		29	02	20		29	09	10		29	14	27		30	17	14		00♑	12	28	
23	00♌	26	00♋		00♍	04	21		00♎	10	10		30	15	28		01♐	18	15	17	01	13	29	
24	01	27	01		01	05	21		01	12	11		01♏	16	29	16	02	19	15		02	14	29	
25	02	29	02		02	06	22		02	13	11		02	17	29		03	20	16		03	14	30	
26	03	30	02	13	03	07	23	13	03	14	12	14	03	18	30	16	04	21	16	17	04	15	00♎	17
27	04	01♍	03		04	08	23		04	15	13		04	19	00♍		05	22	17		05	15	01	
28	05	02	03		05	10	24		05	16	13		05	20	01		06	23	17		06	16	01	
29	06	03	04		06	11	24	14	06	17	14		06	22	01		07	24	18		07	16	01	
30	07	05	05		07	12	25		07	19	14		07	23	02		08	25	18		08	16	02	
31	08	06	06	13	08	13	26	14					08	24	03	16					09	17	02	17

BIRTH TABLES - 1950

Day	JAN ☉	JAN ♀	JAN ♂	JAN ♆	FEB ☉	FEB ♀	FEB ♂	FEB ♆	MAR ☉	MAR ♀	MAR ♂	MAR ♆
01	11♑	17♒	02♎	17♎	12♒	10♒	10♎	17♎	10♓	05♒	09♎	17♎
02	12	17	03		13	09	10		11	05	09	
03	13	18	03		14	09	11		12	05	09	
04	14	18	03		15	08	11		13	06	08	
05	15	18	04		16	08	11		14	06	08	
06	16	18	04	17	17	07	11	17	15	07	08	17
07	17	19	04		18	07	11		16	07	08	
08	18	19	05		19	06	11		17	08	07	
09	19	19	05		20	06	11		18	08	07	
10	20	19	05		21	05	11		19	09	07	
11	21	19	06	17	22	05	11	17	20	09	06	17
12	22	19	06		23	05	11		21	10	06	
13	23	19	06		24	04	11		22	10	06	
14	24	18	07		25	04	11		23	11	05	
15	25	18	07		26	04	11		24	12	05	
16	26	18	07	17	27	03	11	17	25	12	05	17
17	27	18	07		28	03	11		26	13	04	
18	28	17	08		29	03	11		27	14	04	
19	29	17	08		00♓	03	11		28	15	03	16
20	30	17	08		01	03	11		29	15	03	
21	01♒	16	08	17	02	03	10	17	00♈	16	03	16
22	02	16	09		03	03	10		01	17	02	
23	03	15	09		04	03	10		02	18	02	
24	04	15	09		05	03	10		03	18	02	
25	05	14	09		06	04	10		04	19	01	
26	06	14	09	17	07	04	10	17	05	20	01	16
27	07	13	10		08	04	10		06	21	00	
28	08	13	10		09	04	09		07	22	00♎	
29	09	12	10						08	23	30♍	
30	10	11	10						09	23	29	
31	11	11	10	17					10	24	29	16

Day	APR ☉	APR ♀	APR ♂	APR ♆	MAY ☉	MAY ♀	MAY ♂	MAY ♆	JUN ☉	JUN ♀	JUN ♂	JUN ♆
01	11♈	25♒	29♍	16♎	11♉	25♓	22♍	15♎	10♊	30♈	27♍	15♎
02	12	26	28		12	26	22		11	01♉	27	
03	13	27	28		12	28	22		12	02	27	
04	14	28	27		13	29	22		13	03	27	
05	15	29	27		14	30	22		14	04	28	
06	16	30	27	16	15	01♈	22	15	15	06	28	15
07	17	01♓	26		16	02	22		16	07	28	
08	18	02	26		17	03	22		17	08	29	
09	19	03	26		18	04	22		18	09	29	
10	20	04	25		19	05	22		19	10	30	
11	21	05	25	16	20	06	22	15	20	11	30	15
12	22	06	25		21	07	22		21	13	00♎	
13	23	07	25		22	08	23		22	14	01	
14	24	08	24		23	10	23		23	15	01	
15	25	09	24		24	11	23		24	16	01	
16	26	10	24	16	25	12	23	15	25	17	02	15
17	27	11	24		26	13	23		26	18	02	
18	28	12	24		27	14	23		27	20	03	
19	29	13	23		28	15	23		28	21	03	
20	30	14	23		29	16	24		29	22	03	
21	01♉	15	23	16	30	17	24	15	30	23	04	15
22	02	16	23		01♊	19	24		00♋	24	04	
23	03	17	23		02	20	24		01	25	05	
24	04	18	23		03	21	24		02	27	05	
25	05	19	22	15	04	22	25		03	28	06	
26	06	20	22	15	05	23	25	15	04	29	06	15
27	07	21	22		06	24	25		05	00♊	06	
28	08	22	22		07	25	25		06	01	07	
29	09	23	22		08	26	26		07	02	07	
30	10	24	22		09	28	26		08	04	08	
31					09	29	26	15				

Day	JUL ☉	JUL ♀	JUL ♂	JUL ♆	AUG ☉	AUG ♀	AUG ♂	AUG ♆	SEP ☉	SEP ♀	SEP ♂	SEP ♆
01	09♋	05♊	08♎	15♎	09♌	12♋	25♎	15♎	08♍	19♌	14♏	16♎
02	10	06	09		10	13	25		09	21	14	
03	11	07	09		11	14	26		10	22	15	
04	12	08	10		12	15	26		11	23	16	
05	13	10	10		12	17	27		12	24	16	
06	14	11	11	15	13	18	28	15	13	26	17	16
07	15	12	11		14	19	28		14	27	18	
08	16	13	12		15	20	29		15	28	18	
09	17	14	12		16	21	29		16	29	19	
10	18	15	13		17	23	30		17	01♍	20	
11	19	17	13	15	18	24	00♏	15	18	02	20	16
12	20	18	14		19	25	01		19	03	21	
13	21	19	14		20	26	02		20	04	22	
14	21	20	15		21	27	02		21	05	22	
15	22	21	15		22	29	03		22	07	23	
16	23	23	16	15	23	30	04	15	23	08	24	16
17	24	24	16		24	01♌	04		24	09	24	
18	25	25	17		25	02	05		25	10	25	
19	26	26	17		26	04	05		26	12	26	
20	27	27	18		27	05	06		27	13	26	
21	28	29	18	15	28	06	07	15	28	14	27	16
22	29	30	19		29	07	07		29	15	28	
23	00♌	01♋	20		30	08	08		30	17	28	
24	01	02	20		01♍	10	09		01♎	18	29	
25	02	03	21		02	11	09	16	02	19	30	17
26	03	05	21	15	03	12	10	16	03	20	00♐	17
27	04	06	22		04	13	10		04	22	01	
28	05	07	22		05	15	11		05	23	02	
29	06	08	23		06	16	12		06	24	03	
30	07	09	23		07	17	12		07	25	03	
31	08	11	24	15	08	18	13	16				

Day	OCT ☉	OCT ♀	OCT ♂	OCT ♆	NOV ☉	NOV ♀	NOV ♂	NOV ♆	DEC ☉	DEC ♀	DEC ♂	DEC ♆
01	08♎	27♍	04♐	17♎	08♏	05♏	26♐	18♎	09♐	13♐	19♑	19♎
02	09	28	05		09	07	27		10	14	20	
03	10	29	05		10	08	28		11	16	21	
04	11	00♎	06		11	09	29		12	17	22	
05	12	02	07		13	10	29		13	18	22	
06	13	03	08	17	14	12	00♑	18	14	19	23	19
07	14	04	08		15	13	01		15	21	24	
08	15	05	09		16	14	02		16	22	25	
09	16	07	10		17	15	02		17	23	25	
10	17	08	10		18	17	03		18	24	26	
11	18	09	11	17	19	18	04	18	19	26	27	19
12	19	10	12		20	19	05		20	27	28	
13	20	12	13		21	20	05		21	28	29	
14	21	13	13		22	22	06		22	29	29	
15	22	14	14		23	23	07		23	01♑	00♒	
16	23	15	15	17	24	24	08	18	24	02	01	19
17	24	17	15		25	25	08		25	03	02	
18	25	18	16		26	27	09		26	04	02	
19	26	19	17		27	28	10		27	06	03	
20	27	20	18		28	29	11		28	07	04	
21	28	22	18	17	29	00♐	12	19	29	08	05	19
22	29	23	19	18	30	02	12		00♑	09	06	
23	30	24	20		01♐	03	13		01	11	06	
24	01♏	25	21		02	04	14		02	12	07	
25	02	27	21		03	06	15		03	13	08	
26	03	28	22	18	04	07	15	19	04	14	09	19
27	03	29	23		05	08	16		05	16	10	
28	04	00♏	23		06	09	17		06	17	10	
29	05	02	24		07	11	18		07	18	11	
30	06	03	25		08	12	18		08	19	12	
31	07	04	26	18					09	21	13	19

BIRTH TABLES - 1951

	JANUARY				FEBRUARY				MARCH			
Day	☉	♀	♂	♆	☉	♀	♂	♆	☉	♀	♂	♆
01	10♑	22♑	13♒	19♎	12♒	01♓	08♓	20♎	10♓	06♈	30♓	19♎
02	11	23	14		13	02	09		11	07	00♈	
03	12	25	15		14	03	09	19	12	08	01	
04	13	26	16		15	05	10		13	09	02	
05	14	27	17		16	06	11		14	11	03	
06	15	28	17	19	17	07	12	19	15	12	04	19
07	16	30	18		18	08	13		16	13	04	
08	17	01♒	19		19	10	13		17	14	05	
09	18	02	20	20	20	11	14		18	15	06	
10	19	03	21		21	12	15		19	17	07	
11	20	05	21	20	22	13	16	19	20	18	07	19
12	21	06	22		23	15	16		21	19	08	
13	22	07	23		24	16	17		22	20	09	
14	24	08	24		25	17	18		23	22	10	
15	25	10	24		26	18	19		24	23	10	
16	26	11	25	20	27	20	20	19	25	24	11	19
17	27	12	26		28	21	20		26	25	12	
18	28	13	27		29	22	21		27	26	13	
19	29	15	28		00♓	23	22		28	28	14	
20	30	16	28		01	24	23		29	29	14	
21	01♒	17	29	20	02	26	23	19	00♈	00♉	15	19
22	02	18	30		03	27	24		01	01	16	
23	03	20	01♓		04	28	25		02	03	17	
24	04	21	02		05	29	26		03	04	17	
25	05	22	02		06	01♈	27		04	05	18	
26	06	23	03	20	07	02	27	19	05	06	19	19
27	07	25	04		08	03	28		06	07	20	
28	08	26	05		09	04	29		07	09	20	18
29	09	27	05						08	10	21	
30	10	28	06						09	11	22	
31	11	30	07	20					10	12	23	18

	APRIL				MAY				JUNE			
Day	☉	♀	♂	♆	☉	♀	♂	♆	☉	♀	♂	♆
01	11♈	13♉	23♈	18♎	10♉	19♊	16♉	18♎	10♊	24♋	08♊	17♎
02	12	15	24		11	20	16		11	25	08	
03	13	16	25		12	21	17		12	26	09	
04	14	17	26		13	22	18	17	13	27	10	
05	15	18	26		14	24	18		14	28	10	
06	16	19	27	18	15	25	19	17	15	29	11	17
07	17	21	28		16	26	20		16	00♌	12	
08	18	22	29		17	27	21		17	01	13	
09	19	23	29		18	28	21		18	02	13	
10	20	24	00♉		19	29	22		19	03	14	
11	21	25	01	18	20	01♋	23	17	20	04	15	17
12	22	27	02		21	02	23		21	06	15	
13	23	28	02		22	03	24		22	07	16	
14	24	29	03		23	04	25		23	08	17	
15	25	00♊	04		24	05	26		24	09	17	
16	26	01	05	18	25	06	26	17	25	10	18	17
17	27	03	05		26	07	27		25	11	19	
18	28	04	06		27	08	28		26	12	19	
19	29	05	07		28	10	28		27	13	20	
20	30	06	07		29	11	29		28	14	21	
21	01♉	07	08	18	30	12	30	17	29	15	22	17
22	02	08	09		01♊	13	01♊		00♋	16	22	
23	03	10	10		02	14	01		01	17	23	
24	03	11	10		03	15	02		02	18	24	
25	04	12	11		03	16	03		03	19	24	
26	05	13	12	18	04	17	03	17	04	19	25	17
27	06	14	13		05	18	04		05	20	26	
28	07	15	13		06	19	05		06	21	26	
29	08	17	14		07	20	06		07	22	27	
30	09	18	15		08	22	06		08	23	28	
31					09	23	07	17				

JULY

Day	☉	♀	♂	♆
01	09♋	24♌	28♊	17♎
02	10	25	29	
03	11	26	30	
04	12	27	00♋	
05	13	28	01	
06	14	29	02	17
07	15	29	02	
08	16	00♍	03	
09	16	01	04	
10	17	02	04	
11	18	03	05	17
12	19	04	06	
13	20	04	06	
14	21	05	07	
15	22	06	08	
16	23	07	08	17
17	24	07	09	
18	25	08	10	
19	26	09	10	
20	27	09	11	
21	28	10	12	17
22	29	11	12	
23	30	11	13	
24	01♌	12	14	
25	02	12	14	
26	03	13	15	17
27	04	14	16	
28	05	14	16	
29	06	15	17	
30	07	15	18	
31	07	15	18	17

AUGUST

Day	☉	♀	♂	♆
01	08♌	16♍	19♋	17♎
02	09	16	20	
03	10	17	20	
04	11	17	21	
05	12	17	22	
06	13	17	22	17
07	14	18	23	
08	15	18	24	
09	16	18	24	
10	17	18	25	
11	18	18	26	17
12	19	18	26	
13	20	18	27	
14	21	18	27	
15	22	17	28	
16	23	18	29	17
17	24	18	29	
18	25	18	00♌	
19	26	18	01	
20	27	17	01	
21	28	17	02	18
22	29	17	03	
23	30	16	03	
24	01♍	16	04	
25	01	15	05	
26	02	15	05	18
27	03	14	06	
28	04	14	07	
29	05	13	07	
30	06	13	08	
31	07	12	08	18

SEPTEMBER

Day	☉	♀	♂	♆
01	08♍	12♍	09♌	18♎
02	09	11	10	
03	10	10	10	
04	11	10	11	
05	12	09	12	
06	13	09	12	18
07	14	08	13	
08	15	07	13	
09	16	07	14	
10	17	06	15	
11	18	06	15	18
12	19	05	16	
13	20	05	17	
14	21	04	17	
15	22	04	18	
16	23	04	18	18
17	24	03	19	
18	25	03	20	
19	26	03	20	
20	27	03	21	
21	28	02	22	18
22	29	02	22	19
23	30	02	23	
24	01♎	02	23	
25	02	02	24	
26	03	02	25	19
27	04	02	25	
28	05	02	26	
29	06	03	27	
30	07	03	27	

OCTOBER

Day	☉	♀	♂	♆
01	07♎	03♍	28♌	19♎
02	08	03	28	
03	09	03	29	
04	10	04	30	
05	11	04	00♍	
06	12	05	01	19
07	13	05	02	
08	14	05	02	
09	15	06	03	
10	16	06	03	
11	17	07	04	19
12	18	07	04	
13	19	08	05	
14	20	09	06	
15	21	09	06	
16	22	10	07	19
17	23	10	08	
18	24	11	08	
19	25	12	09	
20	26	13	09	
21	27	13	10	20
22	28	14	11	
23	29	15	11	
24	00♏	16	12	
25	01	16	12	
26	02	17	13	20
27	03	18	14	
28	04	19	14	
29	05	20	15	
30	06	21	15	
31	07	21	16	20

NOVEMBER

Day	☉	♀	♂	♆
01	08♏	22♍	17♍	20♎
02	09	23	17	
03	10	24	18	
04	11	25	18	
05	12	26	19	
06	13	27	20	20
07	14	28	20	
08	15	29	21	
09	16	30	21	
10	17	00♎	22	
11	18	02	23	20
12	19	03	23	
13	20	04	24	
14	21	05	24	
15	22	06	25	
16	23	07	26	20
17	24	08	26	21
18	25	09	27	
19	26	10	27	
20	27	11	28	
21	28	12	28	21
22	29	13	29	
23	00♐	14	30	
24	01	15	00♎	
25	02	16	01	
26	03	17	01	21
27	04	18	02	
28	05	19	02	
29	06	21	03	
30	07	22	04	

DECEMBER

Day	☉	♀	♂	♆
01	08♐	23♎	04♎	21♎
02	09	24	05	
03	11	25	05	
04	12	26	06	
05	13	27	06	
06	14	28	07	21
07	15	29	08	
08	16	01♏	08	
09	17	02	09	
10	18	03	09	
11	19	04	10	21
12	20	05	10	
13	21	06	11	
14	22	07	11	
15	23	09	12	
16	24	10	12	21
17	25	11	13	
18	26	12	14	
19	27	13	14	
20	28	14	15	
21	29	16	15	21
22	30	17	16	
23	01♑	18	16	
24	02	19	17	
25	03	20	17	
26	04	21	18	21
27	05	23	18	22
28	06	24	19	
29	07	25	19	
30	08	26	20	
31	09	27	20	22

BIRTH TABLES - 1952

Day	JAN ☉	JAN ♀	JAN ♂	JAN ♆	FEB ☉	FEB ♀	FEB ♂	FEB ♆	MAR ☉	MAR ♀	MAR ♂	MAR ♆
01	10♑	29♏	21♎	22♎	12♒	06♑	05♏	22♎	11♓	11♒	15♏	21♎
02	11	30	21		13	07	06		12	13	16	
03	12	01♐	22		14	08	06		13	14	16	
04	13	02	22		15	10	07		14	15	16	
05	14	03	23		16	11	07		15	16	16	
06	15	04	23	22	17	12	08	22	16	18	16	21
07	16	06	24		18	13	08		17	19	17	
08	17	07	24		19	14	08		18	20	17	
09	18	08	25		20	16	09		19	21	17	
10	19	09	25		21	17	09		20	23	17	
11	20	10	26	22	22	18	09	22	21	24	17	21
12	21	12	26		23	19	10		22	25	17	
13	22	13	27		24	21	10		23	26	18	
14	23	14	27		25	22	11		24	27	18	
15	24	15	28		26	23	11		25	29	18	
16	25	16	28	22	27	24	11	22	26	30	18	21
17	26	18	29		28	25	12		27	01♓	18	
18	27	19	29		29	27	12		28	02	18	
19	28	20	30		30	28	12		29	04	18	
20	29	21	00♏		01♓	29	13		30	05	18	
21	00♒	23	01	22	02	00♒	13	21	01♈	06	18	21
22	01	24	01		03	02	13		02	07	18	
23	02	25	02		04	03	13		03	09	18	
24	03	26	02		05	04	14		04	10	18	
25	04	27	02		06	05	14		05	11	18	
26	05	29	03	22	07	07	14	21	06	12	18	21
27	07	30	03		08	08	15		07	13	18	
28	08	01♑	04		09	09	15		08	15	18	
29	09	02	04		10	10	15		09	16	18	
30	10	03	05						10	17	18	
31	11	05	05	22					11	18	18	21

Day	APR ☉	APR ♀	APR ♂	APR ♆	MAY ☉	MAY ♀	MAY ♂	MAY ♆	JUN ☉	JUN ♀	JUN ♂	JUN ♆
01	12♈	20♓	18♏	21♎	11♉	26♈	11♏	20♎	11♊	05♊	02♏	19♎
02	13	21	18		12	28	10		12	06	02	
03	14	22	18		13	29	10		13	07	01	
04	15	23	18		14	00♉	09		14	08	01	
05	16	25	18		15	01	09		15	09	01	
06	17	26	18	20	16	03	09	20	16	11	01	19
07	18	27	17		17	04	08		17	12	01	
08	19	28	17		18	05	08		18	13	01	
09	20	29	17		19	06	08		19	14	01	
10	21	01♈	17		20	08	07		20	16	01	
11	22	02	17	20	21	09	07	20	21	17	01	19
12	23	03	16		22	10	06		22	18	01	
13	23	04	16		23	11	06		23	19	01	
14	24	06	16		24	12	06		24	21	01	
15	25	07	16		25	14	06		25	22	01	
16	26	08	15	20	26	15	05	19	25	23	01	19
17	27	09	15		27	16	05		26	24	02	
18	28	11	15		27	17	05		27	25	02	
19	29	12	15		28	19	04		28	27	02	
20	00♉	13	14		29	20	04		29	28	02	
21	01	14	14	20	00♊	21	04	19	00♋	29	02	19
22	02	15	14		01	22	04		01	00♋	02	
23	03	17	13		02	23	03		02	02	02	
24	04	18	13		03	25	03		03	03	02	
25	05	19	13		04	26	03		04	04	03	
26	06	20	12	20	05	27	03	19	05	05	03	19
27	07	22	12		06	28	02		06	07	03	
28	08	23	12		07	30	02		07	08	03	
29	09	24	11		08	01♊	02		08	09	04	
30	10	25	11		09	02	02		09	10	04	
31					10	03	02	19				

Day	JULY ☉	♀	♂	♆	AUGUST ☉	♀	♂	♆	SEPTEMBER ☉	♀	♂	♆
01	10♋	11♋	04♏	19♎	09♌	20♌	16♏	19♎	09♍	28♍	03♐	20♎
02	11	13	04		10	21	16		10	29	03	
03	11	14	05		11	22	17		11	00♎	04	
04	12	15	05		12	23	17		12	01	05	
05	13	16	05		13	24	18		13	03	05	
06	14	18	05	19	14	26	18	19	14	04	06	20
07	15	19	06		15	27	19		15	05	07	
08	16	20	06		16	28	19		16	06	07	
09	17	21	06		17	29	20		17	08	08	
10	18	22	07		18	01♍	20		18	09	09	
11	19	24	07	19	19	02	21	19	19	10	09	20
12	20	25	07		20	03	21		20	11	10	
13	21	26	08		21	04	22		21	13	10	
14	22	27	08		22	06	22		22	14	11	
15	23	29	08		23	07	23		23	15	12	
16	24	30	09	19	24	08	23	20	24	16	12	20
17	25	01♌	09		24	09	24		25	17	13	
18	26	02	10		25	11	25		26	19	14	
19	27	04	10		26	12	25		26	20	14	21
20	28	05	10		27	13	26		27	21	15	
21	29	06	11	19	28	14	26	20	28	22	16	21
22	30	07	11		29	15	27		29	24	16	
23	01♌	08	12		00♍	17	27		00♎	25	17	
24	02	10	12		01	18	28		01	26	18	
25	02	11	12		02	19	29		02	27	18	
26	03	12	13	19	03	20	29	20	03	29	19	21
27	04	13	13		04	22	30		04	30	20	
28	05	15	14		05	23	00♐		05	01♏	20	
29	06	16	14		06	24	01		06	02	21	
30	07	17	15		07	25	02		07	03	22	
31	08	18	15	19	08	27	02	20				

Day	OCTOBER ☉	♀	♂	♆	NOVEMBER ☉	♀	♂	♆	DECEMBER ☉	♀	♂	♆
01	08♎	05♏	23♐	21♎	09♏	13♐	15♑	22♎	09♐	19♑	07♒	23♎
02	09	06	23		10	14	16		10	20	08	
03	10	07	24		11	15	16		11	21	09	
04	11	08	25		12	16	17		12	23	10	
05	12	10	25		13	17	18		13	24	10	
06	13	11	26	21	14	19	18	22	14	25	11	23
07	14	12	27		15	20	19		15	26	12	
08	15	13	27		16	21	20		16	27	13	
09	16	14	28		17	22	21		17	28	14	
10	17	16	29		18	24	21		18	30	14	
11	18	17	30	21	19	25	22	22	19	01♒	15	23
12	19	18	00♑		20	26	23		20	02	16	
13	20	19	01		21	27	24	23	21	03	17	
14	21	21	02		22	28	24		22	04	17	
15	22	22	02		23	30	25		23	06	18	
16	23	23	03	22	24	01♑	26	23	24	07	19	23
17	24	24	04		25	02	27		26	08	20	
18	25	25	05		26	03	28		27	09	20	
19	26	27	05		27	04	28		28	10	21	24
20	27	28	06		28	06	29		29	12	22	
21	28	29	07	22	29	07	30	23	30	13	23	24
22	29	00♐	07		00♐	08	01♒		01♑	14	24	
23	00♏	02	08		01	09	01		02	15	24	
24	01	03	09		02	10	02		03	16	25	
25	02	04	10		03	12	03		04	17	26	
26	03	05	10	22	04	13	04	23	05	19	27	24
27	04	07	11		05	14	04		06	20	27	
28	05	08	12		06	15	05		07	21	28	
29	06	09	13		07	17	06		08	22	29	
30	07	10	13		08	18	07		09	23	30	
31	08	11	14	22					10	24	00♓	24

BIRTH TABLES - 1953

Day	JAN ☉	JAN ♀	JAN ♂	JAN ♆	FEB ☉	FEB ♀	FEB ♂	FEB ♆	MAR ☉	MAR ♀	MAR ♂	MAR ♆
01	11♑	25♒	01♓	24♎	12♒	29♓	25♓	24♎	11♓	23♈	16♈	24♎
02	12	27	02		13	00♈	26		12	24	17	
03	13	28	03		14	01	27		13	25	18	
04	14	29	03		15	02	27		14	25	18	23
05	15	00♓	04		16	03	28		15	26	19	
06	16	01	05	24	17	04	29	24	16	26	20	23
07	17	02	06		18	05	30		17	27	21	
08	18	03	07		19	06	00♈		18	27	21	
09	19	05	07		20	07	01		19	28	22	
10	20	06	08		21	08	02		20	28	23	
11	21	07	09	24	22	09	03	24	21	29	24	23
12	22	08	10		23	10	03		22	29	24	
13	23	09	10		25	11	04		23	30	25	
14	24	10	11		26	12	05		24	30	26	
15	25	11	12		27	13	06		25	00♉	27	
16	26	12	13	24	28	13	06	24	26	00	27	23
17	27	13	14		29	14	07		27	01	28	
18	28	15	14		30	15	08		28	01	29	
19	29	16	15		01♓	16	09		29	01	29	
20	00♒	17	16		02	17	09		30	01	00♉	
21	01	18	17	24	03	18	10	24	01♈	01	01	23
22	02	19	17		04	18	11		02	01	02	
23	03	20	18		05	19	12		03	01	02	
24	04	21	19		06	20	12		04	01	03	
25	05	22	20		07	21	13		05	01	04	
26	06	23	20	24	08	21	14	24	06	01	05	23
27	07	24	21		09	22	15		07	01	05	
28	08	25	22		10	23	15		08	01	06	
29	09	26	23						09	01	07	
30	10	27	24						09	00♉	07	
31	11	28	24	24					10	30♈	08	23

Day	APR ☉	APR ♀	APR ♂	APR ♆	MAY ☉	MAY ♀	MAY ♂	MAY ♆	JUN ☉	JUN ♀	JUN ♂	JUN ♆
01	11♈	30♈	09♉	23♎	11♉	15♈	00♊	22♎	11♊	27♈	21♊	21♎
02	12	29	10		12	15	01		12	28	22	
03	13	29	10		13	15	02		13	28	23	
04	14	28	11		14	15	02		14	29	24	
05	15	28	12		15	15	03		15	00♉	24	
06	16	27	12	23	16	15	04	22	15	01	25	21
07	17	27	13		17	15	04		16	02	26	
08	18	26	14		18	15	05		17	02	26	
09	19	25	15		19	15	06		18	03	27	
10	20	25	15		20	16	06		19	04	28	
11	21	24	16	23	20	16	07	22	20	05	28	21
12	22	24	17		21	16	08		21	06	29	
13	23	23	17		22	16	09		22	07	30	
14	24	22	18	22	23	17	09		23	08	00♋	
15	25	22	19		24	17	10		24	09	01	
16	26	21	20	22	25	18	11	22	25	09	02	21
17	27	21	20		26	18	11		26	10	02	
18	28	20	21		27	18	12		27	11	03	
19	29	19	22		28	19	13		28	12	04	
20	00♉	19	22		29	19	13		29	13	04	
21	01	18	23	22	00♊	20	14	22	30	14	05	21
22	02	18	24		01	20	15		01♋	15	06	
23	03	17	25		02	21	15		02	16	06	
24	04	17	25		03	22	16	21	03	17	07	
25	05	17	26		04	22	17		04	18	08	
26	06	16	27	22	05	23	17	21	05	19	08	21
27	07	16	27		06	23	18		06	20	09	
28	08	16	28		07	24	19		06	21	10	
29	09	15	29		08	25	19		07	22	10	
30	10	15	29		09	26	20		08	23	11	
31					10	26	21	21				

Day	JULY				AUGUST				SEPTEMBER			
	☉	♀	♂	Ψ	☉	♀	♂	Ψ	☉	♀	♂	Ψ
01	09♋	24♉	12♋	21♎	09♌	27♊	02♌	21♎	09♍	03♌	22♌	22♎
02	10	25	12		10	28	02		10	04	22	
03	11	26	13		11	29	03		11	05	23	
04	12	27	13		12	01♋	04		12	06	24	
05	13	28	14		13	02	04		13	08	24	
06	14	29	15	21	14	03	05	21	14	09	25	22
07	15	00♊	15		15	04	06		15	10	25	
08	16	01	16		16	05	06		16	11	26	
09	17	02	17		17	06	07	22	17	12	27	
10	18	03	17		18	07	08		17	14	27	
11	19	04	18	21	19	08	08	22	18	15	28	22
12	20	05	19		19	10	09		19	16	29	
13	21	06	19		20	11	09		20	17	29	
14	22	07	20		21	12	10		21	18	30	
15	23	09	21		22	13	11		22	20	01♍	23
16	24	10	21	21	23	14	11	22	23	21	01	23
17	25	11	22		24	15	12		24	22	02	
18	26	12	23		25	17	13		25	23	02	
19	27	13	23		26	18	13		26	24	03	
20	27	14	24		27	19	14		27	26	04	
21	28	15	25	21	28	20	15	22	28	27	04	23
22	29	16	25		29	21	15		29	28	05	
23	00♌	17	26		00♍	22	16		00♎	29	06	
24	01	18	27		01	23	17		01	00♍	06	
25	02	19	27		02	25	17		02	02	07	
26	03	20	28	21	03	26	18	22	03	03	07	23
27	04	22	29		04	27	18		04	04	08	
28	05	23	29		05	28	19		05	05	09	
29	06	24	30		06	29	20		06	07	09	
30	07	25	00♌		07	01♌	20		07	08	10	
31	08	26	01	21	08	02	21	22				

Day	OCTOBER				NOVEMBER				DECEMBER			
	☉	♀	♂	Ψ	☉	♀	♂	Ψ	☉	♀	♂	Ψ
01	08♎	09♍	11♍	23♎	09♏	17♎	30♍	24♎	09♐	25♏	18♎	25♎
02	09	10	11		10	18	01♎		10	26	19	
03	10	11	12		11	20	01		11	27	20	
04	11	13	12		12	21	02		12	29	20	
05	12	14	13		13	22	02		13	30	21	
06	13	15	14	23	14	23	03	25	14	01♐	22	25
07	14	16	14		15	25	04		15	02	22	
08	15	18	15		16	26	04		16	04	23	
09	16	19	16		17	27	05		17	05	23	
10	17	20	16		18	28	06		18	06	24	
11	18	21	17	23	19	30	06	25	19	07	25	25
12	19	22	17		20	01♏	07		20	09	25	
13	20	24	18		21	02	07		21	10	26	
14	21	25	19		22	03	08		22	11	26	26
15	22	26	19		23	05	09		23	12	27	
16	23	27	20	24	24	06	09	25	24	14	28	26
17	24	29	21		25	07	10		25	15	28	
18	25	30	21		26	08	10		26	16	29	
19	26	01♎	22		27	10	11		27	17	29	
20	27	02	22		28	11	12		28	19	00♏	
21	28	04	23	24	29	12	12	25	29	20	01	26
22	29	05	24		30	13	13		00♑	21	01	
23	30	06	24		01♐	15	14		01	22	02	
24	01♏	07	25		02	16	14		02	24	02	
25	02	09	26		03	17	15		03	25	03	
26	03	10	26	24	04	18	15	25	04	26	04	26
27	04	11	27		05	20	16		05	27	04	
28	05	12	27		06	21	17		06	29	05	
29	06	13	28		07	22	17		07	30	05	
30	07	15	29		08	24	18		09	01♑	06	
31	08	16	29	24					10	02	07	26

BIRTH TABLES - 1954

	JANUARY				FEBRUARY				MARCH				APRIL				MAY				JUNE			
	☉	♀	♂	♇	☉	♀	♂	♇	☉	♀	♂	♇	☉	♀	♂	♇	☉	♀	♂	♇	☉	♀	♂	♇
01	11♑	04♑	07♏	26♎	12♒	13♒	25♏	26♎	10♓	18♓	11♐	26♎	11♈	26♈	26♐	25♎	11♉	03♊	06♑	24♎	10♊	11♋	08♑	24♎
02	12	05	08		13	14	26		11	19	11		12	28	26		12	04	06		11	12	08	
03	13	06	08		14	15	26		12	20	12		13	29	26		13	06	06		12	13	08	
04	14	08	09		15	16	27		13	22	12		14	00♉	27		13	07	06		13	14	08	
05	15	09	10		16	18	28		14	23	13		15	01	27		14	08	07		14	15	07	
06	16	10	10	26	17	19	28	26	15	24	13	26	16	02	28	25	15	10	07	24	15	17	07	24
07	17	11	11		18	20	29		16	25	14		17	04	28		16	10	07		16	18	07	23
08	18	13	11		19	21	29		17	27	14		18	05	28		17	12	07		17	19	07	
09	19	14	12		20	23	30		18	28	15		19	06	29		18	13	07		18	20	07	
10	20	15	13		21	24	00♐		19	29	15		20	07	29		19	14	08		19	21	07	
11	21	16	13	26	22	25	01	26	20	00♈	16	26	21	09	30	25	20	15	08	24	20	23	06	23
12	22	18	14		23	27	02		21	02	16		22	10	30		21	17	08		21	24	06	
13	23	19	14		24	28	02		22	03	17		23	11	00♑		22	18	08		22	25	06	
14	24	20	15		25	29	03		23	04	17		24	12	01		23	19	08		23	26	06	
15	25	21	16		26	00♓	03		24	05	18	26	25	14	01		24	20	08		24	27	05	
16	26	23	16	26	27	02	04	26	25	06	18	25	26	15	01	25	25	21	08	24	25	29	05	23
17	27	24	17		28	03	04		26	08	19		27	16	02		26	23	08		26	30	05	
18	28	25	17		29	04	05		27	09	19		28	17	02		27	24	08		27	01♌	05	
19	29	26	18		00♓	05	05		28	10	20		29	18	02		28	25	08		28	02	04	
20	30	28	18		01	07	06		29	11	20		30	20	03		29	26	08		29	03	04	
21	01♒	29	19	26	02	08	06	26	00♈	13	21	25	01♉	21	03	25	30	27	08	24	30	05	04	23
22	02	00♒	20		03	09	07		01	14	21		02	22	03	24	01♊	29	09		01♋	06	03	
23	03	01	20		04	10	07		02	15	22		03	23	04		02	30	09		01	07	03	
24	04	03	21		05	12	08		03	16	22		04	25	04		03	01♋	09		02	08	03	
25	05	04	21		06	13	09		04	18	22		05	26	04		04	02	09		03	09	02	
26	06	05	22	26	07	14	09	26	05	19	23	25	06	27	05	24	05	03	08	24	04	10	02	23
27	07	06	22		08	15	10		06	20	23		07	28	05		06	05	08		05	12	02	
28	08	08	23		09	17	10		07	21	24		08	30	05		07	06	08		06	13	01	
29	09	09	24						08	23	24		09	01♊	05		08	07	08		07	14	01	
30	10	10	24						09	24	25		10	02	06		09	08	08		08	15	01	
31	11	11	25	26					10	25	25	25					09	09	08	24				

Day	Jul ☉	Jul ♀	Jul ♂	Jul ♆	Aug ☉	Aug ♀	Aug ♂	Aug ♆	Sep ☉	Sep ♀	Sep ♂	Sep ♆
01	09♋	16♌	01♑	23♎	09♌	22♍	26♐	24♎	09♍	25♎	03♑	24♎
02	10	17	00		10	23	26		09	26	03	
03	11	19	30♐		11	24	26		10	27	04	
04	12	20	30		12	25	26		11	28	04	
05	13	21	29		13	26	26		12	29	05	
06	14	22	29	23	13	27	26	24	13	30	05	24
07	15	23	29		14	28	26		14	00♏	05	
08	16	24	29		15	29	26		15	01	06	
09	17	25	28		16	01♎	26		16	02	06	
10	18	27	28		17	02	27		17	03	07	
11	19	28	28	23	18	03	27	24	18	04	07	24
12	20	29	28		19	04	27		19	05	08	
13	21	00♍	27		20	05	27		20	06	08	25
14	22	01	27		21	06	27		21	07	09	
15	22	02	27		22	07	28		22	08	09	
16	23	04	27	23	23	08	28	24	23	09	10	25
17	24	05	27		24	09	28		24	10	10	
18	25	06	26		25	10	28		25	11	11	
19	26	07	26		26	11	29		26	11	11	
20	27	08	26		27	12	29		27	12	12	
21	28	09	26	23	28	13	29	24	28	13	12	25
22	29	10	26		29	14	29		29	14	13	
23	00♌	12	26		30	15	30		30	15	13	
24	01	13	26		01♍	17	00♑		01♎	16	14	
25	02	14	26		02	18	00		02	16	14	
26	03	15	26	23	03	19	01	24	03	17	15	25
27	04	16	26		04	20	01		04	18	15	
28	05	17	26		05	21	01		05	19	16	
29	06	18	26		06	22	02		06	19	17	
30	07	19	26		07	23	02		07	20	17	
31	08	21	26	23	08	24	02	24				

Day	Oct ☉	Oct ♀	Oct ♂	Oct ♆	Nov ☉	Nov ♀	Nov ♂	Nov ♆	Dec ☉	Dec ♀	Dec ♂	Dec ♆
01	08♎	21♏	18♑	25♎	09♏	29♏	07♒	26♎	09♐	15♏	28♒	27♎
02	09	21	18		10	29	08		10	15	29	
03	10	22	19		11	29	09		11	15	29	
04	11	23	19		12	28	09		12	15	00♓	
05	12	23	20		13	28	10		13	15	01	
06	13	24	21	25	14	27	11	26	14	15	02	27
07	14	24	21		15	27	11	27	15	15	02	
08	15	25	22		16	26	12		16	15	03	
09	16	26	22		17	26	13		17	15	04	
10	17	26	23		18	25	13		18	15	04	
11	18	27	24	26	19	25	14	27	19	15	05	28
12	19	27	24		20	24	15		20	16	06	
13	20	27	25		21	24	15		21	16	07	
14	21	28	26		22	23	16		22	16	07	
15	22	28	26		23	22	17		23	16	08	
16	23	29	27	26	24	22	17	27	24	17	09	28
17	24	29	27		25	21	18		25	17	09	
18	25	29	28		26	20	19		26	18	10	
19	26	29	29		27	20	20		27	18	11	
20	27	30	29		28	19	20		28	19	12	
21	28	30	30	26	29	19	21	27	29	19	12	28
22	29	30	01♒		30	18	22		00	20	13	
23	30	00♐	01		01♐	18	22		01♑	20	14	
24	01♏	00	02		02	17	23		02	21	14	
25	02	00	03		03	17	24		03	21	15	
26	03	00♐	03	26	04	16	24	27	04	22	16	28
27	04	30♏	04		05	16	25		05	23	17	
28	05	30	05		06	16	26		06	23	17	
29	06	30	05		07	16	27		07	24	18	
30	07	30	06		08	15	27		08	25	19	
31	08	29	07	26					09	25	19	28

BIRTH TABLES - 1955

Day	JAN ☉	JAN ♀	JAN ♂	JAN ♆	FEB ☉	FEB ♀	FEB ♂	FEB ♆	MAR ☉	MAR ♀	MAR ♂	MAR ♆	APR ☉	APR ♀	APR ♂	APR ♆	MAY ☉	MAY ♀	MAY ♂	MAY ♆	JUN ☉	JUN ♀	JUN ♂	JUN ♆
01	10♑	26♍	20♓	28♎	12♒	25♐	12♈	28♎	10♓	26♑	02♉	28♎	11♈	02♓	24♉	27♎	10♉	08♈	14♊	27♎	10♊	16♉	04♋	26♎
02	11	27	21		13	26	13		11	27	03		12	04	24		11	09	14	26	11	17	05	
03	12	28	22		14	27	14		12	28	04		13	05	25		12	11	15		12	18	06	
04	13	29	22		15	28	15		13	30	04		14	06	26		13	12	16		13	19	06	
05	14	29	23		16	29	15		14	01♒	05		15	07	26		14	13	16		14	20	07	
06	15	00♐	24	28	17	00♑	16	28	15	02	06	28	16	09	27	27	15	14	17	26	15	22	08	26
07	16	01	25		18	02	17		16	03	06		17	10	28		16	15	18		16	23	08	
08	17	02	25		19	03	17		17	04	07		18	11	28		17	17	18		17	24	09	
09	18	03	26		20	04	18		18	05	08		19	12	29		18	18	19		18	25	09	
10	19	04	27		21	05	19		19	06	08		20	13	30		19	19	20		19	27	10	
11	20	05	27	28	22	06	19	28	20	08	09	28	21	14	00♊	27	20	20	20	26	20	28	11	26
12	22	05	28		23	07	20		21	09	10		22	16	01		21	21	21		21	29	11	
13	23	06	29		24	08	21		22	10	11		23	17	02		22	23	22		22	00♊	12	
14	24	07	30		25	09	22		23	11	11		24	18	02		23	24	22		23	01	13	
15	25	08	00♈		26	10	22		24	12	12		25	19	03		24	25	23		24	03	13	
16	26	09	01	28	27	11	23	28	25	14	13	28	26	20	04	27	25	26	24	26	25	04	14	26
17	27	10	02		28	13	24		26	15	13		27	21	04		26	28	24		26	05	15	
18	28	11	02		29	14	24		27	16	14		28	23	05		27	29	25		26	06	15	
19	29	12	03		00♓	15	25		28	17	15		29	24	06		28	30	26		27	07	16	
20	30	13	04		01	16	26		29	18	15		30	25	06		29	01♉	26		28	09	17	
21	01♒	14	05	28	02	17	27	28	00♈	19	16	28	01♉	26	07	27	30	02	27	26	29	10	17	26
22	02	15	05		03	18	27		01	21	17		02	27	08		01♊	04	28		00♋	11	18	
23	03	16	06		04	19	28		02	22	17		03	29	08		02	05	28		01	12	19	
24	04	17	07		05	20	29		03	23	18		04	30	09		03	06	29		02	14	19	
25	05	18	07		06	22	29		04	24	19	27	05	01♈	10		04	07	30		03	15	20	
26	06	19	08	28	07	23	00♉	28	05	25	19	27	05	02	10	27	04	08	00♋	26	04	16	20	26
27	07	20	09		08	24	01		06	26	20		06	03	11		05	10	01		05	17	21	
28	08	21	10		09	25	01		07	28	21		07	05	12		06	11	02		06	18	22	
29	09	22	10						08	29	22		08	06	12		07	12	02		07	20	22	25
30	10	23	11						09	00♓	22		09	07	13		08	13	03		08	21	23	
31	11	24	12	28					10	01	23	27					09	14	04	26				

Day	JULY ☉	JULY ♀	JULY ♂	JULY ♆	AUGUST ☉	AUGUST ♀	AUGUST ♂	AUGUST ♆	SEPTEMBER ☉	SEPTEMBER ♀	SEPTEMBER ♂	SEPTEMBER ♆	OCTOBER ☉	OCTOBER ♀	OCTOBER ♂	OCTOBER ♆	NOVEMBER ☉	NOVEMBER ♀	NOVEMBER ♂	NOVEMBER ♆	DECEMBER ☉	DECEMBER ♀	DECEMBER ♂	DECEMBER ♆
01	09♋	22♊	24♋	25♎	08♌	00♌	14♌	26♎	08♍	08♍	03♍	26♎	08♎	16♎	22♍	27	08♏	24♏	12♎	28♎	09♐	02♑	02♏	29♎
02	10	23	24		09	01	14		09	10	04		09	17	23		09	26	13		10	03	02	
03	11	24	25		10	02	15		10	11	05		10	18	24		10	27	14		11	04	03	
04	12	26	26		11	04	15		11	12	05		10	19	24		11	28	14		12	05	04	30
05	13	27	26		12	05	16		12	13	06		11	21	25		12	29	15	29	13	07	04	
06	14	28	27	25	13	06	17	26	13	15	06	26	12	22	26	27	13	01♐	15	29	14	08	05	30
07	15	29	28		14	07	17		14	16	07		13	23	26		14	02	16		15	09	06	
08	16	01♋	28		15	09	18		15	17	08		14	24	27		15	03	17		16	10	06	
09	17	02	29		16	10	19		16	18	08	27	15	26	27	28	16	04	17		17	12	07	
10	17	03	29		17	11	19		17	20	09		16	27	28		17	06	18		18	13	07	
11	18	04	00♌	25	18	12	20	26	18	21	10	27	17	28	29	28	18	07	19	29	19	14	08	30
12	19	05	01		19	14	21		19	22	10		18	29	29		19	08	19		20	15	09	
13	20	07	01		20	15	21		20	23	11		19	01♏	00♎		20	09	20		21	17	09	
14	21	08	02		21	16	22		21	24	12		20	02	01		21	11	21		22	18	10	
15	22	09	03		22	17	22		22	26	12		21	03	01		22	12	21		23	19	11	
16	23	10	03	25	23	19	23	26	23	27	13	27	22	04	02	28	23	13	22	29	24	20	11	30
17	24	12	04		24	20	24		24	28	13		23	06	03		24	14	23		25	22	12	
18	25	13	05		25	21	24		25	29	14		24	07	03		25	15	23		26	23	13	
19	26	14	05	26	26	22	25		26	01♎	15		25	08	04		26	17	24		27	24	13	
20	27	15	06		27	23	26		27	02	15		26	09	05		27	18	24		28	25	14	
21	28	17	06	26	28	25	26	26	28	03	16	27	27	11	05	28	28	19	25	29	29	27	15	30
22	29	18	07		29	26	27		29	04	17		28	12	06		29	20	26		30	28	15	
23	30	19	08		30	27	28		30	06	17		29	13	06		00♐	22	26		01♑	29	16	
24	01♌	20	08		01♍	28	28		01♎	07	18		00♏	14	07		01	23	27		02	00♒	17	00♏
25	02	21	09		02	30	29		02	08	19		01	16	08		02	24	28		03	02	17	
26	03	23	10	26	02	01♍	29	26	03	09	19	27	02	17	08	28	03	25	28	29	04	03	18	00
27	04	24	10		03	02	00♍		04	11	20		03	18	09		04	27	29		05	04	19	
28	05	25	11		04	03	01		05	12	20		04	19	10		05	28	30		06	05	19	
29	06	26	12		05	04	01		06	13	21		05	21	10		06	29	00♏		07	06	20	
30	07	28	12		06	06	02		07	14	22		06	22	11		08	00♑	01		08	08	20	
31	08	29	13	26	07	07	03	26					07	23	12	28					09	09	21	00

BIRTH TABLES - 1956

	JANUARY				FEBRUARY				MARCH				APRIL				MAY				JUNE			
Day	☉	♀	♂	Ψ	☉	♀	♂	Ψ	☉	♀	♂	Ψ	☉	♀	♂	Ψ	☉	♀	♂	Ψ	☉	♀	♂	Ψ
01	10♑	10♒	22♏	00♏	12♒	18♓	12♐	00♏	11♓	23♈	01♑	00♏	12♈	27♉	21♑	30♎	11♉	25♊	11♒	29♎	11♊	09♋	29♒	28♎
02	11	11	22		13	19	13		12	24	02		13	28	22		12	26	11		12	09	30	
03	12	13	23		14	21	14		13	25	02		14	29	23	29	13	27	12		13	09	00♓	
04	13	14	24		15	22	14		14	26	03		15	00♊	23		14	27	12		14	09	01	
05	14	15	24		16	23	15		15	27	04		16	01	24		15	28	13		15	09	01	
06	15	16	25	00	17	24	15	00	16	28	04	00	17	02	24	29	16	29	14	29	16	08	02	28
07	16	18	26		18	25	16		17	30	05		18	03	25		17	30	14		17	08	02	
08	17	19	26		19	27	17		18	01♉	06		19	04	26		18	00♋	15		18	08	03	
09	18	20	27		20	28	17		19	02	06		20	05	26		19	01	15		19	08	03	
10	19	21	28		21	29	18		20	03	07		21	06	27		20	02	16		20	07	04	
11	20	23	28	00	22	00♈	19	00	21	04	08	00	22	07	28	29	21	02	17	28	21	07	04	28
12	21	24	29		23	01	19		22	05	08		23	08	28		22	03	17		21	06	05	
13	22	25	30		24	03	20		23	06	09		24	09	29		23	03	18		22	06	05	
14	23	26	00♐		25	04	21		24	07	10		25	10	30		24	04	18		22	05	06	
15	24	27	01		26	05	21		25	09	10		25	11	00♒		25	04	19		24	05	07	
16	25	29	02	00	27	06	22	00	26	10	11	00	26	12	01	29	26	05	20	28	25	04	07	28
17	26	30	02		28	07	23		27	11	12		27	13	02		27	05	20		26	04	08	
18	27	01♓	03		29	09	23		28	12	12		28	14	02		28	06	21		27	03	08	
19	28	02	04		30	10	24		29	13	13		29	15	03		28	06	21		28	03	09	
20	29	04	04		01♓	11	25		30	14	14		00♉	16	04		29	07	22		29	02	09	
21	00♒	05	05	00	02	12	25	00	01♈	15	14	30♎	01	17	04	29	00♊	07	23	28	00♋	01	10	28
22	01	06	06		03	13	26		02	16	15		02	18	05		01	08	23		01	01	10	
23	02	07	06		04	14	27		03	17	15		03	19	05		02	08	24		02	00	10	
24	03	08	07		05	16	27		04	19	16		04	19	06		03	08	24		03	29♊	11	
25	05	10	07		06	17	28		05	20	17		05	20	07		04	08	25		04	29	11	
26	06	11	08	00	07	18	28	00	06	21	17	30	06	21	07	29	05	09	26	28	05	28	12	28
27	07	12	09		08	19	29		07	22	18		07	22	08		06	09	26		06	28	12	
28	08	13	09		09	20	30		08	23	19		08	23	09		07	09	27		07	27	13	
29	09	15	10		10	21	00♑		09	24	19		09	24	09		08	09	27		08	27	13	
30	10	16	11						10	25	20		10	24	10		09	09	28		09	26	14	
31	11	17	11	00					11	26	21	30					10	09	28	28				

Day	JUL ☉	JUL ♀	JUL ♂	JUL ♆	AUG ☉	AUG ♀	AUG ♂	AUG ♆	SEP ☉	SEP ♀	SEP ♂	SEP ♆
01	10♋	26♊	14♓	28♎	09♌	28♊	23♓	28♎	09♍	23♋	21♓	28♎
02	11	25	15		10	29	23		10	24	20	
03	12	25	15		11	29	23		11	25	20	
04	12	24	15		12	00♋	23		12	26	20	29
05	13	24	16		13	01	23		13	27	20	
06	14	23	16	28	14	01	24	28	14	28	19	29
07	15	23	17		15	02	24		15	29	19	
08	16	23	17		16	03	24		16	00♌	19	
09	17	23	17		17	03	24		17	01	19	
10	18	23	18		18	04	24		18	02	18	
11	19	23	18	28	19	05	24	28	19	03	18	29
12	20	23	18		20	06	24		20	04	18	
13	21	23	19		21	06	24		21	05	17	
14	22	23	19		22	07	24		22	06	17	
15	23	23	19		23	08	24		23	07	17	
16	24	23	20	28	24	09	23	28	24	08	17	29
17	25	23	20		25	10	23		25	09	16	
18	26	23	20		25	10	23		26	11	16	
19	27	23	20		26	11	23		27	12	16	
20	28	23	21		27	12	23		27	13	16	
21	29	24	21	28	28	13	23	28	28	14	15	29
22	30	24	21		29	14	23		29	15	15	
23	01♌	24	21		00♍	15	23		00♎	16	15	
24	02	25	22		01	16	22		01	17	15	
25	02	25	22		02	17	22		02	18	15	
26	03	25	22	28	03	18	22	28	03	19	14	29
27	04	26	22		04	18	22		04	20	14	
28	05	26	22		05	19	22		05	21	14	
29	06	27	23		06	20	21		06	23	14	
30	07	27	23		07	21	21		07	24	14	
31	08	28	23	28	08	22	21	28				

Day	OCT ☉	OCT ♀	OCT ♂	OCT ♆	NOV ☉	NOV ♀	NOV ♂	NOV ♆	DEC ☉	DEC ♀	DEC ♂	DEC ♆
01	08♎	25♌	14♓	29♎	09♏	01♎	16♓	01♏	09♐	07♏	28♓	02♏
02	09	26	14		10	02	17		10	09	28	
03	10	27	13		11	03	17		11	10	29	
04	11	28	13		12	04	17		12	11	29	
05	12	29	13		13	06	17		13	12	30	
06	13	00♍	13	30	14	07	18	01	14	14	00♈	02
07	14	02	13		15	08	18		15	15	01	
08	15	03	13		16	09	18		16	16	01	
09	16	04	13		17	11	19		17	17	02	
10	17	05	13		18	12	19		18	18	02	
11	18	06	13	30	19	13	19	01	19	20	03	02
12	19	07	13		20	14	20		20	21	03	
13	20	08	13		21	15	20		21	22	04	
14	21	10	13		22	17	20		22	23	04	
15	22	11	13		23	18	21		24	25	05	
16	23	12	13	30	24	19	21	01	25	26	05	02
17	24	13	13		25	20	22		26	27	06	
18	25	14	14		26	21	22		27	28	06	
19	26	15	14	00♏	27	23	22		28	30	07	
20	27	17	14		28	24	23		29	01♐	07	
21	28	18	14	00	29	25	23	01	30	02	08	02
22	29	19	14		00♐	26	24		01♑	03	08	
23	00♏	20	14		01	28	24		02	05	09	
24	01	21	14		02	29	24		03	06	10	
25	02	23	15		03	30	25		04	07	10	
26	03	24	15	00	04	01♏	25	01	05	08	11	02
27	04	25	15		05	02	26		06	10	11	
28	05	26	15		06	04	26		07	11	12	
29	06	27	15		07	05	27		08	12	12	
30	07	28	16		08	06	27	02	09	13	13	
31	08	30	16	00					10	15	13	02

BIRTH TABLES - 1957

Day	JAN ☉	♀	♂	♆	FEB ☉	♀	♂	♆	MAR ☉	♀	♂	♆	APR ☉	♀	♂	♆	MAY ☉	♀	♂	♆	JUN ☉	♀	♂	♆
01	11♑	16♐	14♈	02♏	12♒	25♑	02♉	03♏	11♓	30♒	20♉	02♏	11♈	08♈	09♊	02♏	11♉	15♉	28♊	01♏	11♊	23♊	17♋	00♏
02	12	17	15		13	26	03		12	01♓	20		12	09	10		12	17	29		12	24	18	
03	13	18	15		14	27	04		13	02	21		13	11	10		13	18	29		13	26	19	
04	14	20	16		15	28	04		14	03	22		14	12	11		14	19	30		14	27	19	
05	15	21	16		16	30	05		15	05	22		15	13	12		15	20	01♋		15	28	20	
06	16	22	17	02	17	01♒	05	03	16	06	23	02	16	14	12	02	16	21	01	01	16	30	21	00
07	17	23	17		18	02	06		17	07	23		17	16	13		17	23	02		16	01♋	21	
08	18	25	18		19	03	07		18	08	24		18	17	14		18	24	02		17	02	22	
09	19	26	19		20	05	07		19	10	25		19	18	14		19	25	03		18	03	23	
10	20	27	19		22	06	08		20	11	25		20	19	15		20	26	04		19	04	23	
11	21	28	20	02	23	07	09	03	21	12	26	02	21	21	15	02	21	28	04	01	20	06	24	00
12	22	30	20		24	08	09		22	13	27		22	22	16	01	21	29	05		21	07	24	
13	23	01♑	21		25	10	10		23	15	27		23	23	17		22	00♊	06		22	08	25	
14	24	02	22		26	11	10		24	16	28		24	24	17		23	01	06		23	09	26	
15	25	03	22	03	27	12	11		25	17	29		25	26	18		24	03	07		24	11	26	
16	26	05	23	03	28	13	12	03	26	18	29	02	26	27	19	01	25	04	07	01	25	12	27	00
17	27	06	23		29	15	12		27	20	30		27	28	19		26	05	08		26	13	28	30♎
18	28	07	24		30	16	13		28	21	00♊		28	29	20		27	06	09		27	14	28	
19	29	08	25		01♓	17	14		29	22	01		29	00♉	21		28	07	09		28	15	29	
20	00♒	10	25		02	18	14		30	23	02		00♉	02	21		29	09	10		29	17	29	
21	01	11	26	03	03	20	15	03	01♈	24	02	02	01	03	22	01	00♊	10	11	00	30	18	00♌	30
22	02	12	26		04	21	15	02	02	26	03		02	04	22		01	11	11		01♋	19	01	
23	03	13	27		05	22	16		03	27	04		03	05	23		02	12	12		02	20	01	
24	04	15	28		06	23	17		04	28	04		04	07	24		03	14	12		03	22	02	
25	05	16	28		07	25	17		05	29	05		05	08	24		04	15	13		04	23	03	
26	06	17	29	03	08	26	18	02	06	01♈	05	02	06	09	25	01	05	16	14	00	05	24	03	30
27	07	18	29		09	27	18		07	02	06		07	10	26		06	17	14		06	25	04	
28	08	20	30		10	28	19		08	03	07		08	12	26		07	19	15		07	26	04	
29	09	21	01♉						09	04	07		09	13	27		08	20	16		07	27	05	
30	10	22	01						10	06	08		10	14	27		09	21	16		08	29	06	
31	11	23	02	03					11	07	09	02					10	22	17	00				

Day	Jul ☉	Jul ♀	Jul ♂	Jul ♆	Aug ☉	Aug ♀	Aug ♂	Aug ♆	Sep ☉	Sep ♀	Sep ♂	Sep ♆
01	09♋	00♌	06♌	30♎	09♌	08♍	26♌	30♎	09♍	15♎	15♍	01♏
02	10	01	07		10	09	26		10	16	16	
03	11	03	08		11	10	27		11	17	17	
04	12	04	08		12	11	28		12	18	17	
05	13	05	09		13	13	28	00♏	13	20	18	
06	14	06	09	30	14	14	29	00	14	21	19	01
07	15	07	10		15	15	30		15	22	19	
08	16	09	11		16	16	00♍		16	23	20	
09	17	10	11		17	17	01		17	24	21	
10	18	11	12		18	19	01		18	26	21	
11	19	12	13	30	19	20	02	00	18	27	22	01
12	20	13	13		19	21	03		19	28	22	
13	21	15	14		20	22	03		20	29	23	
14	22	16	14		21	23	04		21	00♏	24	
15	23	17	15		22	25	05		22	01	24	
16	24	18	16	30	23	26	05	00	23	03	25	01
17	25	20	16		24	27	06		24	04	26	
18	26	21	17		25	28	07		25	05	26	
19	27	22	18		26	29	07		26	06	27	
20	27	23	18		27	01♎	08		27	07	28	
21	28	24	19	30	28	02	08	00	28	09	28	01
22	29	26	19		29	03	09		29	10	29	
23	00♌	27	20		00♍	04	10		00♎	11	30	
24	01	28	21		01	05	10		01	12	00♎	
25	02	29	21		02	07	11		02	13	01	
26	03	00♍	22	30	03	08	12	00	03	14	02	01
27	04	02	23		04	09	12		04	16	02	
28	05	03	23		05	10	13		05	17	03	
29	06	04	24		06	11	14		06	18	03	
30	07	05	25		07	13	14		07	19	04	
31	08	06	25	30	08	14	15	01				

Day	Oct ☉	Oct ♀	Oct ♂	Oct ♆	Nov ☉	Nov ♀	Nov ♂	Nov ♆	Dec ☉	Dec ♀	Dec ♂	Dec ♆
01	08♎	20♍	05♎	01♏	09♏	25♐	25♎	03♏	09♐	26♑	15♏	04
02	09	21	05		10	26	26		10	26	16	
03	10	22	06	02	11	27	26		11	27	17	
04	11	24	07		12	28	27		12	28	17	
05	12	25	07		13	29	28		13	29	18	
06	13	26	08	02	14	01♑	28	03	14	30	19	04
07	14	27	09		15	02	29		15	01♒	19	
08	15	28	09		16	03	30		16	02	20	
09	16	29	10		17	04	00♏		17	02	21	
10	17	01♐	11		18	05	01		18	03	21	
11	18	02	11	02	19	06	02	03	19	04	22	04
12	19	03	12		20	07	02		20	05	23	
13	20	04	13		21	08	03		21	05	23	
14	21	05	13		22	09	04		22	06	24	
15	22	06	14		23	10	04		23	07	25	
16	23	07	15	02	24	11	05	03	24	08	26	04
17	24	08	15		25	12	06		25	08	26	
18	25	10	16		26	13	06		26	09	27	
19	26	11	17		27	14	07		27	10	28	
20	27	12	17		28	15	08		28	10	28	
21	28	13	18	02	29	16	08	03	29	11	29	04
22	29	14	19		30	17	09		00♑	11	30	
23	30	15	19		01♐	18	10		01	12	00♐	
24	01♏	16	20		02	19	11		02	12	01	
25	02	17	20		03	20	11		03	13	02	
26	03	19	21	02	04	21	12	03	04	13	02	04
27	04	20	22		05	22	13	04	05	14	03	
28	05	21	22		06	23	13		07	14	04	
29	06	22	23		07	24	14		08	15	04	
30	07	23	24	02	08	25	15		09	15	05	
31	08	24	24						10	15	06	04

BIRTH TABLES - 1958

	JANUARY				FEBRUARY				MARCH			
Day	☉	♀	♂	♆	☉	♀	♂	♆	☉	♀	♂	♆
01	11♑	15♒	07♐	04♏	12♒	06♒	28♐	05♏	10♓	03♒	19♑	05♏
02	12	16	07		13	06	29		11	03	19	
03	13	16	08		14	05	30		12	04	20	
04	14	16	09		15	05	01♑		13	04	21	
05	15	16	09	05	16	04	01		14	05	21	
06	16	16	10	05	17	04	02	05	15	05	22	05
07	17	16	11		18	03	03		16	06	23	
08	18	16	11		19	03	03		17	06	24	
09	19	16	12		20	02	04		18	07	24	
10	20	16	13		21	02	05		19	08	25	04
11	21	16	14	05	22	02	06	05	20	08	26	04
12	22	16	14		23	01	06		21	09	27	
13	23	16	15		24	01	07		22	10	27	
14	24	15	16		25	01	08		23	10	28	
15	25	15	16		26	01	08		24	11	29	
16	26	15	17	05	27	01	09	05	25	12	29	04
17	27	14	18		28	01	10		26	12	00♒	
18	28	14	18		29	01	11		27	13	01	
19	29	14	19		00♓	01	11		28	14	02	
20	30	13	20		01	01	12		29	15	02	
21	01♒	13	21	05	02	01	13	05	00♈	16	03	04
22	02	12	21		03	01	13		01	16	04	
23	03	12	22		04	01	14		02	17	05	
24	04	11	23		05	01	15		03	18	05	
25	05	10	23		06	02	16		04	19	06	
26	06	10	24	05	07	02	16	05	05	20	07	04
27	07	09	25		08	02	17		06	21	08	
28	08	09	26		09	03	18		07	22	08	
29	09	08	26						08	22	09	
30	10	07	27						09	23	10	
31	11	07	28	05					10	24	10	04

	APRIL				MAY				JUNE			
Day	☉	♀	♂	♆	☉	♀	♂	♆	☉	♀	♂	♆
01	11♈	25♒	11♒	04♏	11♉	26♓	03♓	03♏	10♊	00♉	26♓	02♏
02	12	26	12		12	27	04		11	02	27	
03	13	27	13		13	28	05		12	03	27	
04	14	28	13		14	29	05		13	04	28	
05	15	29	14		14	00♈	06		14	05	29	
06	16	30	15	04	15	01	07	03	15	06	29♈	02
07	17	01♓	16		16	02	08		16	07	00	
08	18	02	16		17	03	08		17	08	01	
09	19	03	17		18	04	09		18	10	02	
10	20	04	18		19	06	10		19	11	02	
11	21	05	19	04	20	07	11	03	20	12	03	02
12	22	06	19		21	08	11		21	13	04	
13	23	07	20		22	09	12		22	14	04	
14	24	08	21		23	10	13		23	15	05	
15	25	09	21		24	11	14		24	17	06	
16	26	10	22	04	25	12	14	03	25	18	07	02
17	27	11	23		26	13	15		26	19	07	
18	28	12	24		27	14	16		27	20	08	
19	29	13	24		28	16	16		28	21	09	
20	30	14	25		29	17	17		29	22	09	
21	01♉	15	26	04	30	18	18	03	30	24	10	02
22	02	16	27	03	01♊	19	19		01♋	25	11	
23	03	17	27		02	20	19		02	26	11	
24	04	18	28		03	21	20		02	27	12	
25	05	19	29		04	22	21		03	28	13	
26	06	20	30	03	05	24	22	03	04	29	14	02
27	07	21	00♓		06	25	22		05	01♊	14	
28	08	22	01		07	26	23		06	02	15	
29	09	24	02		08	27	24		07	03	16	
30	10	25	03		09	28	24		08	04	16	
31					10	29	25	03				

Each month column group gives ☉ (Sun), ♀ (Venus), ♂ (Mars) and ♆ (Neptune).

JULY

Day	☉	♀	♂	♆
01	09♋	05♊	17♈	02♏
02	10	07	18	
03	11	08	18	
04	12	09	19	
05	13	10	20	
06	14	11	20	02
07	15	12	21	
08	16	14	22	
09	17	15	22	
10	18	16	23	
11	19	17	24	02
12	20	18	24	
13	21	20	25	
14	22	21	26	
15	22	22	26	
16	23	23	27	02
17	24	24	28	
18	25	26	28	
19	26	27	29	
20	27	28	30	
21	28	29	00♉	02
22	29	00♋	01	
23	00♌	02	01	
24	01	03	02	
25	02	04	03	
26	03	05	03	02
27	04	06	04	
28	05	08	04	
29	06	09	05	
30	07	10	06	
31	08	11	06	02

AUGUST

Day	☉	♀	♂	♆
01	09♌	12♋	07♉	02♏
02	10	14	07	
03	11	15	08	
04	12	16	09	
05	13	17	09	
06	14	18	10	02
07	14	20	10	
08	15	21	11	
09	16	22	12	
10	17	23	12	
11	18	24	13	02
12	19	26	13	
13	20	27	14	
14	21	28	14	
15	22	29	15	
16	23	01♌	15	02
17	24	02	16	
18	25	03	16	
19	26	04	17	
20	27	05	17	
21	28	07	18	02
22	29	08	18	
23	30	09	19	
24	01♍	10	19	
25	02	12	20	
26	03	13	20	03
27	04	14	21	
28	05	15	21	
29	06	16	22	
30	07	18	22	
31	08	19	23	03

SEPTEMBER

Day	☉	♀	♂	♆
01	09♍	20♌	23♉	03♏
02	10	21	24	
03	10	23	24	
04	11	24	24	
05	12	25	25	
06	13	26	25	03
07	14	28	26	
08	15	29	26	
09	16	30	26	
10	17	01♍	27	
11	18	02	27	03
12	19	04	27	
13	20	05	28	
14	21	06	28	
15	22	07	28	
16	23	09	28	03
17	24	10	29	
18	25	11	29	
19	26	12	30	
20	27	14	30	
21	28	15	00♊	03
22	29	16	00	
23	30	17	01	
24	01♎	19	01	
25	02	20	01	
26	03	21	01	03
27	04	22	01	
28	05	24	02	
29	06	25	02	
30	07	26	02	04

OCTOBER

Day	☉	♀	♂	♆
01	08♎	27♍	02♊	04♏
02	09	29	02	
03	10	30	02	
04	11	01♎	02	
05	12	02	02	
06	13	04	02	04
07	14	05	02	
08	15	06	03	
09	16	07	03	
10	17	09	03	
11	18	10	03	04
12	19	11	03	
13	20	12	02	
14	21	14	02	
15	22	15	02	
16	23	16	02	04
17	24	17	02	
18	25	19	02	
19	26	20	02	
20	27	21	02	
21	28	22	02	04
22	29	24	01	
23	30	25	01	
24	01♏	26	01	
25	02	27	01	
26	03	29	01	04
27	04	30	00	
28	05	01♏	00	05
29	06	02	30	
30	07	04	30	
31	08	05	29♉	05

NOVEMBER

Day	☉	♀	♂	♆
01	09♏	06♏	29♉	05♏
02	10	07	29	
03	11	09	28	
04	12	10	28	
05	13	11	28	
06	14	12	28	05
07	15	14	27	
08	16	15	27	
09	17	16	26	
10	18	17	26	
11	19	19	26	05
12	20	20	25	
13	21	21	25	
14	22	22	25	
15	23	24	24	
16	24	25	24	05
17	25	26	23	
18	26	27	23	
19	27	29	23	
20	28	30	22	
21	29	01♐	22	05
22	30	02	22	
23	01♐	04	21	
24	02	05	21	06
25	03	06	21	
26	04	08	20	06
27	05	09	20	
28	06	10	20	
29	07	11	20	
30	08	12	19	

DECEMBER

Day	☉	♀	♂	♆
01	09♐	14♐	19♉	06♏
02	10	15	19	
03	11	16	19	
04	12	17	18	
05	13	19	18	
06	14	20	18	06
07	15	21	18	
08	16	23	18	
09	17	24	17	
10	18	25	17	
11	19	26	17	06
12	20	28	17	
13	21	29	17	
14	22	00♑	17	
15	23	01	17	
16	24	03	17	06
17	25	04	17	
18	26	05	17	
19	27	06	17	
20	28	08	17	
21	29	09	17	06
22	00♑	10	17	
23	01	11	17	
24	02	13	17	
25	03	14	17	
26	04	15	17	06
27	05	16	17	
28	06	18	17	
29	07	19	17	07
30	08	20	17	
31	09	21	17	07

BIRTH TABLES - 1959

Day	JAN ☉	JAN ♀	JAN ♂	JAN ♆	FEB ☉	FEB ♀	FEB ♂	FEB ♆	MAR ☉	MAR ♀	MAR ♂	MAR ♆	APR ☉	APR ♀	APR ♂	APR ♆	MAY ☉	MAY ♀	MAY ♂	MAY ♆	JUN ☉	JUN ♀	JUN ♂	JUN ♆
01	10♑	23♑	18♉	07♏	12♒	02♓	26♉	07♏	10♓	06♈	09♊	07♏	11♈	14♉	25♊	06♏	10♉	19♊	12♋	05♏	10♊	24♋	00♌	05♏
02	11	24	18		13	03	27		11	07	09		12	15	26		11	21	13		11	25	01	
03	12	25	18		14	04	27		12	09	10		13	16	27		12	22	13		12	26	01	
04	13	26	18		15	05	27		13	10	10		14	18	27		13	23	14		13	27	02	
05	14	28	18		16	07	28		14	11	11		15	19	27		14	24	14		14	28	03	
06	15	29	18	07	17	08	28	07	15	12	11	07	16	20	28	06	15	25	15	05	15	30	03	05
07	16	00♒	19		18	09	29		16	14	12		17	21	28		16	26	16		16	01♌	04	
08	17	01	19		19	10	29		17	15	12		18	22	29		17	28	16		17	02	04	
09	18	03	19		20	11	30		18	16	13		19	24	30		18	29	17		18	03	05	
10	20	04	19		21	13	30		19	17	13		20	25	00♋		19	30	17		19	04	06	
11	21	05	20	07	22	14	00♊	07	20	19	14	07	21	26	01	06	20	01♋	18	05	20	05	06	05
12	22	06	20		23	15	01		21	20	14		22	27	01		21	02	18		21	06	07	04
13	23	08	20		24	16	01		22	21	15		23	28	02		22	03	19		22	07	07	
14	24	09	20		25	18	02		23	22	15		24	30	02		23	04	20		23	08	08	
15	25	10	21		26	19	02		24	23	16		25	01♊	03		24	05	20		24	09	09	
16	26	12	21	07	27	20	03	07	25	25	16	07	26	02	03	06	25	07	21	05	25	10	09	04
17	27	13	21		28	21	03		26	26	17		27	03	04		26	08	21		26	11	10	
18	28	14	21		29	23	04		27	27	18		28	04	04		27	09	22		27	12	10	
19	29	15	22		00♓	24	04		28	28	18		29	05	05		28	10	23		27	13	11	
20	30	17	22		01	25	04		29	30	19		30	07	06		29	11	23		28	14	12	
21	01♒	18	22	07	02	26	05	07	00♈	01♉	19	07	01♉	08	06	06	30	12	24	05	29	15	12	04
22	02	19	23		03	28	05		01	02	20	06	02	09	07		01♊	13	24		00♋	16	13	
23	03	20	23		04	29	06		02	03	20		03	10	07		02	14	25		01	17	13	
24	04	22	23		05	00♈	06		03	04	21		04	11	08		03	16	26		02	18	14	
25	05	23	24		06	01	07		04	06	21		05	13	09		04	17	26		03	19	15	
26	06	24	24	07	07	03	07	07	05	07	22	06	06	14	09	06	04	18	27	05	04	20	15	04
27	07	25	24		08	04	08		06	08	22		06	15	10		05	19	27		05	20	16	
28	08	27	25		09	05	08		07	09	23		07	16	10		06	20	28		06	21	17	
29	09	28	25						08	10	23		08	17	11		07	21	28		07	22	17	
30	10	29	26						09	12	24		09	18	11		08	22	29		08	23	18	
31	11	00♓	26	07					10	13	25	06					09	23	30	05				

Day	JULY ☉	JULY ♀	JULY ♂	JULY ♆	AUGUST ☉	AUGUST ♀	AUGUST ♂	AUGUST ♆	SEPTEMBER ☉	SEPTEMBER ♀	SEPTEMBER ♂	SEPTEMBER ♆
01	09♋	24♌	18♌	04♏	08♌	15♍	08♍	04♏	08♍	08♍	27♍	05♏
02	10	25	19		09	15	08		09	07	28	
03	11	26	20		10	15	09		10	07	29	
04	12	27	20		11	15	09		11	06	29	
05	13	28	21		12	16	10		12	05	30	
06	14	28	21	04	13	16	11	04	13	05	00♎	05
07	15	29	22		14	16	11		14	04	01	
08	16	30	23		15	16	12		15	04	02	
09	17	01♍	23		16	16	13		16	03	02	
10	17	02	24		17	16	13		17	03	03	
11	18	02	24	04	18	16	14	04	18	02	04	05
12	19	03	25		19	16	14		19	02	04	
13	20	04	26		20	16	15		20	02	05	
14	21	05	26		21	16	16		21	01	06	
15	22	05	27		22	16	16		22	01	06	
16	23	06	28	04	23	16	17	04	23	01	07	05
17	24	07	28		24	15	18		24	00	08	
18	25	07	29		25	15	18		25	00	08	
19	26	08	29		26	15	19	05	26	00	09	
20	27	09	00♍		27	14	19		27	30♌	09	
21	28	09	01	04	28	14	20	05	28	30	10	05
22	29	10	01		29	14	21		29	30	11	
23	30	10	02		30	13	21		30	30	11	
24	01♌	11	03		01♍	13	22		01♎	30♌	12	
25	02	12	03		02	12	23		02	00♍	13	
26	03	12	04	04	03	12	23	05	03	00	13	05
27	04	13	04		03	11	24		04	00	14	
28	05	13	05		04	10	25		05	01	15	
29	06	13	06		05	10	25		06	01	15	
30	07	14	06		06	09	26		07	01	16	
31	08	14	07	04	07	09	27	05				

Day	OCTOBER ☉	OCTOBER ♀	OCTOBER ♂	OCTOBER ♆	NOVEMBER ☉	NOVEMBER ♀	NOVEMBER ♂	NOVEMBER ♆	DECEMBER ☉	DECEMBER ♀	DECEMBER ♂	DECEMBER ♆
01	08♎	01♍	17♎	06♏	08♏	22♍	08♏	07♏	09♐	23♎	28♏	08♏
02	09	02	17		09	23	08		10	24	29	
03	10	02	18		10	24	09		11	25	30	
04	11	02	19		11	25	10		12	26	01♐	
05	12	03	19		12	26	10		13	28	01	
06	12	03	20	06	13	27	11	07	14	29	02	08
07	13	04	21		14	28	12		15	30	03	
08	14	04	21		15	29	12		16	01♏	03	
09	15	05	22		16	30	13		17	02	04	
10	16	05	23		17	01♎	14		18	03	05	
11	17	06	23	06	18	02	14	07	19	04	06	08
12	18	07	24		19	03	15		20	06	06	
13	19	07	25		20	04	16		21	07	07	
14	20	08	25		21	05	17		22	08	08	
15	21	08	26		22	06	17		23	09	08	
16	22	09	27	06	23	07	18	07	24	10	09	08
17	23	10	27		24	08	19		25	11	10	
18	24	11	28		25	09	19		26	12	11	
19	25	11	29		26	10	20		27	14	11	
20	26	12	29		27	11	21		28	15	12	
21	27	13	00♏	06	28	12	21	08	29	16	13	08
22	28	14	01		29	13	22		30	17	13	
23	29	14	01		00♐	14	23		01♑	18	14	09
24	00♏	15	02		01	15	23		02	19	15	
25	01	16	03	07	02	16	24		03	21	16	
26	02	17	03	07	03	18	25	08	04	22	16	09
27	03	18	04		04	19	26		05	23	17	
28	04	19	05		06	20	26		06	24	18	
29	05	19	06		07	21	27		07	25	19	
30	06	20	06		08	22	28		08	27	19	
31	07	21	07	07					09	28	20	09

BIRTH TABLES - 1960

	JANUARY				FEBRUARY				MARCH				APRIL				MAY				JUNE			
	☉	♀	♂	♆	☉	♀	♂	♆	☉	♀	♂	♆	☉	♀	♂	♆	☉	♀	♂	♆	☉	♀	♂	♆
01	10♑	29♏	21♐	09♏	12♒	07♑	14♑	09♏	11♓	12♒	06♒	09♏	12♈	20♓	29♒	08♏	11♉	27♈	23♓	08♏	11♊	05♊	16♈	07♏
02	11	00♐	21		13	08	14		12	13	06		13	21	00♓		12	28	23		12	06	17	
03	12	01	22		14	09	15		13	15	07		14	23	01		13	30	24		13	08	18	
04	13	03	23		15	10	16		14	16	08		15	24	02		14	01♉	25		14	09	18	
05	14	04	24		16	11	17		15	17	09		16	25	03		15	02	26		15	10	19	
06	15	05	24	09	17	13	17	09	16	18	09	09	17	26	03	08	16	03	26	08	16	11	20	07
07	16	06	25		18	14	18		17	19	10		18	28	04		17	05	27		17	13	21	
08	17	07	26		19	15	19		18	21	11		19	29	05		18	06	28	07	18	14	21	
09	18	09	27		20	16	20		19	22	12		20	00♈	06		19	07	29		19	15	22	
10	19	10	27		21	18	20		20	23	13		21	01	06		20	08	29		20	16	23	
11	20	11	28	09	22	19	21	09	21	24	13	09	22	03	07	08	21	09	00♈	07	21	18	23	07
12	21	12	29		23	20	22		22	26	14		23	04	08		22	11	01		21	19	24	
13	22	13	29		24	21	23		23	27	15		24	05	09		23	12	02		22	20	25	
14	23	15	00♑		25	22	23		24	28	16		25	06	09		24	13	02		23	21	26	
15	24	16	01		26	24	24		25	29	16		26	07	10		25	14	03		24	22	26	
16	25	17	02	09	27	25	25	09	26	01♓	17	09	26	09	11	08	26	16	04	07	25	24	27	07
17	26	18	02		28	26	26		27	02	18		27	10	12		27	17	05		26	25	28	
18	27	19	03		29	27	26		28	03	19		28	11	13		28	18	05		27	26	29	
19	28	21	04		30	29	27		29	04	19		29	12	13		28	19	06		28	27	29	
20	29	22	05		01♓	30	28		30	05	20		00♉	14	14		29	20	07		29	29	00♉	
21	00♒	23	05	09	02	01♒	29	09	01♈	07	21	09	01	15	15	08	00♊	22	08	07	00♋	30	01	07
22	01	24	06		03	02	30		02	08	22		02	16	16		01	23	09		01	01♋	02	
23	02	26	07		04	03	00♒		03	09	22		03	17	16		02	24	09		02	02	02	
24	04	27	08		05	05	01		04	10	23		04	19	17		03	25	10		03	03	03	
25	05	28	08		06	06	02		05	12	24		05	20	18		04	27	11		04	05	04	
26	06	29	09	09	07	07	03	09	06	13	25	09	06	21	19	08	05	28	12	07	05	06	04	07
27	07	00♑	10		08	08	03		07	14	26		07	22	19		06	29	12		06	07	05	
28	09	02	11		09	10	04		08	15	26		08	23	20		07	00♊	13		07	08	06	06
29	09	03	11		10	11	05		09	17	27		09	25	21		08	02	14		08	10	07	
30	10	04	12						10	18	28		10	26	22		09	03	15		09	11	07	
31	11	05	13	09					11	19	29	08					10	04	15	07				

Day	JULY				AUGUST				SEPTEMBER				OCTOBER				NOVEMBER				DECEMBER			
	☉	♀	♂	♆	☉	♀	♂	♆	☉	♀	♂	♆	☉	♀	♂	♆	☉	♀	♂	♆	☉	♀	♂	♆
01	10♋	12♋	08♉	06♏	09♌	20♌	30♉	06♏	09♍	28♍	19♊	07♏	08♎	05♏	05♋	08♏	09♏	13♐	16♋	09♏	09♐	19♑	18♋	10♏
02	11	13	09		10	21	00♊		10	30	20		09	06	06		10	14	17		10	21	18	
03	12	15	09		11	23	01		11	01♎	20		10	08	06		11	16	17		11	22	17	
04	12	16	10		12	24	02		12	02	21		11	09	06		12	17	17		12	23	17	
05	13	17	11		13	25	02		13	03	21		12	10	07		13	18	17		13	24	17	
06	14	18	12	06	14	26	03	06	14	05	22	07	13	11	07	08	14	19	17	09	14	25	17	10
07	15	19	12		15	28	04		15	06	23		14	13	08		15	20	18		15	27	17	
08	16	21	13		16	29	04		16	07	23		15	14	08		16	22	18		16	28	16	
09	17	22	14		17	00♍	05	07	17	08	24		16	15	09		17	23	18		17	29	16	
10	18	23	14		18	01	05		18	09	24		17	16	09		18	24	18		18	00♒	16	
11	19	24	15	06	19	03	06	07	19	11	25	07	18	18	09	08	19	25	18	09	19	01	16	10
12	20	26	16		20	04	07		20	12	25		19	19	10		20	27	18		20	03	15	
13	21	27	17		21	05	07		21	13	26		20	20	10		21	28	18		21	04	15	
14	22	28	17		22	06	08		22	14	26		21	21	11		22	29	18		23	05	15	
15	23	29	18		23	07	09		23	16	27		22	22	11		23	00♑	18		24	06	14	
16	24	01♌	19	06	24	09	09	07	24	17	28	07	23	24	11	08	24	01	19	09	25	07	14	10
17	25	02	19		25	10	10		25	18	28		24	25	12		25	03	19		26	08	14	
18	26	03	20		26	11	11		26	19	29		25	26	12		26	04	19	10	27	10	13	11
19	27	04	21		26	12	11		27	21	29		26	27	13		27	05	19		28	11	13	
20	28	05	21		27	14	12		28	22	30		27	29	13		28	06	19		29	12	13	
21	29	07	22	06	28	15	12	07	28	23	00♋	07	28	30	13	09	29	07	19	10	30	13	12	11
22	30	08	23		29	16	13		29	24	01		29	01♐	14		00♐	09	19		01♑	14	12	
23	01♌	09	23		00♍	17	14		00♎	25	01	08	00♏	02	14		01	10	19		02	15	11	
24	02	10	24		01	19	14		01	27	02		01	03	14		02	11	19		03	17	11	
25	03	12	25		02	20	15		02	28	02		02	05	14		03	12	18		04	18	11	
26	03	13	26	06	03	21	16	07	03	29	03	08	03	06	15	09	04	13	18	10	05	19	10	11
27	04	14	26		04	22	16		04	00♏	03		04	07	15		05	14	18		06	20	10	
28	05	15	27		05	23	17		05	02	04		05	08	15		06	16	18		07	21	10	
29	06	17	28		06	25	17		06	03	04		06	10	16		07	17	18		08	22	09	
30	07	18	28		07	26	18		07	04	05		07	11	16		08	18	18		09	24	09	
31	08	19	29	06	08	27	19	07					08	12	16	09					10	25	08	11

BIRTH TABLES - 1961

Day	JAN ☉	JAN ♀	JAN ♂	JAN ♆	FEB ☉	FEB ♀	FEB ♂	FEB ♆	MAR ☉	MAR ♀	MAR ♂	MAR ♆	APR ☉	APR ♀	APR ♂	APR ♆	MAY ☉	MAY ♀	MAY ♂	MAY ♆	JUN ☉	JUN ♀	JUN ♂	JUN ♆
01	11♑	26♒	08♋	11♏	12♒	29♓	00♋	11♏	11♓	23♈	03♋	11♏	12♈	26♈	14♋	11♏	11♉	13♈	28♋	10♏	11♊	27♈	14♌	09♏
02	12	27	08		13	00♈	00		12	23	03		13	26	14		12	13	28		12	27	15	
03	13	28	07		14	01	00		13	24	04		13	25	14		13	13	28		13	28	15	
04	14	29	07		15	02	00		14	24	04		14	25	15		14	13	29		14	29	16	
05	15	00♓	06		16	03	00		15	25	04		15	24	15		15	13	30		15	30	17	
06	16	02	06	11	17	04	00	11	16	25	04	11	16	24	16	11	16	13	00♌	10	16	01♉	17	09
07	17	03	06		18	05	00		17	26	05		17	23	16		17	13	01		16	01	18	
08	18	04	05		20	06	00		18	26	05		18	22	17		18	14	01		17	02	18	
09	19	05	05		21	07	00		19	27	05		19	22	17		19	14	02		18	03	19	
10	20	06	05		22	08	00		20	27	06		20	21	18		20	14	02		19	04	19	
11	21	07	04	11	23	09	00	11	21	27	06	11	21	21	18	10	21	14	03	10	20	05	20	09
12	22	08	04		24	10	00		22	28	06		22	20	18		22	15	03		21	06	20	
13	23	09	04		25	11	00		23	28	06		23	19	19		22	15	04		22	07	21	
14	24	10	03		26	11	00		24	28	07		24	19	19		23	15	04		23	08	22	
15	25	12	03		27	12	01		25	29	07		25	18	20		24	16	05		24	09	22	
16	26	13	03	11	28	13	01	11	26	29	07	11	26	18	20	10	25	16	06	10	25	09	23	09
17	27	14	03		29	14	01		27	29	08		27	17	21		26	17	06	09	26	10	23	
18	28	15	02		30	15	01		28	29	08		28	16	21		27	17	07		27	11	24	
19	29	16	02		01♓	16	01		29	29	09		29	16	21		28	18	07		28	12	24	
20	00♒	17	02		02	16	01		30	29	09		00♉	15	22		29	18	08		29	13	25	
21	01	18	02	11	03	17	01	11	01♈	29	09	11	01	15	23	10	00♊	19	08	09	30	14	26	09
22	02	19	01		04	18	02		02	29	10		02	15	23		01	20	09		01♋	15	26	
23	03	20	01		05	18	02		03	29	10		03	14	24		02	20	09		02	16	27	
24	04	21	01		06	19	02		04	29	10		04	14	24		03	21	10		03	17	27	
25	05	22	01		07	20	02		05	29	11		05	14	25		04	22	10		04	18	28	
26	06	23	01	11	08	21	02	11	06	28	11	11	06	13	25	10	05	22	11	09	05	19	29	09
27	07	24	01		09	21	03		07	28	12		07	13	26		06	23	11		06	20	29	
28	08	25	00		10	22	03		08	28	12		08	13	26		07	24	12		07	21	30	
29	09	26	00						09	28	12		09	13	27		08	24	13		07	22	00♍	
30	10	27	00						10	27	13		10	13	27		09	25	13		08	23	01	
31	11	28	00	11					11	27	13	11					10	26	14	09				

	JULY				AUGUST				SEPTEMBER				OCTOBER				NOVEMBER				DECEMBER			
	☉	♀	♂	♆	☉	♀	♂	♆	☉	♀	♂	♆	☉	♀	♂	♆	☉	♀	♂	♆	☉	♀	♂	♆
01	09♋	24♉	02♍	09♏	09♌	28♊	20♍	09♏	09♍	03♌	10♎	09♏	08♎	10♍	30♎	10♏	09♏	18♎	21♏	11♏	09♐	25♏	13♐	12♏
02	10	25	02		10	29	21		10	05	11		09	11	00♏		10	19	22		10	27	13	
03	11	26	03		11	30	22		11	06	11		10	12	01		11	20	23		11	28	14	
04	12	27	03		12	01♋	22		12	07	12		11	13	02		12	22	23		12	29	15	
05	13	28	04		13	02	23		13	08	13		12	14	02		13	23	24		13	00♐	16	
06	14	29	04	09	14	03	23	09	14	09	13	09	13	16	03	10	14	24	25	11	14	02	16	12
07	15	00♊	05		15	04	24		15	11	14		14	17	04		15	25	25		15	03	17	
08	16	01	06		16	06	24		16	12	14		15	18	05		16	27	26		16	04	18	
09	17	02	06		17	07	25		17	13	15		16	19	05		17	28	27		17	05	19	
10	18	03	07		18	08	26		18	14	16		17	21	06		18	29	28		18	07	19	
11	19	05	07	09	19	09	27	09	19	15	16	09	18	22	07	10	19	00♏	28	11	19	08	20	12
12	20	06	08		20	10	27		19	17	17		19	23	07		20	02	29		20	09	21	
13	21	07	09		20	11	28		20	18	18		20	24	08		21	03	30		21	11	22	
14	22	08	09		21	12	28		21	19	18		21	26	09		22	04	00♐		22	12	22	
15	23	09	10		22	14	29		22	20	19		22	27	09		23	05	01	11	23	13	23	13
16	24	10	10	09	23	15	30	09	23	21	20	09	23	28	10	10	24	07	02	12	24	14	24	13
17	25	11	11		24	16	00♎		24	23	20		24	29	11		25	08	03		25	16	25	
18	26	12	12		25	17	01		25	24	21		25	00♎	11		26	09	03		26	17	25	
19	27	13	12		26	18	02		26	25	22		26	02	12		27	11	04		27	18	26	
20	28	14	13		27	19	02		27	26	22	10	27	03	13	11	28	12	05		28	19	27	
21	28	15	14	09	28	21	03	09	28	27	23	10	28	04	13	11	29	13	05	12	29	21	28	13
22	29	16	14		29	22	03		29	29	24		29	05	14		30	14	06		00♑	22	28	
23	00♌	18	15		00♍	23	04		00♎	30	24		30	07	15		01♐	15	07		01	23	29	
24	01	19	15		01	24	05		01	01♍	25		01♏	08	16		02	17	08		02	24	30	
25	02	20	16		02	25	05		02	02	26		02	09	16		03	18	08		03	26	01♑	
26	03	21	17	09	03	26	06	09	03	03	26	10	03	10	17	11	04	19	09	12	04	27	01	13
27	04	22	17		04	28	07		04	05	27		04	12	18		05	20	10		05	28	02	
28	05	23	18		05	29	07		05	06	28		05	13	18		06	22	11		07	29	03	
29	06	24	18		06	30	08		06	07	28		06	14	19		07	23	11		08	01♑	04	
30	07	25	19		07	01♌	09		07	08	29		07	15	20		08	24	12		09	02	04	
31	08	26	20	09	08	02	09	09					08	17	20	11					10	03	05	13

BIRTH TABLES - 1962

Day	JAN ☉	JAN ♀	JAN ♂	JAN ♆	FEB ☉	FEB ♀	FEB ♂	FEB ♆	MAR ☉	MAR ♀	MAR ♂	MAR ♆
01	11♑	04♑	06♑	13♏	12♒	13♒	30♑	13♏	10♓	18♓	22♒	13♏
02	12	06	07		13	15	00♒		11	20	22	
03	13	07	07		14	16	01		12	21	23	
04	14	08	08		15	17	02		13	22	24	
05	15	09	09		16	18	03		14	23	25	
06	16	11	10	13	17	20	04	13	15	25	25	13
07	17	12	10		18	21	04		16	26	26	
08	18	13	11		19	22	05		17	27	27	
09	19	14	12		20	23	06		18	28	28·	
10	20	16	13		21	25	07		19	30	28	
11	21	17	13	13	22	26	07	13	20	01♈	29	13
12	22	18	14		23	27	08		21	02	00♓	
13	23	20	15		24	28	09		22	03	01	
14	24	21	16		25	30	10		23	05	02	
15	25	22	17		26	01♓	11		24	06	03	
16	26	23	17	13	27	02	11	13	25	07	03	13
17	27	25	18		28	03	12		26	08	04	
18	28	26	19		29	05	13		27	10	05	
19	29	27	20		00♓	06	14		28	11	06	
20	30	28	20		01	07	14		29	12	06	
21	01♒	30	21	13	02	08	15	13	00♈	13	07	13
22	02	01♒	22		03	10	16		01	15	08	
23	03	02	23		04	11	17		02	16	09	
24	04	03	23		05	12	18		03	17	10	
25	05	05	24		06	13	18		04	18	10	
26	06	06	25	13	07	15	19	13	05	20	11	13
27	07	07	26		08	16	20		06	21	12	
28	08	08	27		09	17	21		07	22	13	
29	09	10	27						08	23	13	
30	10	11	28						09	24	14	
31	11	12	29	13					10	26	15	13

Day	APR ☉	APR ♀	APR ♂	APR ♆	MAY ☉	MAY ♀	MAY ♂	MAY ♆	JUN ☉	JUN ♀	JUN ♂	JUN ♆
01	11♈	27♈	16♓	13♏	11♉	04♊	09♈	12♏	11♊	11♋	03♉	11♏
02	12	28	17		12	05	10		11	12	03	
03	13	29	17		13	06	11		12	14	04	
04	14	01♉	18		14	07	11		13	15	05	
05	15	02	19		15	09	12		14	16	06	
06	16	03	20	13	15	10	13	12	15	17	06	11
07	17	04	21		16	11	14		16	18	07	
08	18	06	21		17	12	14		17	20	08	
09	19	07	22		18	14	15		18	21	09	
10	20	08	23		19	15	16		19	22	09	
11	21	09	24	13	20	16	17	12	20	23	10	11
12	22	10	25		21	17	18		21	24	11	
13	23	12	25		22	18	18		22	26	12	
14	24	13	26		23	20	19		23	27	12	
15	25	14	27		24	21	20		24	28	13	
16	26	15	28	12	25	22	21	11	25	29	14	11
17	27	17	28		26	23	21		26	00♌	14	
18	28	18	29		27	24	22		27	02	15	
19	29	19	30		28	26	23		28	03	16	
20	30	20	01♈		29	27	24		29	04	17	
21	01♉	22	01	12	30	28	24	11	30	05	17	11
22	02	23	02		01♊	29	25		01♋	06	18	
23	03	24	03		02	00♋	26		02	07	19	
24	04	25	04		03	02	27		02	09	20	
25	05	26	05		04	03	27		03	10	20	
26	06	28	05	12	05	04	28	11	04	11	21	11
27	07	29	06		06	05	29		05	12	22	
28	08	00♊	07		07	06	30		06	13	22	
29	09	01	08		08	08	00♉		07	15	23	
30	10	03	08		09	09	01		08	16	24	
31					10	10	02	11				

Day	☉ JUL	♀ JUL	♂ JUL	♆ JUL	☉ AUG	♀ AUG	♂ AUG	♆ AUG	☉ SEP	♀ SEP	♂ SEP	♆ SEP	☉ OCT	♀ OCT	♂ OCT	♆ OCT	☉ NOV	♀ NOV	♂ NOV	♆ NOV	☉ DEC	♀ DEC	♂ DEC	♆ DEC
01	09♋	17♌	25♉	11♏	09♌	22♍	16♊	11♏	09♍	25♎	06♋	11♏	08♎	20♏	24♋	12♏	09♏	26♏	10♌	13♏	09♐	12♏	21♌	14♏
02	10	18	25		10	23	17		10	26	07		09	21	25		10	25	11		10	12	22	
03	11	19	26		11	24	18		11	27	08		10	21	25		11	25	11		11	12	22	
04	12	20	27		12	25	18		11	28	08		11	22	26		12	25	12		12	12	22	
05	13	21	27		13	27	19		12	29	09		12	22	27		13	24	12		13	12	22	
06	14	23	28	11	14	28	20	11	13	30	09	11	13	23	27	12	14	24	12	13	14	13	23	14
07	15	24	29		14	29	20		14	01♏	10		14	23	28		15	23	13		15	13	23	
08	16	25	30		15	30	21		15	01	11		15	24	28		16	23	13		16	13	23	
09	17	26	00♊		16	01♎	22		16	02	11		16	24	29		17	22	14		17	13	23	
10	18	27	01		17	02	22		17	03	12		17	25	29		18	21	14		18	13	23	15
11	19	28	02	11	18	03	23	11	18	04	13	11	18	25	30	12	19	21	14	13	19	14	23	15
12	20	30	02		19	04	23		19	05	13		19	25	00♌		20	20	15	14	20	14	24	
13	21	01♍	03		20	05	24		20	06	14		20	26	01		21	20	15		21	14	24	
14	22	02	04		21	06	25		21	07	14		21	26	01		22	19	16		22	15	24	
15	23	03	04		22	07	25		22	08	15		22	27	02		23	18	16		23	15	24	
16	23	04	05	11	23	08	26	11	23	09	16	11	23	27	03	12	24	18	16	14	24	16	24	15
17	24	05	06		24	09	27		24	10	16	12	24	27	03		25	17	17		25	16	24	
18	25	06	07		25	10	27		25	10	17		25	27	03	13	26	17	17		26	16	24	
19	26	08	07		26	12	28		26	11	17		26	27	04		27	16	18		27	17	25	
20	27	09	08		27	13	29		27	12	18		27	28	04		28	16	18		28	18	25	
21	28	10	09	11	28	14	29	11	28	13	19	12	28	28	05	13	29	15	18	14	29	18	25	15
22	29	11	09		29	15	00♋		29	13	19		29	28	05		30	15	19		00♑	19	25	
23	00♌	12	10		30	16	01		30	14	20		30	28	06		01♐	14	19		01	19	25	
24	01	13	11		01♍	17	01		01♎	15	20		01♏	28	06		02	14	19		02	20	25	
25	02	14	11		02	18	02		02	16	21		02	28	07		03	14	20		03	21	25	
26	03	15	12	11	03	19	03	11	03	17	21	12	03	27	07	13	04	14	20	14	04	21	25	15
27	04	17	13		04	20	03		04	17	22		04	27	08		05	13	20		05	22	25	
28	05	18	13		05	21	04		05	18	23		05	27	08		06	13	20		06	23	25	
29	06	19	14		06	22	04		06	19	23		06	27	09		07	13	21		07	23	25	
30	07	20	15		07	23	05		07	19	24		07	27	09		08	13	21		08	24	25	
31	08	21	15	11	08	24	06	11					08	26	10	13					09	25	25	15

BIRTH TABLES - 1963

Day	JANUARY ☉	♀	♂	♆	FEBRUARY ☉	♀	♂	♆	MARCH ☉	♀	♂	♆
01	10♑	26♏	25♌	15♏	12♒	25♐	16♌	16♏	10♓	27♑	07♌	16♏
02	11	27	24		13	26	16		11	28	07	
03	12	27	24		14	27	15		12	29	06	
04	13	28	24		15	29	15		13	00♒	06	
05	14	29	24		16	30	14		14	01	06	
06	15	30	24	15	17	01♑	14	16	15	02	06	16
07	16	00♐	24		18	02	14		16	04	06	
08	17	02	24		19	03	13		17	05	06	
09	19	03	23		20	04	13		18	06	06	
10	20	03	23		21	05	13		19	07	06	
11	21	04	23	15	22	06	12	16	20	08	06	16
12	22	05	23		23	07	12		21	09	05	
13	23	06	23		24	08	11		22	10	05	15
14	24	07	22		25	10	11		23	12	05	
15	25	08	22		26	11	11		24	13	05	
16	26	09	22	15	27	12	10	16	25	14	05	15
17	27	10	22		28	13	10		26	15	05	
18	28	11	21		29	14	10		27	16	05	
19	29	12	21		00♓	15	09		28	18	05	
20	30	13	21		01	16	09		29	19	05	
21	01♒	14	20	15	02	17	09	16	00♈	20	06	15
22	02	15	20		03	19	09		01	21	06	
23	03	16	20		04	20	08		02	22	06	
24	04	17	19		05	21	08		03	23	06	
25	05	18	19	16	06	22	08		04	25	06	
26	06	19	19	16	07	23	07	16	05	26	06	15
27	07	20	18		08	24	07		06	27	06	
28	08	21	18		09	25	07		07	28	06	
29	09	22	17						08	29	06	
30	10	23	17						09	01♓	06	
31	11	24	17	16					10	02	07	15

Day	APRIL ☉	♀	♂	♆	MAY ☉	♀	♂	♆	JUNE ☉	♀	♂	♆
01	11♈	03♓	07♌	15♏	10♉	09♈	15♌	14♏	10♊	16♉	29♌	14♏
02	12	04	07		11	10	16		11	17	30	
03	13	05	07		12	11	16		12	19	00♍	
04	14	07	07		13	12	17		13	20	01	
05	15	08	08		14	14	17		14	21	01	
06	16	09	08	15	15	15	17	14	15	22	02	14
07	17	10	08		16	16	18		16	24	02	
08	18	11	08		17	17	18		17	25	03	
09	19	12	08		18	18	19		18	26	03	
10	20	14	09		19	20	19		19	27	04	
11	21	15	09	15	20	21	19	14	20	28	04	14
12	22	16	09		21	22	20		21	30	05	13
13	23	17	09		22	23	20		22	01♊	05	
14	24	18	10		23	25	21		23	02	06	
15	25	20	10		24	26	21		24	03	06	
16	26	21	10	15	25	27	22	14	25	04	07	13
17	27	22	11		26	28	22		26	06	07	
18	28	23	11		27	29	23		27	07	08	
19	29	24	11		28	01♉	23		27	08	08	
20	30	26	12		29	02	23		28	09	09	
21	01♉	27	12	15	30	03	24	14	29	11	10	13
22	02	28	12		01♊	04	24		00♋	12	10	
23	03	29	13		02	05	25		01	13	11	
24	04	00♈	13		03	07	25		02	14	11	
25	05	02	13		04	08	26		03	15	12	
26	06	03	14	15	05	09	26	14	04	17	12	13
27	07	04	14		05	10	27		05	18	13	
28	07	05	14		06	11	27		06	19	13	
29	08	06	15		07	13	28		07	20	14	
30	09	08	15		08	14	28		08	22	14	
31					09	15	29	14				

JULY

Day	☉	♀	♂	♆
01	09♋	23♊	15♍	13♏
02	10	24	16	
03	11	25	16	
04	12	26	17	
05	13	28	17	
06	14	29	18	13
07	15	00♋	18	
08	16	01	19	
09	17	02	20	
10	18	04	20	
11	18	05	21	13
12	19	06	21	
13	20	07	22	
14	21	09	22	
15	22	10	23	
16	23	11	24	13
17	24	12	24	
18	25	14	25	
19	26	15	25	
20	27	16	26	
21	28	17	27	13
22	29	18	27	
23	30	20	28	
24	01♌	21	28	
25	02	22	29	
26	03	23	30	13
27	04	25	00♎	
28	05	26	01	
29	06	27	01	
30	07	28	02	
31	08	29	03	13

AUGUST

Day	☉	♀	♂	♆
01	08♌	01♌	03♎	13♏
02	09	02	04	
03	10	03	04	
04	11	04	05	
05	12	06	06	
06	13	07	06	13
07	14	08	07	
08	15	09	08	
09	16	11	08	
10	17	12	09	
11	18	13	09	13
12	19	14	10	
13	20	15	11	
14	21	17	11	
15	22	18	12	
16	23	19	13	13
17	24	20	13	
18	25	22	14	
19	26	23	14	
20	27	24	15	
21	28	25	16	13
22	29	27	16	
23	30	28	17	
24	01♍	29	18	
25	02	00♍	18	
26	03	02	19	13
27	04	03	20	
28	04	04	20	
29	05	05	21	
30	06	07	22	
31	07	08	22	13

SEPTEMBER

Day	☉	♀	♂	♆
01	08♍	09♍	23♎	13♏
02	09	10	23	
03	10	11	24	
04	11	13	25	
05	12	14	25	
06	13	15	26	13
07	14	16	27	
08	15	18	27	
09	16	19	28	
10	17	20	29	
11	18	21	29	14
12	19	23	00♏	
13	20	24	01	
14	21	25	01	
15	22	26	02	
16	23	28	03	14
17	24	29	03	
18	25	00♎	04	
19	26	01	05	
20	27	03	05	
21	28	04	06	14
22	29	05	07	
23	30	06	07	
24	01♎	08	08	
25	02	09	09	
26	03	10	10	14
27	04	11	10	
28	05	13	11	
29	06	14	12	
30	07	15	12	

OCTOBER

Day	☉	♀	♂	♆
01	08♎	16♎	13♏	14♏
02	09	18	14	
03	10	19	14	
04	11	20	15	
05	12	21	16	
06	13	23	16	14
07	13	24	17	
08	14	25	18	
09	15	26	19	
10	16	28	19	
11	17	29	20	14
12	18	00♏	21	
13	19	01	21	15
14	20	03	22	
15	21	04	23	
16	22	05	23	15
17	23	06	24	
18	24	07	25	
19	25	09	26	
20	26	10	26	
21	27	11	27	15
22	28	12	28	
23	29	14	28	
24	00♏	15	29	
25	01	16	30	
26	02	17	01♐	15
27	03	19	01	
28	04	20	02	
29	05	21	03	
30	06	22	03	
31	07	24	04	15

NOVEMBER

Day	☉	♀	♂	♆
01	08♏	24♏	05♐	15♏
02	09	26	06	
03	10	27	06	
04	11	29	07	
05	12	30	08	
06	13	01♐	09	15
07	14	02	09	
08	15	04	10	
09	16	05	11	
10	17	06	11	
11	18	07	12	16
12	19	09	13	
13	20	10	14	
14	21	11	14	
15	22	12	15	
16	23	14	16	16
17	24	15	17	
18	25	16	17	
19	26	17	18	
20	27	19	19	
21	28	20	20	16
22	29	21	20	
23	00♐	22	21	
24	01	24	22	
25	02	25	23	
26	04	26	23	16
27	05	27	24	
28	06	29	25	
29	07	30	26	
30	08	01♑	26	

DECEMBER

Day	☉	♀	♂	♆
01	09♐	02♑	27♐	16♏
02	10	04	28	
03	11	05	29	
04	12	06	29	
05	13	07	00♑	
06	14	09	01	16
07	15	10	02	
08	16	11	02	
09	17	12	03	17
10	18	13	04	
11	19	15	05	17
12	20	16	05	
13	21	17	06	
14	22	19	07	
15	23	20	08	
16	24	21	09	17
17	25	22	09	
18	26	23	10	
19	27	25	11	
20	28	26	12	
21	29	27	12	17
22	30	28	13	
23	01♑	30	14	
24	02	01♒	15	
25	03	02	15	
26	04	03	16	17
27	05	05	17	
28	06	06	18	
29	07	07	19	
30	08	08	19	
31	09	10	20	17

BIRTH TABLES - 1964

Day	JAN ☉	JAN ♀	JAN ♂	JAN ♇	FEB ☉	FEB ♀	FEB ♂	FEB ♇	MAR ☉	MAR ♀	MAR ♂	MAR ♇	APR ☉	APR ♀	APR ♂	APR ♇	MAY ☉	MAY ♀	MAY ♂	MAY ♇	JUN ☉	JUN ♀	JUN ♂	JUN ♇
01	10♑	11♒	21♑	17♏	12♒	19♓	15♒	18♏	11♓	23♈	08♓	18♏	12♈	27♉	02♈	17♏	11♉	25♊	25♈	17♏	11♊	07♋	18♉	16♏
02	11	12	22		13	20	16		12	24	09		13	28	03		12	26	26		12	07	19	
03	12	13	22		14	21	17		13	25	10		14	29	04		13	26	27		13	06	20	
04	13	14	23		15	22	18		14	27	10		15	00♊	05		14	27	28		14	06	21	
05	14	16	24		16	24	18		15	28	11		16	01	05		15	28	28		15	06	21	
06	15	17	25	17	17	25	19	18	16	29	12	18	17	02	06	17	16	28	29	17	16	05	22	16
07	16	18	26		18	26	20		17	30	13		18	03	07		17	29	30		17	05	23	
08	17	19	26		19	27	21		18	01♉	14		19	04	08		18	30	01♉		18	05	24	
09	18	21	27		20	28	21		19	02	14		20	05	09		19	00♋	01		19	04	24	
10	19	22	28		21	30	22		20	03	15		21	06	09		20	01	02		20	04	25	
11	20	23	29	18	22	01♈	23	18	21	05	16	18	22	07	10	17	21	01	03	16	21	03	26	16
12	21	24	29		23	02	24		22	06	17		23	08	11		22	02	04		22	03	26	
13	22	26	00♒		24	03	25		23	07	18		24	09	12		23	02	04		22	02	27	
14	23	27	01		25	04	25		24	08	18		25	10	12		24	03	05		23	02	28	
15	24	28	02		26	06	26		25	09	19		26	11	13		25	03	06		24	01	29	
16	25	29	03	18	27	07	27	18	26	10	20	18	27	12	14	17	26	04	07	16	25	01	29	16
17	26	00♓	03		28	08	28		27	11	21		27	13	15		27	04	07		26	00	00♊	
18	27	02	04		29	09	29		28	12	21		28	14	16		28	05	08		27	29♊	01	
19	28	03	05		30	10	29		29	13	22		29	15	16		29	05	09		28	29	01	
20	29	04	06		01♓	11	00♓		30	15	23		00♉	16	17		29	05	10		29	28	02	
21	00♒	05	07	18	02	13	01	18	01♈	16	24	18	01	17	18	17	00♊	06	10	16	00♋	28	03	16
22	02	07	07		03	14	02		02	17	25		02	17	19		01	06	11		01	27	04	15
23	03	08	08		04	15	03		03	18	25		03	18	19		02	06	12		02	26	04	
24	04	09	09		05	16	03		04	19	26		04	19	20		03	06	13		03	26	05	
25	05	10	10		06	17	04		05	20	27		05	20	21		04	07	13		04	25	06	
26	06	11	10	18	07	18	05	18	06	21	28	18	06	21	22	17	05	07	14	16	05	25	06	15
27	07	13	11		08	20	06		07	22	28		07	22	22		06	07	15		06	24	07	
28	09	14	12		09	21	06		08	23	29		08	23	23		07	07	16		07	24	08	
29	09	15	13		10	22	07		09	24	00♈		09	23	24		08	07	16		08	23	09	
30	10	16	14						10	25	01		10	24	25		09	07	17		09	23	09	
31	11	18	14	18					11	26	02	17					10	07	18	16				

	JULY				AUGUST				SEPTEMBER			
Day	☉	♀	♂	♆	☉	♀	♂	♆	☉	♀	♂	♆
01	10♋	22♊	10♊	15♏	09♌	28♊	01♋	15♏	09♍	23♋	21♋	15♏
02	11	22	11		10	28	02		10	24	22	
03	12	22	11		11	29	03		11	25	23	
04	13	21	12		12	30	03		12	26	23	
05	13	21	13		13	00♋	04		13	27	24	
06	14	21	13	15	14	01	05	15	14	28	25	15
07	15	21	14		15	02	05		15	29	25	
08	16	21	15		16	02	06		16	00♌	26	
09	17	21	15		17	03	07		17	01	26	
10	18	20	16		18	04	07		18	02	27	16
11	19	20	17	15	19	05	08	15	19	03	28	16
12	20	20	18		20	05	08		20	04	28	
13	21	20	18		21	06	09		21	05	29	
14	22	21	19		22	07	10		22	07	30	
15	23	21	20		23	08	10		23	08	00♌	
16	24	21	20	15	24	09	11	15	24	09	01	16
17	25	21	21		25	09	12		25	10	01	
18	26	21	22		26	10	12		26	11	02	
19	27	21	22		27	11	13		27	12	03	
20	28	22	23		28	12	14		28	13	03	
21	29	22	24	15	28	13	14	15	29	14	04	16
22	30	23	24		29	14	15		30	15	04	
23	01♌	23	25		00♍	15	16		00♎	16	05	
24	02	23	26		01	16	16		01	17	06	
25	03	24	26		02	17	17		02	18	06	
26	04	24	27	15	03	18	18	15	03	20	07	16
27	04	25	28		04	18	18		04	21	08	
28	05	25	28		05	19	19		05	22	08	
29	06	26	29		06	20	19		06	23	09	
30	07	26	30		07	21	20		07	24	09	
31	08	27	01♋	15	08	22	21	15				

	OCTOBER				NOVEMBER				DECEMBER			
Day	☉	♀	♂	♆	☉	♀	♂	♆	☉	♀	♂	♆
01	08♎	25♌	10♌	16♏	09♏	02♎	28♌	17♏	09♐	08♏	12♍	18♏
02	09	26	11		10	03	28		10	09	13	
03	10	27	11		11	04	29		11	10	13	19
04	11	29	12		12	05	29		12	12	14	
05	12	30	12		13	06	30		13	13	14	
06	13	01♍	13	16	14	07	00♍	17	14	14	15	19
07	14	02	13		15	09	01		15	15	15	
08	15	03	14		16	10	01		16	17	15	
09	16	04	15		17	11	02	18	17	18	16	
10	17	05	15		18	12	02		18	19	16	
11	18	07	16	16	19	13	03	18	19	20	17	19
12	19	08	16	17	20	15	03		20	22	17	
13	20	09	17		21	16	04		21	23	18	
14	21	10	18		22	17	04		22	24	18	
15	22	11	18		23	18	05		23	25	18	
16	23	12	19	17	24	20	05	18	24	27	19	19
17	24	14	19		25	21	06		25	28	19	
18	25	15	20		26	22	06		26	29	19	
19	26	16	20		27	23	07		27	00♐	20	
20	27	17	21		28	24	07		28	02	20	
21	28	18	21	17	29	26	08	18	29	03	20	19
22	29	20	22		00♐	27	08		01♑	04	21	
23	00♏	21	23		01	28	09		02	05	21	
24	01	22	23		02	29	09		03	06	22	
25	02	23	24		03	01♏	10		04	08	22	
26	03	24	24	17	04	02	10	18	05	09	22	19
27	04	26	25		05	03	11		06	10	22	
28	05	27	25		06	04	11		07	11	23	
29	06	28	26		07	06	12		08	13	23	
30	07	29	26		08	07	12		09	14	23	
31	08	00♎	27	17					10	15	24	19

BIRTH TABLES - 1965

Day	JAN ☉	JAN ♀	JAN ♂	JAN ♆	FEB ☉	FEB ♀	FEB ♂	FEB ♆	MAR ☉	MAR ♀	MAR ♂	MAR ♆	APR ☉	APR ♀	APR ♂	APR ♆	MAY ☉	MAY ♀	MAY ♂	MAY ♆	JUN ☉	JUN ♀	JUN ♂	JUN ♆
01	11♑	16♐	24♍	19♏	12♒	25♑	28♍	20♏	11♓	00♓	22♍	20♏	12♈	09♈	11♍	20♏	11♉	16♉	10♍	19♏	11♊	24♊	18♍	18♏
02	12	17	24		13	27	28		12	01	21		13	10	11		12	17	10		12	25	18	
03	13	19	24		14	28	28		13	03	21		14	11	10		13	18	10		13	26	19	
04	14	20	25		15	00♒	28		14	04	21		15	13	10		14	20	10		14	28	19	
05	15	22	25		16	01	28		15	05	20		16	14	10		15	21	10		15	29	19	
06	16	23	25	19	18	02	28	20	16	06	20	20	16	15	10	20	16	22	10	19	16	00♋	19	18
07	17	24	25	20	19	03	27		17	08	20		17	16	10	19	17	23	10		17	01	20	
08	18	25	26		20	04	27		18	09	19		18	18	10		18	25	11		17	03	20	
09	19	26	26		21	05	27		19	10	19		19	19	09		19	26	11		18	04	20	
10	20	28	26		22	06	27		20	11	18		20	20	09		20	27	11		19	05	21	
11	21	29	26	20	23	08	27	20	21	13	18	20	21	21	09	19	21	28	11	19	20	06	21	18
12	22	00♑	26		24	09	27		22	14	18		22	23	09		22	30	12		21	08	22	
13	23	01	27		25	10	26		23	15	17		23	24	09		23	01♊	12		22	09	22	
14	24	02	27		26	11	26		24	16	17		24	25	09		23	02	12		23	10	23	
15	25	04	27		27	13	26		25	18	16		25	26	09		24	03	12		24	11	24	
16	26	05	27	20	28	14	26	20	26	19	16	20	26	28	09	19	25	04	13	18	25	12	24	18
17	27	06	27		29	15	26		27	20	16		27	29	09		26	06	13		26	14	24	
18	28	08	27		30	17	25		28	21	15		28	30	09		27	07	13		27	15	25	
19	29	09	28		01♓	18	25		29	23	15		29	01♉	09		28	08	13		28	16	25	
20	00♒	10	28		02	19	25		30	24	15		00♉	02	09		29	09	14		29	17	26	
21	01	11	28	20	03	20	24	20	01♈	25	14	20	01	04	09	19	00♊	11	14	18	30	19	26	18
22	02	13	28		04	21	24		02	26	14		02	05	09		01	12	14		01♋	20	27	
23	03	14	28		05	23	24		03	28	14		03	06	09		02	13	15		02	22	27	
24	04	15	28		06	24	24		04	29	13		04	07	09		03	14	15		03	23	28	
25	05	17	28		07	25	23		05	00♈	13		05	09	09		04	15	15		04	24	28	
26	06	18	28	20	08	26	23	20	06	01	13	20	06	10	09	19	05	17	16	18	05	25	29	18
27	07	19	28		09	28	23		07	03	12		07	11	09		06	18	16		06	26	29	
28	08	20	28		10	29	22		08	04	12		08	12	09		07	19	16		07	27	30	17
29	09	22	28						09	05	12		09	13	09		08	20	17		08	29	00♎	
30	10	23	28						10	06	11		10	15	09		09	22	17		09	30	01	
31	11	24	28	20					11	08	11	20					10	23	17	18				

Day	JULY ☉	♀	♂	♆	AUGUST ☉	♀	♂	♆	SEPTEMBER ☉	♀	♂	♆	OCTOBER ☉	♀	♂	♆	NOVEMBER ☉	♀	♂	♆	DECEMBER ☉	♀	♂	♆
01	09♋	01♌	01♎	17♏	09♌	08♍	18♎	17♏	09♍	15♎	08♏	18♏	08♎	21♏	28♏	18♏	09♏	25♐	20♐	19♏	09♐	25♑	13♑	20♏
02	10	02	02		10	10	19		10	17	08		09	22	29		10	26	21		10	26	14	21
03	11	03	02		11	11	20		11	18	09		10	23	29		11	28	22		11	27	15	
04	12	04	03		12	12	20		12	19	10		11	24	00♐		12	29	23		12	28	15	
05	13	06	03		13	13	21		13	20	10		12	25	01		13	30	23	20	13	29	16	
06	14	07	04	17	14	14	22	17	14	21	11	18	13	26	02	18	14	01♑	24	20	14	29	17	21
07	15	08	04		15	16	22		15	23	11		14	27	02		15	02	25		15	30	18	
08	16	09	05		16	17	23		16	24	12		15	29	03		16	03	26		16	01♒	19	
09	17	10	05		17	18	23		17	25	13		16	30	04	19	17	04	26		17	01	19	
10	18	12	06		18	19	24		18	26	14		17	01♐	04		18	05	27		18	03	20	
11	19	13	06	17	19	20	24	17	19	27	14	18	18	02	05	19	19	06	28	20	19	03	21	21
12	20	14	07		20	22	25		20	28	15		19	03	06		20	07	28		20	04	22	
13	21	15	08		21	23	26		20	30	16		20	04	07		21	08	29		21	05	22	
14	22	17	08		21	24	26		21	01♏	16		21	05	07		22	09	00♑		22	05	23	
15	23	18	09		22	25	27		22	02	17		22	07	08		23	10	01		23	06	24	
16	24	19	09	17	23	26	27	17	23	03	18	18	23	08	09	19	24	11	02	20	24	07	25	21
17	25	20	10		24	28	28		24	04	18		24	09	09		25	12	02		25	07	26	
18	26	21	10		25	29	29		25	05	19		25	10	10		26	13	03		26	08	26	
19	27	23	11		26	30	29		26	07	20		26	11	11		27	14	04		27	08	27	
20	28	24	11		27	01♎	30		27	08	20		27	12	12		28	15	05		28	09	28	
21	29	25	12	17	28	02	01♏	17	28	09	21	18	28	13	12	19	29	16	05	20	29	10	28	21
22	29	26	12		29	04	01		29	10	22		29	14	13		30	17	06		00♑	10	29	
23	00♌	27	13		00♍	05	02		00♎	11	22		30	16	14		01♐	18	07		01	11	00♒	
24	01	29	14		01	06	03		01	12	23		01♏	17	14		02	19	08		02	11	01	
25	02	30	14		02	07	03		02	14	24		02	18	15		03	20	09		03	11	02	
26	03	01♍	15	17	03	08	04	17	03	15	24	18	03	19	16	19	04	21	09	20	05	12	03	21
27	04	02	15		04	10	04		04	16	25		04	20	17		05	22	10		06	12	03	
28	05	03	16		05	11	05	18	05	17	26		05	21	17		06	23	11		07	12	04	
29	06	05	17		06	12	06		06	18	27		06	22	18		07	24	12		08	13	05	
30	07	06	17		07	13	06		07	19	27		07	23	19		08	24	12		09	13	06	
31	08	07	18	17	08	14	07	18					08	24	20	19					10	13	07	21

BIRTH TABLES - 1966

Day	JANUARY ☉	♀	♂	♆	FEBRUARY ☉	♀	♂	♆	MARCH ☉	♀	♂	♆
01	11♑	13♒	07♒	22♏	12♒	02♒	02♓	22♏	10♓	01♒	24♓	22♏
02	12	14	08		13	02	03		11	02	25	
03	13	14	09		14	01	03		12	03	25	
04	14	14	10		15	01	04		13	03	26	
05	15	14	10		16	00	05		14	04	27	
06	16	14	11	22	17	30♑	06	22	15	04	28	22
07	17	14	12		18	30	07		16	05	28	
08	18	14	13		19	29	07		17	05	29	
09	19	13	14		20	29	08		18	06	00♈	
10	20	13	14		21	29	09		19	07	01	
11	21	13	15	22	22	29	10	22	20	07	02	22
12	22	13	16		23	28	11		21	08	02	
13	23	13	17		24	28	11		22	09	03	
14	24	12	18		25	28	12		23	10	04	
15	25	12	18		26	28	13		24	10	05	
16	26	11	19	22	27	28	14	22	25	11	05	22
17	27	11	20		28	28	14		26	12	06	
18	28	10	21		29	28	15		27	13	07	
19	29	10	21		00♓	28	16		28	14	08	
20	00♒	09	22		01	29	17		29	14	08	
21	01	09	23	22	02	29	17	22	00♈	15	09	22
22	02	08	24		03	29	18		01	16	10	
23	03	07	25		04	29	19		02	17	11	
24	04	07	25		05	30	20		03	18	12	
25	05	06	26		06	30♑	21		04	19	12	
26	06	06	27	22	07	00♒	21	22	05	19	13	22
27	07	05	28		08	01	22		06	20	14	
28	08	05	29		09	01	23		07	21	14	
29	09	04	29						08	22	15	
30	10	03	00♓						09	23	16	
31	11	03	01	22					10	24	17	22

Day	APRIL ☉	♀	♂	♆	MAY ☉	♀	♂	♆	JUNE ☉	♀	♂	♆
01	11♈	25♒	18♈	22♏	11♉	26♓	10♉	21♏	11♊	01♉	03♊	20♏
02	12	26	18		12	27	11		12	02	03	
03	13	27	19		13	28	12		12	03	04	
04	14	28	20		14	29	12		13	04	05	
05	15	29	21		15	00♈	13		14	06	05	
06	16	30	21	22	16	01	14	21	15	07	06	20
07	17	01♓	22		16	03	15		16	08	07	
08	18	02	23		17	04	15		17	09	08	
09	19	03	24		18	05	16		18	10	08	
10	20	04	25		19	06	17		19	11	09	
11	21	05	25	22	20	07	17	21	20	12	10	20
12	22	06	26		21	08	18		21	14	10	
13	23	07	27		22	09	19		22	15	11	
14	24	08	28		23	10	20		23	16	12	
15	25	09	28		24	11	20		24	17	12	
16	26	10	29	22	25	13	21	21	25	18	13	20
17	27	11	30	21	26	14	22		26	19	14	
18	28	12	00♉		27	15	23		27	21	15	
19	29	13	01		28	16	23		28	22	15	
20	30	14	02		29	17	24		29	23	16	
21	01♉	15	03	21	30	18	25	21	30	24	17	20
22	02	16	03		01♊	19	25		01♋	25	17	
23	03	17	04		02	21	26		02	27	18	
24	04	18	05		03	22	27		03	28	19	
25	05	19	06		04	23	28	20	03	29	19	
26	06	21	06	21	05	24	28	20	04	00♊	20	20
27	07	22	07		06	25	29		05	01	21	
28	08	23	08		07	26	30		06	02	21	
29	09	24	09		08	27	00♊		07	04	22	
30	10	25	09		09	29	01		08	05	23	
31					10	30♈	02	20				

Day	JULY				AUGUST				SEPTEMBER				OCTOBER				NOVEMBER				DECEMBER			
	☉	♀	♂	♆	☉	♀	♂	♆	☉	♀	♂	♆	☉	♀	♂	♆	☉	♀	♂	♆	☉	♀	♂	♆
01	09♋	06♊	23♊	20♏	09♌	13♋	14♋	19♏	09♍	21♌	04♌	20♏	08♎	28♍	23♌	20♏	09♏	07♏	12♏	21♏	09♐	14♐	29♏	23♏
02	10	07	24		10	14	15		10	22	05		09	29	24		10	08	12		10	16	29	
03	11	08	25		11	15	16		11	23	06		10	00♎	24		11	09	13	22	11	17	30	
04	12	09	26		12	17	16		12	24	06		11	02	25		12	11	13		12	18	00♐	
05	13	11	26		13	18	17		12	26	07		12	03	26	21	13	12	14		13	19	01	
06	14	12	27	20	14	19	18	19	13	27	08	20	13	04	26	21	14	13	15	22	14	21	01	23
07	15	13	28		15	20	18		14	28	08		14	05	27		15	14	15		15	22	02	
08	16	14	28		15	21	19		15	29	09		15	07	27		16	16	16		16	23	02	
09	17	15	29		16	23	20		16	01♍	09		16	08	28		17	17	16		17	24	03	
10	18	17	30		17	24	20		17	02	10		17	09	29		18	18	17		18	26	03	
11	19	18	00♋	20	18	25	21	19	18	03	11	20	18	10	29	21	19	19	18	22	19	27	04	23
12	20	19	01		19	26	22		19	05	11		19	12	30		20	21	18		20	28	04	
13	21	20	02		20	28	22		20	06	12		20	13	00♍		21	22	19		21	29	05	
14	22	21	02		21	29	23		21	07	13		21	14	01		22	23	19		22	01♑	06	
15	23	23	03	19	22	30	23	20	22	08	13		22	15	02		23	24	20		23	02	06	
16	24	24	04	19	23	01♌	24	20	23	09	14	20	23	17	02	21	24	26	20	22	24	03	07	23
17	24	25	04		24	02	25		24	11	14		24	18	03		25	27	21		25	05	07	
18	25	26	05		25	04	25		25	12	15		25	19	03		26	28	22		26	06	08	
19	26	27	06		26	05	26		26	13	16		26	20	04		27	29	22		27	07	08	
20	27	29	06		27	06	27		27	14	16		27	22	05		28	01♐	23		28	08	09	
21	28	30	07	19	28	07	27	20	28	16	17	20	28	23	05	21	29	02	23	22	29	10	09	23
22	29	01♋	08		29	09	28		29	17	18		29	24	06		30	03	24		00♑	11	10	
23	00♌	02	08		30	10	29		00♎	18	18		30	25	06		01♐	04	24		01	12	10	
24	01	03	09		01♍	11	29		01	19	19		01♏	27	07		02	06	25		02	13	11	
25	02	05	10		02	12	30		02	20	19		02	28	08		03	07	25		03	15	11	
26	03	06	10	19	03	13	01♌	20	03	22	20	20	03	29	08	21	04	08	26	22	04	16	11	23
27	04	07	11		04	15	01		04	23	21		04	00♏	09		05	09	26		05	17	12	
28	05	08	12		05	16	02		05	24	21		05	02	09		06	11	27		06	18	12	
29	06	09	12		06	17	02		06	25	22		06	03	10		07	12	28		07	20	13	
30	07	11	13		07	18	03		07	27	23		07	04	11		08	13	28	23	08	21	13	24
31	08	12	14	19	08	20	04	20					08	05	11	21					09	22	14	24

BIRTH TABLES - 1967

	JANUARY				FEBRUARY				MARCH				APRIL				MAY				JUNE			
	☉	♀	♂	♆	☉	♀	♂	♆	☉	♀	♂	♆	☉	♀	♂	♆	☉	♀	♂	♆	☉	♀	♂	♆
01	10♑	23♑	14♎	24♏	12♒	02♓	27♎	24♏	10♓	07♈	03♏	24♏	11♈	15♉	30♎	24♏	10♉	20♊	19♎	23♏	10♊	25♋	15♎	23♏
02	11	25	15		13	03	27		11	08	03		12	16	29		11	21	19		11	26	15	22
03	12	26	15		14	04	27		12	09	03		13	17	29		12	22	18		12	27	15	
04	13	27	16		15	05	28		13	11	03		14	18	29		13	23	18		13	28	16	
05	14	28	16		16	07	28		14	12	03		15	19	28		14	25	18		14	29	16	
06	15	30	17	24	17	08	28	24	15	13	03	24	16	21	28	24	15	26	18	23	15	30	16	22
07	17	01♒	17		18	10	29		16	14	03		17	22	28		16	27	17		16	01♌	16	
08	18	02	18		19	11	29		17	15	03		18	23	27		17	28	17		17	02	16	
09	19	03	18		20	12	29		18	17	03		19	24	27		18	29	17		18	03	16	
10	20	04	18		21	13	30		19	18	03		20	25	27		19	00♋	17		19	04	16	
11	21	06	19	24	22	15	30	24	20	19	03	24	21	27	26	24	20	01	16	23	20	05	17	22
12	22	07	19		23	16	00♏		21	20	03		22	28	26		21	03	16		21	06	17	
13	23	08	20		24	17	00		22	22	03		23	29	25		22	04	16		22	07	17	
14	24	10	20		25	18	01		23	23	03		24	00♊	25		23	05	16		23	08	17	
15	25	11	21		26	20	01		24	24	03		25	01	25		24	06	16		24	09	17	
16	26	12	21	24	27	21	01	24	25	25	03	24	26	02	24	24	25	07	16	23	25	10	18	22
17	27	13	21		28	22	01		26	26	03		27	04	24		26	08	16		26	11	18	
18	28	15	22		29	23	01		27	28	03		28	05	24		27	09	15		27	12	18	
19	29	16	22		00♓	25	02		28	29	02		29	06	23		28	10	15		28	13	18	
20	30	17	23		01	26	02		29	00♉	02		30	07	23		29	11	15		28	14	19	
21	01♒	18	23	24	02	27	02	24	00♈	01	02	24	01♉	08	22	24	30	13	15	23	29	15	19	22
22	02	20	23		03	28	02		01	03	02		02	10	22		01♊	14	15		00♋	16	19	
23	03	21	24		04	29	02		02	04	02		03	11	22		02	15	15		01	17	20	
24	04	22	24		05	01♈	02		03	05	02		04	12	21		03	16	15		02	18	20	
25	05	23	24		06	02	02		04	06	01		05	13	21		04	17	15		03	19	20	
26	06	25	25	24	07	03	03	24	05	07	01	24	06	14	21	23	05	18	15	23	04	19	21	22
27	07	26	25		08	04	03		06	09	01		07	15	20		06	19	15		05	20	21	
28	08	27	25		09	06	03		07	10	01		08	16	20		06	20	15		06	21	21	
29	09	28	26						08	11	00		08	18	20		07	21	15		07	22	22	
30	10	30	26						09	12	00♏		09	19	19		08	22	15		08	23	22	
31	11	01♓	27	24					10	13	30♎	24					09	23	15	23				

Day	JULY ☉	♀	♂	♆	AUGUST ☉	♀	♂	♆	SEPTEMBER ☉	♀	♂	♆	OCTOBER ☉	♀	♂	♆	NOVEMBER ☉	♀	♂	♆	DECEMBER ☉	♀	♂	♆
01	09♋	24♌	22♎	22♏	09♌	13♍	06♏	22♏	08♍	04♍	24♏	22♏	08♎	30♌	15♐	23♏	08♏	22♍	07♑	24♏	09♐	23♎	30♑	25♏
02	10	25	23		10	13	07		09	04	25		09	00♍	15		09	23	08		10	24	01♒	
03	11	26	23		10	13	07		10	03	26		10	01	16		10	24	08		11	26	01	
04	12	26	23		11	14	08		11	02	26		11	01	16		11	25	09		12	27	02	
05	13	27	24		12	14	08		12	02	27		12	02	17		12	26	10		13	28	03	
06	14	28	24	22	13	14	09	22	13	01	28	22	13	02	18	23	13	27	11	24	14	29	04	25
07	15	29	25		14	14	10		14	01	28		14	03	19		14	28	11		15	00♏	04	
08	16	30	25		15	14	10		15	00	29		15	03	19		15	29	12		16	01	05	
09	17	00♍	25		16	14	11		16	30♌	30		16	04	20		16	30	13		17	02	06	
10	18	01	26		17	14	11		17	30	00♐		16	04	21		17	01♎	14		18	04	07	
11	19	02	26	22	18	14	12	22	18	29	01	22	17	05	22	23	18	02	14	24	19	05	08	25
12	19	03	27		19	14	12		19	29	02		18	06	22		19	03	15		20	06	08	
13	20	03	27		20	13	13		20	29	02		19	06	23		20	04	16		21	07	09	
14	21	04	27		21	13	14		21	28	03		20	07	24		21	05	17		22	08	10	
15	22	05	28		22	13	14		22	28	04		21	08	24		22	06	18		23	09	11	
16	23	05	28	22	23	13	15	22	23	28	04	22	22	08	25	23	23	07	18	24	24	11	11	25
17	24	06	29		24	12	15		24	28	05		23	09	26		24	08	19		25	12	12	
18	25	07	29		25	12	16		25	28	06		24	10	27		25	09	20		26	13	13	
19	26	07	30		26	12	16		26	28	06		25	11	27		26	10	21		27	14	14	
20	27	07	00♏		27	11	17		27	28	07		26	12	28		27	11	21		28	15	15	
21	28	08	01	22	28	11	18	22	28	28	08	22	27	12	29	23	28	12	22	24	29	16	15	25
22	29	08	01		29	10	18		29	28	08		28	13	30		29	13	23		30	18	16	
23	30	09	02		30	10	19		30	28	09		29	14	00♑		01♐	15	24		01♑	19	17	
24	01♌	10	02		01♍	09	19		01♎	28	10		00♏	15	01		02	16	24		02	20	18	
25	02	10	03		02	08	20		02	28	10		01	16	02		03	17	25		03	21	18	
26	03	11	03	22	03	08	21	22	03	28	11	22	02	17	03	23	04	18	26	24	04	22	19	26
27	04	11	04		04	07	21		04	29	12		03	17	03		05	19	27		05	24	20	
28	05	12	04		05	07	22		05	29	12		04	18	04		06	20	27	25	06	25	21	
29	06	12	05		05	06	23		06	29	13		05	19	05		07	21	28		07	26	22	
30	07	12	05		06	05	23		07	29	14		06	20	06	24	08	22	29		08	27	22	
31	08	13	06	22	07	05	24	22					07	21	06	24					09	28	23	26

BIRTH TABLES - 1968

Day	JANUARY ☉	♀	♂	♆	FEBRUARY ☉	♀	♂	♆	MARCH ☉	♀	♂	♆
01	10♑	30♏	24♒	26♏	12♒	07♑	18♓	26♏	11♓	13♒	10♈	27♏
02	11	01♐	25		13	08	19		12	14	11	
03	12	02	25		14	10	19		13	15	12	
04	13	03	26		15	11	20		14	16	12	
05	14	04	27		16	12	21		15	18	13	
06	15	05	28	26	17	13	22	26	16	19	14	27
07	16	07	29		18	14	23		17	20	15	
08	17	08	29		19	16	23		18	21	16	
09	18	09	00♓		20	17	24		19	23	16	
10	19	10	01		21	18	25		20	24	17	
11	20	12	02	26	22	19	26	26	21	25	18	27
12	21	13	02		23	21	26	27	22	26	19	
13	22	14	03		24	22	27		23	27	19	
14	23	15	04		25	23	28		24	29	20	
15	24	16	05		26	24	29		25	30	21	26
16	25	18	05	26	27	25	30	27	26	01♓	21	26
17	26	19	06		28	27	00♈		27	02	22	
18	27	20	07		29	28	01		28	04	23	
19	28	21	08		30	29	02		29	05	24	
20	29	22	09		01♓	00♒	03		30	06	24	
21	01♒	24	09	26	02	02	03	27	01♈	07	25	26
22	02	25	10		03	03	04		02	09	26	
23	03	26	11		04	04	05		03	10	27	
24	04	27	12		05	05	06		04	11	27	
25	05	28	13		06	07	06		05	12	28	
26	06	30	13	26	07	08	07	27	06	13	29	26
27	07	01♑	14		08	09	08		07	15	30	
28	08	02	15		09	10	09		08	16	00♉	
29	09	03	16		10	11	09		09	17	01	
30	10	04	16						10	18	02	
31	11	06	17	26					11	20	03	26

Day	APRIL ☉	♀	♂	♆	MAY ☉	♀	♂	♆	JUNE ☉	♀	♂	♆
01	12♈	21♓	03♉	26♏	11♉	28♈	25♉	26♏	11♊	06♊	17♊	25♏
02	13	22	04		12	29	26		12	07	17	
03	14	23	05		13	00♉	26		13	08	18	
04	15	25	06		14	02	27	25	14	10	19	
05	16	26	06		15	03	28		15	11	19	
06	17	27	07	26	16	04	29	25	16	12	20	25
07	18	28	08		17	05	29		17	13	21	
08	19	29	08		18	06	30		18	14	21	
09	20	01♈	09		19	08	01♊		19	16	22	
10	21	02	10		20	09	01		20	17	23	
11	22	03	11	26	21	10	02	25	21	18	23	25
12	23	04	11		22	11	03		22	19	24	24
13	24	06	12		23	13	03		23	21	25	
14	25	07	13		24	14	04		23	22	26	
15	26	08	14		25	15	05		24	23	26	
16	27	09	14	26	26	16	06	25	25	24	27	24
17	28	11	15		27	17	06		26	26	28	
18	29	12	16		28	19	07		27	27	28	
19	29	13	16		29	20	07		28	28	29	
20	00♉	14	17		30	21	08		29	29	30	
21	01	16	18	26	00♊	22	09	25	00♋	00♋	00♋	24
22	02	17	19		01	24	10		01	02	01	
23	03	18	19		02	25	10		02	03	02	
24	04	19	20		03	26	11		03	04	02	
25	05	20	21		04	27	12		04	05	03	
26	06	22	21	26	05	29	12	25	05	07	04	24
27	07	23	22		06	30	13		06	08	04	
28	08	24	23		07	01♊	14		07	09	05	
29	09	25	24		08	02	15		08	10	06	
30	10	27	24		09	03	15		09	12	06	
31					10	05	16	25				

	JULY				AUGUST				SEPTEMBER				OCTOBER				NOVEMBER				DECEMBER			
Day	☉	♀	♂	♆	☉	♀	♂	♆	☉	♀	♂	♆	☉	♀	♂	♆	☉	♀	♂	♆	☉	♀	♂	♆
01	10♋	13♋	07♋	24♏	09♌	21♌	27♋	24♏	09♍	29♍	17♌	24♏	08♎	06♏	06♍	25♏	09♏	14♐	25♍	26♏	09♐	20♑	13♎	27♏
02	11	14	08		10	22	28		10	00♎	18		09	07	07		10	15	26		10	21	14	
03	12	15	08		11	23	29		11	01	18		10	08	07		11	16	26		11	22	15	
04	13	16	09		12	25	29		12	03	19		11	10	08		12	17	27		12	24	15	
05	14	18	10		13	26	30		13	04	20		12	11	09		13	19	28		13	25	16	
06	14	19	10	24	14	27	01♌	24	14	05	20	24	13	12	09	25	14	20	28	26	14	26	16	27
07	15	20	11		15	28	01		15	06	21		14	13	10		15	21	29		15	27	17	
08	16	21	12		16	30	02		16	08	22		15	14	10		16	22	30		16	28	18	
09	17	23	12		17	01♍	02		17	09	22		16	16	11		17	23	00♎		17	29	18	
10	18	24	13		18	02	03		18	10	23		17	17	12		18	25	01		18	01♒	19	
11	19	25	14	24	19	03	04	24	19	11	24	24	18	18	12	25	19	26	01	26	20	02	19	27
12	20	26	14		20	04	04		20	13	24		19	19	13		20	27	02		21	03	20	
13	21	28	15		21	06	05		21	14	25		20	21	13		21	28	03		22	04	20	
14	22	29	16		22	07	06		22	15	25		21	22	14		22	30	03		23	05	21	
15	23	30	16		23	08	06		23	16	26		22	23	15		23	01♑	04		24	07	22	
16	24	01♌	17	24	24	09	07	24	24	18	27	24	23	24	15	25	24	02	04	26	25	08	22	27
17	25	02	17		25	11	08		25	19	27		24	25	16		25	03	05		26	09	23	
18	26	04	18		26	12	08		26	20	28		25	27	17		26	04	06		27	10	23	
19	27	05	19		27	13	09		27	21	29		26	28	17		27	06	06		28	11	24	
20	28	06	19		28	14	10		28	22	29		27	29	18		28	07	07		29	12	25	
21	29	07	20	24	28	16	10	24	29	24	30	24	28	00♐	19	25	29	08	07	26	30	14	25	27
22	30	09	21		29	17	11		30	25	00♍		29	02	19		00♐	09	08		01♑	15	26	
23	01♌	10	21		00♍	18	11		01♎	26	01		00♏	03	20		01	10	09		02	16	26	
24	02	11	22		01	19	12		01	27	02		01	04	20		02	12	09		03	17	27	
25	03	12	23		02	20	13		02	29	02		02	05	21		03	13	10		04	18	27	
26	04	14	23	24	03	22	13	24	03	30	03	24	03	06	22	25	04	14	10	27	05	19	28	28
27	04	15	24		04	23	14		04	01♏	04	25	04	08	22		05	15	11		06	21	29	
28	05	16	25		05	24	15		05	02	04		05	09	23		06	16	12		07	22	29	
29	06	17	25		06	25	15		06	03	05		06	10	23		07	18	12		08	23	30	
30	07	18	26		07	27	16		07	05	05		07	11	24		08	19	13		09	24	00♏	
31	08	20	27	24	08	28	17	24					08	13	25	26					10	25	01	28

BIRTH TABLES - 1969

Day	JANUARY				FEBRUARY				MARCH				APRIL				MAY				JUNE			
	☉	♀	♂	♆	☉	♀	♂	♆	☉	♀	♂	♆	☉	♀	♂	♆	☉	♀	♂	♆	☉	♀	♂	♆
01	11♑	26♒	01♏	28♏	12♒	29♓	18♏	29♏	11♓	22♈	02♐	29♏	12♈	23♈	13♐	28♏	11♉	11♈	17♐	28♏	11♊	26♈	10♐	27♏
02	12	27	02		13	00♈	19		12	22	02		13	22	13		12	11	17		12	27	09	
03	13	29	03		14	01	19		13	23	03		14	22	14		13	11	17		13	28	09	
04	14	30	03		16	02	20		14	23	03		15	21	14		14	11	16		14	29	09	
05	15	01	04		17	03	20		15	24	04		16	21	14		15	11	16		15	30	08	
06	16	02	04	28	18	04	21	29	16	24	04	29	17	20	14	28	16	11	16	28	16	00♉	08	27
07	17	03	05		19	05	22		17	25	04		17	19	15		17	12	16		17	01	08	
08	18	04	05		20	06	22		18	25	05		18	19	15		18	12	16		18	02	07	
09	19	05	06		21	07	23		19	25	05		19	18	15		19	12	16		18	03	07	
10	20	06	07		22	08	23		20	26	06		20	17	15		20	13	16		19	04	07	
11	21	07	07	28	23	09	24	29	21	26	06	29	21	17	15	28	21	13	16	28	20	05	06	27
12	22	09	08		24	09	24		22	26	06		22	16	15		22	13	15		21	06	06	
13	23	10	08		25	10	25		23	26	07		23	16	16		23	14	15	27	22	07	06	
14	24	11	09		26	11	25		24	26	07		24	15	16		24	14	15		23	08	05	
15	25	12	09		27	12	25		25	27	08		25	14	16		24	15	15		24	09	05	
16	26	13	10	28	28	13	26	29	26	27	08	29	26	14	16	28	25	15	15	27	25	09	05	27
17	27	14	10		29	14	26		27	27	08		27	14	16		26	16	14		26	10	05	
18	28	15	11		30	14	26		28	27	09		28	13	16		27	16	14		27	11	04	
19	29	16	12		01♓	15	27		29	27	09		29	13	16		28	17	14		28	12	04	
20	00♒	17	12		02	16	28		30	27	09		00♉	12	16		29	18	13		29	13	04	
21	01	18	13	28	03	17	28	29	01♈	27	10	29	01	12	17	28	00♊	18	13	27	30	14	04	26
22	02	19	13		04	17	29		02	26	10		02	12	17		01	19	13		01♋	15	03	
23	03	20	14		05	18	29		03	26	10		03	11	17		02	20	13		02	16	03	
24	04	21	14		06	19	30		04	26	11		04	11	17		03	20	12		03	17	03	
25	05	22	15		07	19	00♐		05	26	11		05	11	17		04	21	12		04	18	03	
26	06	23	15	28	08	20	01	29	06	25	11	29	06	11	17	28	05	22	12	27	05	19	03	26
27	07	24	16		09	21	01		07	25	12		07	11	17		06	22	11		06	20	02	
28	08	25	16		10	21	01		08	25	12		08	11	17		07	23	11		07	21	02	
29	09	26	17						09	24	12		09	11	17		08	24	11		08	22	02	
30	10	27	17						10	24	13		10	11	17		09	25	10		09	23	02	
31	11	28	18	29					11	23	13	29					10	25	10	27				

Day	Jul ☉	Jul ♀	Jul ♂	Jul ♆	Aug ☉	Aug ♀	Aug ♂	Aug ♆	Sep ☉	Sep ♀	Sep ♂	Sep ♆
01	09♋	24♉	02♐	26♏	09♌	28♊	05♐	26♏	09♍	04♌	19♐	26♏
02	10	25	02		10	29	06		10	05	19	
03	11	26	02		11	00♋	06		11	06	20	
04	12	28	02		12	01	06		12	08	20	
05	13	29	02		13	03	07		13	09	21	
06	14	30	02	26	14	04	07	26	14	10	21	26
07	15	01♊	02		15	05	07		15	11	22	
08	16	02	02		16	06	08		16	12	22	
09	17	03	02		17	07	08		17	14	23	
10	18	04	02		18	08	09		18	15	24	
11	19	05	02	26	19	09	09	26	19	16	24	26
12	20	06	02		20	11	09		20	17	25	
13	21	07	02		21	12	10		21	18	25	
14	22	08	02		22	13	10		21	20	26	
15	23	09	02		23	14	11		22	21	26	
16	24	10	02	26	24	15	11	26	23	22	27	26
17	25	11	02		25	16	11		24	23	28	
18	26	12	02		26	18	12		25	24	28	
19	27	14	03		27	19	12		26	26	29	
20	28	15	03		28	20	13		27	27	30	
21	29	16	03	26	29	21	13	26	28	28	00♑	26
22	29	17	03		30	22	14		29	29	01	
23	00♌	18	03		00♍	23	14		00♎	00♍	01	
24	01	19	03		01	25	15		01	02	02	
25	02	20	04		02	26	15		02	03	03	
26	03	21	04	26	03	27	15	26	03	04	03	27
27	04	22	04		04	28	16		04	05	04	
28	05	24	04		05	29	17		05	07	04	
29	06	25	05		06	00♌	17		06	08	05	
30	07	26	05		07	02	18		07	09	06	
31	08	27	05	26	08	03	18	26				

Day	Oct ☉	Oct ♀	Oct ♂	Oct ♆	Nov ☉	Nov ♀	Nov ♂	Nov ♆	Dec ☉	Dec ♀	Dec ♂	Dec ♆
01	08♎	10♍	06♑	27♏	09♏	19♎	28♑	28♏	09♐	25♏	20♒	29♏
02	09	11	07		10	20	28		10	27	20	
03	10	13	08		11	21	29		11	29	21	
04	11	14	08		12	22	30		12	30	22	
05	12	15	09		13	23	01♒		13	01♐	22	
06	13	16	10	27	14	25	01	28	14	02	23	29
07	14	18	10		15	26	02		15	04	24	
08	15	19	11		16	27	03		16	05	25	
09	16	20	12		17	28	03		17	06	25	
10	17	21	12		18	30	04		18	07	26	
11	18	23	13	27	19	01♏	05	28	19	09	27	29
12	19	24	14		20	02	06		20	10	28	
13	20	25	14		21	04	06		21	11	28	
14	21	26	15		22	05	07		22	12	29	
15	22	27	16		23	05	08		23	14	30	
16	23	29	17	27	24	07	09	28	24	15	01♓	29
17	24	30	17		25	09	09		25	16	01	
18	25	01♎	18		26	10	10		26	17	02	
19	26	02	18		27	11	11		27	19	03	
20	27	04	19		28	12	11		28	20	04	
21	28	05	20	27	29	14	12	28	29	21	04	30
22	29	06	21		30	15	13		00♑	23	05	
23	30	07	21		01♐	16	14		01	24	06	
24	01♏	09	22		02	17	14		02	25	07	
25	02	10	23		03	19	15		04	26	07	
26	03	11	23	28	04	20	16	29	05	27	08	30
27	04	12	24		05	21	17		06	29	09	
28	05	14	25		06	22	17		07	00♑	10	
29	06	15	26		07	24	18		08	01	10	
30	07	16	26		08	25	19		09	03	11	
31	08	17	27	28					10	04	12	30

BIRTH TABLES - 1970

Day	JANUARY				FEBRUARY				MARCH			
	☉	♀	♂	♆	☉	♀	♂	♆	☉	♀	♂	♆
01	11♑	05♑	13♓	30♏	12♒	14♒	06♈	01♐	10♓	19♓	26♈	01♐
02	12	06	13		13	15	06		11	20	27	
03	13	08	14		14	17	07		12	22	27	
04	14	09	15		15	18	08		13	23	28	
05	15	10	16	00♐	16	19	09		14	24	29	
06	16	11	16	00	17	20	09	01	16	25	30	01
07	17	13	17		18	22	10		17	27	00♉	
08	18	14	18		19	23	11		18	28	01	
09	19	15	19		20	24	11		19	29	02	
10	20	16	19		21	25	12		20	00♈	02	
11	21	18	20	00	22	27	13	01	21	02	03	01
12	22	19	21		23	28	14		21	03	04	
13	23	20	22		24	29	14		22	04	05	
14	24	21	22		25	00♓	15		23	05	05	
15	25	23	23		26	02	16		24	07	06	
16	26	24	24	00	27	03	17	01	25	08	07	01
17	27	25	25		28	04	17		26	09	07	
18	28	26	25		29	05	18		27	10	08	
19	29	28	26		00♓	07	19		28	12	09	
20	00♒	29	27		01	08	29		29	13	10	
21	01	00♒	27	00	02	09	21	01	00♈	14	10	01
22	02	02	28		03	10	22		01	15	11	
23	03	03	29		04	11	22		02	17	12	
24	04	04	30	01	05	13	23		03	18	12	
25	05	05	00♈		06	14	24		04	19	13	
26	06	07	01	01	07	15	24	01	05	20	14	01
27	07	08	02		08	17	25		06	21	15	
28	08	09	03		09	18	25		07	23	15	
29	09	10	03						08	24	16	
30	10	12	04						09	25	17	
31	11	13	05	01					10	26	17	01

Day	APRIL				MAY				JUNE			
	☉	♀	♂	♆	☉	♀	♂	♆	☉	♀	♂	♆
01	11♈	28♈	18♉	01♐	11♉	04♊	09♊	00♐	11♊	12♋	29♊	29♏
02	12	29	19		12	06	09		12	13	00♋	
03	13	00♉	19		13	07	10	30♏	12	14	01	
04	14	01	20		14	08	11		13	15	01	
05	15	03	21		15	09	11		14	17	02	
06	16	04	22	01	16	11	12	30	15	18	03	29
07	17	05	22		17	12	13		16	19	03	
08	18	06	23		17	13	13		17	20	04	
09	19	08	24		18	14	14		18	21	05	
10	20	09	24		19	15	15		19	23	05	
11	21	10	25	00	20	17	15	30	20	24	06	29
12	22	11	26		21	18	16		21	25	07	
13	23	12	26		22	19	17		22	26	07	
14	24	14	27		23	20	17		23	27	08	
15	25	15	28		24	21	18		24	29	09	
16	26	16	28	00	25	23	19	30	25	30	09	29
17	27	17	29		26	24	19		26	00♌	10	
18	28	19	30		27	25	20		27	02	11	
19	29	20	00♊		28	26	21		28	03	11	
20	30	21	01		29	27	22		29	04	12	
21	01♉	22	02	00	00♊	29	22	30	30	06	13	29
22	02	23	03		01	30	23	29	01♋	07	13	
23	03	25	03		02	01♋	24		02	08	14	
24	04	26	04		03	02	24		03	09	14	
25	05	27	05		04	03	25		04	10	15	
26	06	28	05	00	05	05	26	29	04	11	16	29
27	07	30	06		06	06	26		05	13	17	
28	08	01♊	07		07	07	27		06	14	17	
29	09	02	07		08	08	27		07	15	18	
30	10	03	08		09	09	28		08	16	19	
31					10	11	29	29				

Day	JULY ☉	♀	♂	♆	AUGUST ☉	♀	♂	♆	SEPTEMBER ☉	♀	♂	♆
01	09♋	17♌	19♋	29♏	09♌	22♍	09♌	28♏	09♍	25♎	29♌	28♏
02	10	18	20		10	24	10		10	26	30	
03	11	20	20	28	11	25	10		11	27	00♍	
04	12	21	21		12	26	11		12	28	01	
05	13	22	22		13	27	12		13	29	01	
06	14	23	22	28	14	28	12	28	13	29	02	28
07	15	24	23		15	29	13		14	00♏	03	
08	16	25	24		16	00♎	14		15	01	03	
09	17	27	24		17	01	14		16	02	04	
10	18	28	25		17	02	15		17	03	05	
11	19	29	26	28	18	03	16	28	18	04	05	28
12	20	30	26		19	04	16		19	05	06	
13	21	01♍	27		20	05	17		20	06	07	
14	22	02	27		21	07	17		21	07	07	
15	23	03	28		22	08	18		22	07	08	
16	24	05	29	28	23	09	19	28	23	08	08	29
17	24	06	30		24	10	19		24	09	09	
18	25	07	00♌		25	11	20		25	10	10	
19	26	08	01		26	12	21		26	11	10	
20	27	09	01		27	13	21		27	11	11	
21	28	10	02	28	28	14	22	28	28	12	12	29
22	29	11	03		29	15	23		29	13	12	
23	00♌	12	03		30	16	23		00♎	14	13	
24	01	14	04		01♍	17	24		01	14	14	
25	02	15	05		02	18	24		02	15	14	
26	03	16	05	28	03	19	25	28	03	16	15	29
27	04	17	06		04	20	26		04	17	15	
28	05	18	07		05	21	26		05	17	16	
29	06	19	07		06	22	27		06	18	17	
30	07	20	08		07	23	28		07	18	17	
31	08	21	09	28	08	24	28	28				

Day	OCTOBER ☉	♀	♂	♆	NOVEMBER ☉	♀	♂	♆	DECEMBER ☉	♀	♂	♆
01	08♎	19♏	18♍	29♏	09♏	22♍	08♎	30♏	09♐	10♍	27♎	01♐
02	09	20	19		10	22	08		10	10	27	
03	10	20	19		11	22	09		11	10	28	
04	11	21	20		12	21	10		12	10	29	
05	12	21	21		13	20	10		13	10	29	
06	13	22	21	29	14	20	11	00♐	14	10	30	01
07	14	22	22		15	19	11		15	11	01♏	
08	15	23	22		16	19	12		16	11	01	
09	16	23	23		17	18	13		17	11	02	
10	17	23	24		18	17	13		18	12	02	
11	18	24	24	29	19	17	14	00	19	12	03	01
12	19	24	25		20	16	15		20	12	04	
13	20	24	26		21	16	15		21	13	04	
14	21	25	26		22	15	16		22	13	05	
15	22	25	27		23	15	17		23	14	06	
16	23	25	27	29	24	14	17	00	24	14	06	01
17	24	25	28		25	13	18		25	15	07	02
18	25	25	29		26	13	18		26	15	08	
19	26	25	29		27	13	19		27	16	08	
20	27	25	00♎		28	12	20		28	16	09	
21	28	25	01	29	29	12	20	01	29	17	09	02
22	29	25	01		30♏	11	21		00♑	18	10	
23	30	25	02	30	01♐	11	22		01	18	11	
24	01♏	25	03		02	11	22		02	19	11	
25	02	25	03		03	10	23		03	20	12	
26	03	25	04	30	04	10	24	01	04	21	13	02
27	04	24	04		05	10	24		-5	21	13	
28	05	24	05		06	10	25		06	22	14	
29	06	24	06		07	10	25		07	23	14	
30	07	23	06		08	10	26		08	24	15	
31	08	23	07	30					09	24	16	02

PART THREE

Days and Nights
For Making Love
1980-1981

ARIES

0 ♈

1980   Feb. 9; Mar. 19; May 12, 13; June 3, 4, 20; July 10, 11, 22; Aug. 6; Sept. 7, 22; Oct. 11, 12, 29; Nov. 21; Dec. 17, 21

1981   Jan. 10; Mar. 16, 20, 23, 24; June 4, 21; July 17, 18, 22; Aug. 17; Sept. 1, 2, 22; Oct. 8; Nov. 4, 21; Dec. 15, 16, 21.

1 ♈

1980   Feb. 10; Mar. 20; May 14, 15, 16; June 1, 2, 21; July 11, 12, 23; Aug. 7; Sept. 8, 23; Oct. 13, 30; Nov. 22, 23; Dec. 18, 22.

1981   Jan. 11; Mar. 17, 18, 21, 24, 25; June 5, 22; July 19, 23; Aug. 18, Sept. 3, 23; Oct. 9; Nov. 5, 22; Dec. 17, 18, 22.

2 ♈

1980   Feb. 11; Mar. 21; May 17, 18, 19, 20, 21, 22, 23, 24 25, 26, 27, 28, 29, 30 31; June 22; July 13, 24; Sept. 9, 24; Oct. 14, 15, 31; Nov. 19, 23.

1981   Jan. 12; March 19, 22, 25; June 6, 23; July 20, 21, 24; Sept. 4, 24; Oct. 10; Nov. 6, 23; Dec. 19, 20, 21, 23.

3 ♈

1980   Feb. 12; Mar. 22; May 23, 24, 25, 26; June 23; July 14, 15, 16, 25; Sept. 10, 25; Oct. 16; Nov. 1, 24, 25; Dec. 20, 24.

1981   Jan. 13; Mar. 20, 23, 26; June 7, 24; July 22, 25; Sept. 5, 6, 25; Oct. 11; Nov. 7, 24; Dec. 22, 23, 24, 25.

4 ♈

1980   Feb. 12; Mar. 23; June 24; July 17, 18, 26; Sept. 11, 26; Oct. 17; Nov. 2, 25, 26, 27; Dec. 20, 25.

1981   Jan. 13; Mar 21, 22, 24, 27; June 8, 25; July 23, 24, 26; Sept. 7, 8, 26; Oct. 12; Nov. 9, 26; Dec. 26, 27.

5 ♈

1980   Feb 13; Mar. 24, 25, June 25, 26; July 19, 27; Sept. 12, 27; Oct. 18; Nov. 3, 26, 28; Dec. 21, 26.

1981   Jan. 14; Mar. 23, 25, 27; June 8, 26; July 25, 27; Sept. 9, 27; Oct. 12; Nov. 9, 26; 27.

6 ♈

1980   Feb. 14; Mar. 26; June 27; July 20, 28; Sept. 12, 28; Oct. 19, 20; Nov. 3, 27, 29; Dec. 22, 27.

1981   Jan. 15; Mar. 24, 26 28; June 9, 27; July 26, 27, 28; Sept. 10, 11, 28; Oct. 13; Nov. 10, 27; Dec. 27, 28, 29 30.

7 ♈

1980   Feb. 15; Mar. 27; June 28; July 21, 22, 23, 29; Sept. 13, 29; Oct 21; Nov. 4, 28, 30; Dec. 1, 23, 28.

1981   Jan. 16; Mar. 25, 27, 29; June 10, 28; July 28, 29; Sept. 12, 29; Oct. 14; Nov. 11, 28; Dec. 28, 31.

8 ♈

1890   Feb. 16; Mar. 28; June 29; July 24, 30; Sept. 14, 30; Oct. 22, 23; Nov. 5, 29; Dec. 2, 24, 29.

1981   Jan. 17; Mar. 26, 27, 28, 30; June 11, 29; July 29, 30; Sept. 13, 14, 30; Oct. 15; Nov. 12, 29; Dec. 29.

9 ♈

1980   Feb. 17; Mar. 29; June 30; July 25, 26, 31; Sept. 15; Oct. 1, 24; Nov. 6, 30; Dec. 3, 24, 30.

1981   Jan. 17; Mar. 28, 29, 31; June 12, 30; July 30, **31;** Sept. 15, 16; Oct. 1, 16; Nov. 13, 30; Dec. 30.

10 ♈

1980   Feb. 17; Mar. 30; July 1, 27, 28; Aug. 1; Sept. 16; Oct. 2, 25, 26; Nov. 7; Dec. 1, 4, 25, 31.

1981   Jan 18; Mar. 29, 30, 31; June 12; July 1; Aug. **1**, Sept. 17, 18; Oct. 2, 17; Nov. 14; Dec. 1, 31.

11 ♈

1980   Jan. 1; Feb. 18; Mar. 31; July 2, 29; Aug. 2; Sept. 17; Oct. 3, 27; Nov. 8; Dec. 2, 5, 26.

1981   Jan. 1, 19; Mar. 30, 31; Apr. 1; June 13; July 2; Aug. **2**, 3; Sept. 19; Oct. 3, 18; Nov. 15; Dec. 2.

12 ♈
1980   Jan. 2; Feb. 19; Apr. 1; July 3, 30, 31; Aug. 3; Sept. 18; Oct. 4, 28; Nov. 8; Dec. 3, 6, 7, 27.

1981   Jan. 1, 20; Mar. 31; Apr. **1**, 2; June 14; July 3; Aug. 3,**4**; Sept. 20, 21; Oct. 4, 19; Nov. 16, 17; Dec. 3.

13 ♈
1980   Jan. 3; Feb. 20; Apr. 2; July 4; Aug. 1, 2, 4; Sept. 19; Oct. 5, 29, 30; Nov. 9; Dec. 4, 8, 28.

1981   Jan. 2, 21; Feb. **2,** 3; June 15; July 4; Aug. **5**, 6; Sept. 22; Oct. 5, 20; Nov. 18; Dec. 4

14 ♈
1980   Jan. 4; Feb. 21; Apr. 3; July 5; Aug, 3, 5; Sept. 20; Oct. 6, 31; Nov. 10; Dec. 5, 9, 10, 28.

1981   Jan. 3, 21; Feb. **3**, 4; June 16; July 5; Aug. 6, 7; Sept. 23, 24; Oct. 6, 21; Nov. 19; Dec. 5.

15 ♈
1980   Jan. 5; Feb. 22; Apr. 4; July 6; Aug. 4, 5, 6; Sept. 21; Oct. 7; Nov. 1, 2, 11; Dec. 6, 11, 29.

1981   Jan. 4, 22; Apr. **4**, 5; June 17; July 6; Aug. 7, 8, 9; Sept. 25; Oct. 7, 21; Nov. 20; Dec. 6.

16 ♈
1980   Jan. 6; Feb. 23, Apr. 5; July 7; Aug. 6, **7**; Sept. 22; Oct. 8; Nov. 3, 12; Dec. 7, 12, 30.

1981   Jan. 5, 23; Apr. **5**, 6; June 17; July 7; Aug. 8, 10; Sept. 26, 27; Oct. 8, 22; Nov. 21; Dec. 7.

17 ♈
1980   Jan. 7; Feb. 23; Apr. 6; July 8; Aug. **8**, 9; Sept. 22, 23; Oct. 9; Nov. 4, 12; Dec. 8, 13, 14, 31.

1981   Jan. 6, 24; Apr. **6**, 7; June 18; July 8; Aug. 9, 11, 12; Sept. 28, 29; Oct. 9, 23; Nov. 22; Dec. 8.

18 ♈
1980   Jan. 8; Feb. 24; Apr. 7; July 9; Aug. 9, **10**; Sept. 23; Oct. 10; Nov. 5, 13; Dec. 9, 15.

1981   Jan. 1, 7, 25; Apr. **7**, 8; June 19; July 9; Aug. 10, 13; Sept. 30; Oct. 10, 24; Nov. 23; Dec. 9.

19 ♈

1980   Jan. 9; Feb. 25; Apr. 8; July 10; Aug. **11**, 12; Sept. 24; Oct. 11; Nov. 6, 7, 14; Dec. 10, 16.

1981   Jan. 1, 8, 25; Apr. **8**, 9, 10; June 20; July 10; Aug. 11, 14, 15; Oct. 1, 11, 25; Nov. 24; Dec. 10.

20 ♈

1980   Jan. 10; Feb. 26; Apr. 9; July 11; Aug. 12, 13; Sept. 25; Oct. 12; Nov. 8, 15; Dec. 11, 17.

1981   Jan. 2, 9, 26; Apr. 8, 9, 11; June 21; July 11; Aug. 12, 16; Oct. 2, 3, 12, 26; Nov. 25; Dec. 11.

21 ♈

1980   Jan. 11; Feb. 27; Apr. 10; July 12; Aug. 13, 14, 15; Sept. 26; Oct. 13: Nov. 9, 16; Dec. 12, 18, 19.

1981   Jan. 3, 10, 27; Apr. 9, 10, 12, 13; June 21; July 12, 13; Aug. 13, 17, 18; Oct. 4, 13, 17; Nov. 26; Dec. 12.

22 ♈

1980   Jan. 12; Feb. 28; Apr. 11; July 13; Aug. 14, 16; Sept. 27; Oct. 14; Nov. 10, 11, 17; Dec. 13, 20.

1981   Jan. 4, 11, 28; Apr. 10, 11, 14; June 22; July 14; Aug. 14, 19, 20; Oct. 5, 6, 14, 28; Nov. 27, 28; Dec. 13.

23 ♈

1980   Jan. 13; Feb. 29; Apr. 12; July 14; Aug. 15, 17, 18; Sept. 28; Oct. 15; Nov. 12, 17; Dec. 14, 21.

1981   Jan. 5, 12, 29; Apr. 11, 12, 15; June 23; July 15; Aug. 15, 21; Oct. 7, 8, 15, 29; Nov. 29; Dec. 14.

24 ♈

1980   Jan. 14; March 1; Apr. 13; July 15; Aug. 16, 19, 20; Sept. 29; Oct. 16; Nov. 13, 18; Dec. 15, 22.

1981   Jan. 5, 13, 29; Apr. 12, 13, 16, 17; June 24; July 16; Aug. 16, 22, 23; Oct. 9, 10, 16, 30; Nov. 30; Dec. 15.

25 ♈

1980   Jan. 15; Mar. 1; Apr. 1, 2, 3, 4, 5, 6, 7, 8, 9, 14; July 16; Aug. 17, 21; Sept. 30; Oct. 17; Nov. 14, 15, 19; Dec. 16, 23, 24.

1981   Jan. 6, 14, 30; Apr. 12, 14, 18; June 25; July 17; Aug. 17, 24; Oct. 11, 12, 17, 31; Dec. 1, 16.

26 ♈
1980 Jan. 16; Mar. 2, 23, 24, 25, 26, 27, 28, 29, 30, 31; Apr. 10, 11, 12, 13, 14, **15**, 16, 17, 18; July 17, 18; Aug. 18, 22, 23; Oct. 1, 18; Nov. 16, 20; Dec. 17, 25.

1981 Jan. 7, 15, 31; Apr. 13, 15, 19; June 26; July 18; Aug. 18, 25, 26; Oct. 13, 18; Nov. 1; Dec. 2, 17.

27 ♈
1980 Jan. 17; Mar. 3, 18, 19, 29, 21, 22; Apr. 16, 19, 20, 21, 22, 23, 24; July 19; Aug. 19, 24; Oct. 1, 19; Nov. 17, 21; Dec. 18, 26.

1981 Jan. 8, 16; Feb. 1; Apr. 14, 16, 20, 21; June 26; July 19; Aug. 19, 27; Oct. 14, 15, 19, 20; Nov. 2; Dec. 3, 4, 18.

28 ♈
1980 Jan. 18; Mar. 4, 15, 16, 17; Apr. 17, 25, 26, 27, 28; July 20; Aug. 20, 25, 26; Oct. 2, 20; Nov. 18, 19, 21; Dec. 19, 27.

1981 Jan. 9, 17; Feb. 2; Apr. 15, 17, 22; June 28; July 20; Aug. 20, 28, 29; Oct. 16, 17, 21; Nov. 3; Dec. 5, 19.

29 ♈
1980 Jan. 19; Mar. 5, 11, 12, 13; Apr. 18, 29, 30, 31; May 1, 2; July 21; Aug. 21, 27; Oct. 3, 21; Nov. 20, 22; Dec. 20, 23.

1981 Jan. 9, 18; Feb. 2; Apr. 16, 18, 23; June 29; July 21; Aug. 21, 30; Oct. 18, 19, 22; Nov. 4; Dec. 6, 7, 20.

TAURUS

0 ♉

1980   Jan. 20; Mar. 6, 8, 9, 10; Apr. 19; May 3, 4, 5, 6; July 22; Aug. 22, 28, 29; Sept. 7; Oct. 4, 22; Nov. 21, 23; Dec. 21, 30, 31.

1981   Jan. 10; Feb. 3; Apr. 16, 19, 24, 25; July 22, 24; Aug. 22; Sept. 1, 2, 12; Oct. 20, 21, 23; Nov. 5; Dec. 8, 21.

1 ♉

1980   Jan. 21; Mar. 5, 6, **7**; Apr. 20; May 7, 8, 9; July 23; Aug. 23, 30; Sept. 8; Oct. 5, 23; Nov. 22, 23, 24; Dec. 22.

1981   Jan. 11; Feb. 4; Apr. 17, 20, 26; July 23, 24; Aug. 23; Sept. 3, 13; Oct. 22, 24; Nov. 5; Dec. 9, 10, 22.

2 ♉

1980   Jan. 22; Mar. 3, 4, 8; Apr. 21; May 10, 11, 12; July 24; Aug. 24, 31; Sept. 1, 9; Oct. 6, 24; Nov. 24, 25; Dec. 23.

1981   Jan. 1, 2, 12; Feb. 5; Apr. 18, 21, 27; July 24, 25; Aug. 24; Sept. 4, 5, 14; Oct. 23, 24, 25; Nov. 6; Dec. 11, 23.

3 ♉

1980   Jan. 23; Feb. 29; Mar. 1, 8; Apr. 22; May 13, 14, 15; July 25; Aug. 25; Sept. 2, 10; Oct. 7, 25; Nov. **25**; Dec. 24.

1981   Jan. 3, 13; Feb. 6; Apr. 19, 22, 28, 29; July 25, 26; Aug. 25; Sept. 6, 15; Oct. 25, **26**; Nov. 7; Dec. 12, 13, 24.

4 ♉

1980   Jan. 24; Feb. 26, 27, 28; Mar. 9; Apr. 23; May 16, 17; July 26; Aug. 26; Sept. 3, 4, 11; Oct. 7, 26; Nov. **26,** 27; Dec. 25.

1981   Jan. 4, 13; Feb. 6; Apr. 20, 23, 30; July 26, 27; Aug. 26; Sept. 7, 8, 16; Oct. **27** 28; Nov. 8; Dec. 14, 15, 25.

5 ♉
1980 Jan. 25; Feb. 24, 25; Mar. 10; Apr. 24; May 18, 19, 20; July 27; Aug. 27; Sept. 5, 11; Oct. 8, 27; Nov. 27, 28; Dec. 26.

1981 Jan. 5, 6, 14; Feb. 7; Apr. 21, 24; May 1; July 27, 28; Aug. 27; Sept. 9, 10, 16; Oct. 28, 29; Nov. 9; Dec. 16, 17, 26.

6 ♉
1980 Jan. 26; Feb. 24, 25; Mar. 11; Apr. 25; May 21, 22, 23; July 28; Aug. 28; Sept. 6, 7, 12; Oct. 9, 28; Nov. 28, 29; Dec. 27.

1981 Jan. 7, 15; Feb. 8; Apr. 21, 25; May 2, 3; July 28, 29; Aug. 28; Sept. 11, 17; Oct. 29, 30, 31; Nov. 10; Dec. 18, 19, 20, 27.

7 ♉
1980 Jan. 27; Feb. 19, 20; Mar. 12; Apr. 26; May 24, 25; July 29; Aug. 29; Sept. 8, 13; Oct. 10, 29; Nov. 29, 30; Dec. 1, 28.

1981 Jan. 8, l1; Feb. 9; Apr. 22, 26; May 4; July **16**; Aug. 29; Sept. 12, 13, 18; Oct. 30; Nov. 1, 2, 11; Dec. 21, 22, 23, 28.

8 ♉
1980 Jan. 28; Feb. 16, 17, 18; Mar. 13; Apr. 27; May 26, 27; July 30; Aug. 30; Sept. 9, 10, 14; Oct. 11, 30; Nov. 30; Dec. 2, 29.

1981 Jan. 9, 17; Feb. 10; Apr. 23, 27; May 5; July **30**; Aug. 30, 31; Sept. 14, 19; Oct. 31; Nov. 3, 4, 12; Dec. 24, 25, 26, 27, 28, **29**, 30, 31.

9 ♉
1980 Jan. 29; Feb. 13, 14, 15; Mar. 14; Apr. 28; May 28, 29, 30; July 31; Aug. 31; Sept. 11, 15; Oct. 12, 31; Nov. 30; Dec. 3, 30.

1981 Jan. 10, 11, 17; Feb. 10; Apr. 24, 28; May 6, 7; July **31**; Sept. 1, 15, 16, 20; Nov. 1, 5, 6, 13; Dec. 30.

10 ♉
1980 Jan. 30; Feb. 10, 11, 12; Mar. 15; Apr. 29; May 31; June 1; Aug. 1; Sept. 1, 12, 13, 16; Oct. 13; Nov. **1**; Dec. 4, 31.

1981 Jan. 12, 18; Feb. 11; Apr. 25, 29; May 8; Aug. **1**; Sept. 2, 17, 18, 21; Nov. 2, 7, 14; Dec. 31.

11 ♉
1980 Jan. 1, 31; Feb. 7, 8, 9; Mar. 16; Apr. 30; June 2, 3; Aug. 2; Sept. 2, 14, 17; Oct. 13; Nov. **2**;Dec. 5, 6.

1981 Jan. 1, 13, 19; Feb. 12; Apr. 25, 30; May 9; Aug. **2**; Sept. 3, 19, 21; Nov. 3, 8, 9, 15.

12 ♉

1980   Jan. 2; Feb. 1, 3, 4, 5, 6; Mar. 17; May 1; June 4, 5, 6; Aug. 3; Sept. 3, 15, 16, 18; Oct. 14; Nov. **3**; Dec. 7.

1981   Jan. 1, 14, 20, Feb. 13; Apr. 26; May 1, 2, 10, 11; Aug. **3**, 4; Sept. 4, 20, 21, 22; Nov. 4, 10, 11, 16, 17.

13 ♉

1980   Jan. 1, 3, 30, 31; Feb. 1, 2; Mar. 18; May 2; June 7, 8; Aug. 4; Sept. 4, 17, 19; Oct. 15; Nov. **4**; Dec. 8.

1981   Jan. 2, 15, 16, 21; Feb. 14; Apr. 27; May 3, 12; Aug. 3, 5; Sept. 5, 22, 23; Nov. 5, 12, 13, 18.

14 ♉

1980   Jan. 1, **2**, 3, **4**, 5, 6, 7; Feb. 3; Mar. 18; May 3; June 9, 10; Aug. 5; Sept. 5, 18, 19, 20; Oct. 16; Nov. 4, 5; Dec. 9, 10.

1981   Jan. 3, 17, 21; Feb. 14; Apr. 28; May 4, 13, 14; Aug. 4, 6; Sept. 6, 23, **24**; Nov. 6, 14, 15, 19.

15 ♉

1980   Jan. 3, 5, 8, 9, 10, 11, 12, 13, 14, 15, 16, 17, 18, 19, 20, 21, 22, 23; Feb. 4; Mar. 19; May 4; June 11, 12; Aug. 6; Sept. 6, 20, 21; Oct. 17; Nov. 5, 6; Dec. 11.

1981   Jan. 4, 18, 22; Feb. 15; Apr. 29; May 5, 15; Aug. 5, 7; Sept. 7, **25**, 26; Nov. 7, 16, 20.

16 ♉

1980   Jan. 4, 6; Feb. 5; Mar. 20; May 5; June 13, 14; Aug. 7; Sept. 7, 8, 21, **22**; Oct. 18; Nov. 6, 7; Dec. 12.

1981   Jan. 5, 19, 23; Feb. 16; Apr. 29; May 6, 16; Aug. 6, 8; Sept. 8, 26, 27; Nov. 8, 19, 20, 22.

17 ♉

1980   Jan. 5, 7; Feb. 6; Mar. 21; May 6; June 15, 16; Aug. 8; Sept. 9, 22, 23; Oct. 19; Nov. 7, 8; Dec. 13, 14.

1981   Jan. 6, 20, 21, 24; Feb. 17; Apr. 30; May 7, 17, 18; Aug. 7, 9; Sept. 9, 27, 28, 29; Nov. 8, 17, 18, 21.

18 ♉

1980   Jan. 5, 8; Feb. 7; Mar. 22; May 7; June 17, 18; Aug. 9, 10; Sept. 10, 23, 24, 25; Oct. 19; Nov. 8, 9; Dec. 15.

1981   Jan. 7, 22, 25; Feb. 18; May 1, 8, 19; Aug. 8, 10; Sept. 10, 27, 30; Nov. 9, 21, 22, 23.

19 ♉
1980   Jan. 6, 9; Feb. 8; Mar. 23; May 8; June 18, 19; Aug. 11; Sept. 11, 24, 26; Oct. 20; Nov. 8, 10; Dec. 16.

1981   Jan. 8, 23, 25; Feb. 18; May 2, 9, 20; Aug. 8, 11; Sept. 11, 28; Oct. 2; Nov. 10, 23, **24.**

20 ♉
1980   Jan. 7, 10; Feb. 9; Mar. 24; May 9, 10; June 20, 2l; Aug. 12; Sept. 12, 25, 27; Oct. 21; Nov. 9, 11; Dec. 17.

1981   Jan. 9, 24, 25, 26; Feb. 19; May 3, 10, 21, 22; Aug. 9, 12; Sept. 12, 29; Oct. 3, 4; Nov. 11, **25**, 26.

21 ♉
1980   Jan. 8, 11; Feb. 10; Mar. 25; May 11; June 22, 23, 24; Aug. 13; Sept. 13, 26, 28, 29; Oct. 22; Nov. 10, 12; Dec. 18, 19.

1981   Jan. 10, 26, 27; Feb. 20; May 4, 11, 23; Aug. 10, 13; Sept. 13, 30; Oct. 5, 6; Nov. 12, 26, **27**, 28.

22 ♉
1980   Jan. 9, 12; Feb. 11; Mar. 26; May 12; June 25, 26;Aug. 14; Sept. 14, 27, 30; Oct. 23; Nov. 11, 13; Dec. 20.

1981   Jan. 11, 27, 28; Feb. 21; May 4, 12, 24; Aug. 11, 14; Sept. 14; Oct. 1, 7; Nov. 13, 28, 29, 30.

23 ♉
1980   Jan. 9, 13; Feb. 12; Mar. 27; May 13; June 27, 28; Aug. 15; Sept. 15, 28; Oct. 1, 2, 24; Nov. 12, 14; Dec. 21.

1981   Jan. 12, 28, 29; Feb. 22; May 5, 13, 25, 26; Aug. 12, 15; Sept. 15; Oct. 2, 8, 9; Nov. 14, 29; Dec. 1, 2.

24 ♉
1980   Jan. 10, 14; Feb. 13; Mar. 28; May 14; June 29, 30; Aug. 16; Sept. 16, 29; Oct. 3, 24; Nov. 12, 15; Dec. 22, 23.

1981   Jan. 13, **29**, 30; Feb. 22; May 6, 14, 27; Aug. 13, 16; Sept. 16; Oct. 3, 10, 11; Nov. 15, 30; Dec. 3, 4.

25 ♉
1980   Jan. 11, 15; Feb. 14; Mar. 29; Apr. 1, 2, 3, 4, 5, 6, 7, 8, 9; May 15; July 1; Aug. 17; Sept. 17, 30; Oct. 4, 5, 25; Nov. 13, 16; Dec. 24.

1981   Jan. 14, 30, 31; Feb. 23; May 7, 15, 28, 29; Aug. 13, 17; Sept. 17; Oct. 4, 12; Nov. 16; Dec. 1, 5, 6.

26 ♉

1980 Jan. 12, 16; Feb. 15; Mar. 23, 24, 25, 26, 27, 28, 29, **30**, 31; Apr. 10, 11, 12, 13, 14, 15, 16, 17, 18; May 16; July 2, 3; Aug. 18; Sept. 18, 30; Oct. 6, 26; Nov. 14, 17; Dec. 25.

1981 Jan. 15, 31; Feb. 1, 24; May 8, 16, 30; Aug. 14, 18; Sept. 18; Oct. 4, 13, 14; Nov. 17; Dec. 2, 7, 8.

27 ♉

1980 Jan. 13, 17; Feb. 16; Mar. 18, 19, 20, 21, 22, 31; Apr. 19, 20, 21, 22, 23, 24; May 17; July 4, 5; Aug. 19; Sept. 19; Oct. 1, 7, 27; Nov. 15, 18; Dec. 26.

1981 Jan. 16; Feb. 1, 2, 25; May 8, 17, 31; Aug. 15, 19; Sept. 19; Oct. 5, 15, 16; Nov. 18, Dec. 3, 4, 9, 10.

28 ♉

1980 Jan. 14, 18; Feb. 17; Mar. 14, 15, 16 ,17; Apr. 1, 25, 26, 27, 28; May 18; July 6, 7; Aug. 20; Sept. 20; Oct. 2, 8, 9, 28; Nov. 16, 19; Dec. 27, 28.

1981 Jan. 17; Feb. 2, 3, 4, 26; May 9, 18; June 1, 2; Aug. 16, 20; Sept. 20; Oct. 6, 17; Nov. 19; Dec. 5, 11, 12.

29 ♉

1980 Jan. 14, 19; Feb. 18; Mar. 11, 12, 13; Apr. 2, 29, 30; May 1, 2, 19; July 8, 9; Aug. 21; Sept. 21; Oct. 3, 10, 29; Nov. 16, 20; Dec. 29.

1981 Jan. 18; Feb. 2, 5, 26; May 10, 19; June 3; Aug. 17, 21; Sept. 21; Oct. 7, 18, 19; Nov. 20; Dec. 6, 13, 14.

GEMINI

0 Ⅱ

1980   Jan. 15, 20; Feb. 19; Mar. 8, 9, 10; Apr. 3; May 3, 4, 5, 6, 20; July 10, 11; Aug. 22; Sept. 22; Oct. 4, 11, 12, **29;** Nov. 21; Dec. 17, 30.

1981   Jan. 19; Feb. 3, 6, 18; May 11, 20; June 4, 5; July 24; Aug. 18, 22; Sept. 22; Oct. 8, 20, 21, 23; Nov. 21; Dec. 8, 15, 16.

1 Ⅱ

1980   Jan. 16, 21; Feb. 19; Mar. 5, 6, 7; Apr. 4; May 7, 8, 9, 21; July 12; Aug. 23; Sept. 23; Oct. 5, 13, 30; Nov. 22; Dec. 18, 31

1981   Jan. 20; Feb. 4, 7, 19; May 12, 21; June 6; July 24; Aug. 18, 23; Sept. 23; Oct. 9, 22, 24; Nov. 22; Dec. 9, 10, 17, 18.

2 Ⅱ

1980   Jan. 17, 22; Feb. 20; Mar. 2, 3, 4; Apr. 5; May 10, 11, 12, 22; July 13, 14; Aug. 24; Sept. 24; Oct. 6, 14, 31; Nov. 23; Dec. 19.

1981   Jan. 1, 2, 21; Feb. 5, 8, 9, 20; May 12, 22; June 7; July 25; Aug. 19, 24; Sept. 24; Oct. 10, 23, 24, 25; Nov. 23; Dec. 11, 12, 19, 20, 21.

3 Ⅱ

1980   Jan. 18, 23; Feb. 21, 29; Mar. 1; Apr. 6; May 13, 14, 15, 23; July 15, 16; Aug. 25; Sept. 25; Oct. 7, 15, 16; Nov. 1, 24; Dec. 20.

1981   Jan. 3, 22; Feb. 6, 10, 21; May 13, 23; June 8, 9; July 26; Aug. 20, 25; Sept. 25; Oct. 11, 25, **26;** Nov. 24; Dec. 13, 22, 23.

4 Ⅱ

1980   Jan. 18, 24; Feb. 22, 26, 27, 28; Apr. 7; May 16, 17, 24; July 17, 18; Aug. 26; Sept. 26; Oct. 7, 17; Nov. 2, 25; Dec. 20.

1981   Jan. 4, 23; Feb. 6, 11, 22; May 14, 24; June 10; July 27; Aug. 21, 26; Sept. 26; Oct. 12, **27**, 28; Nov. 25; Dec. 14, 15, 24, 25.

5 ♊
1980   Jan. 19, 25; Feb. 23, 24, 25; Apr. 8; May 18, 19, 20, 25; July 19; Aug. 27; Sept. 27; Oct. 8, 18, 19; Nov. 3, 26; Dec. 21.

1981   Jan. 5, 6, 24; Feb. 7, 12, 13, 23; May 15, 25; June 11, 12; July 28; Aug. 22, 27; Sept. 27; Oct. 12, 18, 29; Nov. 26; Dec. 16, 17, 26, 27.

6 ♊
1980   Jan. 20, 26; Feb. 21, 22, 23, 24; Apr. 9; May 21, 22, 23, 26; July 20, 21; Aug. 28; Sept. 28; Oct. 9, 20; Nov. 3, 27; Dec. 22.

1981   Jan. 7, 25; Feb. 8, 14, 24; May 16, 26; June 13; July 29; Aug. 23, 28; Sept. 28; Oct. 13, 29, 30, 31; Nov. 27; Dec. 18, 19, 20, 28, 29, 30.

7 ♊
1980   Jan. 21, 27; Feb. 19, 20, 25; Apr. 10; May 24, 25, 27; July 22, 23; Aug. 29; Sept. 29; Oct. 10, 21; Nov. 4, 28; Dec. 23.

1981   Jan. 8, 26; Feb. 9, 15, 25; May 17, 27; June 14; July 29; Aug. 23, 29, 30; Sept. 29; Oct. 14, 30; Nov. 1, 2, 28; Dec. 21, 22, 23, 31.

8 ♊
1980   Jan. 22, 28; Feb. 16, 17, 18, 26; Apr. 11; May 26, 27, 28; July 24; Aug. 30; Sept. 30; Oct. 11, 22, 23; Nov. 5, 29; Dec. 24.

1981   Jan. 9, 27; Feb. 10, 16, 26; May 17, 28, 29; June 15, 16; July 30; Aug. 24, 31; Sept. 30; Oct. 15, 31; Nov. 3, 4, 29; Dec. 24, 25, 26, 27, 28, 29, 30, 31.

9 ♊
1980   Jan. 23, 29; Feb. 13, 14, 15, 27; Apr. 12; May 28, **29,** 30; July 25, 26; Aug. 31; Oct. 1, 12, 24; Nov. 6, 30; Dec. 24.

1981   Jan. 10, 11, 28; Feb. 10, 17, 18, 27; May 18, 30; June 17; July 31; Aug. 25; Sept. 1; Oct. 1, 16; Nov. 1, 5, 6, 30

10 ♊
1980   Jan. 23, 30; Feb. 10, 11, 12, 28; Apr. 13; May 30, 31; July 27, 28; Sept. 1; Oct. 2, 13, 25, 26; Nov. 7; Dec. 1, 25.

1981   Jan. 12, 29; Feb. 11, 19, 28; May 19, 31; June 18, 19; Aug. 1, 26; Sept. 2; Oct. 2, 17; Nov. 2, 7; Dec. 1.

11 ♊
1980   Jan. 24, 31; Feb. 7, 8, 9, 29; Apr. 14, 15; May 31; June 2, 3; July 29; Sept. 2; Oct. 3, 13, 27; Nov. 8; Dec. 2, 26.

1981   Jan. 13, 30; Feb. 12, 20; Mar. 1; May 20; June 1, 20; Aug. 2, 27; Sept. 3; Oct. 3, 18; Nov. 3, 8, 9; Dec.2.

12 ♊
1980   Jan. 25; Feb. 1, 3, 4, 5, 6; Mar. 1; Apr. 16; June 1, 4, 5, 6; July 30, 31; Sept. 3; Oct. 4, 14, 28; Nov. 8; Dec. 3, 27.

1981   Jan. 14, 31; Feb. 13, 21; Mar. 2; May 21; June 2, 21, 22; Aug. 3, 28; Sept. 4; Oct. 4, 19; Nov. 4, 10, 11; Dec. 3.

13 ♊
1980   Jan. 1, 26, 30, 31; Feb. 1, **2**; Mar. 2; Apr. 17; June 2, 7, 8; Aug. 1, 2; Sept. 4; Oct. 5, 15, 29, 30; Nov. 9; Dec. 4, 28.

1981   Jan. 15, 16; Feb. 1, 14, 22, 23; Mar. 3; May 21; June 3, 23; Aug. 3, 29; Sept. 5; Oct. 5, 20, Nov. 5, 12, 13; Dec. 4.

14 ♊
1980   Jan. 1, **2**, 3, 4, 5, 6, 7, 23, 24, 25, 26, **27**, 28, 29; Feb. 3; Mar. 3; Apr. 18; June 3, 4, 9, 10; Aug. 3; Sept. 5; Oct. 6, 16, 31; Nov. 10; Dec. 5, 28.

1981   Jan. 17; Feb. 2, 14, 24; Mar. 4; May 22; June 4, 24; Aug. 4, 29; Sept. 6; Oct. 6, 21; Nov. 6, 14, 15; Dec. 5.

15 ♊
1980   Jan. 3, 8, 9, 10, 11, 12, 13, 14, 15, 16, 17, 18, 19, 20, 21, 22, 27; Feb. 4; Mar. 4; Apr. 19; June 5, 11, 12; Aug. 4, 5; Sept. 6, 7; Oct. 7, 17; Nov. 1, 11; Dec. 6, 29.

1981   Jan. 18; Feb. 3, 15, 25; Mar. 5; May 23; June 5, 25, 26; Aug. 5, 30; Sept. 7; Oct. 7, 21; Nov. 7, 16; Dec. 6.

16 ♊
1980   Jan. 4, 28; Feb. 5; Mar. 5; Apr. 20; June 6, 13, 14, 29, 30, 31; July 1, 2, 3, 4, 5, 6, 7, 8, 9, 10, 11, 12; Aug. 6, 7; Sept. 8; Oct. 8, 18; Nov. 2, 3, 12; Dec. 7, 30.

1981   Jan. 19, 20; Feb. 4, 16, 26, 27; Mar. 6; May 24; June 6, 27; Aug. 6, 31; Sept. 8; Oct. 8, 22; Nov. 8, 17, 18; Dec. 7.

17 ♊
1980   Jan. 5, 29; Feb. 6; Mar. 6; Apr. 11, 21; June 7, 15, 16, 26, 27, 28; July 13, 14, 15; Aug. 8; Sept. 9; Oct. 9, 19; Nov. 4, 12; Dec. 8, 31.

1981   Jan. 21; Feb. 5, 17, 28; Mar. 7; May 25; June 7, 28, 29; Aug. 7; Sept. 1, 9; Oct. 9, 23; Nov. 8, 19, 20; Dec. 8.

18 ♊
1980   Jan. 5, 30; Feb. 7; Mar. 7; Apr. 23; June 8, 17, 18, 24, 25; July 16, 17, 18; Aug. 9, 10; Sept. 10; Oct. 10, 19; Nov. 5, 13; Dec. 9.

1981   Jan. 1, 22; Feb. 6, 18; Mar. 1, 8; May 25; June 8, 30; Aug. 8; Sept. 2, 10; Oct. 10, 24; Nov. 9, 21, 22; Dec. 9.

19 ♊
1980   Jan. 6, 31; Feb. 8; Mar. 8; Apr. 24; June 9, 19, 20, 22, 23; July 19, 20; Aug. 11, 12; Sept. 11; Oct. 11, 20; Nov. 6, 7, 14; Dec. 10.

1981   Jan. 1, 23; Feb. 7, 18; Mar. 2, 9; May 26; June 9; July 1, 2; Aug. 8; Sept. 3, 11; Oct. 11, 25; Nov. 10, 23, 24; Dec. 10.

20 ♊
1980   Jan. 7; Feb. 1, 9; Mar. 9; Apr. 25; June 10, 20, **21**, 22; July 21, 22; Aug. 13; Sept. 12; Oct. 12, 21; Nov. 8, 15; Dec. 11

1981   Jan. 2, 24, 25; Feb. 8, 19; Mar. 3, 4, 10; May 27; June 10; July 3; Aug. 9; Sept. 3, 12; Oct. 12, 26; Nov. 11, 25, 26; Dec. 11.

21 ♊
1980   Jan. 8; Feb. 1, 10; Mar. 10; Apr. 26, 27; June 11, 18, 19, 23, 24; July 23, 24; Aug. 14, 15; Sept. 13; Oct. 13, 22, Nov. 9, 16; Dec. 12.

1981   Jan. 3, 26; Feb. 9, 20; Mar. 5, 11; May 28; June 11; July 4, 5; Aug. 10; Sept. 4, 13; Oct. 13, 27; Nov. 12, 27, 28; Dec. 12.

22 ♊
1980   Jan. 9; Feb. 2, 11; Mar. 11; Apr. 28; June 12, 16, 17, 25, 26; July 25, 26; Aug. 16; Sept. 14; Oct. 14, 23; Nov. 10, 11, 17; Dec. 13.

1981   Jan. 4, 27; Feb. 10, 21; Mar. 6, 12; May 29; June 12; July 6; Aug. 11; Sept. 5, 14; Oct. 14, 28; Nov. 13, 29, 30; Dec. 13.

23 ♊
1980   Jan. 9; Feb. 3, 12; Mar. 12; Apr. 29; June 13, 15, 27, 28; July 27; Aug. 17, 18; Sept. 15; Oct. 15, 24; Nov. 12, 17; Dec. 14.

1981   Jan. 5, 28; Feb. 11, 22; Mar. 7, 13; May 30; June 13; July 7, 8; Aug. 12; Sept. 6, 15; Oct. 15, 29; Nov. 14; Dec. 1, 2, 14.

24 ♊
1980   Jan. 10; Feb. 4, 13; Mar 13; Apr. 30; May 1; June 13, **14**, 29, 30; July 28, 29; Aug. 19; Sept. 16; Oct. 16, 24; Nov. 13, 18;Dec. 15.

1981   Jan. 5, 29, 30; Feb. 12, 22; Mar. 8, 9, 14; May 30; June 14; July 9; Aug. 13; Sept. 7, 16; Oct. 16, 30; Nov. 15; Dec. 3, 4, 15.

25 ♊
1980   Jan. 11; Feb. 5, 14; Mar. 14; May 2, 3; June 12, 15; July 1, 30; Aug. 20, 21; Sept. 17; Oct. 17, 25; Nov. 14, 15, 19; Dec. 16.

1981   Jan. 6, 31; Feb. 13, 23; Mar. 10, 15; May 31; June 15; July 10; Aug. 13; Sept. 8, 17; Oct. 17, 31; Nov. 16; Dec. 5, 6, 16.

26 ♊
1980   Jan. 12; Feb. 6, 15; Mar. 15; May 4, 5; June 10, 11, 16; July 2, 3, 31; Aug. 1, 22, 23; Sept. 18; Oct. 18, 26; Nov. 16; 20; Dec. 17.

1981   Jan. 7; Feb. 1, 14, 24; Mar. 11, 16; June 1, 16; July 11, 12; Aug. 14; Sept. 9, 18; Oct. 18; Nov. 1, 17; Dec. 7, 8, 17.

27 ♊
1980   Jan. 13; Feb. 6, 16; Mar. 16; May 6, 7; June 8, 9, 17; July 4, 5; Aug. 2, 24; Sept. 19; Oct. 19, 27; Nov. 17, 21; Dec. 18.

1981   Jan. 8; Feb. 2, 15, 25; Mar. 12, 13, 17; June 2, 17; July 13; Aug. 15; Sept. 9, 19; Oct. 19, 20; Nov. 2, 18; Dec. 9, 10, 18.

28 ♊
1980   Jan. 14; Feb. 7, 17; Mar. 17; May 8, 9; June 6, 7, 18; Aug. 3, 25, 26; Sept. 20; Oct. 20, 28; Nov. 18, 19, 21; Dec. 19.

1981   Jan. 9; Feb. 3, 4, 16, 26; Mar. 14, 18; June 3, 18; July 14, 15; Aug. 16; Sept. 10, 20; Oct. 21; Nov. 3, 19; Dec. 11, 12, 19.

29 ♊
1980   Jan. 14; Feb. 8, 18; Mar. 18; June 4, 5, 19; July 8, 9; Aug. 4, 5, 27; Sept. 21; Oct. 21, 29; Nov. 20, 22; Dec. 20.

1981   Jan. 9; Feb. 5, 17, 26; Mar. 15, 19; June 3, 19; July 16; Aug. 17; Sept. 11, 21; Oct. 22; Nov. 4, 20; Dec. 13, 14, 20.

CANCER

0 ♋

1980   Jan. 15; Feb. 9, 19; Mar. 19; May 12, 13, 14; June 2, 3, 4, 20; July 10, 11; Aug. 6, 28, 29; Sept. 22; Oct. 22, 29; Nov. 21, 23; Dec. 21.

1981   Jan. 10; Feb. 6, 18, 27; Mar. 16, 20, 23; June 4, 20, 21; Aug. 17; Sept. 12, 22; Oct. 23; Nov. 5; Dec. 15, 16.

1 ♋

1980   Jan. 16; Feb. 10, 19; Mar. 20; May 15, 16, 17, 29, 30, 31; June 1, 21; July 12; Aug. 7, 30; Sept. 23; Oct. 23, 30; Nov. 22, 23, 24; Dec. 22.

1981   Jan. 11; Feb. 7, 19, 28; Mar. 17, 18, 21, 24; June 5, 22; July 19; Aug. 18; Sept. 13, 23; Oct. 24; Nov. 5; Dec. 17, 18.

2 ♋

1980   Jan. 17; Feb. 11, 20; Mar. 21; May 18, 19, 20, 21, 22, 23, 24, 25, 26, 27, 28; June 22; July 13, 14; Aug. 8, 31; Sept. 1, 24; Oct. 24, 31; Nov. 24, 25; Dec. 23.

1981   Jan. 12; Feb. 8, 9, 20; Mar. 1, 19, 22, 25; June 6, 23; July 20, 21; Aug. 19; Sept. 14, 24; Oct. 25; Nov. 6; Dec. 19, 20, 21.

3 ♋

1980   Jan. 18; Feb. 12, 21; Mar. 22; June 23; July 15, 16; Aug. 9, 10; Sept. 2, 25; Oct. 25; Nov. 1, **25**; Dec. 24.

1981   Jan. 13; Feb. 10, 21; Mar. 2, 20, 23, 26; June 7, 24; July 22; Aug. 20; Sept. 15, 25; Oct. 26; Nov. 7; Dec. 22, 23.

4 ♋

1980   Jan. 18; Feb. 12, 22; Mar. 23, 24; June 24; July 17, 18; Aug. 11; Sept. 3, 4, 26; Oct. 26; Nov. 2, **26**, 27; Dec. 25.

1981   Jan. 13, Feb, 11, 22; Mar. 2, 21, 22, 24, 27; June 8, 25; July 23, 24; Aug. 21; Sept. 15, 26; Oct. 27; Nov. 8; Dec. 24, 25.

5 ♋
1980 Jan. 19; Feb. 13, 23; Mar. 25; June 25, 26; July 19; Aug. 12; Sept. 5, 27; Oct. 27; Nov. 3, 27, 28; Dec. 26.

1981 Jan. 14; Feb. 12, 13, 23; Mar. 3, 23, 25, 27; June 8, 26; July 25; Aug. 22; Sept. 16, 27; Oct. 28; Nov. 9; Dec. 26. 27.

6 ♋
1980 Jan. 20; Feb. 14, 24; Mar. 26; June 27; July 20, 21; Aug 13; Oct. 6, 7, 28; Oct. 28; Nov. 3, 28, 29; Dec. 27.

1981 Jan. 15; Feb. 14, 24; Mar. 4, 24, 26, 28; June 9, 27; July 26, 27; Aug. 23; Sept. 17, 28; Oct. 29; Nov. 10; Dec. 28, 29, 30.

7 ♋
1980 Jan. 21; Feb. 15, 25; Mar. 27; June 28; July 22, 23; Aug. 14; Sept. 8, 29; Oct. 29; Nov. 4, 29, 30; Dec. 1, 22.

1981 Jan. 16; Feb. 15, 25; Mar. 5, 25, 27, 29; June 10, 28; July 28; Aug. 23; Sept. 18, 29; Oct. 30; Nov. 11; Dec. 31.

8 ♋
1980 Jan. 22; Feb. 16, 26; Mar. 28; June 29; July 24; Aug. 15; Sept. 9, 10, 30; Oct. 30; Nov. 5, 30; Dec. 2, 29.

1981 Jan. 17; Feb. 16, 26; Mar. 6, 26, 27, 28, 30; June 11, 29; July 29, 30; Aug. 24; Sept. 19, 30; Oct. 31; Nov. 12.

9 ♋
1980 Jan. 23; Feb. 17, 27; Mar. 29; June 30; July 25, 26; Aug. 16; Sept. 11; Oct. 1, 31; Nov. 6, 30; Dec. 3, 30.

1981 Jan. 17, Feb. 17, 18, 27; Mar. 6, 28, 29, 31; June 12, 30; July 31; Aug. 25; Sept. 20; Oct. 1; Nov. 1, 13.

10 ♋
1980 Jan. 23; Feb. 17, 28; Mar. 30; July 1, 27, 28; Aug. 17; Sept. 12, 13; Oct. 2; Nov. 1, 7; Dec. 1, 4, 31.

1981 Jan. 18; Feb. 19, 28; Mar. 7, 29, 30, 31; June 12; July 1; Aug. 1, 2, 26; Sept. 21; Oct. 2; Nov. 2, 14.

11 ♋
1980 Jan. 1, 24; Feb. 18, 29; Mar. 31; July 29; Aug. 18, 19; Sept. 14; Oct. 3; Nov. 2, 8; Dec. 2, 5, 6.

1981 Jan. 1, 19; Feb. 20; Mar. 1, 8, 30, **31**; Apr. 1; June 13; July 2; Aug. 3, 27; Sept. 21; Oct. 3; Nov. 3, 15, 16.

12♋
1980   Jan. 2, 25; Feb. 19; Mar. 1; Apr. 1; July 3, 30, 31; Aug. 20; Sept. 15, 16; Oct. 4; Nov. 3, 8; Dec. 3, 7.

1981   Jan. 1, 20; Feb. 21; Mar. 2, 9; Apr. **1**, 2; June 14; July 3; Aug. 4, 5, 28; Sept. 22; Oct. 4; Nov. 4, 17.

13♋
1980   Jan. 3, 26; Feb. 20; Mar. 2; Apr. 2; July 4; Aug. 1, 2, 21; Sept. 17; Oct. 5; Nov. 4, 9; Dec. 4, 8.

1981   Jan. 2, 21; Feb. 22, 23; Mar. 3, 10; Apr. **2**, 3; June 15; July 4; Aug. 6, 29; Sept. 23; Oct. 5; Nov. 5, 18.

14♋
1980   Jan. 4, 27; Feb. 21; Mar. 3; Apr. 3; July 5; Aug. 3, 22; Sept. 18, 19; Oct. 6; Nov. 5, 10; Dec. 4, 9, 10.

1981   Jan. 3, 21; Feb. 24; Mar. 4, 10; Apr.**3, 4**; June 16; July 5; Aug. 7, 8, 29; Sept. 24; Oct. 6; Nov. 6, 19.

15♋
1980   Jan. 5, 27; Feb. 22; Mar. 4; Apr. 4; July 6; Aug. 4, 5, 23; Sept. 20; Oct.7; Nov. 6, 11; Dec. 5, 11.

1981   Jan. 4, 22; Feb. 25; Mar. 5, 11; Apr. **4**, 5; June 17; July 6; Aug. 9, 30; Sept. 25; Oct. 7; Nov. 7, 20.

16♋
1980   Jan. 6, 28; Feb. 23; Mar. 5; Apr. 5; July 7; Aug. 6, 7, 24; Sept. 20, 21; Oct. 8; Nov. 7, 12; Dec. 6, 12.

1981   Jan. 5, 23; Feb. 26; Mar. 6, 12; Apr. **5**, 6; June 17; July 7; Aug. 10, 11, 31; Sept. 26; Oct. 8, 21.

17♋
1980   Jan. 7, 29; Feb. 23; Mar. 6; Apr. 6; July 8; Aug. 8, 25; Sept. 23; Oct. 9; Nov. 8, 12; Dec. 7, 13, 14.

1981   Jan. 6, 24; Feb. 27, 28; Mar. 7, 13; Apr. **6**, 7; June 18; July 8; Aug. 12; Sept. 1, 27; Oct. 9; Nov. 8, 22.

18♋
1980   Jan. 8, 30; Feb. 24; Mar. 7; Apr. 7; July 9; Aug. 9, 10, 26; Sept. 24, 25; Oct. 10; Nov. 9, 13; Dec. 8, 15.

1981   Jan. 7, 25; Mar. 1, 8, 14; Apr. **7**, 8, 9; June 19; July 9; Aug. 13, 14; Sept. 2, 27; Oct. 10; Nov. 9, 23.

19 ♋
1980   Jan. 9, 31; Feb. 25; Mar. 8; Apr. 8; July 10; Aug. 11, 12, 27; Sept. 26; Oct. 11; Nov. 10, 14; Dec. 8, 16.

1981   Jan. 8, 25; Mar, 2, 9, 14; Apr. **8**, 10; June 20; July 10; Aug. 15, 16; Sept. 3, 28; Oct. 11; Nov. 10, 24.

20 ♋
1980   Jan. 10; Feb. 1, 26; Mar. 9; Apr. 9; July 11; Aug. 13, 28; Sept. 27; Oct. 12; Nov. 11, 15; Dec. 9, 17.

1981   Jan. 9, 26; Mar. 3, 4, 10, 15; Apr. 8, 9, 11; June 21; July 11, 12; Aug. 17; Sept. 3, 29; Oct. 12; Nov. 11, 25.

21 ♋
1980   Jan. 11; Feb. 1, 27; Mar. 10; Apr. 10; July 12; Aug. 14, 15, 29; Sept. 28, 29; Oct. 13; Nov. 12, 16; Dec. 10, 18, 19.

1981   Jan. 10, 27; Mar. 5, 11, 16; Apr. 9, 10, 12, 13; June 21; July 13; Aug. 18, 19; Sept. 4, 30; Oct. 13; Nov. 12, 26, 27.

22 ♋
1980   Jan. 12; Feb. 2, 28; Mar. 11; Apr. 11; July 13; Aug. 16, 30; Sept. 30; Oct. 14; Nov. 13, 17; Dec. 11, 20.

1981   Jan. 11, 28; Mar. 6, 12, 17; Apr. 10, 11, 14; June 22; July 14; Aug. 20; Sept. 5; Oct. 1, 14; Nov. 13, 28.

23 ♋
1980   Jan. 13; Feb. 3, 29; Mar. 12; Apr. 12; July 14; Aug. 17, 18, 31; Oct. 1, 2, 15; Nov. 14, 17; Dec. 12, 21.

1981   Jan. 12, 29; Mar. 7, 13, 18; Apr. 11, 12, 15; June 23; July 15; Aug. 21, 22; Sept. 6; Oct. 2, 15; Nov. 14, 29; Dec. 1, 2.

24 ♋
1980   Jan. 14; Feb. 4; Mar. 1, 13; Apr. 13; July 15; Aug. 19; Sept. 1; Oct. 3, 16; Nov. 15, 18; Dec. 12, 22, 23.

1981   Jan. 13, 29; Mar. 8, 9, 14, 18; Apr. 12, 13, 16, 17; June 24; July 16; Aug; Aug. 23; Sept. 7; Oct. 3, 16; Nov. 15, 30; Dec. 3, 4.

25 ♋
1980   Jan. 15; Feb. 5; Mar. 1, 14; Apr. 14; July 16, 17; Aug. 20, 21; Sept. 2; Oct. 4, 5, 17; Nov. 16, 19; Dec. 13, 24.

1981   Jan. 14, 30; Mar. 10, 15, 19; Apr. 12, 14, 18; June 25; July 17; Aug. 24, 25; Sept. 8; Oct. 4, 17; Nov. 16; Dec. 1, 5, 6.

26♋

1980   Jan. 16; Feb. 6; Mar. 2, 15; Apr. 15; July 18; Aug. 22, 23; Sept. 3; Oct. 6, 18; Nov. 17, 20; Dec. 14, 25.

1981   Jan. 15, 31; Mar. 11, 16, 20; Apr. 13, 15, 19; June 26; July 18; Aug. 26; Sept. 9; Oct. 4, 18; Nov. 17; Dec. 2, 3, 7, 8.

27♋

1980   Jan. 17; Feb. 6; Mar. 3, 16; Apr. 16; July 19; Aug. 24; Sept. 4; Oct. 7, 19; Nov. 18, 21; Dec. 15, 26.

1981   Jan. 16; Feb. 1; Mar. 12, 13, 17, 21; Apr. 14, 16, 20, 21; June 26; July 19; Aug. 27, 28; Sept. 9; Oct. 5, 19, 20; Nov. 18; Dec. 4, 9, 10.

28♋

1980   Jan. 18; Feb. 7; Mar. 4, 17; Apr. 17; July 20; Aug. 25, 26; Sept. 5; Oct. 8, 9, 20; Nov. 19, 21; Dec. 16, 27, 28.

1981   Jan. 17; Feb. 2; Mar. 14, 18, 22; Apr. 15, 17, 22; June 27; July 20; Aug. 29; Sept. 10; Oct. 6, 21; Nov. 19; Dec. 5, 11, 12.

29♋

1980   Jan. 19; Feb. 8; Mar. 5, 18; Apr. 18; July 21; Aug. 27; Sept. 6; Oct. 10, 21; Nov. 20, 22; Dec. 16, 29.

1981   Jan. 18; Feb. 2; Mar. 15, 19, 23; Apr. 16, 18, 23; June 28; July 21; Aug. 30; Sept. 11; Oct. 7, 22; Nov. 20; Dec. 6, 7, 13, 14.

LEO

0 ♌

1980   Jan. 20; Feb. 9; Mar. 6, 19; Apr. 19; July 22; Aug. 28, 29; Sept. 7; Oct. 11, 12, 22; Nov. 21, 23; Dec. 17, 30, 31.

1981   Jan. 19; Feb. 3; Mar. 16, 20, 23; Apr. 16, 17, 19, 24, 25; June 29; July 22; Sept. 1, 2, 12; Oct. 8, 23; Nov. 21; Dec. 8.

1 ♌

1980   Jan. 21; Feb. 10; Mar. 7, 20; Apr. 20; July 23; Aug. 30; Sept. 8; Oct. 13, 23; Nov. 22, 24; Dec. 18.

1981   Jan. 20; Feb. 4; Mar. 17, 18, 21, 24; Apr. 17, 20, 26; June 30; July 23; Sept. 3, 13; Oct. 9, 24; Nov. 22; Dec. 9, 10.

2 ♌

1980   Jan. 22; Feb. 11; Mar. 8, 21; Apr. 21; July 24; Aug. 31; Sept. 1, 9; Oct. 14, 24; Nov. 23, 25; Dec. 19.

1981   Jan. 1, 2, 21; Feb. 5; Mar. 19, 22, 25; Apr. 18, 21, 27; June 30; July 24; Sept. 4, 5, 14; Oct. 10, 25; Nov. 23; Dec. 11, 12.

3 ♌

1980   Jan. 23; Feb. 12; Mar. 8, 22; Apr. 22; July 25; Sept. 2, 10; Oct. 15, 16, 25; Nov. 24, 25; Dec. 20.

1981   Jan. 3, 22; Feb. 6; Mar. 20, 23, 26; Apr. 19, 22, 28, 29; July 1, 25; Sept. 6, 15; Oct. 11, 26; Nov. 24; Dec. 13.

4 ♌

1980   Jan. 24; Feb. 12; Mar. 9, 23, 24; Apr. 23; July 26; Sept. 3, 4, 11; Oct. 17, 26; Nov. 25, 26; Dec. 20.

1981   Jan. 4, 23; Feb. 6; Mar. 21, 22, 24, 27; Apr. 20, 23, 30; July 2, 26; Sept. 7, 8, 15; Oct. 12, 27; Nov. 25; Dec. 14, 15.

5 ♌

1980   Jan. 25; Feb. 13; Mar. 10, 25; Apr. 24; July 27; Sept. 5, 11; Oct. 18, 19, 27; Nov. 26, 27; Dec. 21.

1981   Jan. 5, 6, 24; Feb. 7; Mar. 23, 25, 27; Apr. 21, 24; July 3, 27; Sept. 9, 10, 16; Oct. 12, 28; Nov. 26; Dec. 16, 17.

6 ♌

1980   Jan. 26; Feb. 14; Mar. 11, 26; Apr. 25; July 28; Sept. 6, 7, 12; Oct. 20, 28; Nov. 27, 28; Dec. 22.

1981   Jan. 7, 25; Feb. 8; Mar. 24, 26, 28; Apr. 21, 25; May 2, 3; July 4, 28; Sept. 11, 17; Oct. 13, 29; Nov. 27; Dec. 18, 19, 20.

7 ♌

1980   Jan. 27; Feb. 15; Mar. 12, 27; Apr. 26; July 29; Sept. 8, 13; Oct. 21, 29; Nov. 28, 29; Dec. 23.

1981   Jan. 8, 26; Feb. 9; Mar. 25, 27, 29; Apr. 22, 26; May 4; July 5, 29; Sept. 12, 13, 18; Oct. 14, 30; Nov. 28; Dec. 21, 22, 23.

8 ♌

1980   Jan 28; Feb. 16; Mar. 13, 28; Apr. 27; July 30; Sept. 9, 10, 14; Oct. 22, 23, 30; Nov. 29, 30; Dec. 24.

1981   Jan. 9, 27; Feb. 10; Mar. 26, 27, 28, 30; Apr. 23, 27; May 5; July 5, 30; Sept. 14, 19; Oct. 15, 31; Nov. 29; Dec. 24, 25, 26, 27, 28, 29, 30, 31.

9 ♌

1980   Jan. 26; Feb. 17; Mar. 14, 29; Apr. 28; July 31; Sept. 11, 15; Oct. 24, 31; Nov. **30**; Dec. 24.

1981   Jan. 10, 11, 28; Feb. 10; Mar. 28, 29, 31; Apr. 24, 28; May 6, 7; July 6, 31; Sept. 15, 16, 20; Oct. 16; Nov. 1, 30.

10 ♌

1980   Jan. 30; Feb. 17; Mar. 15, 30; Apr. 29; Aug. 1; Sept. 12, 13, 16; Oct. 25, 26; Nov. 1; Dec. **1**, 25.

1981   Jan. 12, 29; Feb. 11; Mar. 29, 30, 31; Apr. 25, 29; May 8; July 7; Aug. 1; Sept. 17, 18, 21; Oct. 17; Nov. 2; Dec. 1.

11 ♌

1980   Jan. 31; Feb. 18; Mar. 16, 31; Apr. 30; Aug. 2; Sept. 14, 27; Oct. 27; Nov. 2; Dec. **2**, 26.

1981   Jan. 13, 30; Feb. 12; Mar. 30, **31**; Apr. 1, 25, 30; May 1, 9; July 8; Aug. 2; Sept. 19, 21; Oct. 18; Nov. 3; Dec. 2.

12 ♌
1980   Feb. 1, 19; Mar. 17; Apr. 1; May 1; Aug. 3; Sept. 15, 16, 18; Oct. 28; Nov. 3; Dec. **3**, 27.

1981   Jan. 14, 21; Feb. 13; Apr. **1**, 2, 26; May 2, 10, 11; July 9; Aug. 3, 4; Sept. 20, 21, 22; Oct. 19; Nov. 4; Dec. 3.

13 ♌
1980   Feb. 2, 20; Mar. 18; Apr. 2; May 2; Aug. 4; Oct. 17, 19; Oct. 29, 30; Nov. 4; Dec. **4**, 28.

1981   Jan. 15, 16; Feb. 1, 14; Apr. **2**, 3, 27; May 3, 12; July 10; Aug. 5; Sept. 22, 23; Oct. 20; Nov. 5; Dec. 4.

14 ♌
1980   Feb. 3, 21; Mar. 18; Apr. 3; May 3; Aug. 5; Sept. 18, 19, 20; Oct. 31; Nov. 5; Dec. 4, 5, 28.

1981   Jan. 17; Feb. 2, 14; Apr. **3, 4**, 28; May 4, 13, 14; July 10; Aug. 6; Sept. 23, **24**; Oct. 21; Nov. 6; Dec. 5.

15 ♌
1980   Feb. 4, 22; Mar. 19; Apr. 4; May 4; Aug. 6; Sept. 20, 21; Nov. 1, 6; Dec. 5, 6, 29.

1981   Jan. 18; Feb. 3, 15; Apr. **4**, 5, 29; May 5, 15; July 11; Aug. 7; Sept. **25**, 26; Oct. 21; Nov. 7; Dec. 6.

16 ♌
1980   Feb. 5, 23; Mar. 20; Apr. 5; May 5; Aug. 7; Sept. 21, **22**; Nov. 2, 3, 7; Dec. 6, 7, 30.

1981   Jan. 19, 20; Feb. 4, 16; Apr. **5**, 6, 29; May 6, 16; July 12; Aug. 8; Sept. 26, 27; Oct. 22; Nov. 8; Dec. 7.

17 ♌
1980   Feb. 6, 23; Mar. 21; Apr. 6; May 6; Aug. 8; Sept. 22, 23; Nov. 4, 8; Dec. 7, 8, 31.

1981   Jan. 21; Feb. 5, 17; Apr. **6**, 7, 30; May 7, 17, 18; July 13; Aug. 9; Sept. 27, 28, 29; Oct. 23; Nov. 8; Dec. 8.

18 ♌
1980   Feb. 7, 24; Mar. 22; Apr. 7; May 7; Aug. 9, 10; Sept. 23, 24, 25; Nov. 5, 9; Dec. 8, 9.

1981   Jan. 1, 22; Feb. 6, 18; Apr. **7**, 8, 9; May 1, 8, 19; July 14; Aug. 10; Sept. 27, 30; Oct. 24; Nov. 9; Dec. 9.

19 ♌

1980   Feb. 8, 25; Mar. 23; Apr. 8; May 8, 9; Aug. 11; Sept. 24, 26; Nov. 6, 7, 10; Dec. 8, 10.

1981   Jan. 1, 23; Feb. 6, 18; Apr. **8**, 10; May 2, 9, 20; July 14; Aug. 11; Sept. 28; Oct. 1, 2, 25; Nov. 10; Dec. 10.

20 ♌

1980   Feb. 9, 26; Mar. 24; Apr. 9; May 10; Aug. 12; Sept. 25, 27; Nov. 8, 11; Dec. 9, 11.

1981   Jan. 2, 24, 25; Feb. 8, 19; Apr. 8, 9, 11; May 3, 10, 21, 22; July 15; Aug. 12; Sept. 29; Oct. 3, 4, 26; Nov. 11; Dec. 11.

21 ♌

1980   Feb. 10, 17; Mar. 25; Apr. 10; May 11; Aug. 13; Sept. 26, 28, 29; Nov. 9, 12; Dec. 10, 12.

1981   Jan. 3, 26; Feb. 9, 20; Apr. 9, 10, 12, 13; May 4, 11, 22; July 16; Aug. 13; Sept. 30; Oct. 5, 6, 27; Nov. 12; Dec. 12.

22 ♌

1980   Feb. 11, 28; Mar. 26; Apr. 11; May 12; Aug. 14; Sept. 27, 30; Nov. 10, 11, 13; Dec. 11, 13.

1981   Jan. 4, 27; Feb. 10, 21; Apr. 10, 11, 14; May 4, 12, 24; July 17; Aug. 14; Oct. 1, 7, 28; Nov. 13; Dec. 13.

23 ♌

1980   Feb. 12, 29; Mar. 27; Apr. 12; May 13; Aug. 15; Sept. 28; Oct. 1, 2; Nov. 12, 14; Dec. 12, 14.

1981   Jan. 5, 28; Feb. 11, 22; Apr. 11, 12, 15; May 5, 13, 15, 26; July 18; Aug. 15; Oct. 2, 8, 9, 29; Nov. 14; Dec. 14.

24 ♌

1980   Feb. 13; Mar. 1, 28; Apr. 13; May 14; Aug. 16; Sept. 29; Oct. 3; Nov. 13, 15; Dec. 12, 15.

1981   Jan. 5, 29, 30; Feb. 12, 23; Apr. 12, 13, 16, 17; May 6, 14, 27; July 19; Aug. 16; Oct. 3, 10, 11, 30; Nov. 15; Dec. 15.

25 ♌

1980   Feb. 14; Mar. 1, 29; Apr. 1, 2, 3, 4, 5, 6, 7, 8, 9, 14; May 15; Aug. 17; Sept. 30; Oct. 4, 5; Nov. 14, 15, 16; Dec. 13, 16.

1981   Jan. 6, 31; Feb. 13, 23; Apr. 12, 14, 18; May 7, 15, 18, 29; July 19; Aug. 17; Oct. 4, 12, 31; Nov. 16; Dec. 16.

26 ♌

1980 Feb. 15; Mar. 2, 23, 24, 25, 26, 27, 28, 29, **30**, 31; Apr. 10, 11, 12, 13, 14, **15**, 16, 17, 18; May 16; Aug. 18; Sept. 30; Oct. 6; Nov. 16, 17; Dec. 14, 17.

1981 Jan. 7; Feb. 1, 14, 24; Apr. 13, 15, 19; May 8, 16, 30; July 20; Aug. 18; Oct. 4, 13, 14; Nov. 1, 17; Dec. 17.

27 ♌

1980 Feb. 16; Mar. 3, 18, 19, 20, 21, 22, 31; Apr. 16, 19, 20, 21, 22, 23, 24; May 17; Aug. 19; Oct. 1, 7; Nov. 17, 18; Dec. 15, 18.

1981 Jan. 8; Feb. 2, 15, 25; Apr. 14, 16, 20, 21; May 8, 17, 31; July 21; Aug. 19; Oct. 5, 15, 16; Nov. 2, 18; Dec. 18.

28 ♌

1980 Feb. 17; Mar. 4, 14, 15, 16, 17; Apr. 1, 17, 25, 26, 27, 28; Aug. 20; Oct. 2, 8, 9; Nov. 18, **19**; Dec. 16, 19.

1981 Jan. 9; Feb. 3, 4, 16, 26; Apr. 15, 17, 22; May 9, 18; June 1, 2; July 22; Aug. 20; Oct. 6, 17; Nov. 3, 19; Dec. 19.

29 ♌

1980 Feb. 18; Mar. 5, 11, 12, 13; Apr. 2, 18, 29, 30; May 1, 2, 19; Aug. 21; Oct. 3, 10; Nov. **20**; Dec. 16, 20.

1981 Jan. 9; Feb. 5, 17, 26; Apr. 16, 18, 23; May 10, 19; June 3; July 23; Aug. 21; Oct. 7, 18, 19; Nov. 4, 20; Dec. 20.

VIRGO

0 ♍
1980 Jan. 15; Feb. 19; Mar. 6, 8, 9, 10; May 3, 4, 5, 6, 20; Aug. 22; Oct. 4, 11, 12; Nov. **21;** Dec. 17, 21.

1981 Jan. 10; Feb. 6, 18, 27; Apr. 16, 19, 24, 25; May 11, 20; June 4, 5; July 24; Aug. 22; Oct. 8, 20, 21; Nov. 5, 21; Dec. 21.

1 ♍
1980 Jan. 16; Feb. 19; Mar. 5, 6, **7;** Apr. 4, 20; May 7, 8, 9, 21; Aug. 23; Oct. 5, 13; Nov. **22,** 23; Dec. 18, 22.

1981 Jan. 11; Feb. 7, 19, 28; Apr. 17, 20, 26; May 12, 21; June 6; July 24; Aug. 23; Oct. 9, 22; Nov. 5, 22; Dec. 22.

2 ♍
1980 Jan. 17; Feb. 20; Mar. 2, 3, 4, 8; Apr. 5, 21; May 10, 11, 12, 22; Aug. 24; Oct. 6, 14; Nov. 23, 24; Dec. 19, 23.

1981 Jan. 12; Feb. 8, 9, 20; Mar. 1; Apr. 18, 21, 27; May 12, 22; June 7; July 25; Aug. 24; Oct. 10, 23, 24; Nov. 6, 23; Dec. 23.

3 ♍
1980 Jan. 18; Feb. 21, 19; Mar. 1, 8; Apr. 6, 22; May 13, 14, 15, 23; Aug. 25; Oct. 7, 15, 16; Nov. 24, 25; Dec. 20, 24.

1981 Jan. 13; Feb. 10, 21; Mar. 2; Apr. 19, 22, 28, 29; May 13, 23; June 8, 9; July 26; Aug. 25; Oct. 11, 25, 26; Nov. 7, 24; Dec. 24.

4 ♍
1980 Jan. 18; Feb. 22, 26, 27, 28; Mar. 9; Apr. 7, 23; May 16, 17, 24; Aug. 26; Oct. 7, 17; Oct. 25, 26, 27; Dec. 20, 25.

1981 Jan. 13; Feb. 11, 22; Mar. 2; Apr. 20, 23, 30; May 14, 24; June 10; July 27; Aug. 26; Oct. 12, 27, 28; Nov. 8, 25; Dec. 25.

5 ♍
1980   Jan. 19; Feb. 23, 24, 25; Mar. 10; Apr. 8, 24; May 18, 19, 20, 25; Aug. 27; Oct. 8, 18, 19; Nov. 26, 28; Dec. 21, 26.

1981   Jan. 14; Feb. 12, 13, 23; Mar. 3; Apr. 21, 24; May 1, 15, 25; June 11, 12; July 28; Aug. 27; Oct. 12, 29; Nov. 9, 26; Dec. 26.

6 ♍
1980   Jan. 20; Feb. 21, 22, 23, 24; Mar. 11; Apr. 9, 25; May 21, 22, 23, 26; Aug. 28; Oct. 9, 20; Nov. 27, 29; Dec. 22, 27.

1981   Jan. 15; Feb. 14, 24; Mar. 4; Apr. 21, 25; May 2, 3, 16, 26; June 13; July 29; Aug. 28; Oct. 13, 30, 31; Nov. 10, 27; Dec. 27.

7 ♍
1980   Jan. 21; Feb. 19, 20, 25; Mar. 12; Apr. 10, 26; May 24, 25, 27; Aug. 29; Oct. 10, 21; Nov. 28, 30; Dec. 1, 23, 28.

1981   Jan. 16; Feb. 15, 25; Mar. 5; Apr. 22, 26; May 4, 17, 27; June 14; July 29; Aug. 29, 30; Oct. 14; Nov. 1, 2, 11, 28; Dec. 28,

8 ♍
1980   Jan. 22; Feb. 16, 17, 18, 26; Mar. 13; Apr. 11, 27; May 26, 27, 28; Aug. 30; Oct. 11, 22, 23; Nov. 29; Dec. 2, 24, 29.

1981   Jan. 17; Feb. 16, 26; Mar. 6; Apr. 23, 27; May 5, 17, 28, 29; June 15, 16; July 30; Aug. 31; Oct. 15; Nov. 3, 4, 12, 29; Dec. 29.

9 ♍
1980   Jan. 23; Feb. 13, 14, 15, 27; Mar. 14; Apr. 12, 28; May 28, **29**, 30; Aug. 31; Oct. 12, 24; Nov. 30; Dec. 3, 24, 30.

1981   Jan. 17; Feb. 17, 18, 27; Mar. 6; Apr. 24, 28; May 6, 7, 18, 30; June 17; July 31; Sept. 1; Oct. 16; Nov. 5, 6, 13, 30; Dec. 30.

10 ♍
1980   Jan. 23; Feb. 10, 11, 12, 28; Mar. 15; Apr. 13, 29; May 30, 31; Sept. 1; Oct. 13, 25, 26; Dec. 1, 4, 25, 31.

1981   Jan. 18; Feb. 19, 28; Mar. 7; Apr. 25, 29; May 8, 19, 31; June 18, 19; Aug. 1; Sept. 2; Oct. 17; Nov. 7, 14; Dec. 1, 31.

11 ♍
1980   Jan. 1, 24; Feb. 7, 8, 9, 29; Mar. 16; Apr. 14, 15, 30; May 31; June 2, 3; Sept. 2; Oct. 13, 27; Dec. 2, 5, 6, 26.

1981   Jan. 1, 19; Feb. 20; Mar. 1, 8; Apr. 25, 30; May 1, 9, 20; June 1, 20; Aug. 2; Sept. 3; Oct. 18; Nov. 8, 9, 15, 16; Dec. 2.

12♍
1980   Jan. 2, 25; Feb. 3, 4, 5, 6; Mar. 1, 17; Apr. 16; May 1; June 1, 4, 5, 6; Sept. 3; Oct. 14, 28; Dec. 3, 7, 27.

1981   Jan. 1, 20; Feb. 21; Mar. 2, 9; Apr. 26; May 2, 10, 11, 21; June 2, 21, 22; Aug. 3; Sept. 4; Oct. 19; Nov. 10, 11, 17; Dec. 3.

13♍
1980   Jan. 3, 26, 30. 31; Feb. 1, 2; Mar. 2, 18; Apr. 17; May 2; June 2, 7, 8; Sept. 4; Oct. 15, 29, 30; Dec. 4, 8, 28.

1981   Jan. 2, 21; Feb. 22, 23; Mar. 3, 10; Apr. 27; May 3, 12, 21; June 3, 23; Aug. 3, Sept. 5; Oct. 20; Nov. 12, 13, 18; Dec. 4.

14♍
1980   Jan. 1, 2, 3, **4,** 5, 6, 7, 23, 24, 25, 26, **27**, 28, 29; Mar. 3, 18; Apr. 18; May 3; June 3, 4, 9, 10; Sept. 5; Oct. 16, 31; Dec. 5, 9, 10, 28.

1981   Jan. 3, 21; Feb. 24; Mar. 4, 10; Apr. 28; May 4, 13, 14, 22; June 4, 24; Aug. 4; Sept. 6; Oct. 21; Nov. 14, 15, 19; Dec. 5.

15♍
1980   Jan, 5, 8, 9, 10, 11, 12, 13, 14, 15, 16, 17, 18, 19, 20, 21, 22, 27; Mar. 4, 19; Apr. 19; May 4; June 5, 11, 12; Sept, 6, 7; Oct. 17; Nov. 1; Dec. 6, 11, 29.

1981   Jan. 4, 22; Feb. 25; Mar, 5, 11; Apr. 29; May 5, 15, 23; June 5, 25, 26; Aug. 5; Sept, 7; Oct. 21; Nov. 16, 20; Dec. 6.

16♍
1980   Jan. 6, 28; Mar. 5, 20; Apr. 20; May 5; June 6, 13, 14, 29, 30; July 1, 2, 3, 4, 5, 6, 7, 8, ;9, 10, 11, 12; Sept. 8; Oct. 18; Nov. 2, 3; Dec. 7, 12, 30.

1981   Jan. 5, 23; Feb. 26; Mar. 6, 12; Apr. 29; May 6, 16, 24; June 6, 27; Aug. 6; Sept 8; Oct. 22; Nov. 17, 18, 21; Dec. 7.

17♍
1980   Jan. 7, 29; Mar. 6, 21; Apr. 21, 22; May 6; June 7, 15, 16, 26, 27, 28; July 13, 14, 15; Sept. 9; Oct. 19; Nov. 4; Dec. 8, 13, 14, 31.

1981   Jan. 6, 24; Feb. 27, 28; Mar. 7, 13; Apr. 30; May 7, 17, 18, 25; June 7, 28, 29; Aug. 7; Sept. 9; Oct. 23; Nov. 19, 20, 22; Dec. 8.

18♍
1980   Jan. 8, 30; Mar. 7, 22; Apr. 23; May 7; June 8, 17, 18, 24, 25; July 16, 17, 18; Sept. 10; Oct. 19; Nov. 5; Dec. 9, 15.

1981   Jan. 1, 7, 25; Mar. 1, 8, 14; May 1, 8, 19, 25; June 8, 30; Aug. 8; Sept. 10; Oct. 24; Nov. 21, 22, 23; Dec. 9.

19 ♍
1980   Jan. 9, 31; Mar. 8, 23; Apr. 24; May 8, 9; June 9, 19, 20, 22, 23; July 19, 20; Sept. 11; Oct. 20; Nov. 6, 7; Dec. 10, 16.

1981   Jan. 1, 8, 25; Mar. 2, 14, 19; May 2, 9, 20, 26; June 9; July 1, 2; Aug. 8; Sept. 11; Oct. 25; Nov. 23, **24;** Dec. 10.

20 ♍
1980   Jan. 10; Feb. 1; Mar. 9, 24; Apr. 25, 26; May 8, 10; June 10, 20, **21,** 22; July 21, 22; Sept. 12; Oct. 21; Nov. 8; Dec. 11, 17.

1981   Jan. 2, 9, 26; Mar. 3, 4, 10, 15; May 3, 10, 21, 22, 27; June 10; July 3; Aug. 9; Sept. 12; Oct. 26; Nov. **25,** 26; Dec. 11.

21 ♍
1980   Jan. 11; Feb. 1; Mar. 10, 25; Apr. 27; May 11,; Jun 11, 18, 19, 23, 24; July 23, 24; Sept. 14; Oct. 23; Nov. 10, 11; Dec. 13, 20.

1981   Jan. 3, 10, 27; Mar. 5, 11, 16; May 4, 11, 23, 28; June 11; July 4, 5; Aug. 10; Sept. 13; Oct. 27; Nov. 26, **27,** 28; Dec. 12.

22 ♍
1980   Jan. 12; Feb. 2; Mar. 11, 26; Apr. 28; May 12; June 12, 16, 17, 25, 26; July 25, 26; Sept. 14; Oct. 23; Nov. 10, 11; Dec. 13, 20.

1981   Jan. 4, 11, 28; Mar. 6, 12, 17; May 4, 12, 24, 29; June 12; July 6; Aug. 11; Sept. 14; Oct. 28; No. 28, 29, 30; Dec. 13.

23 ♍
1980   Jan. 13 Feb. 3; Mar. 12, 27; Apr. 29, 30; May 13; June 13, 15, 27, 28; July 27; Sept. 15; Oct. 24; Nov. 12; Dec. 14, 21.

1981   Jan. 5, 12, 29; Mar. 7, 13, 18; May 5, 13, 25, 26, 30; June 13; July 7, 8; Aug. 12; Sept. 15; Oct. 29; Nov. 29; Dec. 1, 2, 14.

24 ♍
1980   Jan. 14; Feb. 4; Mar. 13, 28; May 12, 14; June 13, **14,** 29, 30; July 28, 29; Sept. 16; Oct. 24; Nov. 13; Dec. 15, 22, 23.

1981   Jan. 5, 13, 29; Mar. 8, 9, 14, 18; May 6, 14, 20, 27; June 14; July 9; Aug. 13; Sept. 16; Oct. 30; Nov. 30; Dec. 3, 4, 15.

25 ♍
1980   Jan. 15; Feb. 5; Mar. 14, 29; May 2, 3, 15; June 12, 15; July 1, 30; Sept. 17; Oct. 25; Nov. 14, 15; Dec. 16, 24.

1981   Jan. 6, 14, 30; Mar. 10, 15, 19; May 7, 15, 28, 29, 31; June 15; July 10; Aug. 13; Sept. 17; Oct. 31; Dec. 1, 5, 6, 16.

26♍

1980   Jan. 16; Feb. 6; Mar. 15, 30; May 4, 5, 16; June 10, 11, 16; July 2, 3, 31; Aug. 1; Sept. 18; Oct. 26; Nov. 16; Dec. 17, 25.

1981   Jan. 7, 15, 31; Mar. 11, 16, 20; May 8, 16, 30; June 1, 16; July 11, 12; Aug. 14; Sept. 18; Nov. 1; Dec. 2, 3, 7, 8, 17.

27♍

1980   Jan. 17; Feb. 6; Mar. 16, 31; May 6, 7, 17; June 8, 9, 17; July 4, 5; Aug. 2; Sept. 19; Oct. 27; Nov. 17; Dec. 18, 26.

1981   Jan. 8, 16; Feb. 1; Mar. 12, 13, 17, 21; May 8, 17, 31; June 2, 17; July 13; Aug. 15; Sept. 19; Nov. 2; Dec. 4, 9, 10, 18.

28♍

1980   Jan. 18; Feb. 7; Mar. 17; Apr. 1; May 8, 9, 18; June 6, 7, 18; July 6, 7; Aug. 3; Sept. 20; Oct. 28; Nov. 18, 19; Dec. 19, 27, 28.

1981   Jan. 9, 17; Feb. 2; Mar. 14, 18, 22; May 9, 18; June 1, 2, 3, 18; July 14, 15; Aug. 16; Sept. 20; Nov. 3; Dec. 5, 11, 12, 19.

29♍

1980   Jan. 19; Feb. 8; Mar. 18; Apr. 2; May 10, 19; June 4, 5, 19; July 8. 9; Aug. 4; Sept. 21; Oct. 29; Nov. 20; Dec. 20. 29.

1981   Jan. 9, 18; Feb. 2; Mar. 15, 19, 23; May 10, 19; June 3, 19; July 16; Aug. 17; Sept. 21; Nov. 4; Dec. 6, 13, 14, 20.

LIBRA

0 ♎

1980   Jan. 20; Feb. 9; Mar. 19; Apr. 3; May 12, 13, 14, 20; June 2, 3, 20; July 10, 11; Aug. 6; Sept. 22; Oct. 29; Nov. 21; Dec. 21, 30.

1981   Jan. 10, 19; Feb. 3; Mar. 16, 20, 23; May 11, 20; June **4,** 5, 20, 21; July 17, 18; Aug. 18; Sept. 22; Nov. 5; Dec. 8, 15, 16, 21.

1 ♎

1980   Jan. 21; Feb. 10; Mar. 20; Apr. 4; May 13, 16, 17, 21, 29, 30. 31; June 1, 21; July 12; Aug. 7; Sept. 23; Oct. 30; Nov. 22, 23; Dec. 22, 31.

1981   Jan. 11, 20; Feb. 4; Mar. 17, 18, 21, 24; May 12, 21; June 5, 6, 22; July 19; Aug. 18; Sept. 23; Nov. 5; Dec. 9, 10, 17, 18, 22.

2 ♎

1980   Jan. 22; Feb. 11; Mar. 21; Apr. 5; May 18, 19, 20, 21, **22,** 23, 24, 25, 26, 27, 28; June 22; July 13, 14; Aug. 8; Sept. 24; Oct. 31; Nov. 24; Dec. 23.

1981   Jan. 1, 2, 12, 21; Feb. 5; Mar. 19, 22, 25; May 12, 22; June 6, 7, 23; July 20, 21; Aug. 19; Sept. 24; Nov. 6; Dec. 11, 12, 19, 20, 21, 23.

3 ♎

1980   Jan. 23; Feb. 12; Mar. 22, 23; Apr. 6; May 23; July 15, 16; Aug. 9, 10; Sept. 25; Nov. 1, 25; Dec. 24.

1981   Jan. 3, 13, 22; Feb. 6; Mar. 20, 23, 26; May 13, 23; June 7, 8, 9, 24; July 22; Aug. 20; Sept. 25; Nov. 7; Dec. 13, 22, 23, 24.

4 ♎

1980   Jan. 24; Feb. 12; Mar. 24; Apr. 7; May 24; June 24; July 17, 18; Aug. 11; Sept. 26; Nov. 2, 26, 27; Dec. 25.

1981   Jan. 4, 13, 23; Feb. 6; Mar. 21, 22, 24, 27; May 14, 24; June 8, 10, 25; July 23, 24; Aug. 21; Sept. 26; Nov. 8; Dec. 14, 15, 24, **25.**

5 ≏

1980   Jan. 25; Feb. 13; Mar. 25; Apr. 8; May 25; June 25, 26; July 19; Aug. 12; Sept. 27; Nov. 3, 28; Dec. 26.

1981   Jan. 5, 6, 14, 24; Feb. 7; Mar. 23, 25, 27; May 15, 25; June 8, 11, 12, 26; July 25; Aug. 22; Sept. 27; Nov. 9; Dec. 16, 17, **26** ,27.

6 ≏

1980   Jan. 26; Feb. 14; Mar. 26; Apr. 9; May 26; June 27; July 20, 21; Aug. 13; Sept. 28; Nov. 3, 29; Dec. 27.

1981   Jan. 7, 15, 25; Feb. 8; Mar. 24, 26, 28; May 16, 26; June 9, 13, 27; July 26, 27; Aug. 23; Sept. 28; Nov. 10; Dec. 18, 19, 20, 27, 28, 29, 30.

7 ≏

1980   Jan. 27; Feb. 15; Mar. 27; Apr. 10; May 27; June 28; July 22, 23; Aug. 14; Sept. 29; Nov. 4, 30; Dec. 1, 30.

1981   Jan. 8, 16, 26; Feb. 9; Mar. 25, 27, 29; May 17, 27; June 10, 14, 28; July 28; Aug. 23; Sept 29; Nov. 11; Dec. 21, 22, 23, 28, 31.

8 ≏

1980   Jan. 28; Feb. 16; Mar. 28; Apr. 11; May 28; June 29; July 24; Aug. 15; Sept. 30; Nov. 5; Dec. 2, 31

1981   Jan. 9, 17, 27; Feb. 10; Mar. 26, 27, 28, 30; May 17, 28, 29; June 11, 15, 16, 29; July 29, 30; Aug. 24; Sept. 30; Nov. 12; Dec. 24, 25, 26, 27, 28, **29**, 30, 31.

9 ≏

1980   Jan. 29; Feb. 17; Mar. 29; Apr. 12; May 29; June 30; July 25, 26; Aug. 16; Oct. 1; Nov. 6; Dec. 3.

1981   Jan. 10, 11, 17, 28; Feb. 10; Mar. 28, 29, 31; May 18, 30; June 12, 17, 30; July 31; Aug. 25; Oct 1; Nov. 13; Dec. 30.

10 ≏

1980   Jan. 30; Feb. 17; Mar. 30; Apr. 13; May 30; July 1, 27, 28; Aug. 17, 18; Oct. 2; Nov. 7; Dec. 4.

1981   Jan. 12, 18, 29; Feb. 11; Mar. 29, 30, 31; May 19, 31; June 12, 18, 19; July 1; Aug. 1, 2, 26; Oct. 2; Nov. 14; Dec. 31.

11 ≏

1980   Jan. 1, 31; Feb. 18; Mar. 31; Apr. 14, 15; May 31; July 2, 29; Aug. 19; Oct. 3; Nov. 8; Dec. 5, 6.

1981   Jan. 1, 13, 19, 30; Feb. 12; Mar. 30. **31**; Apr. 1; May 20; Jun 1, 13, 20; July 2; Aug. 3, 27; Oct. 3; Nov. 15, 16.

12 ♎
1980   Jan. 2; Feb. 1, 19; Apr. 1, 16; June 1; July 3, 30 31; Aug. 20; Oct. 4; Nov. 8; Dec. 7.

1981   Jan. 1, 14, 20, 31; Feb. 13; Apr. **1,** 2; May 21; June 2, 14, 21, 22; July 3; Aug. 4, 5, 28; Oct. 4; Nov. 17.

13 ♎
1980   Jan. 3; Feb. 2, 20; Apr. 2, 17; June 2; July 4; Aug. 1, 2, 21; Oct. 5; Nov. 9; Dec. 8.

1981   Jan. 2, 15, 16, 21; Feb. 1, 14; Apr. **2,** 3; May 21; June 3, 15, 23; July 4; Aug. 6, 29; Oct. 5; Nov. 18.

14 ♎
1980   Jan. 4; Feb. 3, 21; Apr. 3, 18; June 3, 4; July 5; Aug. 3, 22; Oct. 6; Nov. 10; Dec. 9. 10.

1981   Jan. 3, 17, 21; Feb. 2, 14. Apr. **, 3, 4;** May 22; June 4, 16, 24; July 5; Aug. 7, 8, 29; Oct. 6; Nov. 19.

15 ♎
1980   Jan. 5; Feb. 4, 22; Apr. 4, 19; June 5; July 6; Aug. 4, 5, 23; Oct. 7; Nov. 11; Dec. II.

1981   Jan. 4, 18, 22; Feb. 3, 15; Apr. **4,** 5; May 23; June 5, 17, 25, 26; July 6; Aug. 9, 30; Oct. 7; Nov. 20.

16 ♎
1980   Jan. 6; Feb. 5, 23; Apr. 5, 20; June 6, 29, 30; July 1, 2, 3, 4, 5, 6, **7,** 8, 9, 10, 11, 12; Aug. 6, 7, 24; Oct. 8; Nov. 12; Dec. 12.

1981   Jan. 5, 19, 20, 23; Feb. 4, 16; Apr. **5,** 6; May 24; June 6, 17, 27; July 7; Aug. 10, 11, 31; Oct. 8; Nov. 21.

17 ♎
1980   Jan. 7; Feb. 6, 23; Apr. 6, 21, 22; June 7, 26, 27, 28; July 8, 13, 14, 15; Aug. 8; 25; Oct. 9; Nov. 12; Dec. 13, 14.

1981   Jan. 6, 21, 24; Feb. 5, 17; Apr. **6,** 7; May 25; June 7, 18, 28, 29; July 8; Aug. 12; Sept. 1; Oct. 9; Nov. 22.

18 ♎
1980   Jan. 8; Feb. 7, 24; Apr. 7, 23; June 8, 24, 25; July 9, 16, 17, 18; Aug. 9, 10, 26; Oct. 10; Nov. 13; Dec. 15.

1981   Jan. 7, 22, 25; Feb. 6, 18; Apr. **7,** 8, 9; May 25; June 8, 19, 30; July 9; Aug. 13, 14; Sept. 2; Oct. 10; Nov. 23.

19 ♎

1980   Jan. 9; Feb. 8, 25; Apr. 8, 24; June 9, 22, 23; July 10, 19, 20; Aug. 11, 12, 27; Oct. 11; Nov. 14; Dec. 19.

1981   Jan. 8, 23, 25; Feb. 7, 18; Apr. **8,** 10; May 26; June 9, 20; July 1, 2, 10; Aug. 15, 16; Sept. 3; Oct. 11; Nov. 24.

20 ♎

1980   Jan. 10; Feb. 9, 26; Apr. 9, 25, 26; June 10, 20, 21; July 11, 21, 22; Aug. 13, 28; Oct. 12; Nov. 15; Dec. 17.

1981   Jan. 9, 24, 25, 26; Feb. 8, 19; Apr. 8, 9, 11; May 27; June 10, 21; July 3, 11, 12; Aug. 17; Sept. 3; Oct. 12; Nov. 25.

21 ♎

1980   Jan. 11; Feb. 10. 27; Apr. 10, 27; June 11, 18, 19; July 12, 23, 24; Aug. 14, 15, 29; Oct. 13; Nov. 16; Dec. 18, 19.

1981   Jan. 10, 26, 27; Feb. 9, 20; Apr. 9, 10, 12, 13; May 28; June 11, 21; July 4, 5, 13; Aug. 18, 19; Sept. 4; Oct. 13; Nov. 26, 27.

22 ♎

1980   Jan. 12; Feb. 11, 28; Apr. 11, 28; June 12, 16, 17; July 13, 25, 26; Aug. 16, 30; Oct. 14; Nov. 17; Dec. 20.

1981   Jan. 11, 27, 28; Feb. 10, 21; Apr. 10, 11, 14; May 29; June 12, 22; July 6, 14; Aug. 20; Sept. 5; Oct. 14; Nov. 28.

23 ♎

1980   Jan. 13; Feb. 12, 29; Apr. 12, 29, 30; June 13, 15; July 14, 27; Aug. 17, 18, 31; Oct. 15; Nov. 17; Dec. 21.

1981   Jan. 12, 28, 29; Feb. 11, 22; Apr. 11, 12, 15; May 30; June 13, 23; July 7, 8, 15; Aug. 21, 22; Sept. 6; Oct. 15, 16; Nov. 29.

24 ♎

1980   Jan. 14; Feb. 13; Mar. 1; Apr. 13; May 1; June 13, **14;** July 15, 28, 29; Aug. 19; Sept. 1; Oct. 16; Nov. 18; Dec. 22, 23.

1981   Jan. 13, **29,** 30; Feb. 12, 22; Apr. 12, 13, 16, 17; May 30; June 14, 24; July 9, 16; Aug. 23; Sept. 7; Oct. 16; Nov. 30.

25 ♎

1980   Jan. 15; Feb. 14; Mar. 1; Apr. 14; May 2, 3; June 12, 15; July 16, 17, 30; Aug. 20, 21; Sept. 2; Oct. 17; Nov. 19; Dec. 24.

1981   Jan. 14, 30. 31; Feb. 13, 23; Apr. 12, 14, 18, May 31; June 15, 25; July 10, 17; Aug. 24, 25; Sept. 8; Oct. 17; Dec. 1.

26 ♎

1980 Jan. 16; Feb. 15; Mar. 2; Apr. 15; May 4, 5; June 10, 11, 16; July 18, 31; Aug. 1, 22, 23; Sept. 3; Oct. 18; Nov. 20; Dec. 25.

1981 Jan. 15, 31; Feb. 1, 14, 24; Apr. 13, 15, 19; June 1, 16, 26; July 11, 12, 18; Aug. 26; Sept. 9; Oct. 18; Dec. 2, 3.

27 ♎

1980 Jan. 17; Feb. 16; Mar. 3; Apr. 16; May 6, 7; June 8, 9, 17; July 19; Aug. 2, 24; Sept. 4; Oct. 19; Nov. 21; Dec. 26.

1981 Jan. 16; Feb. 1, 2, 15, 25; Apr. 14, 16, 20, 21; June 2, 17, 26; July 13, 19; Aug. 27, 28; Sept. 9; Oct. 19, 20; Dec. 4.

28 ♎

1980 Jan. 18; Feb. 17; Mar. 4; Apr. 17; May 8; June 6, 7, 18; July 20; Aug. 3, 25, 26; Sept. 5; Oct. 20; Nov. 21; Dec. 27, 28.

1981 Jan. 17; Feb. 2, 3, 4, 16, 26; Apr. 15, 17, 22; June 3, 18, 27; July 14, 15, 20; Aug. 29; Sept. 10; Oct. 21; Dec. 5.

29 ♎

1980 Jan. 19; Feb. 18; Mar. 5; Apr. 18; May 9; June 4, 5, 19; July 21; Aug. 4, 5, 27; Sept. 6; Oct. 21; Nov. 22; Dec. 29.

1981 Jan. 18; Feb. 2, 5, 17, 26; Apr. 16, 18, 23; June 3, 19, 28; July 16, 21; Aug. 30, 31; Sept. 11; Oct. 22; Dec. 6, 7.

SCORPIO

0 ♏

1980 Jan. 15, 20; Feb. 19; Mar. 6; Apr. 19; May 2, 3, 12, 13, 14; June 20; July 22; Aug. 6, 28, 29; Sept. 7; Oct. 22; Nov. 23; Dec. 30.

1981 Jan. 19; Feb. 3, 6, 18, 27; Apr. 16, 19, 24, 25; June 4, 20, 21, 29; July 17, 18, 22; Sept. 1, 2, 12; Oct. 23, 24; Dec. 8.

1 ♏

1980 Jan. 16, 21; Feb. 19, Mar. 7; Apr. 20; May 15, 16, 17, 29, 30, 31; June 1, 21; July 23; Aug. 7, 30; Sept. 8; Oct. 23; Nov. 24; Dec. 31.

1981 Jan. 20; Feb. 4, 7, 19, 28; Apr. 17, 20, 26; June 5, 22, 30; July 19, 23; Sept. 3, 13; Oct. 24; Dec. 9, 10.

2 ♏

1980 Jan. 17, 22; Feb. 20; Mar. 8; Apr. 21; May 18, 19, 20, 21, 22, 23, 24, 25, 26, 27, 28; June 22; July 24; Aug. 8, 31; Sept 1, 9; Oct. 24; Nov. 25.

1981 Jan. 1, 2, 21; Feb. 5, 8, 9, 20; Mar. 1; Apr. 18, 21, 27; June 6, 23, 30; July 20, 21, 24; Sept. 4, 5, 14; Oct. 25; Dec. 11, 12.

3 ♏

1980 Jan. 18, 23; Feb. 21; Mar. 8; Apr. 22; June 23; July 25; Aug. 9, 10; Sept. 2, 10; Oct. 25; Nov. 25.

1981 Jan. 3, 22; Feb. 6, 10, 21; Mar. 2; Apr. 19, 22, 28, 29; June 7, 24; July 1, 22, 25; Sept. 6, 15; Oct. 26; Dec. 13.

4 ♏

1980 Jan. 18, 24; Feb. 22; Mar. 9; Apr. 23; June 24; July 26; Aug. 11; Sept. 3, 4, 11; Oct. 26; Nov. 26.

1981 Jan. 4. 23; Feb. 6, 11, 22; Mar. 2; Apr. 20, 23, 30; June 8, 25; July 2, 23, 24, 26; Sept. 7, 8, 15; Oct. 27; Dec. 14, 15.

5 ♏
1980   Jan. 19, 25; Feb. 23; Mar. 10; Apr. 24; June 25, 26; July 27; Aug. 12; Sept. 5, 11; Oct. 27; Nov. 27.

1981   Jan. 5, 6, 24; Feb. 7, 12, 13, 23; Mar. 3; Apr. 21, 24; May 1; June 8, 26; July 3, 25, 27; Sept. 9, 10, 16; Oct. 28; Dec. 16, 17.

6 ♏
1980   Jan. 20, 26; Feb. 24; Mar. 11; Apr. 25; June 27; July 28; Aug. 13; Sept. 6, 7, 12; Oct. 28; Nov. 28.

1981   Jan. 7, 25; Feb. 8, 14, 24; Mar. 4; Apr. 21, 25; May 2, 3; June 9, 27; July 4, 26, 27, 28; Sept. 11, 17; Oct. 29; Dec. 18, 19, 20.

7 ♏
1980   Jan. 21, 27; Feb. 25; Mar. 12; Apr. 26; June 28; July 29; Aug. 14; Sept. 8, 13; Oct. 29; Nov. 29.

1981   Jan. 8, 26; Feb. 9, 15, 25; Mar. 5; Apr. 22, 26; May 4; June 10, 28; July 5, 28, 29; Sept. 12, 13, 18; Oct. 30; Dec. 21, 22, 23,

8 ♏
1980   Jan. 22, 28; Feb. 26; Mar. 13; Apr. 27; June 29; July 30; Aug. 15; Sept. 9, 10, 14; Oct. 30; Nov. 30.

1981   Jan. 9, 27; Feb. 10, 16, 26; Mar. 6; Apr. 23, 27; May 5; June 11, 29; July 5, 29, **30,** Sept. 14, 19; Oct. 31; Dec. 24, 25, 26, 27, 28, 29, 30, 31.

9 ♏
1980   Jan. 23, 29; Feb. 27; Mar. 14; Apr. 28; June 30; July 31; Aug. 16; Sept. 11, 15; Oct. 31; Nov. 30.

1981   Jan. 10, 11, 28; Feb. 10, 17, 18, 27; Mar. 6; Apr. 24, 28; May 6, 7; June 12, 30; July 6, **31;** Sept. 15, 16, 20; Nov. 1.

10 ♏
1980   Jan. 23, 30; Feb. 28; Mar. 15; Apr. 29; July 1; Aug. 1, 17, 18; Sept. 12, 13, 16; Nov. 1; Dec. 1.

1981   Jan. 12, 29; Feb. 11, 19, 28; Mar. 7; Apr. 25, 29; May 8; June 12; July 1, 7; Aug. **1,** 2; Sept. 17, 18, 21; Nov. 2.

11 ♏
1980   Jan. 24, 31; Feb. 29; Mar. 16; Apr. 30; July 2; Aug. 2, 19; Sept. 14, 17; Nov. 2; Dec. 2.

1981   Jan. 13, 30; Feb. 12, 20; Mar. 1, 8; Apr. 25, 30; May 1, 9; June 13; July 2, 8; Aug. 2, **3;** Sept. 19, 21; Nov. 3.

12 ♏
1980   Jan. 25; Feb. 1; Mar. 1, 17; May 1; July 3; Aug. 3, 20; Sept. 15, 16, 18; Nov. 3; Dec. 3.

1981   Jan. 14, 31; Feb. 13, 21; Mar. 2, 9; Apr. 26; May 2, 10, 11; June 14; July 3, 9; Aug. 3, **4,** 5; Sept. 20, 21, 22; Nov. 4.

13 ♏
1980   Jan. 1, 26; Feb. 2; Mar. 2, 18; July 4; Aug. 4, 21; Sept. 17, 19; Nov. 4; Dec. 4.

1981   Jan. 15, 16; Feb. 1, 14, 22, 23; Mar. 3, 10; Apr. 27; May 3, 12; June 15; July 4, 10; Aug. 5, 6; Sept. 22, 23; Nov. 5.

14 ♏
1980   Jan. 2, 27; Feb. 3; Mar. 3, 18; May 3; July 5; Aug. 5, 22; Sept. 18, 19, 20; Nov. 5; Dec. 4.

1981   Jan. 17; Feb. 2, 14, 24; Mar. 4, 10; Apr. 28; May 4, 13, 14; June 16; July 5, 10; Aug. 6, 7, 8; Sept. 23, **24;** Nov. 6.

15 ♏
1980   Jan. 3, 27; Feb. 4; Mar. 4, 19; May 4; July 6; Aug. 6, 23; Sept. 20, 21; Nov. 6; Dec. 5.

1981   Jan. 18; Feb. 3, 15, 25; Mar. 5, 11; Apr. 29; May 5, 15; June 17; July 6, 11; Aug. 7, 9; Sept. **25,** 26; Nov. 7, 8.

16 ♏
·1980   Jan. 4, 28; Feb. 5; Mar. 5, 20; May 5; July 7; Aug. 7, 24; Sept. 21, **22;** Nov. 7; Dec. 6.

1981   Jan. 19, 20; Feb. 4, 16, 26; Mar. 6, 12; Apr. 29; May 6, 16; June 17; July 7, 12; Aug. 8, 10, 11; Sept. 26, 27; Nov. 8, 9.

17 ♏
1980   Jan. 5, 29; Feb. 6; Mar. 6, 21; May 6; July 8; Aug. 8, 9, 25; Sept. 22, 23; Nov. 8; Dec. 7.

1981   Jan. 21; Feb. 5, 17, 27, 28; Mar. 7, 13; Apr. 30; May 7, 17, 18; June 18; July 8, 13; Aug. 9, 12; Sept. 27, 28, 29; Nov. 9.

18 ♏
1980   Jan. 5, 30; Feb. 7; Mar. 7, 22; May 7; July 9; Aug. 10, 26; Sept. 23, 24, 25; Nov. 9; Dec. 8.

1981   Jan. 22; Feb. 6, 18; Mar. 1, 8, 14; May 1, 8, 19; June 19; July 9, 14; Aug. 10, 13, 14; Sept. 27, 30; Oct. 1; Nov. 10.

19 ♏
1980   Jan. 6, 31; Feb. 8; Mar. 8, 23; May 8, 9; July 10; Aug. 11, 27; Sept. 24, 26; Nov. 10; Dec. 8.

1981   Jan. 23; Feb. 7, 18; Mar. 2, 9, 14; May 2, 9, 20; June 20; July 10, 14; Aug. 11, 15, 16; Sept. 28; Oct. 2; Nov. 10.

20 ♏
1980   Jan. 7; Feb. 1, 9; Mar. 9, 24; May 10; July 11; Aug. 12, 28; Sept. 25, 27; Nov. 11; Dec. 9.

1981   Jan. 24, 25; Feb. 8, 19; Mar. 3, 4, 10, 15; May 3, 10, 21; June 21; July 11, 12, 15; Aug. 12, 17; Sept. 29; Oct. 3, 4; Nov. 11.

21 ♏
1980   Jan. 8; Feb. 1, 10; Mar. 10, 25; May 11; July 12; Aug. 13, 29; Sept. 26, 28, 29; Nov. 12; Dec. 10.

1981   Jan. 26; Feb. 9, 20; Mar. 5, 11, 16; May 4, 11, 23; June 21; July 13, 16; Aug. 13, 18, 19; Sept. 30; Oct. 5, 6; Nov. 12.

22 ♏
1980   Jan. 9; Feb. 2, 11; Mar. 11, 26; May 12; July 13; Aug. 14, 30; Sept. 27, 30; Nov. 13; Dec. 11.

1981   Jan. 27; Feb. 10, 21; Mar. 6, 12, 17; May 4, 12, 24; June 22; July 14, 17; Aug. 14, 20; Oct. 1, 7; Nov. 13.

23 ♏
1980   Jan. 9; Feb. 3, 12; Mar. 12, 27; May 13; July 14; Aug. 15, 31; Sept. 28; Oct. 1, 2; Nov. 14; Dec. 12.

1981   Jan. 28; Feb. 11, 22; Mar. 7, 13, 18; May 5, 13, 25, 26; June 23; July 15, 18; Aug. 15, 21, 22; Oct. 2, 8, 9; Nov. 14.

24 ♏
1980   Jan. 10; Feb. 4, 13; Mar. 13, 28; May 14; July 15; Aug. 16; Sept. 1, 29; Oct. 3; Nov. 15; Dec. 12.

1981   Jan. 29, 30; Feb. 12, 22; Mar. 8, 9, 14, 18; May 6, 14, 27; June 24; July 16, 19; Aug. 16, 23; Oct. 3, 10, 11; Nov. 15.

25 ♏
1980   Jan. 11; Feb. 5, 14; Mar. 14, 29; Apr. 1, 2, 3, 4, 5, 6, 7, 8, 9; May 15; July 16, 17; Aug. 17; Sept. 2, 30; Oct. 4, 5; Nov. 16; Dec. 13.

1981   Jan. 31; Feb. 13, 23; Mar. 10, 15, 19; May 7, 15, 28, 29; June 25; July 17, 19; Aug. 17, 24, 25; Oct. 4, 12; Nov. 16.

26 ♏

1980   Jan. 12; Feb. 6, 15; Mar. 15, 23, 25, 26, 27, 28, 29, **30,** 31; Apr. 10, 11, 12, 13, 14, 15, 16, 17, 18; May 16; July 18; Aug. 18; Sept. 3, 30; Oct. 6; Nov. 17; Dec. 14.

1981   Feb. 1, 14, 24; Mar. 11, 16, 20; May 8, 16, 30; June 26; July 18, 20; Aug. 18, 26; Oct. 4, 13, 14; Nov. 17.

27 ♏

1980   Jan. 13; Feb. 6, 16; Mar. 16, 18, 19, 20, 21, 22, 31; Apr. 19, 20, 21, 22, 23, 24; May 17; July 19; Aug. 19; Sept. 4; Oct. 1, 7; Nov. 18; Dec. 15.

1981   Feb. 2, 15, 25; Mar. 12, 13, 17, 21; May 8, 17, 31; June 26; July 19, 21; Aug. 19, 27, 28; Oct. 5, 15, 16; Nov. 18.

28 ♏

1980   Jan. 14; Feb. 7, 17; Mar. 14, 15, 16, **17;** Apr. 1, 25, 26, 27, 28; May 18; July 20; Aug. 20; Sept. 5; Oct. 2, 8, 9; Nov. 19; Dec. 16.

1981   Feb. 3, 4, 16, 26; Mar. 14, 18, 22; May 9, 18; June 1, 2, 27; July 20, 22; Aug. 20, 29; Oct. 6, 17; Nov. 19.

29 ♏

1980   Jan. 14; Feb. 8, 18; Mar. 11, 12, 13, 18; Apr. 2, 29, 30; May 1, 2, 19; July 21; Aug. 21; Sept. 6; Oct. 10, 13; Nov. 20; Dec. 16.

1981   Feb. 5, 17, 26; Mar. 15, 19, 23; May 10, 19; June 3, 28; July 21, 23; Aug. 21, 30 31; Oct. 7, 18, 19; Nov. 20.

SAGITTARIUS

0 ↗
1980   Jan. 15; Feb. 9, 19; Mar. 8, 9, 10, 19; Apr. 3; May 3, 4, 5, 6, 20; July 22; Aug. 22; Sept. 7; Oct. 4, 11, 12; Nov. 21; Dec. 17.

1981   Feb. 6, 18, 27; Mar. 16, 20, 23; May 11, 20; June 4, 5, 29; July 22, 24; Aug. 22; Sept. 1, 2; Oct. 8, 20, 21; Nov. 21.

1 ↗
1980   Jan. 16; Feb. 10, 19; Mar. 5, 6, 7, 20; Apr. 4; May 7, 8, 9, 21; July 23; Aug. 23; Sept. 8; Oct. 5, 13; Nov. 22; Dec. 18.

1980   Feb. 7, 19, 28; Mar. 17, 18, 21, 24; May 12, 21; June 6, 30; July 23, 24; Aug. 23; Sept. 3; Oct. 9, 22; Nov. 22.

2 ↗
1980   Jan. 17; Feb. 11, 20; Mar. 2, 3, 4, 21; Apr. 5; May 10, 11, 12, 22; July 24; Aug. 24; Sept. 9; Oct. 6, 14; Nov. 23; Dec. 19.

1981   Feb. 8, 9, 20; Mar. 1, 19, 22, 25; May 12, 22; June 7, 30; July 24, 25; Aug 24; Sept. 4, 5; Oct. 10, 23, 24; Nov. 23.

3 ↗
1980   Jan. 18; Feb. 12, 21, 29; Mar. 1, 22; Apr. 6; May 13, 14, 15, 23; July 25; Aug. 25; Sept. 10; Oct. 7, 15, 16; Nov. 24; Dec. 20.

1981   Feb. 10, 21; Mar. 2, 20, 23, 26; May 13, 23; June 8, 9; July 1, 25, 26; Aug. 25; Sept. 6; Oct. 11, 25, 26; Nov. 24.

4 ↗
1980   Jan. 18; Feb. 12, 22, 26, 27, 28; Mar. 23, 24; Apr. 7; May 16, 17, 24; July 26; Aug. 26; Sept. 11; Oct. 7, 17; Nov. 25; Dec. 20.

1981   Feb. 11, 22; Mar. 2, 21, 22, 24, 27; May 14, 24; June 10; July 2, 26, 27; Aug. 26; Sept. 7, 8; Oct. 12, 27, 28; Nov. 25

293

5 ♐

1980   Jan. 19; Feb. 13, 23, 24, 25; Mar. 25; Apr. 8; May 18, 19, 20, 25; July 27; Aug. 27; Sept. 11; Oct. 8, 18, 19; Nov. 26; Dec. 21.

1981   Feb. 12, 13, 23; Mar. 3, 23, 25, 27; May 15, 25; June 11, 12; July 3, 27, 28; Aug. 27; Sept. 9, 10; Oct. 12, 29; Nov. 26.

6 ♐

1980   Jan. 20; Feb. 14, 21, 22, 23, 24; Mar. 26; Apr. 9; May 21, 22, 23, 26; July 28; Aug. 28; Sept. 12; Oct. 9, 20; Nov. 27; Dec. 22.

1981   Feb. 14, 24; Mar. 4, 24, 26, 28; May 16, 26; June 13; July 4, 28, 29; Aug. 28; Sept. 11; Oct. 13, 30, 31; Nov. 27.

7 ♐

1980   Jan. 21; Feb. 15, 19, 20, 25; Mar. 27; Apr. 10; May 24, 25, 27; July 29; Aug. 29; Sept. 13; Oct. 10, 21; Nov. 28; Dec. 23.

1981   Feb. 15, 25; Mar. 5, 25, 27, 29; May 17, 27; June 14; July 5, **29**; Aug. 29, 30; Sept. 12, 13; Oct. 14; Nov. 1, 2, 28.

8 ♐

1980   Jan. 22; Feb. **16**, 17, 18, 26; Mar. 28; Apr. 11; May 26, 27, 28; July 30; Aug. 30; Sept. 14; Oct. 11, 22, 23; Nov. 29; Dec. 24.

1981   Feb. 16, 26; Mar. 6, 26, 27, 28, 30; May 17, 28, 29; June 15, 16; July 5, **30**; Aug. 31; Sept. 14; Oct. 15; Nov. 3, 4, 29.

9 ♐

1980   Jan. 23; Feb. 13, 14, 15, 17, 27; Mar. 29; Apr. 12; May 28, **29**, 30; July 31; Aug. 31; Sept. 15; Oct. 12, 24; Nov. 30; Dec. 24.

1981   Feb. 17, 18, 27; Mar. 6, 28, 29, 31; May 18, 30; June 17; July 6, **31**; Sept. 1, 15, 16; Oct. 16, Nov. 5, 6, 30.

10 ♐

1980   Jan. 23; Feb. 10, 11, 12, 17, 28; Mar. 30; Apr. 13; May 30, 31; June 1; Aug. 1; Sept. 1, 16; Oct. 13, 25, 26; Dec. 1, 25.

1981   Feb. 19, 28; Mar. 7, 29, 30, 31; May 19, 31; June 18, 19; July 7; Aug. **1**; Sept. 2, 17, 18; Oct. 17, Nov. 7; Dec. 1.

11 ♐

1980   Jan. 24; Feb. 7, 8, 9, 18, 29; Mar. 31; Apr. 14, 15; May 31; June 2, 3; Aug. 2; Sept. 2, 17; Oct. 13, 27; Dec. 2, 26.

1981   Feb. 20; Mar. 1, 8, 30, **31**; Apr. 1; May 20; June 1, 20; July 8; Aug. **2**; Sept. 3, 19; Oct. 18; Nov. 8, 9; Dec. 2.

12 ♐
1980   Jan. 25; Feb. 3, 4, 5, 6, 19; Mar. 1; Apr. 1, 16; June 1, 4, 5, 6; Aug. 3; Sept. 3, 18; Oct. 14, 28; Dec. 3, 27.

1981   Feb. 21; Mar. 2, 9; Apr. **1**, 2; May 21; June 2, 21, 22; July 9; Aug. **3**, 4; Sept. 4, 20, 21; Oct. 19; Nov. 10, 11; Dec. 3.

13 ♐
1980   Jan. 26, 30, 31; Feb. 1, 2, 20; Mar. 2; Apr. 2, 17; June 2, 7, 8; Aug. 4; Sept. 4, 19; Oct. 15, 29, 30; Dec. 4, 28.

1981   Feb. 22, 23; Mar. 3, 10; Apr. **2**, 3; May 21; June 3, 23; July 10; Aug. 3, 5; Sept. 5, 22; Oct. 20, Nov. 12, 13; Dec. 4.

14 ♐
1980   Jan. 1, 2, 3, 4, 5, 6, 7, 23, 24, 25, 26, **27**, 28, 29; Feb. 21; Mar. 3; Apr. 3, 18; June 3, 4, 9, 10; Aug. 5; Sept. 5, 6, 20; Oct. 16, 31; Dec. 5, 28.

1981   Feb. 24; Mar. 4, 10; Apr. **3, 4**; May 22; June 4, 24; July 10; Aug. 4, 6; Sept. 6, 23, 24; Oct. 21; Nov. 14, 15; Dec. 5

15 ♐
1980   Jan. 8, 9, 10, 11, 12, 13, 14, 15, 16, 17, 18, 19, 20, 21, 22, 27; Feb. 22; Mar. 4; Apr. 4, 19; June 5, 11, 12; Aug. 6; Sept. 6, 7, 21; Oct. 17; Nov. 1; Dec. 6, 29.

1981   Feb. 25; Mar. 5, 11, Apr. **4**, 5; May 23; June 5, 25, 26; July 11; Aug. 5, 7; Sept. 7, 25, 26; Oct. 21; Nov. 16; Dec. 6.

16 ♐
1980   Jan. 28; Feb. 23; Mar. 5; Apr. 5, 20; June 6, 13, 14, 29, 30; July 1, 2, 3, 4, 5, 6, 7, 8, 9, 10, 11, 12; Aug. 7; Sept. 8, 22; Oct. 18; Nov. 2, 3; Dec. 7, 30.

1981   Feb. 26; Mar. 6, 12; Apr. **5**, 6; May 24; June 6, 27; July 12; Aug. 6, 8; Sept. 8, 27; Oct. 22; Nov. 17, 18; Dec. 7.

17 ♐
1980   Jan. 29; Feb. 23; Mar. 6; Apr. 6, 21, 22; June 7, 15, 16, 26, 27, 28; July 13, 14, 15; Aug. 8, 9; Sept. 9, 22; Oct. 19; Nov. 4; Dec. 8, 31.

1981   Feb. 27, 28; Mar. 7, 13; Apr. **6**, 7; May 25; June 7, 28, 29; July 13; Aug. 7, 9; Sept. 9, 28, 29; Oc.t 23; Nov. 19, 20; Dec. 8.

18 ♐

1980   Jan. 30; Feb. 24; Mar. 7; Apr. 7, 23; June 8, 17, 18, 24, 25; July 16, 17, 18; Aug. 10; Sept. 10, 23; Oct. 19; Nov. 5; Dec. 9.

1981   Jan. 1; Mar. 1, 8, 14; Apr. **7**, 8, 9; May 25; June 8, 30; July 14; Aug. 8, 10; Sept. 10, 30; Oct. 1, 24; Nov. 21, 22; Dec. 9

19 ♐

1980   Jan. 31; Feb. 25; Mar. 8; Apr. 8, 24; June 9, 19, 20, 22, 23; July 19, 20; Aug. 11; Sept. 11, 24; Oct. 20; Nov. 6, 7; Dec. 10.

1981   Jan. 1; Mar. 2, 9, 14; Apr. **8**, 10; May 26; June 9; July 1, 2, 14; Aug. 8, 11; Sept. 11; Oct. 2, 25; Nov. 23, 24; Dec. 10.

20 ♐

1980   Feb. 1, 26; Mar. 9; Apr. 9, 25, 26; June 10, 20, 21, 22; July 21, 22; Aug. 12; Sept. 12, 25; Oct. 21; Nov. 8; Dec. 11.

1981   Jan. 2; Mar. 3, 4, 10, 15; Apr. 8, 9, 11; May 27; June 10; July 3, 15; Aug. 9, 12; Sept. 12; Oct. 3, 4, 26; Nov. 25, 26; Dec. 11.

21 ♐

1980   Feb. 1, 27; Mar. 10; Apr. 10, 27; June 11, 18, 19, 23, 24; July 23, 24; Aug. 13; Sept. 13, 26; Oct. 22; Nov. 9; Dec. 12.

1981   Jan. 3; Mar. 5, 11, 16; Apr. 9, 10, 12, 13; May 28; June 11; July 4, 5, 16; Aug. 10, 13; Sept. 13; Oct. 5, 6, 27; Nov. 27, 28; Dec. 12.

22 ♐

1980   Feb. 2, 28; Mar. 11; Apr. 11, 28; June 12, 16, 17, 25, 26; July 25, 26; Aug. 14; Sept. 14, 27; Oct. 23; Nov. 10, 11; Dec. 13.

1981   Jan. 4; Mar. 6, 12, 17; Apr. 10, 11, 14; May 29; June 12; July 6, 17; Aug. 11, 14; Sept. 14; Oct.7, 28; Nov. 29, 30; Dec. 13.

23 ♐

1980   Feb. 3, 29; Mar. 12; Apr. 12, 29, 30; June 13, 15, 27, 28; July 27; Aug. 15; Sept. 15, 18; Oct. 24; Nov. 12; Dec. 14.

1981   Jan. 5; Mar. 7, 13, 18; Apr. 11, 12, 15; May 30; June 13; July 7, 8, 18; Aug. 12, 15; Sept. 15; Oct. 8, 9, 29; Dec. 1, 2, 14.

24 ♐

1980   Feb. 4; Mar. 1, 13; Apr. 13; May 1; June 13, **14**, 29, 30; July 28, 29; Aug. 16; Sept. 16, 29; Oct. 24; Nov. 13; Dec. 15.

1981   Jan. 5; Mar. 8, 9, 14, 18; Apr. 12, 13, 16, 17; May 30; June 14; July 9, 19; Aug. 13, 16; Sept. 16; Oct. 10, 11, 30; Dec. 3, 4, 15.

25 ♐

1980 Feb. 5; Mar. 1, 14; Apr. 1, 2, 3, 4, 5, 6, 7, 8, 9, 14; May 2, 3; June 12, 15; July 1, 30; Aug. 17; Sept. 17, 30; Oct. 25; Nov. 14, 15; Dec. 16.

1981 Jan. 6; Mar. 10, 15, 19; Apr. 12, 14, 18; May 31; June 15; July 10, 19; Aug. 13, 17; Sept. 17; Oct. 12, 31; Dec. 5, 6, 16.

26 ♐

1980 Feb. 6; Mar. 2, 15, 23, 24, 25, 26, 27, 28, 29, 30, 31; Apr. 10, 11, 12, 13, 14, **15**, 16, 17, 18; May 4, 5; June 10, 11, 16; July 2, 3, 31; Aug. 1, 18; Sept. 18, 30; Oct. 26; Nov. 16; Dec. 17.

1981 Jan. 7; Mar. 11, 16, 20; Apr. 13, 15, 19; June 1, 16; July 11, 12, 20; Aug. 14, 18; Sept. 18; Oct. 13, 14; Nov. 1; Dec. 7, 8.

27 ♐

1980 Feb. 6; Mar. 3, 16, 18, 19, 20, 21, 22; Apr. 16, 19, 20, 21, 22, 23, 24; May 6, 7; June 8, 9, 17; July 4, 5; Aug. 2, 19; Sept. 19; Oct. 1, 27; Nov. 17; Dec. 18.

1981 Jan. 8; Mar. 12, 13, 17, 21; Apr. 14, 16, 20, 21; June 2, 17; July 13, 21; Aug. 15, 19; Sept. 19; Oct. 15, 16; Nov. 2; Dec. 9, 10, 18.

28 ♐

1980 Feb. 7; Mar. 4, 14, 15, 16, **17**; Apr. 17, 25, 26, 27, 28; May 8, 9; June 6, 7, 18; July 6, 7; Aug. 3, 20; Sept. 20; Oct. 2, 28; Nov. 18, 19; Dec. 19.

1981 Jan. 9; Mar. 14, 18, 22; Apr. 15, 17, 22; June 3, 18; July 14, 15, 22; Aug. 16, 20; Sept. 20; Oct. 17; Nov. 3; Dec. 11, 12, 19.

29 ♐

1980 Feb. 8; Mar. 5, 11, 12, 13, 18; Apr. 18, 29, 30; May 1, 2, 10, 11; June 4, 5, 19; July 8, 9; Aug. 4, 5, 21; Sept. 21; Oct. 3, 29; Nov. 20; Dec. 20.

1981 Jan. 9; Mar. 15, 19, 23; Apr. 16, 18, 23; June 3, 19; July 16, 23; Aug. 17, 21; Sept. 21; Oct. 18, 19; Nov. 4; Dec. 13, 14, 20.

CAPRICORN

0 ♑

1980 Feb. 9; Mar. 6, 8, 9, 10, 19; Apr. 19; May 3, 4, 5, 6, 12, 13, 14; June 2, 3, 20; July 10, 11; Aug. 6, 22; Sept. 22; Oct. 4, 29; Nov. 21; Dec. 21.

1981 Jan. 10; Mar. 16, 20, 23; Apr. 16, 19, 24, 25; June 4, 20, 21; July 17, 18, 24; Aug. 18, 22; Sept. 22; Oct. 20, 21; Nov. 5; Dec. 15, 16, 21.

1 ♑

1980 Feb. 10; Mar. 5, 6, 7, 20; Apr. 20; May 7, 8, 9, 15, 16, 17, 29, 30, 31; June 21; July 12; Aug. 7, 23; Sept. 23; Oct. 5, 30; Nov. 22, 23; Dec. 22.

1981 Jan. 11; Mar. 17, 18, 21, 24; Apr. 17, 20, 26; June 5, 22; July 19, 24; Aug. 18, 23; Sept. 23; Oct. 22; Nov. 5; Dec. 17, 18, 22.

2 ♑

1980 Feb. 11; Mar. 2, 3, 4, 8, 21; Apr. 21; May 10, 11, 12, 18, 19, 20, 21, 22, 23, 24, 25, 26, 27, 28; June 22; July 13, 14; Aug. 8, 24; Sept. 24; Oct. 6, 31; Nov. 24; Dec. 23.

1981 Jan. 12; Mar. 19, 22, 25; Apr. 18, 21, 27; June 6, 23; July 20, 21, 25; Aug. 19, 24; Sept. 24; Oct. 23, 24; Nov. 6; Dec. 19, 20, 21, 23.

3 ♑

1980 Feb. 12, 29; Mar. 1, 8, 22; Apr. 22; May 13, 14, 15; June 23; July 15, 16; Aug. 9, 19, 25; Sept. 25; Oct. 7; Nov. 1, 25; Dec. 24.

1981 Jan. 13; Mar. 20, 23, 26; Apr. 19, 22, 28, 29; June 7, 24; July 22, 26; Aug. 20, 25; Sept. 25; Oct. 25, 26; Nov. 7; Dec. 22, 23, 24.

4 ♑

1980 Feb. 12, 26, 27, 28; Mar. 9, 23, 24; Apr. 23; May 16, 17; June 24; July 17, 18; Aug. 11, 26; Sept. 26; Oct. 7; Nov. 2, 26, 27; Dec. 25.

1981 Jan. 13; Mar. 21, 22, 24, 27; Apr. 20, 23, 30; June 8, 25; July 23, 24, 27; Aug. 21, 26; Sept. 26; Oct. 27, 28; Nov. 8; Dec. 24, **25**.

5 ♑

1980   Feb. 13, 24, 25; Mar. 10, 25; Apr. 24; May 18, 19, 20; June 25, 26; July 19; Aug. 12, 27; Sept. 27; Oct. 8; Nov. 3, 28; Dec. 26.

1981   Jan. 14; Mar. 23, 25, 27; Apr. 21, 24; May 1; June 8, 26; July 25, 28; Aug. 22, 27; Sept. 27; Oct. 29; Nov. 9; Dec. **26**, 27.

6 ♑

1980   Feb. 14, 21, 22, 23; Mar. 11, 26; Apr. 25; May 21, 22, 23; June 27; July 20, 21; Aug. 13, 28; Sept. 28; Oct. 9; Nov. 3, 29; Dec. 27.

1981   Jan. 15; Mar. 24, 26, 28; Apr. 21, 25; May 2, 3; June 9, 27; July 26, 27, 29; Aug. 23, 28; Sept. 28; Oct. 30, 31; Nov. 10; Dec. 27, 28, 29.

7 ♑

1980   Feb. 15, 19, 20; Mar. 12, 27; Apr. 26; May 24, 25; June 28; July 22, 23; Aug. 14, 29; Sept. 29; Oct. 10; Nov. 4, 30; Dec. 1, 28.

1981   Jan. 16; Mar. 25, 27, 29; Apr. 22, 26; May 4; June 10, 28; July 28, 29; Aug. 23, 29, 30; Sept. 29; Nov. 1, 2, 11; Dec. 28, 30, 31.

8 ♑

1980   Feb. **16**, 17, 18; Mar. 13, 28; Apr. 27; May 26, 27; June 29; July 24; Aug. 15, 30; Sept. 30; Oct. 11, Nov. 5; Dec. 2, 29.

1981   Jan. 17; Mar. 26, 27, 28, 30; Apr. 23, 27; May 5; June 11, 29; July 29, **30**; Aug. 24, 31; Sept. 30; Nov. 3, 4, 12; Dec. 29.

9 ♑

1980   Feb. 13, 14, 15, 17; Mar. 14, 29; Apr. 28; May 28, 29, 30; June 30; July 25, 26; Aug. 16, 31; Oct. 1, 12; Nov. 6; Dec. 3, 30.

1981   Jan. 17; Mar. 28, 29, 31; Apr. 24, 28; May 6, 7; June 12, 30; July **31**; Aug. 25; Sept. 1; Oct. 1; Nov. 5, 6, 13; Dec. 30.

10♑

1980   Feb. 10, 11, 12, 17; Mar. 15, 30; Apr. 29; May 31; June 1; July 1, 27, 28; Aug. 17, 18; Sept. 1; Oct. 2, 13; Nov. 7; Dec. 4, 31.

1981   Jan. 18; Mar. 29, 30, 31; Apr. 25, 29; May 8; June 12; July 1; Aug. **1**, 2, 26; Sept. 2; Oct. 2; Nov. 7, 14; Dec. 31.

11♑

1980   Jan. 1; Feb. 7, 8, 9, 18; Mar. 16, 31; Apr. 30; June 2, 3; July 2, 29; Aug. 19; Sept. 2; Oct. 3, 13; Nov. 8; Dec. 5, 6.

1981   Jan. 1, 19; Mar. 30, **31**; Apr. 1, 25, 30; May 1, 9; June 13, July 2; Aug. 2, 3, 27; Sept. 3; Oct. 3; Nov. 8, 9, 15, 16.

12♑

1980   Jan. 2; Feb. 3, 4, 5, 6, 19; Mar. 17; Apr. 1; May 1; June 4, 5, 6; July 3, 30, 31; Aug. 20; Sept. 3; Oct. 4, 14; Nov. 8; Dec. 7.

1981   Jan. 1, 20, Apr. **1**, 2, 26; May 2, 10, 11; June 14; July 3; Aug. 3, 4, 5, 28; Sept. 4; Oct. 4; Nov. 10, 11, 17.

13♑

1980   Jan. 3, 30, 31; Feb. 1, 2, 20; Mar. 18; Apr. 2; May 2; June 7, 8; July 4; Aug. 1, 2, 21; Sept. 4; Oct. 5, 15; Nov. 9; Dec. 8.

1981   Jan. 2, 21; Apr. **2**, 3, 27; May 3, 12; June 15; July 4; Aug. 3, 6, 29; Sept. 5; Oct. 5; Nov. 12, 13, 18.

14 ♑

1980   Jan. 1, 2, 3, **4,**5, 6, 7, 23, 24, 25, 26, 27, 28, 29; Feb. 21; Mar. 18; Apr. 3; May 3; June 9, 10; July 5; Aug. 3, 22; Sept. 5; Oct. 6, 16; Nov. 10; Dec. 9, 10.

1981   Jan. 3, 21; Apr. **3, 4,** 28; May 4, 13, 14; June 16; July 5; Aug. 4, 7, 8, 29; Sept. 6; Oct. 6; Nov. 14, 15, 19.

15 ♑

1980   Jan. 5, 8, 9, 10, 11, 12, 13, 14, 15, 16, 17, 18, 19, 19, 21, 22; Feb. 22; Mar. 19; Apr. 4; May 4; June 11, 12; July 6; Aug. 4, 5, 23; Sept. 6, 7; Oct. 7, 17; Nov. 11; Dec. 11

1981   Jan. 4, 22; Apr. **4**, 5, 29; May 5, 15; June 17; July 6; Aug. 5, 9, 30; Sept. 7; Oct. 7; Nov. 16, 20.

16♑

1980   Jan. 6; Feb. 23; Mar. 20; Apr. 5; May 5; June 13, 14; July 7; Aug. 6, 7, 24; Sept. 8; Oct. 8, 18; Nov. 12; Dec. 12

1981   Jan. 5, 23; Apr. **5**, 6, 29; May 6, 16; June 17; July 7; Aug. 6, 10, 11, 31; Sept. 8; Oct. 8; Nov. 17, 18, 21.

17♑

1980   Jan. 7; Feb. 23; Mar. 21; Apr. 6; May 6; June 15, 16; July 8; Aug. 8, 25; Sept. 9; Oct. 9, 19; Nov. 12; Dec. 13, 14.

1981   Jan. 6, 24; Apr. **6,** 7, 30; May 7, 17, 18; June 18; July 8; Aug. 7, 12; Sept. 1, 9; Oct. 9; Nov. 19, 20, 22.

18 ♑
1980 Jan. 8; Feb. 24; Mar. 22; Apr. 7; May 7; June 17, 18; July 9; Aug. 9, 10, 26; Sept. 10; Oct. 10, 19; Nov. 13; Dec. 15.

1981 Jan. 7, 25; Apr. **7**, 8, 9; May 1, 8, 19; June 19; July 9; Aug. 8, 13, 14; Sept. 2, 10; Oct. 10; Nov. 21, 22, 23.

19 ♑
1980 Jan. 9; Feb. 25; Mar. 23; Apr. 8; May 8, 9; June 19, 20; July 10; Aug. 11, 12, 27; Sept. 11; Oct. 11, 20; Nov. 14; Dec. 16.

1981 Jan. 8, 25; Apr. **8**, 10; May 2, 9, 20; June 20; July 10; Aug. 8, 15, 16; Sept. 3, 11; Oct. 11; Nov. 23, **24**.

20 ♑
1980 Jan. 10; Feb. 26; Mar. 24; Apr. 9; May 10; June 21, 22, July 11; Aug. 13, 28; Sept. 12; Oct. 12, 21; Nov. 15; Dec. 17.

1981 Jan. 9, 26; Apr. 8, 9, 11; May 3, 10, 21, 22; June 21; July 11, 12; Aug. 9, 17; Sept. 3, 12; Oct. 12; Nov. **25**, 26.

21 ♑
1980 Jan. 11; Feb. 27; Mar. 25; Apr. 10; May 11; June 23, 24; July 12; Aug. 14, 15, 29; Sept. 13; Oct. 13, 22; Nov. 16; Dec. 18, 19.

1981 Jan. 10, 27; Apr. 9, 10, 12, 13; May 4, 11, 23; June 21; July 13; Aug. 10, 18, 19; Sept. 4, 13; Oct. 13; Nov. 26, **27**, 28.

22 ♑
1980 Jan. 12; Feb. 28; Mar. 26; Apr. 11; May 12; June 25, 26; July 13; Aug. 16, 30; Sept. 14; Oct. 14, 23; Nov. 17; Dec. 20.

1981 Jan. 11, 28; Apr. 10, 11, 14; May 4, 12, 24; June 22; July 14; Aug. 11, 20; Sept. 5; 14; Oct. 14; Nov. 28, 29, 30.

23 ♑
1980 Jan. 13; Feb. 29; Mar. 27; Apr. 12; May 13; June 27, 28; July 14; Aug. 17, 18, 31; Sept. 15; Oct. 15, 24; Nov. 17; Dec. 21.

1981 Jan. 12, 29; Apr. 11, 12, 15; May 5, 13, 25, 26; June 23; July 15; Aug. 12, 21, 22; Sept. 6, 15; Oct. 15; Nov. 29; Dec. 1, 2.

24 ♑
1980 Jan. 14; Mar. 1, 28; Apr. 13; May 14; June 29, 30; July 15; Aug. 19; Sept. 1, 16; Oct. 16, 24; Nov. 18; Dec. 22, 23.

1981 Jan. 13, 29; Apr. 12, 13, 16, 17; May 6, 14, 27; June 24; July 16; Aug. 13, 23; Sept. 7, 16; Oct. 16; Nov. 30; Dec. 3, 4.

25
1980   Jan. 15; Mar. 1, 29; Apr. 14; May 15; July 1, 16, 17; Aug. 20, 21; Sept. 2, 17; Oct. 17, 25; Nov. 19; Dec. 24

1981   Jan. 14, 30; Apr. 12, 14, 18; May 7, 15, 28, 29; June 25; July 17; Aug. 13, 24, 25; Sept. 8, 17; Oct. 17; Dec. 1, 5, 6.

26 ♑
1980   Jan. 16; Mar. 2, 30; Apr. 15; May 16; July 2, 3, 18; Aug. 22, 23; Sept. 3, 18; Oct. 18, 26; Nov. 20; Dec. 25.

1981   Jan. 15, 31; Apr. 13, 15, 19; May 8, 16, 30; June 26; July 18; Aug. 14, 26; Sept. 9, 18; Oct. 18, 19; Dec. 2, 3, 7, 8.

27 ♑
1980   Jan. 17; Mar. 3, 31; Apr. 16; May 17; July 4, 5, 19; Aug. 24; Sept. 4, 19; Oct. 19, 27; Nov. 21; Dec. 26.

1981   Jan. 16; Feb. 1; Apr. 14, 16, 20, 21; May 8, 17, 31; June 26; July 19; Aug. 15, 27, 28; Sept. 9, 19; Oct. 20; Dec. 4, 9, 10.

28 ♑
1980   Jan. 18; Mar. 4; Apr. 1, 17; May 18; July 6, 7, 20; Aug. 25, 26; Sept. 5, 20; Oct. 20, 28; Nov. 21; Dec. 27, 28.

1981   Jan. 17; Feb. 2; Apr. 15, 17, 22; May 9, 18; June 1, 2, 27; July 20; Aug. 16, 29; Sept. 10, 20; Oct. 21; Dec. 5, 11, 12.

29 ♑
1980   Jan. 19; Mar. 5; Apr. 2, 18; May 19; July 8, 9, 21; Aug. 27; Sept. 6, 21; Oct. 21, 29; Nov. 22; Dec. 29.

1981   Jan. 18; Feb. 2; Apr. 16, 18, 23; May 10, 19; June 3, 28; July 21; Aug. 17, 30; Sept. 11, 21; Oct. 22; Dec. 6, 7, 13, 14.

AQUARIUS

0 ♒

1980   Jan. 20; Mar. 6; Apr. 3, 19; May 20; July 10, 11, 22; Aug. 28, 29; Sept. 7, 22; Oct. 22, 29; Nov. 23; Dec. 30.

1981   Jan. 19; Feb. 3; Apr. 16, 19, 24, 25; May 11, 20; June 4, 5, 29; July 22; Aug. 18; Sept. 1, 2, 12, 22; Oct. 23; Dec. 8, 15, 16.

1 ♒

1980   Jan. 21; Mar. 7; Apr. 4, 20; May 21; July 12, 23; Aug. 30; Sept. 8, 23, Oct. 23, 30; Nov. 24; Dec. 31.

1981   Jan. 20; Feb. 4; Apr. 17, 20, 26; May 12, 21; June 6, 30; July 23; Aug. 18; Sept. 3, 13, 23; Oct. 24; Dec. 9, 10, 17, 18.

2 ♒

1980   Jan. 22; Mar. 8; Apr. 5, 21; May 22; July 13, 14, 24; Aug. 31; Sept. 1, 9, 24; Oct. 24, 31; Nov. 25.

1981   Jan. 1, 2, 21; Feb. 5; Apr. 18, 21, 27; May 12, 22; June 7, 30; July 24; Aug. 19; Sept. 4, 5, 14, 24; Oct. 25; Dec. 11, 12, 19, 20, 21.

3 ♒

1980   Jan. 23; Mar. 8; Apr. 6, 22; May 23; July 15, 16, 25; Sept. 2, 10, 25; Oct. 25; Nov. 1, 25.

1981   Jan. 3, 22; Feb. 6; Apr. 19, 22, 28, 29; May 13, 23; June 8, 9; July 1, 25; Aug. 20; Sept. 6, 15, 25; Oct. 26; Dec. 13, 22, 23.

4 ♒

1980   Jan. 24; Mar. 9; Apr. 7, 23; May 24; July 17, 18, 26; Sept. 3, 4, 11, 26; Oct. 26; Nov. 2, 26.

1981   Jan. 4, 23; Feb. 6; Apr. 20, 23, 30; May 14, 24; June 10; July 2, 26; Aug. 21; Sept. 7, 8, 15, 26; Oct. 27; Dec. 14, 15, 24, 26.

5 ♒

1980   Jan. 25; Mar. 10; Apr. 8, 24; May 25; July 19, 27; Sept. 5, 11, 27; Oct. 27; Nov. 3, 27.

1981   Jan. 5, 6, 24; Feb. 7; Apr. 21, 24; May 1, 15, 25; June 11, 12; July 3, 27; Aug. 22; Sept. 9, 10, 16, 27; Oct. 28; Dec. 16, 17, 26, 27.

6 ♒

1980   Jan. 26; Mar. 11; Apr. 9, 25; May 26; July 20, 21, 28; Sept. 6, 7, 12, 28; Oct. 28; Nov. 3, 28.

1981   Jan. 7, 25; Feb. 8; Apr. 21, 25; May 2, 3, 16, 26; June 13; July 4, 28; Aug. 23; Sept. 11, 17, 28; Oct. 29; Dec. 18, 19, 20, 28, 29, 30.

7 ♒

1980   Jan. 27; Mar. 12; Apr. 10, 26; May 27; July 22, 23, 29; Sept. 8, 13, 29; Oct. 29; Nov. 4, 29.

1981   Jan. 8, 26; Feb. 9; Apr. 22, 26; May 4, 17, 27; June 14; July 5, 29; Aug. 23; Sept. 12, 13, 18, 29; Oct. 30; Dec. 21, 22, 23, 31.

8 ♒

1980   Jan. 28; Mar. 13; Apr. 11, 27; May 28; July 24, 30; Sept. 9, 10, 14, 30; Oct. 30; Nov. 5, 30.

1981   Jan. 9, 27; Feb. 10; Apr. 23, 27; May 5, 17, 28, 29; June 15, 16; July 5, 30; Aug. 24; Sept. 14, 19, 30; Oct. 31; Dec. 24, 25, 26, 27, 28, 29, 30, 31.

9 ♒

1980   Jan. 29; Mar. 14; Apr. 12, 28; May 29; July 25, 26, 31; Sept. 11, 15; Oct. 1, 31; Nov. 6, 30.

1981   Jan. 10, 11, 28; Feb. 10; Apr. 24, 28; May 6, 7, 18, 30; June 17; July 6, 31; Aug. 25; Sept. 15, 16, 20; Oct. 1, Nov. 1.

10 ♒

1980   Jan. 30; Mar. 15; Apr. 13, 29; May 30; July 27, 28; Aug. 1; Sept. 12, 13, 16; Oct. 2; Nov. 1, 7; Dec. 1.

1981   Jan. 12, 29; Feb. 11; Apr. 25, 29; May 8, 19, 31; June 18, 19; July 7; Aug. 1, 26; Sept. 17, 18, 21; Oct. 2, Nov. 2.

11 ♒

1980   Jan. 31; Mar. 16; Apr. 14, 15, 30; May 31; July 29; Aug. 2; Sept. 14, 17; Oct. 3; Nov. 2, 8; Dec. 2.

1981   Jan. 13, 30; Feb. 12; Apr. 25, 30; May 1, 9, 20; June 1, 20; July 8; Aug. 2, 27; Sept. 19, 21; Oct. 3; Nov. 3.

12≈
1980 Feb. 1; Mar. 17; Apr. 16; May 1; June 1; July 30, 31; Aug. 3; Sept. 15,16, 18; Oct. 4; Nov. 3, 8; Dec. 3.

1981 Jan. 14, 31; Feb. 13; Apr. 26; May 2, 10, 11, 21; June 2, 21, 22; July 9; Aug. 3, 4, 28; Sept. 20, 21, 22; Oct. 4; Nov. 4.

13≈
1980 Jan. 1; Feb. 2; Mar. 18; Apr. 17; May 2; June 2; Aug. 1, 2, 4; Sept. 17, 19; Oct. 5; Nov. 4, 9; Dec. 4.

1981 Jan. 15, 16; Feb. 1, 14; Apr. 27; May 3, 12, 21; June 3, 23; July 10; Aug. 5, 29; Sept. 22, 23; Oct. 5; Nov. 5.

14≈
1980 Jan. 2; Feb. 3; Mar. 18; Apr. 18; May 3; June 3, 4; Aug. 3, 5; Sept. 18, 19, 20; Oct. 6; Nov. 5, 10; Dec. 4.

1981 Jan. 17; Feb. 2, 14; Apr. 28; May 4, 13, 14, 22; June 4, 24; July 10; Aug. 6, 29; Sept. 23, **24**, Oct. 6; Nov. 6.

15≈
1980 Jan. 3; Feb. 4; Mar. 19; Apr. 19; May 4; June 5; Aug. 4, 5, 6; Sept. 20, 21; Oct. 7; Nov. 6, 11; Dec. 5.

1981 Jan. 18; Feb. 3, 15; Apr. 29; May 5, 15, 23; June 5, 25, 26; July 11; Aug. 7, 30; Sept. **25**, 26; Oct. 7; Nov. 7.

16≈
1980 Jan. 4; Feb. 5; Mar. 20; Apr. 20; May 5; June 6, 29, 30; July 1, 2, 3, 4, 5, 6, 7, 8, 9, 10, 11, 12; Aug. 6, **7**; Sept. 21, **22**; Oct. 8; Nov. 7, 12; Dec. 6.

1981 Jan. 19, 20; Feb. 4, 16; Apr. 29; May 6, 16, 24; June 6, 27; July 12; Aug. 8, 31; Sept. 26, 27; Oct. 8; Nov. 8.

17≈
1980 Jan. 5; Feb. 6; Mar. 21; Apr. 21, 22; May 6; June 7, 26, 27, 28; July 13, 14, 15; Aug. **8**, 9; Sept. 22, 23; Oct. 9; Nov. 8, 12; Dec. 7.

1981 Jan. 21; Feb. 5, 17; Apr. 30; May 7, 17, 18, 25; June 7, 28, 29; July 13; Aug. 9; Sept. 1, 27, 28, 29; Oct. 9; Nov. 8.

18≈
1980 Jan. 5; Feb. 7; Mar. 22; Apr. 23; May 7; June 8, 24, 25; July 16, 17, 18; Aug. 9, **10**; Sept. 23, 24, 25; Oct. 10; Nov. 9, 13; Dec. 8.

1981 Jan. 22; Feb. 6, 18; May 1, 8, 19, 25; June 8, 30; July 14; Aug. 10; Sept. 2, 27, 30; Oct. 10; Nov. 9.

19 ♒

1980 Jan. 6; Feb. 8; Mar. 23; Apr. 24; May 8, 9; June 9, 22, 23; July 19, 20; Aug. **11**, 12; Sept. 24, 26; Oct. 11; Nov. 10, 14; Dec. 8.

1981 Jan. 23; Feb. 7, 18; May 2, 9, 20, 26; June 9; July 1, 2, 14; Aug. 11; Sept. 3, 28; Oct. 1, 2, 11; Nov. 10.

20 ♒

1980 Jan. 7; Feb. 9; Mar. 24; Apr. 25, 26; May 10; June 10, 20, 21; July 21, 22; Aug. 12, 13; Sept. 25, 27; Oct. 12; Nov. 11, 15; Dec. 9.

1981 Jan. 24, 25; Feb. 8, 19; May 3, 10, 21, 22, 27; June 10; July 3, 15; Aug. 12; Sept. 3, 29; Oct. 3, 4, 12; Nov. 11.

21 ♒

1980 Jan. 8; Feb. 10; Mar. 25; Apr. 27; May 11; June 11, 18, 19; July 23, 24; Aug. 13, 14, 15; Sept. 26, 28, 29; Oct. 13; Nov. 12, 16; Dec. 10.

1981 Jan. 26; Feb. 9, 20; May 4, 11, 23, 28; June 11; July 4, 5, 16; Aug. 13; Sept. 4, 30; Oct. 5, 6, 13; Nov. 12.

22 ♒

1980 Jan. 9; Feb. 11; Mar. 26; Apr. 28; May 12; June 12, 16, 17; July 25, 26; Aug. 14, 16; Sept. 27, 30; Oct. 14; Nov. 13, 17; Dec. 11.

1981 Jan. 27, Feb. 10, 21; May 4, 12, 24, 29; June 12; July 6, 17; Aug. 14; Sept. 5; Oct. 1, 7, 14; Nov. 13.

23 ♒

1980 Jan. 9; Feb. 12; Mar. 27; Apr. 29, 30; May 13; June 13, 15; July 27; Aug. 15, 17, 18; Sept. 28; Oct. 1, 2, 15; Nov. 14, 17; Dec. 12.

1981 Jan. 28; Feb. 11, 22; May 5, 13, 25, 26, 30; June 13; July 7, 8, 18; Aug. 15; Sept. 6; Oct. 2, 8, 9, 15; Nov. 14.

24 ♒

1980 Jan. 10; Feb. 13; Mar. 28; May 1, 14; June 13, **14**, July 28, 29; Aug. 16, 19; Sept. 29; Oct. 3, 16; Nov. 15, 18; Dec. 12.

1981 Jan. 29, 30; Feb. 12, 22; May 6, 14, 27, 30; June 14; July 9, 19; Aug. 16; Sept. 7; Oct. 3, 10, 11, 16; Nov. 15.

25 ♒

1980 Jan. 11; Feb. 14; Mar. 29; Apr. 1, 2, 3, 4, 5, 6, 7, 8, 9; May 2, 3, 15; June 12, 15; July 30; Aug. 17, 20, 21; Sept. 30; Oct. 4, 5, 17; Nov. 16, 19; Dec. 13.

1981 Jan. 31; Feb. 13, 23; May 7, 15, 28, 29, 31; June 15; July 10, 19; Aug. 17; Sept. 8; Oct. 4, 12, 17; Nov. 16.

26 ♒

1980   Jan. 12; Feb. 15; Mar. 22, 23, 24, 25, 26, 27, 28, 29, **30**, 31; Apr. 10, 11, 12, 13, 14, 15, 16, 17, 18; May 4, 5, 16; June 10, 11, 16; July 31; Aug. 1, 18, 22, 23; Sept. 30; Oct. 6, 18; Nov. 17, 20; Dec. 14.

1981   Feb. 1, 14, 24; May 8, 16, 30; June 1, 16; July 11, 12, 20; Aug. 18; Sept. 9; Oct. 4, 13, 14, 18, 19; Nov. 17.

27 ♒

1980   Jan. 13; Feb. 16; Mar. 18, 19, 20, 21, 22, 31; Apr. 19, 20, 21, 22, 23, 24; May 6, 7, 17; June 8, 9, 17; Aug. 2, 19, 24; Oct. 1, 7, 19; Nov. 18, 21; Dec. 15.

1981   Feb. 2, 15, 25; May 8, 17, 31; June 2, 17; July 13, 21; Aug. 19; Sept. 9; Oct. 5, 15, 16, 19, 20; Nov. 18.

28 ♒

1980   Jan. 14; Feb. 17; Mar. 14, 15, 16, 17; Apr. 1, 25, 26, 27, 28; May 8, 9, 18; June 6, 7, 18; Aug. 3, 20, 25, 26; Oct. 2, 8, 9, 20; Nov. 19, 21; Dec. 16.

1981   Feb. 3, 4, 16, 26; May 9, 18; June 1, 2, 3, 18; July 14, 15, 22; Aug. 20; Sept. 10; Oct. 6, 17, 21; Nov. 19.

29 ♒

1980   Jan. 14; Feb. 18; Mar. 11, 12, 13; Apr. 2, 29, 30; May 1, 2, 10, 11, 19; June 4, 5, 19; Aug. 4, 5, 21, 27; Oct. 3, 10, 21; Nov. 20, 22; Dec. 16.

1981   Feb. 5, 17, 26; May 10, 19; June **3**, 19; July 16, 23; Aug. 21; Sept. 11; Oct. 7, 18, 19, 22; Nov. 20.

PISCES

0 ♓

1980 Jan. 15; Feb. 19; Mar. 8, 9, 10; Apr. 3; May 3, 4, 5, 6, 12, 13, 14, 20; June 2, 3, 20; Aug. 6, 22, 28, 29; Oct. 4, 11, 12, 22; Nov. 21, 23; Dec. 17.

1981 Feb. 6, 18, 27; May 11, 20; June **4**, 5, 20, 21; June 17, 18, 24; Aug. 22; Sept. 12; Oct. 8, 20, 21, 23; Nov. 21.

1 ♓

1980 Jan. 16; Feb. 19; Mar. 5, 6, 7; Apr. 4; May 7, 8, 9, 15, 16, 17, 21, 28, 29, 30, 31; June 1, 21; Aug. 7, 23, 30; Oct. 5, 13, 23; Nov. 22, 24; Dec. 18.

1981 Feb. 7, 19, 28; May 12, 21; June 5, 6, 22; July 19, 24; Aug. 23; Sept. 13; Oct. 9, 22, 24; Nov. 22.

2 ♓

1980 Jan. 17; Feb. 20; Mar. 2, 3, 4; Apr. 5; May 10, 11, 12, 18, 19, 20, 21,**22**, 23, 24, 25, 26, 27, 28; June 22; Aug. 8, 24, 31; Sept. 1; Oct. 6, 14, 24; Nov. 23, 25; Dec. 19.

1981 Feb. 8, 9, 20; Mar. 1; May 12, 22; June 6, 7, 23; July 20, 21, 25; Aug. 24; Sept. 14; Oct. 10, 23, 24, 25; Nov. 23.

3 ♓

1980 Jan. 18; Feb. 21, 29; Mar. 1; Apr. 6; May 13, 14, 15, 23; June 23; Aug. 9, 10, 25; Sept. 2; Oct. 7, 15, 16, 25; Nov. 24, 25; Dec. 20.

1981 Feb. 10, 21; Mar. 2; May 13, 23; June 7, 8, 9, 24; July 22, 26; Aug. 25; Sept. 15; Oct. 11, 25, **26**; Nov. 24.

4 ♓

1980 Jan. 18; Feb. 22, 26, 27, 28; Apr. 7; May 16, 17, 24; June 24; Aug. 11, 26; Sept. 3, 4; Oct. 7, 17, 26; Nov. 25, 26; Dec. 20.

1981 Feb. 11, 22; Mar. 2; May 14, 24; June 8, 10, 25; July 23, 24, 27; Aug. 26; Sept. 15; Oct. 12, **27**, 28; Nov. 25.

5 ♓
1980   Jan. 19; Feb. 23, 24, 25; Apr. 8; May 18, 19, 20, 25; June 25, 26; Aug. 12, 27; Sept. 5; Oct. 8, 18, 19, 27; Nov. 26, 27; Dec. 21.

1981   Feb. 12, 13, 23; Mar. 3; May 15, 25; June 8, 11, 12, 26; July 25, 28; Aug. 27; Sept. 16; Oct. 12, 28, 29; Nov. 26.

6 ♓
1980   Jan. 20; Feb. 21, 22, 23, 24; Apr. 9; May 21, 22, 23, 26; June 27; Aug. 13, 28; Sept. 6, 7; Oct. 9, 20, 28; Nov. 27, 28; Dec. 22.

1981   Feb. 14, 24; Mar. 4; May 16, 26; June 9, 13, 27; July 26, 27, 29; Aug. 28; Sept. 17; Oct. 13, 29, 30, 31; Nov. 27.

7 ♓
1980   Jan. 21; Feb. 19, 20, 25; Apr. 10; May 24, 25, 27; June 28; Aug. 14, 29; Sept. 8; Oct. 10, 21, 29; Nov. 28, 29; Dec. 23.

1981   Feb. 15, 25; Mar. 5; May 17, 27; June 10, 14, 28; July 28, 29; Aug. 29, 30; Sept. 18; Oct. 14, 30; Nov. 1, 2, 28.

8 ♓
1980   Jan. 22; Feb. 16, 17, 18, 26; Apr. 11; May 26, 27, 28; June 29; Aug. 15, 30; Sept. 9, 10; Oct. 11, 22, 23, 30; Nov. 29, 30; Dec. 24.

1981   Feb. 16, 26; Mar. 6; May 17, 28, 29; June 11, 15, 16, 29; July 29, **30;** Aug. 31; Sept. 19; Oct. 15, 31; Nov. 3, 4, 29.

9 ♓
1980   Jan. 23; Feb. 13, 14, 15, 27; Apr. 12; May 28, **29**, 30; June 30; Aug. 16, 31; Sept. 11; Oct. 12, 24, 31; Nov. **30**; Dec. 24.

1981   Feb. 17, 18, 27; Mar. 6; May 18, 30; June 12, 17, 30; July **31;** Sept. 1, 20; Oct. 16; Nov. 1, 5, 6, 30.

10 ♓
1980   Jan. 23; Feb. 10, 11, 12, 28; Apr. 13; May 30, 31; June 1; July 1; Aug. 17, 18; Sept. 1, 12, 13; Oct. 13, 25, 26; Nov. 1; Dec. **1**, 25.

1981   Feb. 19, 28; Mar. 7; May 19, 31; June 12, 18, 19; July 1, Aug. **1**, 2; Sept. 2, 21; Oct. 17; Nov. 2, 7; Dec. 1.

11 ♓
1980   Jan. 24; Feb. 7, 8, 9, 29; Apr. 14, 15; May 31; June 2, 3; July 2; Aug. 19; Sept. 2, 14; Oct. 13, 27; Nov. 2; Dec. **2**, 26.

1981   Feb. 20; Mar. 1, 8; May 20; June 1, 13, 20; July 2; Aug. 2, 3; Sept. 3, 21; Oct. 18; Nov. 3, 8, 9; Dec. 2.

12 ♓

1980   Jan. 25; Feb. 3, 4, 5, 6; Mar. 1; Apr. 16; June 1, 4, 5, 6; July 3; Aug. 20; Sept. 3, 15, 16; Oct. 14, 28; Nov. 3; Dec. **3**, 27.

1981   Feb. 21; Mar. 2, 9; May 21; June 2, 14, 21, 22; July 3; Aug. 3, 4, 5; Sept. 4, 22; Oct. 19; Nov. 4, 10, 11; Dec. 3.

13 ♓

1980   Jan. 26, 30, 31; Feb. 1, 2; Mar. 2; Apr. 17; June 2, 7, 8; July 4; Aug. 21; Sept. 4, 17; Oct. 15, 29, 30; Nov. 4; Dec. **4**, 28.

1981   Feb. 22, 23; Mar. 3, 10; May 21; June 3, 15, 23; July 4; Aug. 3, 6; Sept. 5, 23; Oct. 20; Nov. 5, 12, 13; Dec. 4.

14 ♓

1980   Jan. 1, 2, 3, 4, 5, 6, 7, 23, 24, 25, 26, **27**, 28, 29; Mar. 3; Apr. 18; June 3, 4, 9, 10; July 5; Aug. 22; Sept. 5, 18, 19; Oct. 16, 31; Nov. 5; Dec. 4, 5, 28.

1981   Feb. 24; Mar. 4, 10; May 22; June 4, 16, 24; July 5; Aug. 4, 7, 8; Sept. 6, 24; Oct. 21; Nov. 6, 14, 15; Dec. 5.

15 ♓

1980   Jan. 8, 9, 10, 11, 12, 13, 14, 15, 16, 17, 18, 19, 20, 21, 22, 27; Mar. 4; Apr. 19; June 5, 11, 12; July 6; Aug. 23; Sept. 6, 7, 20; Oct. 17; Nov. 1, 6; Dec. 5, 6, 29.

1981   Feb. 25; Mar. 5, 11; May 23; June 5, 17, 25, 26; July 6; Aug. 5, 9; Sept. 7, 25; Oct. 21; Nov. 7, 8, 16; Dec. 6.

16 ♓

1980   Jan. 28; Mar. 5; Apr. 20; June 6, 13, 14, 29, 30; July 1, 2, 3, 4, 5, 6, **7**,, 8, 9, 10, 11, 12; Aug. 24; Sept. 8, 21, 22; Oct. 18; Nov. 2, 3, 7; Dec. 6, 7, 30.

1981   Feb. 26; Mar. 6, 12; May 24; June 6, 17, 27; July 7; Aug. 6, 10, 11; Sept. 8, 26; Oct. 22; Nov. 8, 17, 18; Dec. 7.

17 ♓

1980   Jan. 29; Mar. 6; Apr. 21, 22; June 7, 15, 16, 26, 27, 28; July 8, 13, 14, 15; Aug. 25; Sept. 9, 23; Oct. 19; Nov. 4, 8; Dec. 7, 8, 31.

1981   Feb. 27, 28; Mar. 7, 13; May 25; June 7, 18, 28, 29; July 8, Aug. 7, 12; Sept. 9, 27; Oct. 23; Nov. 9, 19, 20; Dec. 8.

18 ♓

1980   Jan. 30; Mar. 7; Apr. 23; June 8, 17, 18, 24, 25; July 9, 16, 17, 18; Aug. 26; Sept. 10, 24, 25; Oct. 19; Nov. 5, 9; Dec. 8, 9.

1981   Jan. 1; Mar. 1, 8, 14; May 25; June 8, 19, 30; July 9; Aug. 8, 13, 14; Sept. 10, 27; Oct. 24; Nov. 9, 21, 22; Dec. 9.

19 ♓

1980   Jan. 31; Mar. 8; Apr. 24; June 9, 19, 20, 22, 23; July 10, 19, 20; Aug. 27; Sept. 11, 26; Oct. 20; Nov. 6, 7, 10; Dec. 8, 10.

1981   Jan. 1; Mar. 2, 9, 14; May 26; June 9, 20; July 1, 2, 10; Aug. 8, 15, 16; Sept. 11, 28; Oct. 25; Nov. 10, 23, 24; Dec. 10.

20 ♓

1980   Feb. 1; Mar. 9; Apr. 25, 26; June 10, 20, **21**, 22; July 11, 21, 22; Aug. 28; Sept. 12, 27; Oct. 21; Nov. 8, 11; Dec. 9, 11.

1981   Jan. 2; Mar. 3, 4, 10, 15; May 27; June 10, 21; July 3, 11, 12; Aug. 9, 17; Sept. 12, 29; Oct. 26; Nov. 11, 25, 26; Dec. 11.

21 ♓

1980   Feb. 1; Mar. 10; Apr. 27; June 11, 18, 19, 23, 24; July 12, 23, 24; Aug. 29; Sept. 13, 28, 29; Oct. 22; Nov. 9, 12; Dec. 10, 12.

1981   Jan. 3; Mar. 5, 11, 16; May 28; June 11, 21; July 4, 5, 13; Aug. 10, 18, 19; Sept. 13, 30; Oct 27; Nov. 12, 27, 28; Dec. 12.

22 ♓

1980   Feb. 2; Mar. 11; Apr. 28; June 12, 16, 17, 25, 26; July 13, 25, 26; Aug. 30; Sept. 14, 30; Oct. 23; Nov. 10, 11, 13; Dec. 11, 13

1981   Jan. 4; Mar. 6, 12, 17; May 29; June 12, 22; July 6, 14; Aug. 11, 20; Sept. 14; Oct. 1, 28; Nov. 13, 29, 30; Dec. 13.

23 ♓

1980   Feb. 3; Mar. 12; Apr. 29, 30; June 13, 15, 27, 28; July 14, 27; Aug. 31; Sept. 15; Oct. 1, 2, 24; Nov. 12, 14; Dec. 12, 14.

1981   Jan. 5; Mar. 7, 13, 18; May 30; June 13, 23; July 7, 8, 15; Aug. 12, 21; Sept. 15; Oct. 2, 29; Nov. 14; Dec. 1, 2, 14.

24 ♓

1980   Feb. 4; Mar. 13; May 1; June 13, **14**, 29, 30; July 15, 28, 29; Sept. 1, 16; Oct. 3, 24; Nov. 13, 15; Dec. 12, 15.

1981   Jan. 5; Mar. 8, 9, 14, 18; May 30; June 14, 24; July 9, 16; Aug. 13, 23; Sept. 16; Oct. 3, 30; Nov. 15; Dec. 3, 4, 15.

25♓

1980   Feb. 5; Mar. 14; May 2, 3; June 12, 15; July 1, 16, 17, 30; Sept. 2, 17; Oct. 4, 5, 25; Nov. 14, 15, 16; Dec. 13, 16.

1981   Jan. 6; Mar. 10, 15, 19; May 31; June 15, 25; July 10, 17; Aug. 13, 24, 25; Sept. 17; Oct. 4, 31; Nov. 16; Dec. 5, 6, 16.

26♓

1980   Feb. 6; Mar. 15; May 4, 5; June 10, 11, 16; July 2, 3, 18, 31; Aug. 1; Sept. 3, 18; Oct. 6, 26; Nov. 16, 17; Dec. 14, 17.

1981   Jan. 7; Mar. 11, 16, 20; June 1, 16, 26; July 11, 12, 18; Aug. 14, 26; Sept. 18; Oct. 4; Nov. 1, 17; Dec. 7, 8, 17.

27♓

1980   Feb. 6; Mar. 16; May 6, 7; June 8, 9, 17; July 4, 5, 19; Aug. 2; Sept. 4, 19; Oct. 7, 27; Nov. 17, 18; Dec. 15, 18.

1981   Jan 8; Mar. 12, 13, 17, 21; June 2, 17, 26; July 13, 19; Aug. 15, 27, 28; Sept. 19; Oct. 5; Nov. 2, 18; Dec. 9, 10, 18.

28♓

1980   Feb. 7; Mar. 17; May 8, 9; June 6, 7, 18; July 6, 7, 20; Aug. 3; Sept. 5, 20; Oct. 8, 9, 28; Nov. 18, **19**; Dec. 16, 19.

1981   Jan. 9; Mar. 14, 18, 22; June 3, 18, 27; July 14, 15, 20; Aug. 16, 29; Sept. 20; Oct. 6; Nov. 3, 19; Dec. 11, 12, 19.

29♓

1980   Feb. 8; Mar. 18; May 10, 11; June 4, 5, 19; July 8, 9, 21; Aug. 4, 5; Sept. 6, 21; Oct. 10, 29; Nov. **20**; Dec. 16, 20.

1981   Jan. 9; Mar. 15, 19, 23; June 3, 19, 28; July 16, 21; Aug. 17, 30, 31; Sept. 21; Oct. 7; Nov. 4, 20; Dec. 13, 14, 20.

PART FOUR

Love and Sex
Analysis
during 1980-1981

Love and Sex Analysis during 1980-1981

A totally thorough analysis of what you can expect in the way of love and sex during 1980 and 1981 is impossible without an understanding of every factor involved in your horoscope, but now that you know the sign and degree of your Venus and Mars, you can be presented with a fairly accurate road map. The planet Venus rules love and romance, so find the sign and degree of your Venus in the left hand column and read the designated paragraph. Don't forget to note whether it applies to 1980 or 1981. If you follow the same procedure for Mars, the planet of sex, you will have a pretty good thumbnail sketch of your personal days and nights for making love...

VENUS
The Planet of Love

Sign and Degree of Your Venus		Read These Paragraphs	
		1980	1981
ARIES			
0 - 3	degrees	A*, B*	A*, B*
4 - 8		A*, B	A*, B
9 - 10		A	A, B
11 - 14		A	A
15 - 24		A, F*	A, F*
25 - 27		A, F	A, F
28 - 29		K	A, F
TAURUS			
0 - 4	degrees	K	A
5 - 16		K	K
17 - 29		C*	C*

*This influence started affecting you in 1979, so this is just a continuation.

Sign and Degree of Your Venus		Read These Paragraphs	
		1980	**1981**
GEMINI			
0 - 3	degrees	C*	C*
4 - 8		C	C
9 - 15		A*	K
16 - 24		A*, D*, E*	A*, D*, E*
25 - 27		A*, D, E	A*, D, E
28 - 29		A*	A*, D, E
CANCER			
0 - 8	degrees	A*	A*
9 - 15		A	A
16 - 17		A, F*	A
18 - 24		A, B*, F*	A, B*, F*
25 - 27		A, B*, F	A, B*, F
28 - 29		B*	A, B*, F
LEO			
0 - 4	degrees	B*	A, B*
5 - 8		B	B
9 - 10		K	B
11 - 15		K	K
16 - 24		C*, E*	C*, E*
25 - 27		C*, E	C*, E
28 - 29		C*	C*, E
VIRGO			
0 - 3	degrees	C*	C*
4 - 8		C	C
9 - 10		A*	C
11 - 15		A*	K
16 - 17		A*, D*	K
18 - 24		A*, B*, D*	A*, B*, D*
25 - 29		A*, B*, D*	A*, B*, D

This influence started affecting you in 1979, so this is just a continuation.

Sign and Degree of Your Venus

Read These Paragraphs

LIBRA

	1980	1981
0 - 3 degrees	A*, B*	A*, B*
4 - 8	A*, B	A*, B
9 - 10	A	A, B
11 - 14	A	A
15 - 24	A, F*	A, F*
25 - 27	A, F	A, F
28 - 29	K	A, F

SCORPIO

	1980	1981
0 - 4 degrees	K	A
5 - 16	K	K
17 - 29	C*	C*

SAGITTARIUS

	1980	1981
0 - 3 degrees	C*	C*
4 - 8	C	C
9 - 15	A*	K
16 - 24	A*, D*, E*	A*, D*, E*
25 - 27	A*, D, E	A*, D, E
28 - 29	A*	A*, D, E

CAPRICORN

	1980	1981
0 - 8 degrees	A*	A*
9 - 15	A	A
16 - 17	A, F*	A
18 - 24	A, B*, F*	A, B*, F*
25 - 27	A, B*, F	A, B*, F
28 - 29	B*	B*, F

This influence started affecting you in 1979, so this is just a continuation.

Sign and Degree of Your Venus		Read These Paragraphs	
AQUARIUS		**1980**	**1981**
0 - 4	degrees	B*	A, B*
5 - 8		B	B
9 - 10		K	B
11 - 14		K	K
15 - 17		E*	E*
18 - 24		C*, E*	C, E*
25 - 27		C*, E	C*, E
28 - 29		C*	C*, E
PISCES			
0 - 3	degrees	C*	C*
4 - 8		C	C
9 - 10		A*	C
11 - 15		A*	K
16 - 17		A*, D*	K
18 - 24		A*, B*, D*	A*, B*, D*
25 - 29		A*, B*, D	A*, B*, D

MARS
The Planet of Sex

Sign and Degree of Your Mars		Read These Paragraphs	
ARIES		**1980**	**1981**
0 - 3	degrees	G*, H*	G*, H*
4 - 8		G*, H	G*, H
9 - 10		G	G, H
11 - 14		G	G
15 - 24		G, J*	G, J*
25 - 27		G, J	G, J
28 - 29		L	G, J

**This influence started affecting you in 1979, so this is just a continuation.*

Sign and Degree of Your Mars		Read These Paragraphs	
TAURUS		**1980**	**1981**
0 - 4	degrees	L	G
5 - 16		L	L
17 - 29		I*	I*
GEMINI			
0 - 3	degrees	I*	I*
4 - 8		I	I
9 - 22		G*	L
23 - 29		G*	G*
CANCER			
0 - 8	degrees	G*	G*
9 - 15		G	G
16 - 17		G, J*	G
18 - 24		G, H*, J*	G, H*, J*
25 - 27		G, H*, J	G, H*, J
28 - 29		H*	G, H*, J
LEO			
0 - 4	degrees	H*	G, H*
5 - 8		H	H
9 - 10		L	H
11 - 17		L	L
18 - 29		I*	I*

This influence started affecting you in 1979, so this is just a continuation.

Sign and Degree of Your Mars		Read These Paragraphs	
VIRGO		**1980**	**1981**
0 - 3	degrees	I*	I*
4 - 8		I	I
9 - 10		G*	I
11 - 17		G*	K
18 - 24		G*, H*	G*, H*
25 - 29		G*, H*	G*, H*
LIBRA			
0 - 3	degrees	G*, H*	G*, H*
4 - 8		G*, H	G*, H
9 - 10		G	G, H
11 - 14		G	G
15 - 24		G, J*	G, J*
25 - 27		G, J	G, J
28 - 29		L	G, J
SCORPIO			
0 - 4	degrees	L	G
5 - 16		L	L
17 - 29		I*	I*
SAGITTARIUS			
0 - 3	degrees	I*	I*
4 - 8		I	I
9 - 22		G*	L
23 - 29		G*	G*

This influence started affecting you in 1979, so this is just a continuation.

Sign and Degree of Your Mars		Read These Paragraphs	
		1980	**1981**
CAPRICORN			
0 - 8	degrees	G*	G*
9 - 15		G	G
16 - 17		G, J*	G
18 - 24		G, H*, J*	G, H*, J*
25 - 27		G, H*, J	G, H*, J
28 - 29		H*	G, H*, J
AQUARIUS			
0 - 4	degrees	H*	G, H*
5 - 8		H	H
9 - 10		L	H
11 - 14		L	L
15 - 17		I*	L
18 - 29		I*	I*
PISCES			
0 - 3	degrees	I*	I*
4 - 8		I	I
9 - 10		G*	I
11 - 17		G*	K
18 - 24		G*, H*	G*, H*
25 - 29		G*, H*	G*, H*

This influence started affecting you in 1979, so this is just a continuation.

PARAGRAPH A.

This may be a case of water, water everywhere and not a drop to drink. Not that love and romance will be non-existent, it's just that heavy relationship problems can be a drag, or you'll want more—or less— of what is being offered to you. For example, the foxy individual you're dying to meet is either married or dating someone else. Or some fabulous creature you've been out with a few times and can't wait to see again happens to live 1,000 miles away, works 18 hours a day or doesn't dig you.

Meanwhile, you're attracting every social *reject* from the local lonely hearts' club and running out of excuses because you don't want to hurt anyone. So while you're pining away for the one you think could make all your fantasies come true, everyone you don't want to talk to rings the phone off the wall. Your only choice may be catching up on your needlepoint or going out with someone you feel about as much attraction for a Fu Manchu or Olive Oyl.

Some of you will be ending a marriage or a serious affair, leaving a space in your life that feels as empty as the Grand Canyon. Whether you're the lover who leaves or the lover who is left, there's bound to be a sense of disappointment while one of you is "Trying to Get the Feeling Again". If you're the one who's been hurt, you're hesitant to get involved again for fear it could happen all over.

Many of you, however, are simply focusing your energy in other directions. A creative endeavor or a career goal may seem so important, you're afraid a romantic involvement might distract you or water down your drive. Actually this is a period when you can make enormous strides in a new professional area you've never had the courage to try before.

Since you'll be feeling extremely emotional and sentimental, you may wonder why love is eluding you, why your Prince or Princess Charming doesn't materialize to rescue you from your insecurity or loneliness. Actually, the explanation is fairly simple: the real block is within you. Your emotional brakes are on—for a variety of reasons—and besides that, you may not be feeling too good about yourself. Whatever imperfection has bothered you in the past can seem as glaring as a cucumber growing out of your ear. Although you may not actually do it at this time, you could start contemplating anything from a face lift or hair transplant to a total overhaul in Baja California or Zurich.

If you're considering marriage during this period, although it could conceivably be a good, solid relationship, it's probably not the romance of the century. After all, people get married for a lot of reasons: financial security, emotional security, convenience, to get away from parents, to avoid being alone. If one of these fits, just be sure you understand your true motives and exactly what type of love you're giving and receiving.

NOTE: If your Venus is 21 degrees or less of Gemini, Virgo, Sagittarius or Pisces, this influence ends for you in June 1980.

If your Venus is 3 degrees or less of Aries, Cancer, Libra or Capricorn or is in any degree of Gemini, Virgo, Sagittarius or Pisces, this influence ends for you in June 1981.

PARAGRAPH B.

If you're still single, this period could usher in the main event, especially if your Venus is in Leo, Sagittarius or Aquarius. When the most magnificent pair of eyes this side of the moon meets yours across a crowded room—or even an empty lot—you'll know this is it, and every other prior relationship will seem like a dress rehearsal in comparison. Most of you will wind up in a state of wedded bliss, unwedded bliss or, at the very least, an affair you'll never forget. If your Venus is in Aries or Libra, you'll have a few obstacles to surmount, but if you hang in, this relationship could be strong enough to survive the severest tests.

If you're already married, or attached, you won't miss a thing. The impetus is still towards falling in love, so when your relationship suddenly starts to sparkle with more romance than you've experienced since your honeymoon, don't fight it. Even if you have a brief affair at this time, it could add spice to your life without threatening the stability of your marriage, because you won't go to extremes. Some of you will only get mentally involved, but the delicious fantasies you dream up will be enough to light up all the other areas of your life. Friends will rave about how great you look. Creativity is heightened and many of you will fall in love with an idea, a sport, philosophy or hobby that provides all of the stimulation and none of the aggravation of a sexual adventure.

NOTE: If your Venus is in 21 degrees or less of Cancer, Virgo, Capricorn or Pisces, this influence ends for you in August 1980.
If your Venus is 22-25 degrees of Cancer, Virgo, Capricorn or Pisces, this influence ends for you in August 1981.

PARAGRAPH C.

Fasten your safety belt because if you're looking for romance, this is about as exciting as it gets. Whatever infatuations you've had in the past will seem like child's play compared to the wild ride you're in for this year. And if you've never had a real blockbuster, this is a great place to start. The only catch is, even though it feels good, this isn't necessarily the stuff that permanent, 'til-death-do-you-part' relationships are built on. But you won't believe that until it all comes to a screeching halt at the end of the line. You're headed for the weak-in-the-knees, head-in-the-clouds, can't-smile-without-you type of roller coaster ride that seems as if it's never going to stop. And no one will be able to tell you any different. Not that marriage isn't possible; as a matter of fact, it's quite likely. What's unlikely is that it will last after the thrill is gone. Actually, the safest step is living together, which is almost a guarantee if you're still single and searching.

The story generally goes something like this: by some unusual set of circumstances (it's always an unusual set of circumstances), you happen to be working on Saturday and you just happen to stop by a quaint little restaurant for a late lunch and this person just happens to come along at the precise moment you spill the entire contents of your purse or briefcase on the sidewalk while trying to open the door. By the time lunch is over you feel you've known each other for 100 years, and by the time you finally tear yourselves apart on Sunday night, you're totally hooked. You've never met anyone like him (or her) and nothing can dampen your enthusiasm. It won't matter if your beloved is twenty years younger or older, a different race, religion or nationality, is married or has a wooden leg. All you want is to feel the glow. From here on it's like a sighing oboe from the moment you part to the moment you see each other again. You'll think of nothng else and, even if you're normally as secretive as an undercover agent, you'll proceed to bore all your friends with every thrilling detail of the romance. As we said, many of you will form a legal tie—impulsively or compulsively—and it could last (especially if your Venus is in Scorpio or Sagittarius), but we wouldn't want to place any bets.

Now if you're married, or have been living with someone for a few years, you could have a problem. You'll be just as magnetic as those unattached people, so a wild, passionate love affair could be difficult (if not impossible) to resist. And since your emotions are likely to be involved, the situation may not be as simple as a purely sexual adventure. That's where the trouble lies. You think you're in love. You feel just as certain of it as those single swingers we just described. In fact, you could play the same scene. And not realizing that it probably won't last, you could conceivably break up a relatively stable relationship to follow your heart to a place where you believe honeymoons last forever. In some cases, it won't take an extracurricular affair to sever an old tie. A compelling urge for new loves to conquer could suddenly prompt you to leave (under the guise of another reason, of course), or you may be the one who's left holding the bag. But if you are, read this paragraph over again from the top and see how much fun you have in store!

NOTE: If your Venus is in 21 degrees or less of Taurus, Leo, Scorpio or Aquarius, this influence ends for you in August 1980.

If your Venus is 22-25 degrees of Taurus, Leo, Scorpio or Aquarius, this influence ends for you in August 1981.

PARAGRAPH D.

The story usually goes something like this: you meet this devastating creature who happens to have the face or the figure or the wavy blond hair or some other enchanting characteristic of your very own Prince Charming or Fairy Princess. That part may be real, but it's probably the only part that is. The rest will be supplied by your creative imagination. For example, suppose you're also looking for someone who's intelligent, honest, thrifty and kind, or someone who would make a good mother and housekeeper, or provide all the financial security you've always dreamed of. You will automatically imbue this person with all those attributes, along with enough higher virtues to quality for sainthood. You'll see what you want to see and hear what you want to hear, (meaning all the nonsense that comes out of the mouth of this walking bundle of perfection). Even when you discover your beloved has strayed just a bit from the truth, you'll be forgiving. When you hear the same old promises to be faithful or to reform bad habits, recited for the tenth time, you'll believe them. Because you want to. You'll confuse sympathy with love, and in the final analysis, about all you'll succeed in accomplishing with your faith and understanding will be to make your loved one weaker. You, on the othe had, will probably get stronger. You'll also get smarter, But that comes later.

Along with the veil of secrets between you, there could be certain reasons you'll need to be discreet about this relationship—like one of you is married or involved with someone else, you both work for a company that frowns on fraternizing, or your parents wouldn't approve. In the meantime, we can't deny the fact that you'll have some beautiful feelings and experiences in Never-Never Land. If your Venus is in Sagittarius you'll have a little better perspective on the situation and, if you're over 30, it helps a little, but not much. However, trying to build a solid union out of this cobweb of illusions is about a risky as erecting a skyscraper on quicksand.

NOTE: If your Venus is in 18 degrees or less of Gemini, Virgo, Sagittarius or Pisces, this influence ends for you in September 1980.
If your Venus is 19-20 degrees of Gemini, Virgo, Sagittarius or Pisces, this influence ends for you in September 1981.

PARAGRAPH E.

This is the kind of relationship that sneaks up on you. It's not frenzied, it's not passionate, it's not trippy. You won't find yourself coughing away like Camille, swimming the Hellespont like Leander, or having the tough sledding of Ethan Frome. It's the kind of love that starts slowly, builds slowly and often lasts a lot longer than the wild sort. Naturally, it all depends on the other influences affecting your horoscope, but generally speaking, it produces feelings of stability and warmth, rather than lust and obsession. Whatever your age, you might find the right person for the long haul. If you've already lived, loved and agonized, you must have learned something—and a relationship initiated under this planetary configuration could be your Legion of Honor. If you're still very young, it's just possible you won't have to suffer the slings and arrows of outrageous passion before you find the person who has been fashioned for you.

As we said, this isn't the type of thing that hits like summer lightning (and ends the same way). It's a union that gains momentum until one day you suddenly realize this is exactly what you've been looking for after all. It's possible that this individual has been right under your nose all along—a friend of a friend, a boss, a co-worker, or someone you knew years ago who wanders back into your life. For those of you who have sworn you're through with love, this is the best influence to bring back those fabulous feelings you'd almost forgotten.

If you already made your commitment long ago, you could rediscover value in the relationship you thought had eroded with time. Those who feel they're drifting away from each other are brought back together under this influence and listless affairs are revitalized.

NOTE: If your Venus is 21 degrees or less of Gemini, Virgo, Sagittarius or Pisces, this influence ends for you in June 1980.

If your Venus is 3 degrees or less of Aries, Cancer, Libra or Capricorn or is in any degree of Gemini, Virgo, Sagittarius or Pisces, this influence ends for you in June 1981.

PARAGRAPH F.

Horticulturally speaking, this year's romantic bouquet won't be your basic garden of posies. It's a period of emotional extremes, so expect anything from a greenhouse full of Cattleya orchids to a truckload of dandelions. In other words, it's the top of the world or the pits. And in some cases, all of the above. If you're not an extremist by nature, you won't know what hit you when a new love walks in and turns your whole life inside out, or an old love walks out and does the same thing. Either way, the impact could send you reeling. One thing is certain — you'll find out you're stronger than you thought you were. If a relationship is severed with someone you felt you couldn't live without, you'll be amazed to discover you can survive just as well, (and sometimes even better) on your own. On the other hand, if you're still searching for your soul mate you could attract a new romance that's so compelling it will feel like shooting the rapids on a broomstick. While this person is bound to be different from anyone you've ever met, what's even more significant is that your reactions will be different too. You may be totally aware of powerful destructive or compulsive tendencies, yet feel you have no alternative but to stay on course, even if your broomstick is smashed into a thousand pieces.

While your love life is being transformed on the outside, your basic romantic nature will be going through a metamorphosis on the inside. You'll learn things about yourself you never faced before, especially on an emotional level. You'll notice your values changing, along with your beliefs and tastes. Old concepts will tremble, almost imperceptively at first, then come toppling down like a house of cards. You'll be drawn to subjects, objects, and individuals that never interested you before; or people from your past will suddenly pop back into your life, forcing you to re-evaluate these old relationships. When the rebuilding starts, it's like pulling apart cemented alphabet blocks and arranging them into different words.

Permanent relationships *can* be initiated at this time, but it's rare.

The reason is that after this period is over, (which takes about three years), you'll probably want someone different than the type of person you were looking for previously. Or your mate will want some one different than the person you've turned out to be. Nevertheless, by the time you finally emerge from the emotional shell you considered your protection, you'll discover it was also your prison and, as vulnerable as you might feel, you'll never choose to go back.

NOTE: If your Venus is in 16 degrees or less of Aries, Cancer, Libra or Capricorn, this influence ends for you in July 1980.

If your Venus is 17-18 degrees of Aries, Cancer, Libra or Capricorn, this influence ends for you in July 1981.

PARAGRAPH G.

Let's face it, your sex life has seen more exciting periods than this one, but trust us—there are better times ahead. Meanwhile, you have a problem, which simply means something is out of harmony. The degree of this discord can vary from major to minor, but here are some of the grimmer possibilities. (And if these don't occur, think how lucky you'll feel knowing whatever you're going through could be a whole lot worse!)

1. You can't get laid. (Your lover is frigid or impotent, is out of town, studying for a master's degree, working night and day or you don't know anyone).
2. You're getting laid, but the pickins are slim and when it does happen, it isn't worth the effort. (You're a lusty Taurus hooked up with a non-physical Gemini).
3. You're angry or jealous and you're out to punish someone. (Including yourself).
4. You're getting laid too much. (You're a non-physical Gemini hooked up with a lusty Taurus).
5. You're totally turned off. (*You're* frigid or impotent, working night and day, or you've just joined a monastery).

Whether you're the actor or the reactor in this drama determines the kind of feelings you'll experience. If you identify with No. 1, 2 or 3, you could be wallowing around in resentment and frustration. But if you relate to No. 4 or 5, it's a combination of indifference and guilt, depending upon whether someone else is making demands of you. Even if you're the type who wants sex every night and twice on Sunday, heavy business pressures could be draining your energy during this period, cutting your playtime down to once a week or less. On the other hand, if you're working on something that really grabs you, it could mean you're sublimating your sex drive into a creative outlet. Feelings of jealousy, anger or being used, (sexually, financially or some other way), can be devastating to your relationship. If honest communication is lacking, emotional and physical estrangements can result, if not an actual break-up. Don't fall into the trap of making everyone else wrong at this time (which is exactly what you'd like to do). If you take responsibility for your feelings and actions in both your personal and professional life, you'll grow a lot stronger as a result of this planetary influence, instead of playing victim.

NOTE: If your Mars in in 21 degrees or less of Gemini, Virgo, Sagittarius or Pisces, this influence ends for you in June 1980.

If your Venus is 3 degrees or less of Aries, Cancer, Libra or Capricorn or in any degree of Gemini, Virgo, Sagittarius or Pisces, this influence ends for you in June 1981.

PARAGRAPH H.

Sexually, you've got it made this year. You don't have to be a Playboy or Cosmopolitan centerfold, drive a custom Ferrari or sing with the Jefferson Starship. All you have to do is whistle. And while you're feasting on this bacchanalian banquet of sensual delights, your playmates will find you as irresistible as pheasant under glass. Your timing is perfect and your stamina will range from good to incredible, since you won't be scattering your energies in a dozen different directions at once. You'll be treated to all of the thrills and none of the spills of more frantically passionate periods, and those of you who are weary of the sexual obstacle course will welcome a ride without the bumps and the dead end streets. On the other hand, if you're the type who thrives on the highs and lows of a romantic loop-the-loop, you may have to work harder to create the kind of excitement that keeps you from getting bored.

Now remember, this influence relates primarily to physical chemistry and doesn't necessarily mean you'll be falling in love, unless the stars are also smiling on your Venus at this time. If so, consider yourself lucky. You'll probably be contemplating a permanent relationship and since chances are you've got your head on reasonably straight, you won't make this decision in the middle of the first night of sex. You just may have found your perfect physical counterpart and this spark could still be sizzling until you're both too old to stoke the fire.

NOTE: If your Mars is in 21 degrees or less of Cancer, Virgo, Capricorn or Pisces, this influence ends for you in August 1980.

If your Mars is 22-25 degrees of Cancer, Virgo, Capricorn or Pisces, this influence ends for you in August 1981.

PARAGRAPH I.

This period can be summed up by the old saying, "Don't knock it 'til you try it." If you're under 35, you've probably never been hornier or more sexually adventurous in your life. If you're over 35, just remember back about 21 years and you'll understand what we mean. New experiences invariably include a few you always considered unconventional, daring, avant garde or even kinky. But it's all relative to *your* life—your morals, your past and the degree of your adventurousness and sexual interest. However, even if you've only been mildly interested before, you could be turned on to a point that shocks you. Reactions like, "I never thought I'd ever be doing *this*!", or "I never dreamed this would feel so good!" are par for the course.

Now if you're conservative, middle-aged lady or gentleman from Poughkeepsie, you might read "The Joy of Sex" or "The Sensuous Woman" while you're pretending to weed the begonias and your spouse will wonder why you suddenly want to try some new position you always thought was perverted. On the other hand, if you're an experienced pro, you could suddenly get very excited looking at pictures of tigers. Between these two extremes is a potpourri of sexual delights that, under normal circumstances, would stagger your imagination (or never even occur to you), from swapping, swinging, tub parties, homosexual experiences, oral and anal sex to—who knows?—bondage or bestiality. In other words, if you're ever going to stick your neck out and venture into any of these areas, it will probably be now.

If you've never had a climax, this period can provide a breakthrough. If you've never had sex at all, by the time this year is over, you'll feel you've invented it. One of the pitfalls, however, is that it's easy to confuse lust with love, so if you're getting to the point of reserving the wedding chapel, slow down a minute. The intensity is similar to being in heat and since you're bound to cool off sooner or later, be sure there's something more between you and your playmate than a lot of sexual magnetism. Your affair could be excruciatingly exciting, with enough breaking up and making up to keep things lively. But in reality, your craving for variety and new experiences may be more compelling at this time than your passionate promises of fidelity.

If you're already married or living with someone, this could be a difficult period. Since you'll be subject to all the feelings and urges described above, your mate may need to be as understanding as St. Francis of Assisi or Joyce Brothers. Your restlessness and nervous energy can manifest itself in many forms, from changing your job or residence to joining a health club, but it all stems from increased sexual energy, which requires a good deal of effort to direct into channels that don't threaten your relationship. The line of least resistance is infidelity, but new alliances of the stable or long lasting variety will be as rare during this period as finding a pearl in a kumquat!

NOTE: If your Mars is in 21 degrees or less of Taurus, Leo, Scorpio or Aquarius, this influence ends for you in August 1980.

If your Mars is 22-25 degrees of Taurus, Leo, Scorpio or Aquarius, this influence ends for you in August 1981.

PARAGRAPH J.

Whatever biological or psychological problems you've tried to ignore (and thought you'd never have to deal with) could be this year's surprise package at the bottom of your own sexual cauldron. If it feels a little like exploratory surgery, it is—and the surgeon is you. Subtle influences start slowly on the inside before anything becomes apparent, but when the simmering kettle finally comes to a full boil, it can create dramatic changes and transformations in your sex life. It all depends on your past experiences and how much guilt, desire, frustration, hostility, fear and restriction you've stashed away in that cauldron. And how many old wives' tales. Also for how long. Sound pretty heavy? Well, the older you are and the more hang-ups you have, the heavier it can feel.

That doesn't mean your sex life is doomed this year. Far from it. In fact, you could have some of the most mind-blowing experiences of your life, and they'll all contribute to the process of weeding out old habits and replanting new ones. Important relationships may need to be dissolved or drastically altered to keep pace with the changes brewing in the inner sanctum of your psyche. Though you'll find it difficult to explain to others what you're going through, sharing some of your discoveries with someone close will help you handle this period with a lot less strain and pain. You'll only have this opportunity once in your life, so make the most of it. When it's over, you'll feel like you've shed a skin that doesn't fit anymore—and you won't even care.

NOTE: If your Mars is in 16 degrees or less of Aries, Cancer, Libra or Capricorn, this influence ends for you in July 1980.

If your Mars is 17-18 degrees of Aries, Cancer, Libra or Capricorn, this influence ends for you in July 1981.

PARAGRAPH K.

Although there are no major planetary influences affecting your Venus during this period, that doesn't necessarily mean nothing is going on in your love life. There could be a number of reasons you won't be first out of the starting gate for the romantic race this year:

1. You've just come through a long seige of dramatic or traumatic experiences and you need a rest.
2. You've found what you were looking for.
3. You're too busy to look.

However, before you toss out your sexy negligees or your little black book, check your Mars influences. You might be busier than you think.

PARAGRAPH L.

Although there are no major planetary influences affecting your Mars this year, that doesn't mean there's a problem. On the contrary—it usually means there *isn't* a problem. True, some of the fireworks are missing, but so are the disappointments. So relax and enjoy it, but first check out your Venus. If this is your year to fall in love, it's just possible you've got it made!

♈   ♉   ♊   ♋   ♌   ♍

JANUARY

S	M	T	W	T	F	S
		1	2	3	4	5
6	7	8	9	10	11	12
13	14	15	16	17	18	19
20	21	22	23	24	25	26
27	28	29	30	31		

FEBRUARY

S	M	T	W	T	F	S
					1	2
3	4	5	6	7	8	9
10	11	12	13	14	15	16
17	18	19	20	21	22	23
24	25	26	27	28	29	

MARCH

S	M	T	W	T	F	S
						1
2	3	4	5	6	7	8
9	10	11	12	13	14	15
16	17	18	19	20	21	22
23	24	25	26	27	28	29
30	31					

APRIL

S	M	T	W	T	F	S
		1	2	3	4	5
6	7	8	9	10	11	12
13	14	15	16	17	18	19
20	21	22	23	24	25	26
27	28	29	30			

MAY

S	M	T	W	T	F	S
				1	2	3
4	5	6	7	8	9	10
11	12	13	14	15	16	17
18	19	20	21	22	23	24
25	26	27	28	29	30	31

JUNE

S	M	T	W	T	F	S
1	2	3	4	5	6	7
8	9	10	11	12	13	14
15	16	17	18	19	20	21
22	23	24	25	26	27	28
29	30					

JULY

S	M	T	W	T	F	S
		1	2	3	4	5
6	7	8	9	10	11	12
13	14	15	16	17	18	19
20	21	22	23	24	25	26
27	28	29	30	31		

AUGUST

S	M	T	W	T	F	S
					1	2
3	4	5	6	7	8	9
10	11	12	13	14	15	16
17	18	19	20	21	22	23
24	25	26	27	28	29	30
31						

SEPTEMBER

S	M	T	W	T	F	S
	1	2	3	4	5	6
7	8	9	10	11	12	13
14	15	16	17	18	19	20
21	22	23	24	25	26	27
28	29	30				

OCTOBER

S	M	T	W	T	F	S
			1	2	3	4
5	6	7	8	9	10	11
12	13	14	15	16	17	18
19	20	21	22	23	24	25
26	27	28	29	30	31	

NOVEMBER

S	M	T	W	T	F	S
						1
2	3	4	5	6	7	8
9	10	11	12	13	14	15
16	17	18	19	20	21	22
23	24	25	26	27	28	29
30						

DECEMBER

S	M	T	W	T	F	S
	1	2	3	4	5	6
7	8	9	10	11	12	13
14	15	16	17	18	19	20
21	22	23	24	25	26	27
28	29	30	31			

♈   ♉   ♊   ♋   ♌   ♍

JANUARY

S	M	T	W	T	F	S
				1	2	3
4	5	6	7	8	9	10
11	12	13	14	15	16	17
18	19	20	21	22	23	24
25	26	27	28	29	30	31

FEBRUARY

S	M	T	W	T	F	S
1	2	3	4	5	6	7
8	9	10	11	12	13	14
15	16	17	18	19	20	21
22	23	24	25	26	27	28

MARCH

S	M	T	W	T	F	S
1	2	3	4	5	6	7
8	9	10	11	12	13	14
15	16	17	18	19	20	21
22	23	24	25	26	27	28
29	30	31				

APRIL

S	M	T	W	T	F	S
			1	2	3	4
5	6	7	8	9	10	11
12	13	14	15	16	17	18
19	20	21	22	23	24	25
26	27	28	29	30		

MAY

S	M	T	W	T	F	S
					1	2
3	4	5	6	7	8	9
10	11	12	13	14	15	16
17	18	19	20	21	22	23
24	25	26	27	28	29	30
31						

JUNE

S	M	T	W	T	F	S
	1	2	3	4	5	6
7	8	9	10	11	12	13
14	15	16	17	18	19	20
21	22	23	24	25	26	27
28	29	30				

JULY

S	M	T	W	T	F	S
			1	2	3	4
5	6	7	8	9	10	11
12	13	14	15	16	17	18
19	20	21	22	23	24	25
26	27	28	29	30	31	

AUGUST

S	M	T	W	T	F	S
						1
2	3	4	5	6	7	8
9	10	11	12	13	14	15
16	17	18	19	20	21	22
23	24	25	26	27	28	29
30	31					

SEPTEMBER

S	M	T	W	T	F	S
		1	2	3	4	5
6	7	8	9	10	11	12
13	14	15	16	17	18	19
20	21	22	23	24	25	26
27	28	29	30			

OCTOBER

S	M	T	W	T	F	S
				1	2	3
4	5	6	7	8	9	10
11	12	13	14	15	16	17
18	19	20	21	22	23	24
25	26	27	28	29	30	31

NOVEMBER

S	M	T	W	T	F	S
1	2	3	4	5	6	7
8	9	10	11	12	13	14
15	16	17	18	19	20	21
22	23	24	25	26	27	28
29	30					

DECEMBER

S	M	T	W	T	F	S
		1	2	3	4	5
6	7	8	9	10	11	12
13	14	15	16	17	18	19
20	21	22	23	24	25	26
27	28	29	30	31		

NOTES